THE
PAPAL
"NO"

THE PAPAL "NO"

A COMPREHENSIVE GUIDE TO THE VATICAN'S REJECTION OF WOMEN'S ORDINATION

DEBORAH HALTER

A Crossroad Book
The Crossroad Publishing Company
New York

The Crossroad Publishing Company
16 Penn Plaza, 481 Eighth Avenue
New York, NY 10001

Library of Congress Cataloging-in-Publication Data

Halter, Deborah.
  The papal "No" : a comprehensive guide to the Vatican's rejection of women's ordination / Deborah Halter.
    p. cm.
  Includes bibliographical references and index.
  ISBN 0-8245-2271-0 (alk. paper)
  1. Ordination of women – Catholic Church – History of doctrines.   I. Title.
BX1912.2.H35 2004
262'.142 – dc22

                                                                                2004014725

1   2   3   4   5   6   7   8   9   10   10   09   08   07   06   05   04

To Monsignor "Father John" O'Donnell,
who bid me gaze through his third eye
to find there vista'd hopes

For Saint Thérèse of Lisieux
and every woman who finds
her call to priesthood stillborn

In accord with the knowledge, competence and preeminence which they possess, the Christian faithful have the right and even at times a duty to manifest to the sacred pastors their opinion on matters which pertain to the good of the Church, and they have a right to make their opinion known to the other Christian faithful, with due regard for the integrity of faith and morals and reverence towards their pastors, and with consideration for the common good and the dignity of persons.

— CANON 212:3

Contents

Part III
POPE JOHN PAUL II

Part IV
CHANGE AND THE VATICAN

APPENDIX

Preface

If a declared teaching or practice continuously jars our mind as missing the mark . . . it is our responsibility to explore and express the reasons why. This resistance is not to be equated with disloyalty or rebellion, let alone lack of faith, but with a form of loyalty and service.[1]   —Elizabeth A. Johnson, CSJ

"Why are we afraid of ordaining women?" a theologian friend recently asked. "The truth will set us free."

"Maybe we're afraid of the truth," I responded.

"Or," he countered, "maybe we're afraid of the kind of freedom that truth demands."

We were silent after that, but his declaration echoed in my head, then my heart, for days. Freedom born of truth would challenge the belief that God wishes only men to be priests, an idea so deeply ingrained in the Roman Catholic psyche that even the most thoughtful among us assume the male priesthood much the way a fish assumes the water in which it swims. In the world, a woman can be a surgeon, bank president, or truck driver, but a "good Catholic" knows she cannot be a priest and so doesn't think about it.

"Good Catholics" traditionally have not questioned Rome, at least not openly. But after Vatican II in the mid-1960s, some "manly" women (as the fourth-century Cappadocian Fathers called accomplished females) and sympathetic men began to ask questions. At first, their queries were simple. Why *can't* women be priests? Where *does* the Bible say women can't be ordained? Where does the Bible say that Jesus ordained *anybody*? As their questions grew more complex the Vatican's replies took on more and finer points. By the turn of the twenty-first century, teams of theologians were required to translate Vatican declarations for the very bishops to whom they were sent, bishops who in turn found themselves trying to explain the documents to priests. Lay Catholics were left further out of the ever-tightening loop.

This book, then, is intended for anyone who wishes to understand Rome's refusal to ordain women to the priesthood, but who lacks the theological background, access to academic works, or the vast amount of time necessary for extensive research. This work grew out of my own concerns when, during a research project, I discovered that no single volume offered a historical accounting of the shaping and reshaping of Rome's argument against ordaining women (and responses to those arguments), forcing the researcher to wade through piles of books and articles, as well as reams of Vatican declarations, apostolic letters and constitutions, encyclicals, commentaries, press releases, and more. My own search has been an experience in the mosaic art of discovery — but instead of tiles or glass or marble, I have used words and phrases and paragraphs to draw a picture of the papal "No" and the responses to it.

This book is dedicated to Catholics, like me, for whom asking questions about the male-only priesthood is not an act of thoughtless rebellion but rather an act of loyal reflection that leads to and nurtures a mature faith. Although I have no call to priesthood, I've a lifelong yearning to see young girls aspire to be priests, to see women celebrate mass, and to be ministered to by *women and men*. In conscience, I cannot accept Pope John Paul II's verdict that this subject is closed to discussion. The call to serve Christ and God's people can never be silenced.

Having said that, I emphasize that this book is in no way intended as a work of rebellion against Rome. If I wanted to rebel, I would leave the church. To the contrary, this book marks my fifty-year relationship with Catholicism and constitutes for me a renewal of faith in God and trust in the church.

I believe that women's ordination should and will take place within the sacramental life of the church. To date, Roman Catholic women have been ordained only in isolated rituals invalidly performed by estranged bishops. These ordinations serve as important indicators that some women are not willing to wait any longer for priestly ordination, just as similar ordinations preceded the formal approval of female priests in the Presbyterian churches. I believe Rome ultimately will come to understand that priesthood does not have to be an "either-or" condition; rather, it can offer a "both-and" experience of the fullness of humanity, male and female. Likewise, the call for women priests is not a question of *challenging* male priests but of *joining* them. Priesthood should not be about "us and them," but rather "we."

Meanwhile, although public discussion of this issue is currently banned by Rome, Catholics everywhere continue to debate the issue of women's ordination. Advocates have endured round after round of papal rejection and condemnation, until at present they have no "legal" venues in which to articulate their concerns. Opponents of women priests have suffered the decline of the male-only priesthood within the church while seeing more and more parishes run by women, leaving many traditionalist Catholics — especially women — uncertain of their own place in the church.

The reality is that women are more likely than men to oppose women's ordination. In 1974, 35 percent of the men and 25 percent of the women polled in the United States favored women priests. In 1985, 51 percent of the men and 44 percent of the women wanted female clergy.[2] This imbalance is not surprising in an environment where female dependence on male authority has been the norm for many centuries, with the result that women have internalized the idea that they cannot (*must not*) serve as priests. In other words, sometimes it is actually easier for men to envision women as priests because men do not share the experience of subordination that women have traditionally felt.

This phenomenon seems to cut across all Christian denominations struggling with women's ordination. Betty Bone Schiess, ordained an Episcopal priest in the 1970s, recalled the time she was studying in the library when the librarian complained that she was "the reason all the young men were leaving the ministry." When Schiess protested there must be some other cause, the librarian responded, "What other reason could there possibly be?"[3]

As will become clear, the issue of women's ordination has diverse sources of support and opposition, with many reasons on both sides. And, for every forward step taken by the ordination movement, the Vatican has taken two steps backward to further articulate and reiterate its unfolding reasons for a male-only priesthood. This book examines that awkward dance.

Acknowledgments

The themes of this book were nurtured from infancy by people of extraordinary learning and insight. Their scholarly prudence, spiritual wisdom, and visionary understanding of priesthood transformed this project from aspiration to actuality. Dr. Catherine Wessinger of the Department of Religious Studies at Loyola, New Orleans, was a mentor without whom this book surely would not have seen completion. Her willingness to read multiple manuscript drafts, her enthusiasm for the topic, and her many stops at my office door to ask, "How's it going?" kept me moving forward. Reverend Dr. Stephen J. Duffy's command of sacramental history and scholastic theology eased me through a number of complex passages.

Deep thanks to three preeminent scholars for reading an earlier draft of this book: Sister of St. Joseph Dr. Elizabeth A. Johnson of Fordham University, Dr. Anthony T. Padovano, president emeritus of the Association for an Inclusive Priesthood, and Dr. Rosemary Radford Ruether of the Pacific School of Religion/Graduate Theological Union. Their comments were invaluable not only for their scholarship but also because they acknowledged the importance of the project. Also, Sister Christine Schenk, director of FutureChurch, generously provided helpful direction with a very early draft. To these four counselors I am deeply indebted.

Joy Barnes, executive director of the Women's Ordination Conference, endured a parade of e-mails and always responded to information requests quickly and cheerily. Cheryl Kennedy of Little Rock edited multiple drafts with a careful eye and a true friend's willingness to tell me what I didn't want to hear. Krista Kennedy of the University of Minnesota provided shrewd editing and comments. Dr. Andrea Herrmann of the University of Arkansas, Little Rock, provided welcome encouragement. Sharon Orgeron of New Orleans brought a good-humored willingness to the mind-numbing task of checking hundreds of footnotes, bibliography titles, and index entries. Denise Riley of College Park, Maryland, was a source of exceptional wisdom. My editors at Crossroad, John Jones and John Eagleson, brought valuable insights to the text.

Episcopal Church historian Dr. Mary Sudman Donovan, my early teacher, showed me that love for and loyalty to the church often requires asking hard questions of it. And the Society of Jesus (Jesuits), whose writings inspire this work from beginning to end, provided a constant model of priesthood at its finest.

Finally, I am especially grateful to a number of colleagues, readers, and advisors who helped me shape a very technical manuscript into a work of comprehensible prose. Unfortunately, the inclusion of their names here would threaten their employment with the Catholic Church, so I must resort to thanking them under the veil of anonymity. I look forward to a time when they will not have to hide their lights under bushels.

Telling the Story of a Soul

Saint Thérèse of Lisieux (1873–97) called her autobiography *The Story of a Soul.* Her life was indeed the story of a soul, but it was more than that. It was the story of Catholic women's traditional path to sanctity: self-denial. Women's endless caregiving and self-sacrifice were often done joyfully and received with gratitude; the problem was, the Vatican taught that self-denial was women's *only* value. In this model of sanctity, women were defined solely according to their relationships to the men around them — as daughters, wives, and mothers — relationships in which there was little balance.

This stereotype of women changed little in the following century. Vatican statements traditionally spoke of women's "delicate sympathy" and talent for "personal relations." They were "better judges of character" and better suited "to life rather than to structures." While not denying the value of these characteristics, Dominican Sister Nadine Foley wrote that it would be difficult to imagine the Vatican "detailing the characteristics of males in a corresponding way."[4]

As late as 1975, Pope Paul VI wrote about women's virtues that were "in accord with feminine psychology." He praised women for their "sweetness... perseverance... generosity and... humility." A woman was "a vision of virginal purity" who could provide a companion "for man in his loneliness." Her life was "one of unreserved loving dedication" as well as "courageous fidelity and toil," and, finally, "habitual heroic sacrifice." He called upon men to "bow in reverence before her."[5]

It was in this environment that Saint Thérèse of Lisieux was "a cherished icon of Catholic womanhood," whose "little way" of spirituality provided a "model of female sanctity." Catholic Church historian Jay P. Dolan explained that the young Carmelite nun's "model of suffering and self-denial" helped Catholic women to "contend with the social changes that were challenging the domestic ideal" enshrined by the church. One such momentous change came with World War II, when increasing numbers of women entered the work force even while being "continually warned that the proper role for women was marriage and motherhood."[6]

Thérèse knew the frustration of wanting a vocation closed to her. Throughout her life, she wanted to be a priest.[7] She made no secret of her desire, but she declared it from the safety of her Carmelite convent in Lisieux, Normandy, about a hundred miles northwest of Paris. A diminutive young woman who called herself "Little Flower," she seems to have been quite happy as a cloistered nun. Indeed, so faultless was her obedience to authority that the other sisters sometimes called her "Little Sister Amen." She knew, of course, that she could not be a priest, but she never gave up wanting to be ordained. On October 19, 1997, Pope John Paul II bestowed the honor of "Doctor of the Church" upon Thérèse — whose short and unremarkable life led to a surge of religious vocations among women.

At the end of each section of this book, brief vignettes tell the story of Saint Thérèse of Lisieux, whose lifelong desire to be a priest informed the way she saw her church, her faith, and her God.

Part I

TRADITION
AND
VATICAN II

➾ Chapter 1 ⫷

Understanding the Issues

As will become clear in these pages, the magisterium — the teaching authority of the church — holds that women have a threefold mission *determined* by their sex: virgin, wife, and mother.[8] Available to men is a mission *facilitated* by their sex: priesthood. Jesus never mentioned ministerial priesthood, but Catholic teaching developed since Vatican II holds that he established an ordained clergy through his maleness and his choice of only men to join the group of Twelve. To guard this divine will, the church hierarchy reserves the right to test and affirm a man's call to priesthood. Since, according to Catholic teaching, God does not make this call to women, Rome holds itself unable to validate or even acknowledge a woman's call to priesthood.

Herein lies a threefold challenge: Jesus said nothing about a priesthood, the Vatican says only men can be priests, and many Catholics are saying the first two don't add up. Trapped in this scriptural, theological, and ecclesial triangle is conflict concerning the "will" of Jesus, like the baby in Solomon's court, with each side insisting upon the rightness of its claim.

Light and Shadow

In the twenty centuries since Christ's resurrection, depictions of Christian women have been a study in chiaroscuro.[9] History traditionally has been written from a male perspective, and as theologian Elisabeth Schüssler Fiorenza observed: "We cannot reasonably expect to find extensive documentation for the role of women in early Christianity."[10] What few references survive in the New Testament are only a small sample of what we have lost.

In the apostolic church — the self-forming community during the time of the apostles — women served as deacons and performed functions later reserved for priests.[11] Images on catacomb frescoes suggest that women celebrated the eucharist and assumed other ministerial roles until they were prohibited from doing so by a growing patriarchy.[12] For instance, sociologist Ruth A. Wallace's study of a medieval abbess found that her local duties included licensing bishops and priests, suspending them, establishing new parishes, reading the gospel, hearing nuns' confessions, and public preaching. This status actually had been condemned in 1210 by Pope Innocent III (and by others before him), who wrote that abbesses "hear [nuns'] confessions of sin and, reading the Gospel, presume to preach publicly."[13] But women were not *formally* denied this authority until after the French Revolution toppled the church in that country in the late eighteenth century.[14]

Outside the monastery, women's roles in the church were starkly different. Almost immediately in the decades after Christ's resurrection, the Christian view of women became drenched in the dualism of Greco-Roman culture, in which women were considered both pure (because of their feminine nature) and unclean (because of their menstrual cycle). Overall, this negative view was rooted in the legacy of Aristotle, who said, "The female is, as it were, a mutilated male, ... for there is only one thing they have not in them, the principle of soul."[15] From woman's lack of a soul it followed that "the male is by nature superior, and the female inferior; and the one rules, and the other is ruled; this principle, of necessity, extends to all mankind."[16]

Aristotle's "science" of women was packed up tightly and carried forward by Augustine, the fourth-century bishop and theologian whose ideas would permanently mold church teaching on sex roles. Men were primary human beings and women were secondary. By herself, a woman possessed only the image of the body; hence she could not represent God's divine image. Augustine taught that only in her *relationship with a man* could a woman possess the *image of God*.

> The woman, together with her own husband, is the image of God, so that the whole substance may be one image, but when she is referred to separately in her quality as a helpmeet, which regards the woman alone, then she is not the image of God, but, as regards the man alone, he is the image of God as fully and completely as when the woman too is joined with him in one.[17]

The views of women articulated by Aristotle and Augustine were transmitted to the Middle Ages by Thomas Aquinas,[18] who taught that because women were misbegotten males (Aristotle) and secondary beings (Augustine), they were unfit for priesthood.[19] These faulty premises resulted in the conclusion that being female presented an insurmountable impediment to ordination.

The medieval church taught that women were pure daughters of Mary as well as sinful daughters of Eve, a continuation of a long history of gender dualism. In the Middle Ages, however, being female presented an impediment not only to priesthood but also to life itself. In 1484, to further the "good work of the Inquisitors" in rooting out heresy, Pope Innocent VIII appointed two Dominican priests to be professional witch hunters. At the pontiff's behest, the two priests produced *Malleus Maleficarum* ("Witches' Hammer"), the exhaustive and definitive witch-hunter's manual that facilitated a criminal and dangerous environment for persons withholding information about potential witches.[20] For three centuries, this violently sexual book provided prurient descriptions of ways that women copulated with devils. It offered remedies against witches, and described judiciary procedures for trying, judging, sentencing, and executing them.

Men, too, could be possessed by devils and beleaguered by witches. Question II, Chapter IV of *Malleus Maleficarum* explored the remedy for men "who by Prestidigitatory Art [sleight of hand] have lost their Virile Members." Men who had thus lost their sex organs were to make a good confession, be reconciled with God, and "as far as possible come to an amicable agreement with the witch herself."[21]

Of the many thousands of "witches" executed, the vast majority were women, who, according to the Inquisitors, were "chiefly addicted to Evil Superstitions."[22] The medieval view of women — mysterious, enticing, dangerous — saturated church teaching and the sensibilities of men and women alike. In one form or another, this view endured until the 1960s, when Vatican Council II, prompted by the women's movement of that decade, began the long, arduous task of taking "woman" off the purity pedestal while simultaneously removing her medieval horns, yielding a more realistic representation of women. Since then, Rome has consistently and conscientiously continued that effort, even as it aggressively maintains that women cannot experience a valid call to priesthood.

Finding Information

Catholic teaching on the male-only priesthood is prolific.[23] Bishops, theologians, and others have adeptly and passionately addressed various themes of this teaching from both sides, but they have done so in numerous, lengthy documents written in dense, technical language that most Catholics would find inaccessible and unhelpful for developing an understanding of the issue.[24] As a result, most Catholics have only a cloudy picture of the scriptural, traditional, theological, and doctrinal background of this teaching. For many Catholics, this is sufficient. For others, it is not enough. For the latter group, regardless of their fidelity to the church, it is difficult to fully accept a teaching or custom without sufficient knowledge of its roots. Worse, there is no comprehensive, systematic identification of the major components of the teaching.[25]

Beginning with Vatican II, this book explores Rome's major documents arguing against women's ordination, and responses to them. The texts studied here meet at least one of three criteria:

- *Documents written by the pope and curial congregations* (groups within church government) establish the official framework, content, and language for the debate, and they identify appropriate sources of information (scripture, tradition, and church teaching). After Vatican II, popular support for women's ordination grew to such an extent that in 1998, following numerous Vatican attempts to quell the growing movement, Pope John Paul II closed the topic to discussion.[26]

- *Texts of bishops and theologians* frequently reveal the pressure under which these two groups operate. The world's bishops must work in hierarchical tension between the man who governs them (the pope) and the people they govern (the world's priests). Theologians, likewise, often are caught between their local bishops and the people they teach. These circumstances place many bishops and theologians in difficult circumstances, and all the more because taking a pastoral or theological stance against the church hierarchy can carry severe professional and financial consequences.

- *Resolutions, announcements, press releases, and other actions by the laity* include statements by women religious (nuns and sisters, who are vowed but not ordained), pastoral administrators, and other groups or individuals who hold no priestly teaching office but whose teaching ministry is nevertheless affirmed and facilitated by the Catholics they

serve. These groups constitute a unique creative force in the Catholic community insofar as their activities de facto drive the issue of women's ordination, to which Rome
is more reactive than proactive. Yet these groups are accountable to a formidable hierarchy of priests, bishops, curial congregations, and the pope. Unlike members of the
ordained hierarchy, however, lay persons (including nuns and sisters) working for the
church have no lifetime guarantee of employment or continuing financial support to
serve as a safety net if they lose their jobs.

These three documentary sources form a feedback loop that informs and sus-
tains the flow of information in the Roman Catholic Church. Unfortunately, the
flow of information regarding women's ordination has been impeded because of
the Vatican's tight control over information. For the most part, the discussion has
been more *about* women than *with* them.

Claims and Counterclaims

The Vatican documents discussed here reveal the hierarchy's unfolding efforts
to codify and strengthen its position. Framed in highly technical language and
sometimes containing claims couched in obscure or even innovative theory (as
we will see later with a papal congregation's invalid claim of infallibility), Vatican
texts can frustrate even seasoned theologians. Further, the task of tracking specific
arguments over the range of texts through the years is challenging for three
reasons:

- a critical reading of any single document is usually insufficient for understanding Rome's
  position, because Vatican texts rarely appear in isolation but rather in a complex web
  of interdependent documents spanning shifts in time, space, and language;

- every post–Vatican II document on women's ordination has met resistance from many
  of the world's bishops and theologians, prompting Vatican commentators to clarify and
  reinforce the original statements, often substantively expanding and even changing
  theological and scriptural motifs in the original documents; and

- magisterial language on the issue has been in transition since the mid-1970s, when Pope
  Paul VI began a series of attempts (continued by his successor Pope John Paul II) to
  identify women's emerging roles in church and society, sometimes using nontraditional
  language that bewildered theologians and other scholars.

Two words that often confuse many lay Catholics are "doctrine" and "dogma."
The church's definition of "dogma" (Gr. *dokein*, "to think" or "to seem") has
changed over the centuries. Today, it is an authoritative proclamation of a truth
concerning faith or morals. The word "doctrine" (Gr. *didaskelos*, "master" or
"teacher") points to an official teaching of the church. In a practical sense,
these two words often are used interchangeably. Regarding women's ordination,
there have been numerous authoritative proclamations since Vatican II, but many
theologians do not accept that there is any doctrine.

Perhaps the most confusing of all words in the Roman Catholic lexicon is
the word "church" itself. The Latin *ecclesia* derives from the Greek *ekklesia*, an
assembly of worshipers. The Greek *kyiakon* points more to the "house" of the
Lord. The modern English word "church" is used variously to mean a building, a

congregation, an ecclesial governing body, curial congregations and commissions in the Vatican, the magisterium, the pope, and/or the whole people of God. A reader can determine the intended meaning only by placing the word in context (which can make for adventuresome reading). For the benefit of the nonspecialist reader, I use the words "Rome" and "Vatican" to mean a decision-making person, group, or hierarchy within the "Holy See," a more specialized term including the authorities and functions associated with the papacy. Likewise I interchangeably use "nun" (a member of a contemplative religious order) and "sister" (a member of an order active in the world).

Over time, the language used in claims and counterclaims in the ordination debate has become even more intricate. I have tried at every turn to present these arguments in accessible language; however, at some points it is not possible to extricate the issues from the Vatican lexicon without losing meaning, so I have included an exhaustive glossary at the end of this book. I ask the reader's patience with the technical language.

This book examines English translations and responses, primarily (but not exclusively) by American scholars. Biblical passages are taken from the New Revised Standard Version (NRSV) of the Bible. The full English texts of selected documents are included in an appendix (because of space considerations, they appear without footnotes). To facilitate text comparisons, I have numbered the paragraphs of those documents, and I refer to the paragraphs by placing their numbers within parentheses in this text. A thumbnail synopsis of each document appears at the end of this book.

John Paul II attempted to place the entire discussion in parentheses in 1998, when he declared that the debate was closed and that Catholics who insisted upon publicly pursuing the issue would be deserving of a "just penalty." In a practical sense, that penalty is excommunication. That threat notwithstanding, it is the goal of this book to gather up the various strands of the discussion so that Catholics and others might see what they look like all at once, when the big picture becomes manifestly greater than the sum of its parts.

Silence: An Unkind Penalty

Closing discussion of priesthood can also close lives. To illustrate this point, I offer briefly the story of Ludmila Javorova, a Catholic woman living in Communist-controlled Czechoslovakia during the Cold War years following World War II. During that time, Russian leader Joseph Stalin's efforts to crush religion in Czechoslovakia resulted in the 1948 confiscation of church property and the arrest of more than thirteen thousand priests and religious, who were sent to concentration camps. As a result, the Christian resistance movement, most likely with Rome's tacit approval,[27] developed a clandestine church that allowed Catholicism to continue functioning underground. In one account, a cardinal, whose apartment was bugged, secretly ordained priests who were brought blindfolded to his home, where he "put on music and serve[d] them tea. Then, speaking through a long plastic tube, he would whisper the words of ordination to candidates with a Dvorak symphony turned up loud."[28] Such were the realities of Communism and Catholicism in that time and place.

During more than four decades of Communist control in Czechoslovakia, an estimated 220 married men were secretly ordained priests, and of those about 15 were clandestinely ordained as bishops.[29] In 1970, with the country still struggling under Communist rule, Ludmila Javorova was ordained a priest. The impetus for ordaining women was the need for women to minister to other women, particularly women imprisoned by the Communists. At profound risk to her life, Javorova served for twenty years in the underground church and as vicar general for the man who ordained her. Bishop Felix Maria Davidek was a former political prisoner whose validity as bishop was accepted by Rome, and who functioned in the clandestine church with the Vatican's implicit consent to ordain priests to work in secret.[30]

When the Communist regime fell in 1989, the status of priests ordained during those long years had to be negotiated with the Vatican. Priestly ordinations considered legitimate under the forces of Communism now presented a "problem to be solved."[31] Unlike other clandestinely ordained priests, however, Javorova was not invited to any Vatican negotiation. But Rome's rebuff was not the only one, she recalled. "When things began to open up, those priests who knew I was ordained began to distance themselves from me." Her biographer, Medical Mission Sister Miriam Therese Winter, explained that for these priests to "appear supportive of women's ordination in theory or in practice would place another obstacle on the path to their [own] validation."[32]

Javorova began gathering the facts of the underground church to be communicated to Rome. Validation was a tricky business and, according to Winter, not entirely unbiased. The "first line" priests, products of the Communist-controlled seminary and licensed by the government to minister openly, were "quickly reconciled" to Rome. "Among these were a number of clergy who had collaborated with the regime," said Winter. "Second line" clergy, those who had obeyed a Vatican directive prohibiting cooperation with Communists and who ministered in secrecy (without a paper trail) in the underground church "in order to keep the integrity of the Catholic faith alive" were not recognized until Rome could corroborate their ordinations. Priests whose ordinations were of doubtful validity would be reordained *sub conditione* ("subject to condition"), meaning that if their secret ordinations were valid, the new ordinations would have no effect; but, if their original ordinations were not valid, the men would now be newly ordained.[33]

Specifically, Rome dealt with three categories of clandestinely ordained priests:

• Ordinations of unmarried men (if determined by Rome to be valid) were not revoked, and the Vatican assured Czech Catholics that the priestly functions performed by these priests were valid.

• Ordinations of married men (if determined to be valid) were not revoked, but the men were ordered to stop functioning as priests; however, their priestly actions in the underground church were post facto recognized as valid. And, married priests "could be conditionally reordained in a special diocese created for them within the Czech

Republic's Greek Catholic Church, which is affiliated with Rome and allows married priests."[34]

- Ordinations of women were declared "clearly invalid," and their priestly actions were likewise invalid.[35] Thus, said Rome, Catholics to whom these women had ministered under threat of Communist persecution had not, in fact, received valid sacraments.

Javorova sent a letter to John Paul II explaining the extenuating circumstances of her ordination, but he never replied. In 1996, the local bishop notified her that she was "formally prohibited" from exercising priestly duties and instructed her to *keep the details of this prohibition secret.*[36] During the 1990s, as women's ordination movements around the world honored the aging Javorova for her many years of priestly service to a beleaguered church in a Communist-held country, both she and the Vatican remained silent.

As the twentieth century gave way to the twenty-first, Ludmila Javorova was teaching religion to children ages seven to fourteen. Little tangible evidence remained of her priestly ministry: a little box containing a priestly stole "small enough to be hidden in a pocket" in case the Communists came, a tiny brass chalice, a small container for communion hosts, everything small, "so that these things could be hidden, so we could put them in a basket in order to transport them." She could no longer celebrate mass, but she said: "I have been a priest for thirty years and nobody can erase that. They cannot say it did not exist."[37]

Javorova's priesthood illustrates that even in winter, the seed grows. This is a winter of discontent for Catholics who believe that God calls both men and women to serve in priestly ministry. The following pages explore just what Rome has said (and hasn't said) concerning women priests, and responses from theologians, Catholic groups, women religious, bishops, and others. These pages are intended to stoke the fires of faith for Catholics praying for all of women's gifts to be recognized by the church, for women's call to a priestly vocation to be tested, and for women to be granted the same seven sacraments enjoyed by men.

• • •

In spring 1896, during the long, dark night uniting Holy Thursday and Good Friday, Carmelite Sister Thérèse Martin "felt something very hot and wet" percolate into her mouth.[38] *The next morning, she saw that her handkerchief was filled with blood, an ominous symptom. She sensed a "fog" thickening around her.*

By September 1897, she was "dying of not being able to die."[39] *Following many months of vomiting, labored breathing, and loss of consciousness — consumed by tuberculosis — she considered her impending death at age twenty-four a blessing: had she been male, she would have been ordained later that year. She thanked God for taking her early, to spare her the disappointment of not being a priest.*

Thérèse's vows as a Carmelite nun, while sacred, were not sacramental. The church offered no sacrament for a woman wishing to dedicate herself in priestly service to God. Of the seven sacraments, only six were open to women, a reality that caused her great pain.

❧ Chapter 2 ❧

The Hierarchical Priesthood

"An Intimate Sacramental Brotherhood"

Before examining the ordination debate, it will be helpful to explore briefly the history and nature of ordination. Roman Catholic teaching holds that the sacrament of holy orders was instituted by Christ and is conferred by the laying of a bishop's hands on the candidate, who thus receives the Holy Spirit and divine grace necessary to exercise priestly ministry. In the early church, ordination was accomplished by a simple liturgical blessing called *ordinatio* (Lat. *ordinare*, "to create order"),[40] within the Christian community. In contemporary practice, the sacramental rite of ordination is considerably more complex, because "it confers a gift of the Holy Spirit that permits the exercise of a 'sacred power' (*sacra potestas*) that can come only from Christ himself through his Church."[41]

Jesus, however, said nothing about priesthood, and neither did Paul, the "Apostle to the Gentiles" whose work largely shaped the first-century church. According to theologian Richard P. McBrien, at first the church "seems to have had no intention of having a priesthood of its own, distinct from the Jewish priesthood."[42] Moreover, Paul did not rank ministries according to a hierarchy, which would have been useless in any case because he and others expected the imminent return of the glorified Christ. Rather, the hierarchy of holy orders evolved over several centuries and ultimately included three ascending levels of ordination: diaconate, presbyterate, and episcopate.

Threefold Ministry

Diaconate (Gr. *diakonos*, "service"). Dating from the time of the apostles (Phil. 1:1), the diaconate is chronologically the first and hierarchically the lowest level of ordination. Deacons do not consecrate the eucharistic bread and wine but do much of the work of priests: proclaim the gospel, preach, baptize, dispense the eucharist, witness marriages, and officiate at funerals.[43] Paul did not exclude women from serving as deacons (1 Tim. 3:11), but in time the Council of Chalcedon (451) declared: "No woman under forty years of age is to be ordained a deacon, and then only after close scrutiny."[44] Canon 18 of the Second Council of Orleans in 533 decreed, "henceforth no woman may any longer receive diaconal benediction due to the frailty of their sex."[45] Repeated complaints from clergy

12

(Gr. *kleros*, "official") that women had no place in the developing hierarchy put an end to the tradition.[46]

Over the centuries, as the ordained priesthood grew stronger, the diaconate grew weaker and finally became only a ritual stepping-stone to priesthood. In 1967, Pope Paul VI restored the "permanent diaconate" for men who did not intend to become priests.[47] Following the ancient definition of the diaconate as a class of persons dedicated to Christian service (rather than to priestly teaching), these men received the imposition of hands "not unto the priesthood, but unto the ministry."[48] Permanent deacons could be married at the time of their ordination, but were bound to celibacy if they later lost their wives to death or divorce.[49]

Presbyterate (Gr. *presbyteros*, "elder"). Women and men structured the early Christian church at the local level, within their own homes, where women's hospitality and leadership were key components of worship. Over time, worship became more public, leadership became more institutionalized, and the church's increasing absorption of surrounding Greco-Roman values, including women's inferior social status, posed a problem for maintaining women's leadership in the church.[50] Dating from the second century, when these men were compared with the elders chosen by Moses (Num. 11:17–25), the presbyterate (priests) began to exist hierarchically above the diaconate (deacons) but subordinate to the episcopate (bishops). Only after Constantine took Rome under the banner of the cross and in thanksgiving legalized Christianity in 313 did an *ordained* priesthood become firmly established within the institutional church. This development elevated clerics as a "special caste within the church"[51] and introduced sharp divisions between clergy and laity. When the Council of Trent (1545–63) strengthened the ordained priesthood and established a seminary system, the gap widened between priests and the uneducated populations they served. That separation grew throughout the nineteenth and twentieth centuries, as clerical authority became increasingly centralized in local bishops and the bishop of Rome, the pope. By the end of the twentieth century, Rome had revived the neglected idea that through sacramental ordination priests were "configured to Christ" in order to operate *in persona Christi* — in the person and role of Christ. As members of "an intimate sacramental brotherhood" empowered to partake of the "universal mission of salvation,"[52] they became "sharers of the priesthood of Christ Himself."[53]

Episcopate (Gr. *episkopos*, "overseer"). Paul addressed "bishops" (*episkopoi*) according to their function as overseers (Phil. 1:1). He wrote that a bishop should marry only once, be sensible and respectable, avoid drunkenness and violence, and manage his children well, "for if someone does not know how to manage his own household, how can he take care of God's church?" (1 Tim. 3:5). The institutional office of "bishop" (*episkopos*) emerged in the second century and was not used with regularity until the fifth century. The Council of Trent placed bishops hierarchically over priests and deacons, and today the episcopate forms the third and highest office conferred by holy orders, "the acme [*summa*] of the sacred ministry."[54] Bishops are "high priests, principal dispensers of the mysteries of God"[55] commissioned to ordain and consecrate, confirm, teach, and govern. Working in union with (but subordinate to) the pope, they are responsible for most church decision-making and virtually all implementation of church teaching. Bishops, in an "eminent and visible manner, take the place of Christ himself."[56]

Today, the diaconate (deacons) includes men ordained for "service" to the church, while the presbyterate (priests) and the episcopate (bishops) constitute the "ministerial priesthood," which is "sacerdotal" (Lat. *sacerdos,* "priest" or, interestingly, "priestess").[57]

In the New Testament, the term "priest" was applied in only three ways: to Jewish temple priests (Matt. 26:3, 57), to Jesus (as High Priest, Heb. 4:14), and to the community of the faithful (1 Pet. 2:5, 9). Specific tasks, not offices, were created for the service of the Christian community. Gradually, Christian community leadership evolved into a system of titles given and accepted according to ministry. Apostles, including Paul, were ministers of the highest rank, but even they did not assume the office or title of "priest," though the term was readily available (Gr. *hiereus,* Heb. *cohen*).

In the first century, Clement of Rome taught that (still-emerging) leadership offices followed a line of authority from Jesus to the apostles to church leaders and their successors. The interpretation of apostolic *tradition* as constituting a doctrine of "apostolic *succession*" necessary for priesthood would be debated for centuries, although the latter won out. Richard McBrien pointed out, however, that there was no compelling evidence that members of the Twelve presided over the eucharist, "or that a chain of ordination from Apostle to bishop to priest was required for presiding."[58] During the second and third centuries, *presbyteros* (priests) and *episkopos* (bishops) were not yet strictly separate roles, and bishops were elected by the people they served.[59] Likewise, there was little practical difference in the daily lives of laity and clergy.

In the early fourth century, having conquered Rome under the banner of the cross, Constantine opened Rome to religious freedom and conferred civil authority and privilege upon the Christian clergy. The government's favor (and finance) soon transformed the clergy into an elite sociopolitical group. The *presbyteroi* began assuming some of the liturgical functions of the *episkopoi* as the latter took on more administrative and decision-making tasks. As priests and bishops assumed more and more power in the church, the laity became more and more passive.

By the fifth century, the basic structure of priesthood was in place, with special dress, titles, and hierarchical placements. During this time, priests and bishops were still elected by their local communities, and the bishop of Rome was elected by the parish priests of the city and served at the will of the Christian population. In 1059, Pope Nicholas II restricted the privilege of papal election to the cardinals (priests who serve as administrators in the Vatican and as advisors to the pope), even though the body of cardinals would not officially be defined and recognized until 1179, by Lateran Council III.[60]

In the ninth century, religious leaders in the East (Constantinople) and West (Rome) capped a long series of political and religious differences with the Great Schism in 1054. As a result, the church split into the Eastern Orthodox and Roman Catholic expressions of Christianity. This book is concerned with priesthood in the West.

The Sixth Sacrament

Until the twelfth century, the understanding of "ordination" varied according to time and place, but in no case was it sacramental or permanently effective. Primarily, ordination was an assignment of a Christian to a particular church role. Documents from the early Middle Ages show that bishops regularly ordained women as abbesses, deaconesses, and nuns. A tenth-century letter of Bishop Atto of Vercelli said, "For the aid of men, devout women were ordained leaders of worship in the holy Church."[61] Ordination was not formally distinguished according to gender until the twelfth century, when ordination came to be understood as the empowering of a minister to absolve sin and to change bread and wine into the body and blood of Christ. Even then, however, there were considerably diverse opinions over what ordination *was* (for instance, Pope Urban II in 1089 affirmed the archbishop of Rheims's power to ordain the kings and queens of France), and which *kinds* of ordination were considered "clerical."[62]

In 1208, responding to a splinter group's appointment of its own ministers to hold eucharistic services, Pope Innocent III ordered a Crusade against the heretical Waldensians and decreed that priestly ordination henceforth would be necessary to celebrate the eucharist.[63] Three subsequent popes overturned that ruling, but fourteen centuries after Christ, the Council of Florence (1439) decreed that holy orders in fact constituted the sixth sacrament.[64] This fifteenth-century sacramentalization of priesthood further separated the clergy and laity, as well as the male and female.

In 1517, the Augustinian monk and theologian Martin Luther sparked the Protestant Reformation in protest against outrageous abuses of clerical privilege. Largely in reaction against Luther, the Council of Trent (1545–63) issued an official list of seven sacraments for males and six for females. The council declared that the institutional, ordained priesthood was separate from, and superior to, the more biblical priesthood of believers (laity).

Over the centuries these medieval decisions retroactively were laid over the history of the early church, resulting in the widespread assumption among many generations of Catholics that the tradition of ordained priesthood was coexistent with the founding of the church. In fact, however, a rich history of women's participation and leadership existed for more than half of Christian history.

A Reflection of Heavenly Hierarchy

In 1917, the Code of Canon Law — the collection of rules governing church order and discipline — articulated and codified the tradition of a male-only clergy. Canon 968:1 declared, "Only a baptized man [*vir*] validly receives sacred ordination."[65] The words of the ritual, however, were not fixed until 1954, when Pope Pius XII wrote: "The ordained priest is called to be an *official* representative and witness of the Church's priestly charism, while the [lay person] is only a *de facto* witness."[66] These words voiced a traditional assumption: priests were *official* church agents and lay persons were witnesses only in *practice.* This concept reflected the idea articulated in Pius XII's 1947 encyclical *Mediator Dei* ("On the Sacred Liturgy") that the order of priesthood was "a kind of reflection of the heavenly hierarchy"[67] of God and his ranks of angels. This emphasis on hierarchy was rearranged somewhat during Vatican II with a dogmatic constitution (a formal proclamation of dogma) entitled *Lumen Gentium* (literally, "Light of the Nations," but known as the "Dogmatic Constitution on the Church," 1964). This teaching insisted that lay persons were not mere spectators: the whole church constituted *the people of God.*[68] But the roles open to the people of God were divided according to gender. In 1994, the English edition of the *Catechism of the Catholic Church* repeated the 1917 and 1983 canon law codes and further stated that only the Vatican had "the responsibility and right to call someone to receive orders."[69] The call itself came from God, but Rome reserved the right to validate that call and determine who would (and would not) be ordained.

Two ways Rome reserved this right had been explained in 1970 in the Vatican daily newspaper, *L'Osservatore Romano,* in an article spanning a quarter of its front page: "Jesus does not call women to the ministry [and] *does not communicate to women the message he received from the Father.* It is a fact and we are bound to recognize it." Since God had found it necessary "to choose a time and a place" to "make himself a man," it followed that the incarnation of Jesus as savior "would not have been true and real" if God had not submitted to the conditioning of human nature, requiring that Christians not neglect "the conditions of this community."[70] Jesus "obviously had to be either male or female," wrote Bishop Michael Kenny of Juneau, Alaska. Given "the time and culture in which 'the Word was made flesh,' male may have been the best choice. But essential to salvation's story? I don't think so."[71]

Since Christians could not neglect the conditions of Christ's community, it logically followed that they could not neglect the conditions of *any* Christian community, including the present. Over time, the Vatican would adopt the opposite view, saying that Jesus did *not* act according to the values of his day. This about-face was due largely to arguments like the one made by highly regarded Jesuit sociologist Joseph Fichter, who in 1977 quoted sociologist Thomas O'Dea in saying that "structures which emerge in one set of conditions and in response to one set of problems may turn out later to be unwieldy instruments for handling new problems under new conditions."[72] This observation certainly applied to the origins and nature of priesthood.

The 1970 *L'Osservatore Romano* article also had said that ordination constituted a male priesthood according to Christ's "positive will," which "alone could be the sure base of the legitimacy of a priesthood of women." In fact, however, Christ "[did] not communicate to women the message he received from the Father."[73] In time, these statements would provide template-quality justifications *for* the ordination of women: *Could* the mission of Christ continue in the church if the conditions of his community were neglected? *Could* silence tell us anything about the positive will of Christ concerning the gender of ordained priesthood? Could Christ's silence tell us *anything at all* about his will for priesthood? Or that he even *thought* about it?

For the Vatican, Christ's silence posed a particularly troublesome source of support for a male-only priesthood, because theology and tradition were grounded in speculation about (and interpretation of) the unspoken "will" of Jesus. That is, ordained priesthood was built upon the very silence of Christ.

Two Priesthoods:
Common and Ordained

The Vatican II document *Lumen Gentium* ("Dogmatic Constitution on the Church," 1964) also had stressed that the common and ordained priesthoods were different "essentially and not only in degree," and "each in its own way" shared in the "one priesthood of Christ."[74] In addition to the ordained priesthood, "the rest of the Christian faithful... in their own way also have their own part"[75] to play in the Christian life, according to canon law. This "common priesthood of all the faithful" joined with the ordained priesthood to participate "each in its own proper way, in the one priesthood of Christ."[76] But, while "ordered to one another," there was an "essential and vital difference"[77] between the priesthoods. One such difference was that the two priesthoods were born of different sacraments — common priesthood by baptism and ordained priesthood by the sacrament of holy orders. Baptism empowered the Christian to worship and serve Christ, especially by partaking of the eucharist, through which the believer found "union with [Christ] the High Priest."[78] Holy orders, by contrast, had the power to "configure the priest to Christ so as to enable him to act in the person of Christ the head and to exercise the *potestas sacra* [sacred power] to offer sacrifice and forgive sins."[79]

In 2001, Pope John Paul II highlighted this essential difference: "the priest acting *in persona Christi* [in the person of Christ] celebrates the sacrifice of the Mass and administers the sacraments."[80] This speech was part of a paper by the Vatican's Congregation for the Clergy explaining that priestly identity was three-dimensional — a gift of the Holy Spirit, conformation to Christ, and ministry to the church "so as to have Christ" present in the community.

The priest's very being was "ontologically assimilated to Christ."[81] That is, the priest himself was absorbed into Christ. Priests acted *in persona Christi capitis* (in the role of Christ the head),[82] *in nomine ecclesiae* (in the name of the church), and as *alter Christus* ("other" Christ).[83] After Vatican II, *alter Christus* fell into disuse as the hierarchy increasingly employed the term *in persona Christi* to describe the priest's role as acting in the person of Christ.[84] At this point, the Congregation for the Clergy concluded that "a good laity" was "scarcely possible" without "holy priests," without whom "everything is dead."[85]

Hierarchy: An Ordered Body of Clergy

The word "hierarchy" (Gr. *hieros*, "sacred," and *archein*, "rule"), as applied to church leadership, empowers ordained priests (variously as pastors, bishops, or pope) to make church law, determine how it is to be kept, and enforce obedience to it. For this reason, nonordained persons (including nuns and religious sisters and brothers) are not part of the church hierarchy. Following are brief definitions of terms used in this book.

Pope: The bishop of the Diocese of Rome. Since about the eleventh century, the bishop of Rome has served as successor of Peter, the apostle. The pope is the spiritual leader of the world's more than one billion Roman Catholics and the temporal sovereign of Vatican City.

Roman Curia: The collective name for the administrative agencies and officials who carry out the pope's decisions and assist him in governing the church. The curia is comprised of various dicasteries (departments): congregations (executive), pontifical councils (promotional), and tribunals (judicial), with their agencies and commissions. Of these, the Congregation for the Doctrine of the Faith (CDF) is most powerful.

College of Cardinals: Appointed by the pope. Cardinals are bishops who retain their dioceses (some in name only) while advising the pope and assisting him in church administration. As members of the college, the world's cardinals elect the pope but are subordinate to him. This hierarchical arrangement reflects the church's understanding of the relationship of Peter to the other apostles.

Synod of Bishops: A worldwide advisory body to the pope that develops church teaching. This group's power was substantially weakened under Pope John Paul II.

Episcopal Conference: A national or regional body of bishops charged with certain decisions concerning church discipline.

Bishop: A priest consecrated to carry on the work of the apostles. Called an "ordinary," he is responsible for the church government of a diocese (Gr. *dioikesis*, "household management," a geographical area of responsibility). An auxiliary bishop assists the ordinary. The consecrated bishop of a large, metropolitan area (archdiocese) is called an archbishop.

Priest: An ordained minister appointed by a bishop to serve as pastor of a parish. A priest can be "religious" (belonging to a religious order, such as the Benedictines) or "diocesan" (belonging to a diocese).

Deacon: A man ordained for service to the church. A deacon cannot consecrate the bread and wine during mass.

Nuns (Sisters) and Brothers: Women and men religious who live according to communal law, approved by Rome. As nonordained lay persons, they are not part of church hierarchy.

Laity: Nonordained persons who make up the church.

Holy See: From the Latin *sedes* ("seat"), the Diocese of Rome. Also, church government, including the pope, curia, and college of cardinals.

Diocese: A geographic division of the church under the supervision of a bishop.

Parish: A specific community of faithful within a diocese under the supervision of a pastor.

• • •

When Thérèse professed her vows at Carmel of Lisieux in 1890, she stated her mission: "I have come to save souls and, above all, to pray for priests." If she could not fulfill her heart's desire to be a priest, she would devote herself to pray on their behalf.

Yet the priesthood puzzled Thérèse. During a trip to Rome the year before, she had made a discovery:

> Until then, I hadn't been able to understand the main purpose of Carmel. I loved praying for sinners, but I was astounded at having to pray for priests. I thought their souls were without blemish. [In Rome at age fourteen] I met many holy priests [but] I saw that some of them were still men, weak and subject to human frailty, even though the sublime dignity of the priesthood raised them above the angels. Now if prayers are needed for those holy priests whom Jesus called "the salt of the earth," how much more is it needed for priests of lukewarm virtue. [What] a wonderful vocation we Carmelites have! It is up to us to preserve the salt of the earth. We offer our prayers and penance for God's apostles and we are their apostles.[86]

Ever willing to subordinate her wants and needs to authority, Thérèse wrote that though she longed to be a priest, she admired "the humility of St. Francis of Assisi" and believed that she "should imitate him and refuse the sublime dignity of the priesthood."[87] In reality, of course, there was no priesthood open to her refusal.

❧ Chapter 3 ❧

A Window Unopened — Vatican II

October 11, 1962–December 8, 1965

Since this study takes as its springboard the extraordinary occurrence called Vatican II, it will be helpful to examine some relevant events of those fateful four autumns from 1962 to 1965, when church leaders gathered — energetically, optimistically, sometimes uncomfortably — to explore new and uncertain issues and to wrestle with "the problem of where to give in and where to hold fast, how to introduce modernization while preserving tradition."[88] U.S. theologian, and later cardinal, Avery Dulles wrote that the council recognized "the need of setting forth a radically different vision of the Church, more biblical, more historical, more vital and dynamic."[89]

It is important to state at the outset that Vatican II was not a watershed event for women in the church. As Canadian canon lawyer Francis Morrisey pointed out, the word *mulieres* ("women") was not used often in Vatican II documents; rather, it more often was found in the expression *viri et mulieres* ("men and women"). Further, women's activities were usually referred to "in accord with their nature."[90]

But that is not to say that Vatican II had no effect on women's roles in the church. In the late 1950s, with the clerical hierarchy comfortably in place and a pontiff teaching infallibly on matters of faith and morals, the Holy Spirit moved in an unexpected direction. Pope John XXIII, a kind, elderly man from whom little innovation was expected, was an outgoing and sociable person who refused to wear the traditional papal tiara and often mingled with people on the streets of Rome. Soon after his election, he stunned the Catholic world by calling a worldwide meeting of bishops, "against the advice of his Roman bureaucracy."[91] Vatican II was the second such gathering (after Vatican I in 1869–70) since the sixteenth-century Protestant Reformation. Convened for the purpose of *aggiornamento*,[92] or updating the church to the wider outside world, the council exceeded any ecclesiastical initiative in modern Catholic memory with its overview of church teaching and revision of the 1917 Code of Canon Law. Jesuit Ladislas Örsy, a widely respected canon lawyer, wrote that "the achievements of the council could be called, quite legitimately, new discoveries" insofar as the participants "reached new insights into those sacred realities that the church has possessed from its origins."[93] Örsy listed four overarching achievements of the council:

- from *imperium* to *communio,* or from the centralization of power to a more organic structure of a body, where each member was endowed with the power of the Spirit;

- from confessional conflict to ecumenical vision, or from discord to unity among Christian churches;

- from defensive isolation to expansive presence, or from a shocked reaction to the Protestant Reformation to a new and appreciative look at earthly values and human personality; and

- from a static worldview to a dynamic one, or from the Aristotelian idea of unchanging perfection to a contemporary acknowledgment of developmental process.[94]

These achievements, Örsy concluded, occurred because "whenever the fathers reached a new discovery, it was due to their enhanced knowledge and the spirit of inquiry that animated them."[95] In the realm of women's concerns that spirit was not active, but as in so many areas of life, women rode to change on men's coattails.

On the eve of the council, a Swiss attorney named Gertrude Heinzleman submitted a petition to a preparatory commission calling for women's ordination.[96] Predictably, the petition made it no further. During the council's planning stages, according to Vatican observer Peter Steinfels, "the heads of men's orders of priests and brothers were canvassed along with the world's bishops" for their input. "Heads of orders of sisters were not."[97] But in the outside world women's opportunities were rapidly expanding, and the council at least offered hope for expanded church roles for women. Unfortunately, John XXIII died in June 1963, and his successor, Pope Paul VI, was more cautious. Faced with the tremendous task of guiding global change in the church while avoiding excesses, Paul VI was not amenable to expanding women's roles.

Some Devout Ladies

The first challenge women faced at Vatican II was to pry open the door to St. Peter's basilica, where the council met. Rome had formally invited non-Catholic male observers to the proceedings, but Catholic women were not allowed to attend; instead, male auditors (not participants) served as spokesmen for women's organizations.[98] Then, six days before the third session opened in September 1964, having learned that the exclusion of women from the council was being publicly criticized, Pope Paul VI wrote: "We have given orders that some devout ladies" would attend as non-speaking, non-voting auditors for several ceremonies and general assemblies. "Women will thus know just how much honor the church pays to them in the dignity of their being and of their mission on the human and the Christian levels."[99] His gesture came too late for the carefully screened women to arrive in time for his welcoming speech, which was delivered to an empty *auditrices'* box prepared for them.[100]

By the fourth and last session in 1965, twenty-two women were serving as auditors among some three thousand men. Sociologist Ruth Wallace explained that "women were virtually invisible and entirely silent when decisions were made regarding important structural changes affecting all members of the church."[101] Vatican II historian Helen Marie Ciernick wrote that the women were allowed to attend "only those general congregations at which questions regarding women were being debated, meet with council members between meetings, sit beside and not with the male lay auditors, and frequent only the women's coffee bar."[102] With the help of some men present, the women did move somewhat beyond their marginal status, but unfortunately their progress was not recorded in council documents.

The Vatican's treatment of women also pointed to the hierarchy's view of the special "dignity" of women's "being," which the magisterium had long defined in terms of "anthropological subordinationism"[103] promoted by Aristotle, Augustine, and Aquinas. The concept rested on the idea of male headship within the order of creation. Theologian Rosemary Radford Ruether described this phenomenon:

> This notion basically identifies patriarchal social order with the natural or divinely created order. Male headship is thus regarded as rooted in the intrinsic nature of things and willed by God. Any effort to upset this order by giving women autonomy or equal rights would constitute a rebellion against God and would result in moral and social chaos in human society.[104]

Because a woman's natural inferiority could lead to sin when she acted independently — apart from her ties to a man — a key item of subordination was the "scapegoating of woman for the origin of sin. Woman, *acting on her own,* caused the fall of humanity."[105]

When the Second Vatican Council convened in 1962, a Roman Catholic could still pick up the *Catholic Encyclopedia,* published in 1914, and read that women were "inferior in some respects to men both in body and in soul." A woman's "real power" was found in her "indirect influence" (on her husband); even "common sense" supported the Vatican's opposition to the increasingly popular idea of allowing women to vote. Moreover, a woman's struggle for equality in employment was "not compatible with the standard of the gospel," nor could the sexes ever be equal in "studies pursued at a university."[106] After nearly two millennia of this reasoning, it was epoch-making when the Second Vatican Council denounced anthropological subordinationism:

> All women and men are endowed with a rational soul and are created in God's image; they have the same nature and origin and, being redeemed by Christ, they enjoy the same divine calling and destiny; there is here a basic equality between all and it must be accorded ever greater recognition.[107]

The council's acknowledgment that women possessed a "rational soul," with the "same nature and origin" and the "same divine calling and destiny" as men, constituted a clarion (if later muffled) denunciation of subordinationism.

One council document in particular addressed the nature of priesthood. *Presbyterorum Ordinis* ("Decree on the Ministry and Life of Priests") emerged unexpectedly when Council participants realized that existing discussions of priesthood were inadequate for the task of ecclesial renewal.[108] This document crystallized a phrase that would echo in Vatican halls for decades: by the grace of holy orders, priests acted *in persona Christi* — "in the person of Christ."[109] At the time, the male-only priesthood was taken for granted, and this phrase was ascribed little of the meaning it would take on in later arguments prohibiting women priests because *they could not physically resemble Christ.*

Vatican II closed in 1965 with the laity's widespread expectation that their new collaboration with clergy would produce "a thoroughly democratic Catholic Church."[110] That did not happen. In fact, the exhilaration surrounding Vatican II masked a portent of things to come. Women and women's issues had been scarcely addressed in council documents, and thirty years later only three known articles had been published which focused solely on the women at the council.[111]

Another issue was noticeably neglected. According to veteran Vatican observer Peter Hebblethwaite: "Every role and task in the Church was held up for inspection and marked for renewal: priest, lay person, religious, bishop, missionary. But there was one exception: the papal office itself did not come under scrutiny, nor did the college of cardinals."[112] Further, when Vatican II closed just before Christmas 1965, Catholics in the West stood at the threshold of a secular women's movement followed by an "Information Age," a powerful combination; but an unrenewed papacy was poised to revitalize its fight against modernism, especially the idea that woman could be priests.

• • •

On Christmas Day 1886, the Martin family returned home from church in the small French town of Lisieux. For a decade, this had been a single-parent family: Thérèse's mother, a maker of fine lace, had died of breast cancer when Thérèse was four, leaving her father, a watchmaker, to care for five daughters. As was the local tradition, the Martin girls left their shoes on the hearth on Christmas Eve, and the next morning their shoes would be filled with small gifts. Thérèse was now fourteen, an age by which children had usually outgrown the custom; but, always self-interested, she had left her shoes on the hearth, expecting the customary gifts. After mass on Christmas morning, when the family walked into the house, her father looked at the gift-filled shoes: "Thank goodness, it's the last year we shall have to do this kind of thing!"[113]

Thérèse's younger sister, Céline, was standing nearby and steeled herself for one of Thérèse's predictable tantrums, but for some reason it didn't come. As Thérèse would later recall, on that Christmas day Jesus had given her the gift of making her more sensitive to her father's feelings than her own. It was as if she recovered the sense of self she had lost when her mother died. She referred to this "shoe" event as her "conversion." She saw that her old way of seeing things would not suffice for the Christian life she wished to lead and that a more mature faith would require a new vision.

⇒ *Chapter 4* ⇐

A Guide to Post–Vatican II
Themes of the Debate

It can be challenging to grasp the various strands of thought that appear in Vatican teaching about women priests. There is nothing inherently difficult in most of the material, but because it has been presented by different people over time, an idea can take on new shades of meaning from one year to the next. Following are key themes of Vatican teachings presented in the following chapters, where they are explored and amply footnoted.

Creation

Christian anthropology in the narrow sense used here is a creation-based understanding of divinely assigned sex roles. It teaches that Adam (not Eve) physically resembled the savior who was to come, and so only a male, being sexually modeled after Christ, is qualified to be priest.

Complementarity is based upon natural law, in which male and female live in a mutually dependent relationship.

Subordinationism is the teaching of Aristotle, Augustine, and Aquinas, among many others, that women are naturally inferior to men because they are biologically "incomplete males" (Aristotle) or because of their secondary status in the "rib" version of creation. In subordinationism, "complementarity" is defined in unequal terms, with the male as "head" of the female, who is the "body." Vatican Council II (1962–65) repudiated this teaching, but the teaching is still used to reinforce the tradition of male priesthood.

"Feminine genius" is a term frequently used by Pope John Paul II to extol the virtues of women's biological capacities and religious roles as virgin, wife, and mother.

The Church's Divine Constitution

The church was established by Christ, and hence it must be maintained in accordance to Christ's "positive will." In cases where he was silent (as he was on priesthood) the hierarchy reserves the right and duty to determine his will.

The college of twelve apostles comprises Jewish men called by Christ (Luke 6:13) to sit on heavenly thrones and judge the Twelve Tribes of Israel (Matt. 19:28).

Jesus charged these men with carrying the gospel ("good news") to the world. The twelve were entrusted with founding and nurturing the earthly church, including provisions for leadership succession.

A priest is a vehicle of salvation, because through ordination he has been given the ministry entrusted by Christ to Peter, and he exercises the "maternal authority" of Mother Church, obedience to which is required for salvation. Only men may exercise this maternal authority.

Tradition

Church fathers (early teachers of the faith) taught that women were not to be priests. While they employed sexist and even misogynist language, according to the Vatican that did not affect their pastoral practice or teachings.

The deposit of faith is the entire collection of revealed teachings and church tradition whose protection and promulgation is reserved to the church's teaching authority.

Scripture

Scripture alone is not sufficient to show that only males can be priests. However, because much teaching in the past was based on what was then understood about scripture, the teaching about priesthood remains.

Metaphors and Images

The nuptial analogy is a Christian extension of images from the Song of Songs, a love poem in the Old Testament, in which, according to Catholic teaching, the lover is Jesus and the beloved is the church. Jesus is male, and the church is female. Priests represent Christ, and they embody "spiritual fatherhood" as well as the "maternal authority" of the church. In the church, likewise, priests have both male and female roles to play: male as person, female as church member. Women have nothing to represent which they are not; hence they are always only female.

In persona Christi describes the priest's cultic function. He stands in the person and the role of Christ. Maleness is required for this role. A female priest could not be recognized as Christ and would confuse the faithful.

Church-as-woman has Mary the mother of Jesus as its model and norm. The church, like Mary, is passive and receptive.

Sacrament of Holy Orders

The Church has no authority to change the substance of a sacrament, hence holy orders must remain closed to women. There will always be seven sacraments for men and six for women.

Authority

The magisterium, the teaching authority of the church, determines and enforces church law. According to certain procedures, the church teaches "infallibly" and pronounces teachings to be "definitively held." All decision-making power ultimately is tied to priestly ordination.

Discipline and punishment are necessary to preserve the deposit of faith and to fight heresy. These tools include silencing of unorthodox clerics and theologians, and excommunicating Catholics charged with heresy.

Modern World

Women's progress in society prompts the church to examine women's roles more closely and to encourage their accomplishments in society. But women's rights in society are not the same as those in the church, where women's participation is divinely limited.

The priesthood has two kinds of roles to play. Priests are both father and mother, priest and church, head and body, male and female. They must be effective models of each role in relation to its place in the earthly hierarchy, which mirrors the heavenly hierarchy.

Ecumenism is an important element of the ordination issue. Women's ordination poses a serious obstacle to interchurch relations, especially with the Anglican Communion, a sacramental church that ordains women.

Justice

Priesthood is not a matter of justice. No one has a "human right" to ordination.

Reception and Assent

Reception and assent of a teaching by the faithful are required for that teaching to be valid. The faithful receive a teaching and assent to it when they put it into practice. A believer cannot be forced into receiving a doctrine or teaching that seems untrue.

Attached to these themes are numerous lesser concepts, all of which are put into the service of the others when needed to illuminate or reinforce an aspect of the ban on women's ordination. Except for the claim that because Christ was male a priest must be male — which offers no rational grounds for dialogue — these themes oftentimes have been both used and abused. Unfortunately, their service in the debate forum is not finished.

Part II

POPE PAUL VI

> **Chapter 5** ❧

Discontent

The Soul's Language of Self-Discovery

"WOMEN IN CANON LAW"
Canon Law Society of America
October 1975

"WOMEN IN CHURCH AND SOCIETY"
United States Catholic Conference
November 17–20, 1975

FIRST NATIONAL
WOMEN'S ORDINATION CONFERENCE
November 1975

Vatican II ended with a call for Catholics to reexamine their faith in light of contemporary human needs and values. Beginning in the 1970s, scrutiny of the male priesthood resulted from three general sources: (1) Vatican II's call for increased awareness and participation of the laity in church teaching and practice; (2) the call for gender equality by the secular women's movement in the West; and (3) the growing inclusion of women clergy in other Christian denominations, notably the Episcopal Church in the United States and the Canadian Anglican Church.

Women in Canon Law

At the time of Vatican II in the mid-1960s, canon 968:1 of the Code of Canon Law limited holy orders (and its benefits and pensions) to men.[114] Following Vatican II, in the spirit of ecclesial renewal, the Canon Law Society of America (CLSA) created a committee to study the status of women in the church. In its first report in 1975, the committee stated that the church had taken little notice of the women's movement itself and had made "only perfunctory, sporadic and uncoordinated efforts to examine its own practices and attitudes" toward women. In this environment, women did not "share an equal status with men" because church law "fails to recognize the dignity of women as persons and limits their opportunity for service in the church." Indeed, the exclusion of women "from almost all effective decision-making" created a "grave pastoral problem."[115]

In what eventually would become a thorn in the Vatican's ecumenical side, the CLSA report also examined the status of female ministers in Protestant denominations, many of which viewed ministry as rooted not in sacramental priesthood but rather in the general priesthood of believers. The report stated:

> In general, the willingness to admit women to the ministry of the altar corresponds to an individual church's view of what constitutes that ministry: Roman Catholics, Orthodox and Anglicans generally regard orders as a sacrament instituted by Christ and conferring power from God.[116]

Sacramental churches tended to resist women's ordination, but the CLSA concluded that Roman Catholicism's sacramental view of priestly ministry was "not necessarily incompatible with admitting a woman to the apostolic succession of orders."[117] Women could, according to these canon lawyers, at least theoretically be priests.

During Vatican II, Catholic women were not allowed to participate in any aspect of the church lawmaking process, nor did they have access to resources that would help them to even understand the law. Toward the end of the council, Pope Paul VI issued his *Gravissimum Educationis* ("Declaration on Christian Education," 1965), in which he exhorted teachers to "pay due regard in every educational activity to sexual differences and to the special role which divine Providence allots to each sex."[118] At the end of the council there was a closing message to women (but not to men) that addressed women's roles according to their gender and relationships with men, but not their personhood.

Women in Church and Society

Following Vatican II, the U.S. bishops formed the Ad Hoc Committee on Women in Society and the Church to implement related Vatican II directives. At the 1975 annual meeting of the United States Catholic Conference (USCC, the public programming and policy arm of the National Conference of Catholic Bishops), the question of ordaining women arose several times. Committee chair Bishop Michael McAuliffe of Missouri presented the committee's report, explaining that specific issues were "complicated by the diverse spectrum of opinions which surround the role of women ecclesially and socially."[119]

A few weeks before the meeting, USCC president Archbishop Joseph Bernardin of Cincinnati told the press that there seemed to be solid theological evidence against women priests, but that the subject could not be closed to discussion: "Even matters that have been solemnly defined continue to be studied so that our knowledge of them can be deepened or refined."[120] His statement made clear that the purpose of ongoing study was not to gain new knowledge but rather to deepen and refine understanding of the status quo. The ad hoc committee of bishops nevertheless urged the USCC to create a permanent office for women's concerns: "The seriousness of the issues demands urgent and extensive attention from the church at all these levels, and the failure to provide such attention, we believe, may prove costly."[121]

This statement would prove to be prophetic. But Bernardin, who had served in numerous papal congregations (departments dealing with questions brought to Rome for papal consideration), had pointedly stressed that women were "not to be ordained." The USCC rejected the committee's proposal for a permanent office and instead appointed a task force of six women to articulate church-related concerns of Catholic women. The task force identified five major priorities:

- to open the process of theologizing;
- to broaden church images of women;
- to examine traditional classifications of women in the church;
- to examine and reform church processes and structures; and
- to attend to social issues affecting the status of women.[122]

The bishops may have refused to create an office to address women's concerns, but they had at least begun to consider ways to treat women as members, rather than wards, of the church. Their efforts showed good practical judgment. In the early 1990s, according to surveys directed by Holy Cross Sister Francis Bernard O'Connor, a research scholar at the Kellogg Institute for International Studies, more than 60 percent of regular mass attendees were women. When asked "what they would be willing to do to obtain inclusion in the church," over 62 percent said they would be "willing to withhold financial support from the church."[123] Further, many women all over the United States said "they no longer contribute to a church that gives lip service to its message of the equality of men and women."[124] Given the funds required to maintain the Roman Catholic Church and given that women made up the majority of churchgoers, this was no small consideration.

Women's Ordination Conference

At the same time the bishops were meeting in 1975, supporters of women's ordination gathered in Detroit on the first Sunday of Advent to publicly discuss, for the first time, the ordination of women. The first Women's Ordination Conference was attended by more than twelve hundred women, and another five hundred were turned away for lack of seating.[125] During the meeting, some three hundred women stood to indicate their conviction of being called to priesthood.

The conference centered on three themes: concern for bonding among Catholic women; the need to reinterpret priesthood according to contemporary pastoral needs; and emphasis on fidelity to church tradition.[126] From that meeting emerged a commission whose members would become the leadership of the Women's Ordination Conference (WOC).[127] Incorporated in 1977 with an office in Washington, D.C., the organization began coordinating orderly, peaceful, and attention-getting protests at cathedrals around the country, as well as at national bishops' meetings.

Organizers of a second WOC conference, to be held in Baltimore in 1978, invited 350 U.S. bishops to enter into dialogue with participants. Only one bishop, Charles Buswell of Colorado, attended.[128] Political scientist Mary F. Katzenstein wrote that the conference was more "feminist and polemical."[129] Theologian Richard McBrien wrote that this meeting's organizers were younger, and the papers they presented were "less substantive, theologically and historically" than at the 1975 meeting. Both these assessments were supported by conference participants' cool reception to a proposal supporting "standards for the selection, formation, ordination, and performance evaluation." In fact, according to McBrien, the proposal prompted the charge that "only a man" would make such a suggestion, in part because it would "undermine the unity" of the women's movement in the Catholic Church.[130]

This posture served to distance more traditional Catholics wanting to reform the priesthood from within the church. Further, in its first three decades only one male was given a place on the Women's Ordination Conference's board of directors. According to one long-time leader, in the early days of the organization the board "tried out a man to see how it worked. He was fine — quiet, nonintrusive, and stood out like a sore thumb. He also didn't do much for WOC."[131] Had the subject pronoun been changed from "he" to "she," this statement could have been made by any male-only group.

In 1979, during his visit to the United States, the pope addressed the question of women's ordination during stops in Philadelphia and Chicago. The Women's Ordination Conference, among other groups, used the occasion to peacefully protest sexism in the church. Then, on October 7 at the Shrine of the Immaculate Conception in Washington, D.C., Sister of Mercy Theresa Kane, president of the U.S. Leadership Conference of Women Religious (LCWR),[132] delivered a speech to a large gathering of women religious and the pope. Addressing the pontiff, she called for full participation of women in the church:

> As women we have heard the powerful messages of our Church addressing the dignity and reverence for all persons. As women we have pondered upon these words. Our contemplation leads us to state that the Church in its struggle to be faithful to its call for reverence and dignity for all persons must respond by providing the possibility of women as persons being included in all ministries of our Church. I urge you, Your Holiness, to be open to and respond to the voices coming from the women of this country who are desirous of serving in and through the Church as fully participating members.[133]

The pope remained impassive during Kane's speech. Later, he claimed he could not hear her remarks, even though he was sitting nearby.[134] McBrien wrote that Kane's choice of time and place may have been "inappropriate"; however, despite the pope's nearly seventy speeches and sermons during his visit, "never once — except at the Shrine in D.C. — was there even the slightest opportunity for him to receive feedback or to enter into dialogue" with Catholics of varying views.[135]

Kane's direct and very public appeal propelled the issue of women's ordination to a new level of awareness in the minds of American Catholics. According to Vatican observer Peter Hebblethwaite, "encounters with American nuns, nearly all disastrous," would provide an ongoing motive for John Paul II's dedication to the male-only priesthood.[136] Indeed, by the early 1990s, the pope would bemoan the infiltration of liberalism into some communities of nuns, "whose beliefs, attitudes and behavior no longer correspond to what the gospel and the church teach."[137]

During the late 1970s and early 1980s, as John Paul II amplified his opposition to women's ordination, WOC members helped form a coalition of about thirty women's groups,[138] which at the 1983 WOC conference in Chicago would become "Women-Church Convergence," a loosely organized, ecumenical, feminist group.[139] By the end of the decade, this new group had aligned itself with the secular women's movement. By its third meeting in 1993, the Women-Church conference brochure did not use the word "Catholic."[140]

As parts of the ordination movement grew increasingly radical during the 1980s, a long-standing difference of opinion within and among ordination groups became more pronounced. Some activists insisted that women's ordination should take place sacramentally within the church; others argued it should take place by alternative means, because women's ordination should not have to wait decades or centuries for the Vatican to open the priesthood to women. Women-Church identifiers tended toward the latter view. In 1993, Rosemary Radford Ruether wrote:

> A potentially divisive conflict hangs over Women-Church. Is it primarily a reform within the Christian tradition or is it on the way out of the Christian tradition into post-Christian or goddess religion? . . . Women-Church has not made a decision to be either confined to Christianity or to move out of Christianity completely.[141]

In 2003, long-time religion writer Peter Steinfels wrote that in 1993, "Women-Church appeared to have abandoned anything resembling traditional Roman Catholicism except, perhaps, its taste for ritual, now transposed into an inventive New Age key." Indeed, at its 1993 national meeting, a roster of worship services included rituals of Quakers, Native Americans, and goddess worship, but no Catholic mass. A "proposal to include one had been rejected by the planners — a coalition of Catholic feminist groups — who instead provided a 'Catholic-rooted feminist liturgy.' "[142] Steinfels astutely pointed out that Women-Church's "allergic reaction to ordinary Catholicism, its fondness for religious smorgasbords, and its attachment to academic political correctness" tainted other expressions of Catholic feminism "just enough to distance them from many Catholic women."[143]

Women's Ordination Conference members, by contrast, tended to espouse the view that ordination should take place within the church, although Ruether pointed out that planners of the first WOC conference in 1975 had "defined their goals, not simply as the inclusion of women in priestly ministry as it had been traditionally defined but also as the 'renewal of priestly ministry.' "[144] Like other minority groups, persons belonging to these groups did not maintain strict philosophical divisions but rather moved in and out of the groups according to need and circumstance.

In 1995, WOC officially broadened its scope to include a thorough revisioning of priesthood for men and women, as reported by former lay Catholic minister and author Jane Redmont:

> The title of the conference, "Discipleship of Equals: Breaking Bread, Doing Justice," was meant to signal a paradigm shift in the women's ordination movement. It seemed also to indicate a shift in the organization sponsoring the event, the Women's Ordination Conference.... From the start, it has advocated the ordination of women "to a renewed priestly ministry within a renewed church."[145]

This development reflected a divide in the movement between those who believed women should *first* be ordained and *then* tackle the reform of priesthood, and those who believed the priesthood itself was flawed and in need of ground-up reform before *anyone* was ordained. About the latter view, one nun summed up the prevailing mood when she said that to ordain women in an unreformed priesthood would mean having "a masculine structure with feminine bodies in it."[146] While continuing to work for ordination, WOC now assumed this position:[147]

> The "renewed priestly ministry" that we envision and speak of would concentrate more on serving people than administrating a bureaucratic organization. It would call for the end of a hierarchical structure with its attendant evils of racism, classism, sexism and elitism. Instead, there would be more sharing, more cooperation among priests and laity, and more integration of both male and female characteristics in priestly service.[148]

The 1995 WOC conference program claimed that the ordination of women would not resolve the problem, and that "nothing short of a major deconstruction of clericalism, patriarchy, and hierarchy" would suffice. As was becoming more common within institutional organizations of women's ordination supporters, rituals were flourishing but Catholicism was not. Mary F. Katzenstein pointed out "the near-invisibility of Christ within the themes of the conference" and the virtual absence of Christ in the liturgies.[149]

Inside and outside these organizations, mixed opinions and convictions converged in the shared goal of women's full participation in the life of the church, but as time passed the divergences would become more pronounced.

Sister of Loretto Mary Luke Tobin, former LCWR president and one of the female auditors at Vatican II, pointed out that some Catholic women believed ordination was "not the necessary thing" for women, and that "we are better off with a new way of structuring ourselves." But problems with church tradition, she cautioned, were "no reason for throwing the whole thing out."[150] Theologian Lisa Sowle Cahill likewise observed that some Catholics had "ceased to care about ordination in an institution from which they are already so thoroughly alienated that they are seeking innovative forms of Catholic ministry and liturgy where their gifts are recognized."[151]

Others maintained that sacramental ordination *within* the Catholic tradition was the worthier goal. For women to reject the institution was implausible. And wouldn't abandoning the ordination issue play into the hands of those in the church resisting women's advances every step of the way?[152]

Operating under the massive shadow of the Vatican, and with chronically more conviction than funding, women's ordination supporters managed for the moment to subordinate their differences to the larger, primary goal of achieving women's full equality in the church.

In 1996, WOC cofounded and became the first international coordinator for Women's Ordination Worldwide (WOW), the first organized global movement for women's ordination. The movement was particularly strong in (but not limited to) the United States, Canada, Britain,[153] Ireland, Austria, and Germany, corporately representing a huge constituency of Western Catholics. These groups increasingly made public the claim that the male-only priesthood was unjust and unwise. In 2001, the group held its first meeting, in Dublin, to which we will return.

The mid-1970s were heady times for the women's ordination movement. In their enthusiasm, supporters seemed to forget (if indeed they ever knew about) a 1971 International Synod of Bishops' recommendation that a global commission be established to study the situation of women in the church, including the possibility of ordination. After the bishops departed Rome that year (but before the resolution could be delivered to Pope Paul VI), the text mysteriously was changed to make the proposed commission responsible not to the bishops at all, but to the pope.[154] More than thirty years later, no such commission had been created. Nonetheless, with Vatican II's call for an empowered laity still unfolding in the 1970s and the hope of the twenty-first century still ahead, hope for change seemed to be everywhere.

· · ·

By 1887, the Martin family was growing up. Two of Thérèse's older sisters, Marie and Pauline, had already entered the convent at Carmel. Another sister, Léonie, would make three failed attempts at entering a convent before finally being accepted by the Order of the Visitation. The girls were growing into young women, but in March of that year, Louis Martin suffered a stroke that left him temporarily paralyzed. He recovered fairly quickly, but he remained depressed, as he frequently was. On the Feast of Pentecost, May 29, despite her father's precarious health, fourteen-year-old Thérèse, the "little queen" of his life, informed Louis that she wished to enter Carmel when she turned fifteen.

Both her parents had suffered miserable childhoods, for whom religious life must have promised relief. As a young man seeking a religious life, Louis Martin had been turned away by the monks at the local Cistercian monastery for his inadequate education. Likewise, Thérèse's mother, Zelie Guérin, had failed in her attempt to enter a convent. Frustrated in their attempts to enter religious life, the couple set their hearts on a large family with children who would be priests, nuns, and missionaries. Their two sons died before their first birthdays, and the couple lost two daughters. Zelie and Louis raised their remaining five daughters with a keen sensitivity to sacrifice and penance, and with an understanding, so common among Catholics, of the superiority of a religious vocation to married life. So it was no surprise when Louis gave Thérèse permission to enter Carmel.

Next, Thérèse approached the Father Superior of the Carmelites, who held religious jurisdiction over her, for permission to join the convent before the customary age of sixteen. Failing to receive a positive response, on October 31 Thérèse and her father, in a driving rain, approached the bishop's palace, passing through "huge rooms" in which she "felt about the size of an ant." At length, they entered a room where "three vast armchairs stood before a roaring fire."[155] Thérèse, who had put her hair up for the occasion so that she might look older, asked the bishop for permission to enter Carmel when she turned fifteen. The bishop said he would speak to the Father Superior, and sent her away without an answer. Anticipating the verdict the two men would return, Thérèse was crushed.

But a trip to Rome with her father and sister Célie already was in the works for November, and Thérèse was getting ideas. "No" was not the answer she longed to hear. She would keep pursuing "Yes."

✺ Chapter 6 ✸

The Bible Does Not Tell Us So

"REPORT OF THE
PONTIFICAL BIBLICAL COMMISSION"*
July 1976

Before Vatican II, Bible study among Catholic laity had not been widespread. Before the nineteenth century, pervasive illiteracy had made Bible-reading virtually impossible among the masses, and even after the literacy rate in the West mushroomed with the advent of public schools, Rome encouraged the learning of biblical precepts through mass attendance and Vatican-approved catechisms. With the Vatican II–mandated empowerment of the laity, however, Catholics began to read the Bible on their own, although such study received little practical guidance from the church.[156] Of course, the issue of women in the Bible was not in the forefront of scripture study. Likewise, Rome had never depended on scripture to make its case for a male-only priesthood, which was grounded primarily in tradition and male-centered theology.

Insufficient Testimony

In the early 1970s, the Vatican's Doctrinal Congregation directed the Pontifical Biblical Commission (PBC) to study the role of women in the Bible to help determine the place that could be "given to women" in the church (§1). The PBC unanimously declared[157] that the New Testament alone was not sufficient to settle "in a clear way and once and for all" the "problem" of ordaining women (§66).

For one thing, the Bible never used the technical term *hiereus* ("priest") in connection with Christian ministry. Moreover, the New Testament said "very little on the subject of the ministry of the eucharist," and the pastoral letters providing the most detailed picture of Christian leaders never attributed "to them a eucharistic function" (§4–6).

Difficulties arose, the PBC said, from studying biblical data in order to understand eucharistic priesthood, which is a postbiblical concept. This bold and risky claim posed an awkward embarrassment for Pope Paul VI, who responded by

---

*The document is included in the appendix, p. 177.

disbanding the commission. Hence, the report was never officially released. Its contents became known only through a press leak.[158]

The PBC report offered a scriptural background of women's roles in the Old and New Testaments, and its meaning was clear:

> Despite an institutional framework which implies the submission of women to their husbands... [the Bible] supposes between man and woman not only an equality of rights and duties... but also an equality in adoptive sonship [*sic*]... and in the reception of the Spirit who brings about participation in the life of the church (§22).

The PBC concluded that the only certainty about leadership in the early church was that it was "always held by men (in conformity with Jewish custom)" (§53). The commission's strategic addition of the parenthetical remark "in conformity with Jewish custom" suggested that the exclusively male nature of church leadership was neither scriptural nor divine, but merely cultural.

This was not the first time the Vatican found itself reluctantly updating a "normative" position based on an obsolete custom or inadequate theology. Today, some examples of these abandoned church teachings are discomfiting: non-Catholics are bound for hell, slavery is morally just, women are biologically inferior to men, killing a Muslim earns eternal salvation for a Crusader, the sun revolves around the earth, unbaptized infants do not enter heaven, married couples who take pleasure in sex commit a sin... the list goes on.

Further complicating the issue, according to the PBC, was that the texts forbidding women to speak and teach in the assemblies might have referred "only to certain concrete situations and abuses" and might even have been inauthentic (§62).[159]

In time, the books ascribed to Paul most commonly questioned by scripture scholars[160] would prove to be the same books demanding women's submission:

- 1 Timothy (2:12): "I permit no woman to teach or to have authority over a man; she is to keep silent";

- Ephesians (5:22): "Wives, be subject to your husbands as you are to the Lord. For the husband is the head of the wife just as Christ is the head of the church, the body of which he is the Savior"; and

- Titus (2:3, 5): "encourage the young women to love their husbands, to... [be] submissive to their husbands, so that the word of God may not be discredited."

Titus immediately (2:9) commanded the reader: "tell slaves to be submissive to their masters... to show complete and perfect fidelity." The words "wives" and "husbands" could be cleanly inserted for "slaves" and "masters."

Three years before the Pontifical Biblical Commission released its report, the National Conference of Catholic Bishops in the United States had written that Pauline texts should not be cited as arguing against women's ordination because, among other reasons, "these texts are of Pauline authority alone."[161] In other words, Paul's writings were insufficient evidence against women's ordination.

The PBC's findings were not what Pope Paul VI wanted to hear. After all, only eight years earlier, Rome had declared that women lectors, if used at all, were to stand outside the sanctuary.[162] And in 1972, Paul VI had issued a *motu proprio* (on the pope's own initiative) apostolic letter explicitly excluding women from the new lay ministries of lector and altar server,[163] even though neither required ordination but only a ceremonial process called "installation." Now, the PBC report and its surreptitious publication caused a public relations setback for the Vatican, which faced the challenge of undoing the obscure commission's now-public work. But the report could not be undone; further, it would become a staple in the growing arguments *for* women's ordination.

Later that year, the Catholic Biblical Association of America appointed a committee of member scholars to report on the roles of women in early Christianity. In 1979, the committee reported that because of the "process of selection and theological interpretation before and during its literary composition," the New Testament provided "no discussion of the role of women in the ministry of Jesus or the early Church." Ministry was shared in the early church, and priesthood as an institution emerged in its earliest forms only around the beginning of the second century. In Paul's view, an apostle was someone who saw the resurrected Christ and was commissioned to proclaim the gospel. Luke further defined an apostle as someone who accompanied Jesus during his ministry. "Women thus actually met the criteria for apostleship."[164]

In 1979, theologian and New Testament scholar Elisabeth Schüssler Fiorenza wrote:

> According to Paul all those Christians were apostles who fulfilled two conditions: they had to be (1) eyewitnesses to the resurrection and (2) commissioned by the resurrected Lord to missionary work (cf. 1 Cor. 9:4). Luke's requirements for apostleship are somewhat different. He maintains that only those Christians were eligible to replace Judas who had accompanied Jesus in his ministry and had also witnessed the resurrection (Acts 1:21). According to all four Gospels, women fulfilled these criteria of apostleship that Paul and Luke have spelled out. They accompanied Jesus from Galilee to Jerusalem, and they witnessed his death. Moreover, according to all criteria of historical authenticity women were the first witnesses of the resurrection.[165]

Indeed, the gospels say that Jesus' friend Mary of Magdala was the first human being to whom the resurrected Lord showed himself.[166] She was called the "apostle to the apostles," chosen by Christ to proclaim the "good news" of his resurrection to Peter and others. The Catholic Biblical Association of America committee concluded:

- there was no evidence that women were excluded from an early ministry;

- the roles later associated with priesthood "were never limited [and] nowhere in the NT explicitly limited to the Twelve"; and

- the Vatican's claim that Jesus' example and intention provided a "permanent norm excluding women" from priesthood posed a "most serious logical difficulty" because Jesus said nothing about women or a priesthood. This logical difficulty could be seen clearly in the same scenario from a different perspective — "whether in choosing the Twelve Jesus intended to establish a criterion for office in respect to sex, but not in respect to race, ethnic identity, or social identity."

The committee concluded: "All that is known is that there were no women, Gentiles, Samaritans, or, evidently, slaves among the Twelve." It was "not possible to deduce from that fact" that Jesus had a "conscious intention" to exclude any of those groups.[167] Moreover, Jesus chose twelve *Jewish* men to join him in heaven, where they would sit on thrones to "rule the twelve tribes of Israel" (Matt. 19:28). If, as Rome said, it would be difficult to see Christ in a woman, it would be equally difficult to see a tribe of Israel in a French monk or a Brazilian priest.

The reality that Jesus did not call Gentile men to this group would not pose an obstacle to ordaining Gentiles. Paul taught that for a community baptized into Christ: "There is no longer Jew or Greek, there is no longer slave or free, there is no longer male and female, for all of you are one in Christ Jesus" (Gal. 3:28). The developing church would later assume, then, that Gentiles could be ordained into the Christian priesthood. But the church rejected the same teaching for the purpose of ordaining women. Jewishness was required for Jesus' incarnation, but not required for priests. His maleness, which was required for his acceptance in a Jewish kingdom culture, would become required for a Roman Catholic priest to stand in the place of Christ for all times and places.

German theologian Karl Rahner pointed out that the early church might have been "morally required" to exclude women in accord with custom. He pointed out that Jesus likewise made no effort to oppose or abolish slavery at the time. The "transition from the concept of the apostles and the Twelve to the concept of the priest" was "too simple to fit in with knowledge of the origins, structure and organization" of the early church.[168]

The claim that it could not be proven that Jesus willfully intended to exclude women from priesthood was frozen in icy tension with the Vatican's claim that Jesus intended exactly that. The dispute would continue.

• • •

Young Thérèse could not be a priest, but she was intent upon entering Carmel of Lisieux. As a very young nun, she wasn't altogether sure what her vocational focus would be: she had come to realize that a mature faith would require a new vision, but what kind of vision? The gospels showed Thérèse new perspectives on her faith, and she knew that the Kingdom of God was within. In the Gospel of Matthew, she learned that it was "not enough to love," and that she was to love the very people she thought had no regard for her. There were times, though, that she could not "keep strictly to the words of the Gospel" because the gospels were "contrary to human nature," and that "without the help of grace, it would be impossible not only to follow them but even to understand them."[169]

One scripture passage she did understand, however, and it changed her perspective of what her own vocation should be. She still wanted to be a priest — indeed, a saint and a Doctor of the Church — but Paul's first letter to the Corinthians expanded her vision:

> Now you are the body of Christ and individually members of it. And God has appointed in the church first apostles, second prophets, third teachers; then deeds of power, then gifts of healing, forms of assistance, forms of leadership, various kinds of tongues. Are all apostles?

Are all prophets? Are all teachers? Do all work miracles? Do all possess gifts of healing? Do all speak in tongues? Do all interpret? But strive for the greater gifts. And I will show you a still more excellent way. If I speak in the tongues of mortals and of angels, but do not have love, I am a noisy gong or a clanging cymbal. And if I have prophetic powers, and understand all mysteries and all knowledge, and if I have all faith, so as to remove mountains, but do not have love, I am nothing. If I give away all my possessions, and if I hand over my body so that I may boast, but do not have love, I gain nothing. (1 Cor. 12:27–13:3)

"My vocation is love!" she exclaimed.[170] Thérèse wanted everything, and she found that the way to everything was love.

➤ Chapter 7 ⬅

In Persona Christi

In the Person of Christ (a Male)

INTER INSIGNIORES
("Declaration on the Admission of Women
to the Ministerial Priesthood")*
Congregation for the Doctrine of the Faith
October 15, 1976

In order to understand *Inter Insigniores* ("Declaration on the Admission of Women to Ministerial Priesthood"),[171] it will be helpful to review related activities in the Vatican at the time. In 1975, the same year the Canon Law Society of America (CLSA) called the ban on women's ordination a "grave pastoral problem," the Vatican's Commission for the Study of the Role of Women in Society and in the Church attempted to pursue a theological study of the issue. The commission's president, Archbishop Enrico Bartoletti, stressed that the study was not to change the male-only priesthood, but rather to help the faithful understand *why* ordination was "not being granted" to women.[172] He told Pope Paul VI that it was "urgent to give a fully justified answer" to women's exclusion from ordained ministry, and that any papal response should be built upon a solid ecclesiological foundation, rather than being just a "disciplinary *niet.*"[173]

The prospects did not look good. The International Theological Commission had earlier completed a study of women in the diaconate, but its results had been kept secret; and, the Pontifical Biblical Commission's recent report that scripture alone could not settle the matter had become public only through an anonymous press leak. As the Bartoletti commission began its discussion of women's ordination, participants received "a confidential memo, soon leaked, explaining that women's ordination was no part of their brief." The commission thus was written off as a "waste of time," and several commissioners complained they were "treated with suspicion."[174]

Overall, the climate precipitating *Inter Insigniores* was one of increasing calls for women's ordination, and Bartoletti's recommendation for a "solid" answer instead of a disciplinary "no" was a strategic one: only in that way could the

---

*The document is included in the appendix, p. 185.

Vatican avoid intense criticism from women's ordination supporters both outside and inside the church.

From Outside the Church:
An Ecumenical Headache

From the beginning, ecumenical implications for the church were at the top of Rome's concerns about the women's ordination issue. Years of Anglican efforts to ordain women were paying off. In 1974, three retired Episcopal bishops in Philadelphia had ordained eleven women without formal approval. In 1975 in Washington, D.C., a second "irregular" ordination yielded four more female Episcopal priests. At the 1976 General Convention, with several Episcopal diocesan bishops having declared their intention "to ordain women after the 1976 Convention regardless of how the vote went,"[175] the Episcopal Church approved women's ordination,[176] prompting one Vatican official to say that the decision constituted a "real headache from an ecumenical point of view."[177] The first "regular" or legal Episcopalian ordinations of women priests took place the next year.

"We changed a church that would not change itself," said Betty Bone Schiess, one of the first Episcopalian women to be ordained in 1974. "To deny one woman ordination in the Episcopal Church, or in the Anglican-Catholic tradition, which includes Roman Catholicism, is to say something to all women about their second order of creation, and that is inconsistent with the gospel."[178]

In 1971, the Anglican bishop of Hong Kong, where the need for priests was acute, had validly ordained two women deacons to the priesthood with the approval of the international Anglican Consultative Council. The need for priests likewise had fueled the 1944 ordination of a female deacon in war-torn China. After the war, the Lambeth Conference (a regular ten-year meeting of the world's Anglican bishops) requested that she renounce her orders, which she did not do. In 1970, her orders were recognized in Hong Kong.[179] In 1976, Canadian Anglicans approved the ordination of women. In 1992, Anglican synods approved women's ordination in England, Australia, and Southern Africa.[180]

In the United States, the priestly ordination of Episcopalian women resulted in the defection of some church members, including angry male Episcopal priests who abandoned their churches and converted to Catholicism. These men were then ordained as Roman Catholic priests who, unlike their more tenured Catholic colleagues, enjoyed wives and children along with priesthood.

Inter Insigniores acknowledged women's admission to pastoral office in other Christian denominations, saying these ordinations caused both ecumenical and internal problems for Catholics by raising the question whether Rome might "modify her discipline" on male priesthood. This challenge required the Catholic Church to "make her thinking known on it" (§7). The text stressed that churches "stemming from the sixteenth-century Reformation or of later origin" (§6) lacked the validity and depth of tradition enjoyed by Roman Catholicism. That tradition figured prominently in Paul VI's defense of a male priesthood.

The ecumenical issue was discussed in a series of letters between archbishop of Canterbury Donald Coggan and Pope Paul VI. The archbishop informed the pope of the "slow but steady growth of a consensus of opinion within the Anglican Communion that there are no fundamental objections in principle to the ordination of women to the priesthood." Pope Paul VI responded that the Anglican decision to ordain women constituted "an element of grave difficulty" between the two churches.[181]

From Outside the Church:
A Modernist Society

At the time of Vatican II (1962–65), Pope John XXIII had written in his encyclical *Pacem in Terris* ("Peace on Earth," 1963):

> Women are gaining an increasing awareness of their natural dignity. Far from being content with a purely passive role or allowing themselves to be regarded as a kind of instrument, they are demanding both in domestic and in public life the rights and duties which belong to them as human persons.[182]

While John XXIII had acknowledged women's gains in domestic and public life, he had said nothing about their place in the church. Sociologist Mark Chaves pointed out that denominational reports on the church roles of Christian women often began by acknowledging women's rights in society, which raised the issue of women's ordination.[183] Chaves offered the following example:

> The very raising of this question is due, no doubt, to the great changes in the general positions of women, brought about during the last half century or so. Women have been admitted to other professions, formerly practiced by men only, and have proven themselves successful.[184]

That statement was issued by the Central Conference of American Rabbis in 1922.

In *Inter Insigniores*, the Congregation for the Doctrine of the Faith (CDF) acknowledged women's growing leadership in society. Catholic women's rising *social and professional status*, however, made a *corresponding demand upon the church*. The CDF acknowledged the "decisive role and accomplished tasks" of women in the world (especially as mothers, nuns, and saints), and since "in our time women have an ever more active share in the whole life of society, it is very important that they participate more widely also in the various sectors of the Church's apostolate" (§4).

But as women were realizing their strength in the public sphere, the Vatican was emphasizing that Roman Catholics could "never ignore the fact that Christ is a man" or that his role "must be taken by a man." This stemmed not from any "personal superiority of men, but only from a difference of functions and service" (§53), which happened to require maleness. While women's public gains may have outdistanced their place in the church, no human evolution could "abolish, on essential points, the sacramental reference to constitutive events of Christianity and to Christ himself" (§37), one of which was maleness.

Chaves explained that prohibiting female ordination was a way for a denomination to distance itself from the modern world by displaying loyalty to an alternative environment. A formal policy against female clergy was a "symbol of resistance" to formal gender equality being practiced in secular society. In other words, excluding women from priesthood went beyond concern with either priesthood or women, to the concern for using both as shields against encroachment by the modern world.[185]

Inside the Church: A Swelling Ground

In the decade following Vatican II, ecumenical problems and women's advances in society seemed to pose the most immediate threats to the male-only priesthood, but as the 1970s progressed it was becoming clear that growing numbers of lay Catholics, bishops, and theologians were seriously questioning the ban on women priests.

In October 1976, a national justice conference held under the auspices of the U.S. bishops convened in Detroit. Representing dioceses across the United States, the 1,340 delegates called for increased accountability by church authorities and the ordination of married men. Further, they recommended that "sexist language and imagery be eliminated from all official church documents, catechisms, liturgical books, rites and hymnals," that girls be granted the "right and opportunity to serve at the altar," and that "full participation of women in the life and ministry of the church" with "equal access to and full participation in roles of leadership" be given.[186] A bold idea emerged from this meeting: *church teaching on justice depended upon the hierarchy's willingness to be an exemplar of that justice.*

Ordaining women was "more than a matter of simple justice or equal rights," wrote Lutheran theologian and pastor Karen Bloomquist. At stake was the "inclusiveness of the Church, the Gospel and the sacraments." Exclusion of women from the "central word and act of the Church" compromised the church's inclusiveness of "*all* people."[187]

At the time the CDF wrote *Inter Insigniores*, the Vatican faced pressure from three distinct fronts: ecumenical, social, and pastoral. Formerly sporadic and unorganized, Catholic pursuit of women's ordination was becoming a palpable, systematic movement. In response, Pope Paul VI ordered the writing and publication of *Inter Insigniores* to explain and stress the fundamental reasons for the male-only priesthood.

Which Christ? Fidelity to the Example of the Lord

Addressed to the world's bishops, *Inter Insigniores* ("Declaration on the Admission of Women to the Ministerial Priesthood," 1976) was published by the Congregation for the Doctrine of the Faith (CDF),[188] a powerful agency of the Roman curia ("court") charged with promoting and safeguarding Catholic doctrine and morals. The document's stated purpose was "to recall that the Church, in fidelity to the example of the Lord, does not consider herself authorized to admit women to priestly ordination" (§9). The principal reason was that women were unable to act *in persona Christi* — in the person and role of Christ — because they did not resemble Christ in his maleness. This theme contained three interlinked claims:

- the priest acts *in persona Christi*;

- in the person of Christ, the priest is a *sacramental sign* of Christ; and

- as a sign of Christ, the priest *must be male.*

This triple-pronged claim was crucial to Catholicism's male-only priesthood. As Mark Chaves explained, two groups of denominations were particularly resistant to women's ordination: denominations practicing sacramental ritual (e.g., Roman Catholicism) and denominations endorsing biblical inerrancy (e.g., the Southern Baptist Convention). A sacramentalist denomination required an iconic presence, an image representing something beyond itself. For instance, the sacrament of the eucharist required "an agent who resembles Christ, and maleness is an essential component of that representation. By this logic, it is literally impossible for a woman to be a priest; the sacrament, if performed by a female, would be invalid."[189]

Yet baptism could be, and marriage was, administered by women. Vatican II, following Augustine's lead, had declared: "By his power, [Christ] is present in the sacraments so that when anybody baptizes it is really Christ himself who baptizes."[190] Regarding marriage, Pope Pius XII, also echoing Augustine, had declared that spouses were "ministers of grace to each other."[191] In other words, in baptism and marriage Christ acted through *women and men,* but in the sacrament of holy orders he restricted his grace to males.

Thomas Aquinas (1225–74) taught that holy orders conveyed an *active* character and baptism a *passive* one,[192] because the person baptizing was merely a conduit for Christ's saving action. A woman could baptize because the gesture was truly a passive one in which Christ was the actual baptizer. In marriage, the woman could act as a mutual minister with her husband, with whom she was joined as one (that is, in marriage the woman was completed by the husband). In these two (passive) sacraments, being female was not an impediment, but in the other five (active) sacraments, Christ could not be present if administered by a woman. In a syllogism, the claims would look like this:

Christ is present and active in all seven sacraments.

Women may bring Christ to others in only two sacraments.

Christ is neither present nor active in the other five sacraments if administered by women.

A few months before the Vatican released *Inter Insigniores,* an *Anglican Theological Review* article by R. A. Norris Jr. had raised the question of *which* Christ Rome was concerned with representing.

> *In the last resort the question boils down to this: whether it is the Christ of the baptismal mystery whom the ordained person represents, or a Christ who is in fact otherwise understood and qualified.* The Christ of the baptismal mystery — the Christ in whom the new order of creation is embodied and effected — is one in whom male and female, Jew and Greek, slave and free, share a single identity.... To insist, then, that ecclesial priesthood must be male if it is to represent Christ, is to argue that ecclesial priesthood represents a different Christ from the one which the other sacraments of the Church embody and proclaim.[193]

What Christ Did *Not* Do

The Pontifical Biblical Commission had already determined that scripture alone could not exclude women from holy orders and, along with many scripture scholars, it had questioned the authenticity of seemingly misogynistic Pauline passages. Nevertheless, *Inter Insigniores* made numerous references to the Bible, employing the Genesis 2:18–25 account of creation of woman from man's rib to explain Paul's injunction against women teaching in the churches (§32).

Inter Insigniores also stated that any valid appeal to scripture must be understood not only in light of Jesus' actions, but also in light of what Jesus did *not* do. The CDF argued that the church could not ordain women because "Jesus Christ did not call any woman to become part of the Twelve" (§15). Further, Paul "ordained" only men, not for cultural reasons but in respect for divine will.

> When [the apostles] and Paul went beyond the confines of the Jewish world, the preaching of the Gospel and the Christian life in the Greco-Roman civilization impelled them to break with Mosaic practices, sometimes regretfully. They and Paul could therefore have envisaged conferring ordination on women, if they had not been convinced of their duty of fidelity to the Lord on this point (§23).

This paragraph made two concrete but clearly unhistorical assertions:

- the apostles and Paul "conferred ordination" on men; and

- the apostles refused to ordain women in fidelity to Jesus' exclusion of women from the Twelve. "Jesus did not entrust the apostolic charge to women" (§19) and "at no time was there a question of conferring ordination on these women" (§25).[194]

In reality, at no time in the apostolic era was there "a question of conferring ordination" on *anyone*, including the Twelve. *Inter Insigniores* merely articulated a traditional assumption of male priesthood, and it now faced the prickly task of claiming the authority to teach and do what Christ did *not* teach or do, and to define his *nonaction as divine will.*

Having obliquely acknowledged that scripture alone could not settle the issue, having nonetheless quoted scripture at length in defense of its own argument, and having spotlighted the activities of Paul and the Twelve to prove that the church was bound to a divine (if unspoken) will, *Inter Insigniores* turned to the authority of tradition.

The Devil's Gateway

Inter Insigniores recalled activity in the early centuries of Christianity when women's ordination by heretical sects was "immediately noted and condemned by the fathers, who considered it as unacceptable in the Church" (§10). This traditional condemnation of women usurping priestly ministry could be seen in the examples of five men: Irenaeus, Tertullian, Firmilian, Origen, and Epiphanius. But these church fathers (from the second, third, and fourth centuries) actually provided few comments on the subject, and when they did it was usually in reaction against heretical groups. Jesuit theologian and historian Haye van der Meer pointed out that the writers most frequently cited (including these five, above) were usually the same.[195] The texts were embarrassingly misogynist and undeniably opposed a female priesthood but, like children in a house of mirrors, when they were lined up just so, they created an illusion of being much greater than the sum of their parts.

- Irenaeus, a second-century bishop of Lyons, taught (with others of his time) that women were by nature subordinate to men. He is most remembered for his *Adversus Haereses* ("Against Heresies"), which he wrote as a polemic against Gnostic[196] beliefs and rituals laced with magic rites in which women participated. He denounced the participation of women as part of what invalidated Gnosticism.

- Tertullian, a third-century theologian, likewise complained of women teaching and baptizing in heretical groups: "It is not permitted for a woman to speak in church, but neither is it permitted her to teach, nor to baptize, nor to offer, nor to claim for herself any manly function."[197] While Tertullian made valuable contributions to the development of theology, he is also remembered for calling women "the devil's gateway" who "destroyed so easily God's image, man."[198]

- Firmilian, a third-century bishop of Caesarea, once witnessed a woman baptizing using "the customary and legitimate wording," who appeared "to deviate in no particular [way] from ecclesiastical discipline." But her orthodoxy was only a ruse. She was able to "disturb and deceive the brethren" with this ritual orthodoxy only through the "illusions and trickeries of the devil," who had "devised a number of ways for deceiving the faithful."[199]

- Origen, a third-century thinker, was saved from an early death when his mother hid his clothes as he tried to join his father in martyrdom. His theological work was funded by a woman named Juliana, and he is believed to have castrated himself to avoid lust.[200] "It is improper for a woman," he said, "to speak in an assembly no matter what she says, even if she says admirable things or even saintly things; that is of little consequence since they come from the mouth of a woman."[201]

- Epiphanius of Salamis, a fourth-century Christian writer concerned with refuting heresies, expressed his dissatisfaction with the presence of *presbytidae* (priestesses, or presidents of a religious assembly), saying that women should not be given that title lest anyone mistakenly attribute to them the priestly dignity. "They do not have true priestly power, they do not have the right of offering sacrifice to God."[202] This is partly because women are "unstable, prone to error, and mean-spirited," subject to "pride and female madness" which can be dispelled by a "manly frame of mind."[203] Indeed, the "devil seems to vomit out this disorder through women." The "disorder" was a priestly practice among women, who appeared to adore Mary, against which he was reacting. The "folly of these women" could only be rectified by "masculine reasoning."[204]

Inter Insigniores acknowledged the church fathers' undeniable prejudices against women, but it claimed *"these prejudices had hardly any influence on their pastoral activity, and still less on their spiritual direction"* (§10).[205] The CDF did not explain how it is possible to separate one's deeply held cultural biases from one's spiritual activity, beliefs, and mode of governance. Nevertheless, if (as Rome now claimed) these and other church fathers erred in teaching subordinationism, and if this primacy of male over female was their reason for refusing to ordain women, could it not follow that the ban on women priests was in error? This question has never been clarified by the Vatican, which in fact continues to cite the very writers whose misogyny it rejects.

When the Body Overtakes the Head

Having selectively quoted these church fathers to prove the disordered nature of women priests, *Inter Insigniores* cited three ancient texts condemning women for exercising priestly duties.[206]

- The *Didascalia Apostolorum* ("Teaching of the Apostles") was a third-century Syriac document that claimed to be composed by the Twelve. Later shown to be fraudulent, the collection of legal and liturgical matters declared that the church needed both female and male deacons, but women were to restrict their activity to prayer because Christ did not give women the mission to instruct or baptize the people.[207] The latter was "a transgression of the commandment and very dangerous for her who baptizes and her who is baptized."[208]

- The fourth-century Synod of Laodicea issued sixty canons (laws) regulating the behavior of Christians in Asia Minor. Canon 44 declared: "Women are not allowed to approach the altar," either because of their menstrual impurity or the Greek influence against such proximity, or both. Canon 11 stated: "Presbytides, as they are called, or female presidents, are not to be appointed in the Church," perhaps because this privilege had been abused in that area.

- The fourth-century *Constitutiones Apostolicae* ("Apostolic Constitutions") restated much of the material in the *Didascalia Apostolorum*. To allow a woman, "contrary to nature, to hold the office of a priest" would be "a sin of ignorant godless Gentiles, [who] ordain women priests for the female deities," which was not a command of Christ.[209] Men were warned against allowing women to baptize, impart blessings, or do any priestly functions whatsoever, because for a woman to baptize was "wicked and impious," because it would "abrogate the order of creation" by allowing the (female) body to overtake the function of the (male) head. The "principal part" of the woman was the man, "as being her head."[210]

The *Didascalia Apostolorum* and the *Constitutiones Apostolicae* were two examples of how gender-based dualism became foundational to church thinking. According to this dualism, the body (matter, woman) was inferior to the head (mind, priest). To allow the body to "overtake" the head would "set aside the act of creation." In this scenario, the head needed the body to carry out its commands and could even act independently of the body, but the body could never have an idea or act on its own. This theme was carried through the centuries in order to preserve the head (or hierarchy, having roots in the Greek *hieros*, "priest") while

ensuring that the body (or laity, Gr. *laos*, "people") would not overstep its bounds.
While males could rise above the lay state, women could not.

Regulations limiting women's presence and contributions continued through
Christian history. In 494, Pope Gelasius I wrote to Christian communities: "We
have heard to our annoyance that divine affairs have come to such a low state
that women are encouraged to officiate at the sacred altars, and to take part in all
matters imputed to the offices of the male sex, to which they do not belong."[211]

In the sixth century, three bishops of Gaul issued a letter criticizing priests for
"allowing women during eucharistic services to take the chalice in their hands and
to distribute the blood of Christ to the people." The bishops threatened the guilty
priests with "banishment from the ecclesiastical community if they continue[d]
to be assisted by those women, with whom they were living" under an agreement
of celibacy.[212]

The Synod of Paris in the ninth century reported: "In some provinces it happens that women press around the altar, touch the holy vessels, hand the clerics
the priestly vestments, indeed even dispense the body and blood of the Lord to
the people. This is shameful and must not take place."[213]

Popes found it necessary to restate the prohibition against women priests
throughout the Middle Ages, after which time, according to *Inter Insigniores*, "the
question has not been raised again, for the practice [of male priesthood] has enjoyed peaceful and universal acceptance," and the magisterium "has not felt the
need to intervene in order to formulate a principle which was not attacked, or to
defend a law which was not challenged" (§§12–13).[214] Yet the document's claim
that the law was not challenged seemingly was contradicted by its subsequent
claim that while male ordination was "an unbroken tradition throughout the
history of the Church," Rome was "alert to repress abuses immediately" (§39).
If it was necessary to "repress abuses" of the tradition (as did Pope Gelasius,
fifteen hundred years ago), then the tradition could not have been altogether
"unbroken."

German theologian Karl Rahner pointed out that a human tradition in the
church offered "no guarantee of truth" even if it had long been "undisputed and
taken for granted." While Rome claimed divine roots for the male-only priesthood, in fact there had been "scarcely any reflection on the precise nature of this
tradition in actual practice." Indeed, *Inter Insigniores* had omitted "all the difficult questions about the concrete emergence of the Church and its origin from
Jesus."[215]

Christ's "Positive Will"

The tradition of the church's sacramental life, on the other hand, developed
in fits and starts over the centuries, and only in the mid-sixteenth century did
the Council of Trent finalize the list of seven sacraments. *Inter Insigniores* taught
that the magisterium reserved "a certain power" over sacraments, a power used
"down the centuries in order to determine the signs and the conditions of their
administration" (§34). This "certain power" allowed Rome to determine how,

and under what conditions, a sacrament was to be administered. Further, only the male hierarchy was competent to identify the "signs" that could be modified "if circumstances should so suggest" (§69). This meant that the adult Jesus was baptized by immersion, but the Vatican chose to sprinkle the heads of infants. Jesus called married men to the Twelve, but the hierarchy determined that all priests must be celibate.[216]

Rome could modify a sacramental "sign" to accommodate "circumstances, times or places" (§35), but it had no authority to alter "substance" established by Christ. Jesus' stated purpose for choosing twelve Jews was to sit on heavenly thrones and rule the Twelve Tribes of Israel (Matt. 19:28). But when the purpose of his choice no longer fit the "circumstances" of Christianity's developing self-identity, the leaders decided that Jewishness was not required for apostolic succession in the priesthood. Conversely, while Jesus said nothing about maleness or even priesthood, the church hierarchy nevertheless established maleness as the "substance" of the sacrament of holy orders.

However, the document said, the magisterium could have "no power over the substance of the sacraments." The substance was what Christ "determined should be maintained in the sacramental sign" that is "imprinted upon the human psychology" (§§35, 44). Depending upon the requirements of time and place, baptism could take place according to immersion or sprinkling, with an adult or infant; however, Rome had "no authority" (§9) to discontinue the use of water, the "substance" chosen by Christ. Likewise, Christ established the substance of eucharist as bread and wine. Using crackers and grape juice, then, would render the sacrament of the eucharist invalid.

But while the Council of Trent established that a sacramental "substance" was whatever Christ instituted, it left the details of *what* Christ instituted to theologians examining each sacrament. Bernard Leeming, a Jesuit professor of dogmatic theology, explained that other than baptism and eucharist, determining Christ's "positive will" for a sacrament required evidence.

> In other sacraments, given the meaning, the effects, and the assignment of any elements suitable to carry the significance, the institution by Christ, theoretically is safe; what more in fact is required, because of Christ's positive will, must be settled by the evidence in each case.[217]

Here was the source of the hierarchy's power to determine maleness as a sacramental "substance" according to "Christ's positive will" — because of Christ's *silence* on the matter, holy orders could be established as one of the five sacraments for which Christ provided no evidence of "substance." Indeed, Jesus established no priesthood, let alone an unchangeable "substance" of maleness. In such a case, according to traditional Catholic teaching, "Christ's positive will" had to be "settled by the evidence" of the case. It followed that since the "Twelve" were male, and more importantly since Christ was male, ipso facto Christ had a "positive will" for the establishment of a permanent, male priesthood. This presumption provided the rationale for the *tradition* of male priesthood, but only after Vatican II did maleness as sacramental substance become a distinct *theological* inquiry.

Aquinas taught in the thirteenth century that sacramental signs "represent what they signify by natural resemblance" to what they signify (§44). For example, water used in baptism naturally symbolizes a cleansing property. This "natural resemblance," argued *Inter Insigniores*, also was "required for persons as for things":

> When Christ's role in the eucharist is to be expressed sacramentally, there would not be this "natural resemblance" which must exist between Christ and his minister if the role of Christ were not taken by a man: in such a case it would be difficult to see in the [female] minister the image of Christ. (§45)

According to Rome (if not to Christ), maleness was intrinsic to the substance *and* the sign of holy orders. Maleness was part of the "sign" of holy orders because it would be "difficult" for the faithful to see "the image of Christ" in a woman. This claim was neither biblical nor traditional. Rahner argued that there was "no immediate evidence" of a human power over the Eucharist "anywhere in the New Testament."[218]

Signs of the Times:
From *Imago Dei* to *In Persona Christi*

The church had always taught that baptism configures *all* Christians to the image of God — *imago dei*. After Vatican II, as more and more Catholics called for women priests, Rome perceived a need to employ a stronger claim for male priesthood. To this end, post–Vatican II church leaders reinvigorated the priestly concept of *in persona Christi* — in the person and role of Christ. Vatican Council II had addressed the concept of *in persona Christi*[219] as the priest acting in the "person of Christ the head"[220] of the church. *Inter Insigniores* now extended this concept "to the point of being his very image" (§42). This assertion clearly privileged Christ's sex over his humanity. Thomas Newbold and others warned against this reductionism:

> The "natural resemblance" of a "natural symbol" does not require that the symbolic person or function or object be a *literal copy* of the person, function or object sym-bolized. As [Carl] Jung has pointed out, the symbolic manifestation or expression of an archetype loses both vigor and viability, meaning and vitality if it becomes a stereotype. To understand the "natural resemblance" of "natural symbol" in this reduced sense would impoverish its meaning and threaten its viability, making it a stereotype that fails to represent the full range of both meaning and possibility.[221]

Precisely in regard to stereotyping, *Inter Insigniores* prompted a question: "What would be the reaction if one said that a particular race or nationality could not adequately image Christ?"[222] What if the Vatican said that because Christ was neither African nor American, it followed that African Americans could not act *in persona Christi?*

Inter Insigniores did not address this inconsistency, but it did say that the male priesthood did not imply any "natural superiority of man over woman." Its point was that maleness could not be separated from the work of salvation because the "incarnation of the word took place according to the male sex," a fact that was "in harmony with the entirety of God's plan" (§46).

This inference drew widespread, serious criticism. It ignored the central church teaching that salvation comes not from Jesus' *maleness* but from his *humanness.* Nine centuries earlier, Anselm, archbishop of Canterbury and later a Doctor of the Church, had argued that since sin disrupted the order of the universe, some compensation was necessary to restore the divine order. Being finite, humans could not make this compensation to God, who is infinite. In fact, such repayment could be made only by one who was both finite (human) *and* infinite (God). The whole universal order was at stake, and so Jesus was born as a human/god who willingly died for humanity's sins to satisfy the debt once and for all. While this "theory of satisfaction" (as it came to be called) was never made an official teaching of the Church, it pervades mainstream Catholic theology.[223]

Anselm's theory viewed incarnation as a saving event precisely because it included *all* humanity in the person of Jesus. But if, as Rome now claimed, maleness was *intrinsic* to the work of salvation, the logical consequence seemed grim. In the words of theologian Elizabeth A. Johnson, CSJ: "If maleness is constitutive for the incarnation and redemption, female humanity is not assumed and therefore not saved."[224] In brief, if women could not represent Jesus, it followed that Jesus could not represent women. To insist that Jesus (and priests) *could* represent women would require the admission that males were somehow more complete than females, or that males could represent both sexes, while females could represent only themselves.

This claim was strenuously articulated by theologian Hans Urs von Balthasar, who said woman "has nothing to represent which she is not herself, while the male must represent the Origin of all life, which he can never be."[225] Balthasar maintained that *Inter Insigniores* had "penetrated the depths of the mystery" of priesthood (and womanhood) from which "convincing light" shone forth for "the true believer." Those who tried to understand this on a "purely rational plane" could not reach Christ, who was "absolute reason." The mysteries of faith were "accessible and comprehensible only" to *true* believers.[226]

R. A. Norris Jr. remarked that the male priesthood wrongly assumed that maleness was "a necessary precondition of Christ's being what he is and doing what he does." The argument was "virtually unprecedented" and stated none of the "traditional grounds" for a male-only priesthood. The idea that a priest imaged Jesus "in a special way" had "arrived rather late on the scene in Christian history." What was "genuinely novel" in *Inter Insigniores* was the idea that Jesus' sex was "one of the crucial things about him which ecclesial priesthood must image." If this male image had significance, Norris said it must be asked: "Significance for *what?*"[227]

On the other hand, *Inter Insigniores* found avid support among conservative groups such as Women for Faith and Family, which released a statement saying:

[We] recognize that the specific role of ordained priesthood is intrinsically connected with and representative of the begetting creativity of God in which only human males can participate. Human females, who by nature share in the creativity of God by their capacity to bring forth new life ... *can no more be priests than men can be mothers.*[228]

While explicitly rejecting "subordinationism," *Inter Insigniores* implicitly assumed the validity of Aquinas's (Aristotelian) conviction that only males were fully human: since Jesus was incarnated as a human male, he could *subsume* women just as the word "man" was used to *include* "woman." Man was complete in himself, but woman was dependent upon man for her completion. This was another reason why she could not act in the person of Christ.

The concept of the priest acting *in persona Christi* to the point of being Christ's "very image" was crucial to the document's model of sacrament for at least two reasons. First, it provided "a sign that must be perceptible and which the faithful must be able to recognize with ease" (§43). That is, the congregation must be able to look toward the altar and recognize Christ in the male priest — whether he be Nigerian, Vietnamese, or Aleut. Second, according to the CDF, Aquinas had employed the requirement of "signification" (natural resemblance) "precisely in order to reject the ordination of women" (n. 17).

Inter Insigniores acknowledged that the modern ordination ritual was neither apostolic nor biblical, and the laying-on of hands (a critical moment in the sacrament of orders) was not done by the apostles themselves, but rather began with their successors. Still, it was "clearly impossible to prove" that Jesus' selection of only men to the Twelve was inspired "only by social and cultural reasons" (§29). (Of course, the same logic held true for the opposite conclusion.)

While offering numerous reasons for the male-only priesthood, *Inter Insigniores* made a sympathetic reference to the Second Vatican Council's pastoral constitution *Gaudium et Spes* ("On the Church in the Modern World," 1965) and its stated concern for eliminating discrimination against human rights, especially based on sex, which it called contrary to God's plan. The result of eliminating such discrimination, Pope Paul VI later said, would be a world "harmonious and unified, if men and women contribute to it their own resources" (§2).[229] The words "their own resources" here and elsewhere strongly signaled the Vatican's intention to selectively emphasize traditional gender divisions.

"Bridegroom" and "Bride"

One gender division especially captured Rome's imagination and appeared frequently during the second half of the twentieth century. Known as the "nuptial analogy," a "bridegroom"/"bride" image allowed Rome to reinforce male-female relationships within several connected layers. Christ and his church were at the top layer of the bridegroom/bride hierarchy. Next came the priest and laity. Finally, men and women. The "bridegroom" ruled, and the "bride" obeyed.

The nuptial analogy was produced by an unhistorical interpretation of biblical symbolism found in the Old Testament's Song of Songs (also known as Canticle of Canticles and Song of Solomon). This biblical book shared a history with the

Mesopotamian marriage ritual between a fertility god (Dummuzi-Tammuz) and his sister (Inanna-Astarte). Dating from perhaps the fourth century B.C.E. by an unknown author, the book was used in a variety of ways through the centuries.[230] As interpreted by ancient rabbis, it was an allegory of the love between God (YHWH) and Israel. Christians would interpret it as a paean to the love between Christ (male) and the church (female).

In the early Christian interpretation, Christ as "bridegroom" was not identified as "priest," which developed only later. When this metaphor came to rest in its current form, Jesus as priest/male was a stalwart lover and rescuer who remained ever faithful to his beloved church/woman, even when she was sinful. But even this innovative metaphorical extension to Christ and his church was never intended to address a male-only priesthood, or a human priesthood at all.

In chapter 4 of the Song of Songs, the bridegroom speaks of the charms of his beloved, the bride. She is without blemish. Her lips are like a "scarlet thread" dripping honey, and her breasts are "two fawns" of a gazelle. She is a "garden locked, a fountain sealed," awaiting union with her lover. Her "channel is an orchard," and she invites her lover to "eat of its choice fruits."

The use of the "bridegroom"/"bride" analogy in *Inter Insigniores* to reinforce male supremacy in gender relations was unhistorical and unbiblical. The Song of Songs stresses "mutuality and fidelity between lovers." There is no subjection of one sex to the other. The main speaker is a woman, and her lover appears "as both shepherd and king," according to a common literary device in fiction.[231]

According to *Inter Insigniores*, however, this analogy identified the sexes in their "profound identity," an "unfathomable" (§52) distinction between man and woman determining the "identity proper to the person" (§54) in biology and religion. In the church, women and men could not be imagined apart from these gender-based identities.

The magisterium's literalistic, legalistic, and out-of-context use of the Song of Songs imagery to determine the relationship of (1) Jesus to the church, (2) priests to laity, and (3) men to women was seriously questioned. *Commonweal* columnist Sidney Callahan wrote:

> Exaggerated, overblown interpretations of the importance of gender differences and nuptial bodily orientations might make sense if Catholicism were a pagan fertility cult in which a divine couple created the world by sexual intercourse. But in Christianity ... disciples enter into the corporate body of Christ by faith, hope, and charity. The basic sacramental action is to eat a ritual sacred meal together ... and thereby become transformed into Christ as a new creation.[232]

Social Housekeepers

In its concluding paragraph, *Inter Insigniores* came as close as it would come to actually identifying women's roles both in church and society: "The Church desires that Christian women should become fully aware of the greatness of their mission: today their role is of capital importance, both for the renewal and humanization of society and for the rediscovery by believers of the true face of the Church"

(§69). The *"rediscovery* of the *true* face of the Church" implied that women had strayed from the "identity proper" to them, requiring that they rethink their place in the church.

The "renewal and humanization of society" echoed a long-familiar theme in the social ordering of women's spheres. In the nineteenth-century West, women were expected to stay home in the fashion of Coventry Patmore's *Angel in the House,* published in 1854 as a tribute to the perfect Victorian wife. This nineteenth-century "cult of domesticity" was an essentially biological construct in which traditionalists "focused on the concept of domesticity as a means of flattering women but suggesting that they stay at home."[233] As "social housekeepers," however, women could extend their Christian wifely and motherly skills into the public sphere in order to clean up the moral litter generated by the Industrial Revolution's displacement of populations. In this way, women's customary roles as housekeepers and moral guardians could continue in a larger arena.[234]

For nineteenth-century "social housekeepers" to ask for regular employment in the public sector, which belonged to men alone, not only would have contravened divine and human laws but also would have been a blatant display of ambition. And so it was with priesthood, according to *Inter Insigniores:*

> To consider the ministerial priesthood as a human right would be to misjudge its nature completely: baptism does not confer any personal title to public ministry in the Church. The priesthood is not conferred for the honor or advantage of the recipient, but for the service of God and the Church (§63).... The priestly office cannot become the goal of social advancement (§67).

This statement strongly implied that women who discerned God's call to priesthood acted only out of concern with personal titles, honors, and social advancement. No such charge was made regarding men's motives for ordination.

Inter Insigniores continued: ordination could not "provide an excuse for jealousy" by women of men, because the "greatest in the kingdom of heaven are not the ministers but the saints" (§68). This claim eerily echoed the concept of social housekeeping: while male activities such as politics and commerce were closed to women, frustrated females who insisted upon leaving the house could acceptably do so by extending their domestic duties into the public sphere — they could feed the hungry, clothe the poor, teach the ignorant, and perform other works of mercy. They even formed their own infrastructures for networking and mutual support. Historian Mary P. Ryan explained that rather than "invading male territory directly, this remarkable generation of women built a separate female domain in the public sector,"[235] a domain that ultimately equipped them to penetrate the male bastion of education, politics, economics, and eventually religion.

Inter Insigniores said that Catholics supporting women's ordination lacked understanding of the "respective roles of men and women" (§9). Once sex roles were properly understood, the Vatican's teaching against women's ordination would become clear. Once the teaching was manifest, sex roles would be properly understood. Concealed somewhere inside this circular reasoning was the will of God.

Some years later, Benedictine Sister Joan Chittister wrote:

> It would be an inconsistent God indeed who created women and men out of an identical substance, yet supposedly gave one gender control of the other; a God who is all Spirit yet exclusively male; a God who makes both man and woman in the divine image yet defines one as less human than the other; a God who calls us all to knowledge of salvation but gives men alone the right to designate exactly what that means, implies, requires.[236]

Inter Insigniores made clear that Rome would stand firm against any theological rebuttal. This was indicated in part by the document's copious use of a strategic rhetorical device that placed the whole of the argument beyond the sum of its parts. That is, the document frequently grouped various claims within the same sentence, so that to deny one element effectively denied the sentence's claims *in toto*. For instance:

> But over and above considerations inspired by the spirit of the times, one finds expressed — especially in the canonical documents of the Antiochian and Egyptian traditions — this essential reason, namely, that by calling only men to the priestly order and ministry in its true sense, the Church intends to remain faithful to the type of ordained ministry willed by the Lord Jesus Christ and carefully maintained by the apostles (§11).

This sentence contained six elements:

- an appeal to *Eastern tradition*;
- a claim that the male-only call to ordination was *essential*;
- a declaration that men were called to priestly ministry in its *true sense*;
- an assertion that the *church* called these men to true ministry;
- a pledge that the church would be faithful to the *will* of the *Lord*; and
- the church would be faithful to the divine will as *maintained by the apostles*.

These six claims, housed within a single sentence, made it difficult and time-consuming to analyze a single assertion, independent of the others (although it was crystal clear that "church" meant "hierarchy"). Such linguistic challenges were difficult for most Catholics, yet Rome said that only in this way could Catholics "better understand how well-founded is the basis of the Church's practice" and thus conclude that the character of ordination required priests to be "the image and symbol of Christ himself" (§59).

Far from settling the issue, *Inter Insigniores* only ignited more heated controversy. In the wake of the declaration, a 1977 Gallup poll of U.S. Catholics was conducted in three stages: a February 18 survey showed 31 percent in favor of women priests; March 4 — 36 percent; and March 18 — 41 percent. In the four weeks following *Inter Insigniores*, support for women's ordination enjoyed a 10 percent increase.[237]

While most leaders in the 1970s complained about women's ordination supporters in the United States, in reality the phenomenon was not so limited. Cardinal John Krol of Philadelphia observed that the teaching of *Inter Insigniores* stood in "sharp contrast to movements *throughout the world*" to ordain women.[238]

He was right. Theologians everywhere went to work dismantling much of the document's spurious theology and challenging its lack of ecumenical awareness as well as its sexism.[239] Many bishops and theologians struggled just to absorb its content, and like most Vatican documents directly affecting the laity, the text's technical language and circuitous arguments placed it beyond the reach of most Catholics in the pews. In many cases, bishops and priests found themselves able to tell the faithful only that the pope said "No."

• • •

Becoming the "bride of Christ" has traditionally been taken quite literally by women religious, as evidenced by the wedding rings worn on their ring fingers. This relationship was especially deep for Thérèse, who extended the bride/bridegroom motif "to the limits of our reasonable endurance."[240] According to an early biographer, when Thérèse took the habit on January 10, 1889, her father walked her down the aisle "to the altar in her bridal dress . . . on this most beautiful of occasions when a young girl girdled with chastity gives herself to that Bridegroom for whom she will remain forever maiden."[241] Another biographer, however, pointed out that Thérèse's "tough core of heroism" was intact, even if it had to be "disinterred from under layers and layers of cotton wool."[242]

❧ Chapter 8 ❧

Obliged to Intervene

"A COMMENTARY ON THE DECLARATION"*
Prepared by an Expert Theologian at the Request of
the Congregation for the Doctrine of the Faith
January 27, 1977

Worldwide objections to *Inter Insigniores* ("Declaration on the Admission of Women to the Ministerial Priesthood," 1976) prompted the Congregation for the Doctrine of the Faith (CDF) to issue a commentary[243] explaining that *Inter Insigniores* had been published in the first place because of the growing numbers of Catholics supporting women's ordination and of non-Catholic Christian ordinations of women. Now, because of the increasingly vocal frustration among ordination supporters and the growing visibility of the Women's Ordination Conference, the magisterium was "obliged to intervene" (§12).

The CDF was a force to be reckoned with. Founded in 1542 to defend the church from Martin Luther and numerous heretics, it was called the "Sacred Congregation of the Universal Inquisition." In 1908, Pope Pius X changed its name to the "Sacred Congregation of the Holy Office," and in 1965 Pope Paul VI changed it again to the "Congregation for the Doctrine of the Faith." In 1988, Pope John Paul II declared that the CDF's duty was "to promote and safeguard the doctrine on the faith and morals throughout the Catholic world" — including matters of doctrine, discipline, and priestly affairs — "and defend those points of Christian tradition which seem in danger because of new and unacceptable doctrines."[244]

The CDF's "Commentary on the Declaration [*Inter Insigniores*]" — written by an anonymous "expert theologian"[245] — was necessary because it was "difficult to leave unanswered any longer a precise question that is being posed nearly everywhere and which is polarizing attention to the detriment of more urgent endeavors that should be fostered" (§18). The CDF did not list the "more urgent" endeavors, but its acknowledgment that the women's ordination issue was "polarizing attention" of the world's Catholics away from the Vatican's agenda was the strongest suggestion yet that the church hierarchy was, in fact, paying close attention to the growing movement. More than 50 percent longer than *Inter*

---

*The document is included in the appendix, p. 196.

59

Insigniores, the commentary reiterated the reasons women could not be priests: (1) the will of Christ; (2) apostolic practice; (3) church tradition; and (4) the "nuptial" (bridegroom/bride) relationship of Christ and the church.

Of these claims, church tradition caused particular concern among theologians. *Inter Insigniores* included one controversial pronouncement in the form of a question asked by ordination supporters: "What the Church does she can in fact do, since she has the assistance of the Holy Spirit" (§25). "But what the Church has never done — is this any proof that she cannot do it in the future?" (§26). Rome's answer was an immediate and vehement *yes.* What the church had never done *was* proof that the church could never do it. Tradition was "received from Christ and the apostles" and the church was "bound" to it (§30).[246] This assertion, of course, contradicted a long history of changes in church thinking and practice over the centuries (slavery is justified, women must cover their heads in church, unbaptized babies go to "Limbo") and threatened to place Catholics in an intellectual and devotional straitjacket.

In case the argument from tradition failed to convince, the commentary said that even if a woman heard "as it were a call in the depths of [her] soul," the vocation to priesthood could be authentic only from the moment it was "authenticated by the external call of the Church" (§107). For women, such authentication was impossible: the hierarchy had never ordained women, and what the hierarchy had never done, it could never do. The circle was complete.

Scrutinizing the Lord's Thought

In addition to validating the call to priesthood, Rome reserved the sole right to authenticate the interpretation of scripture. Echoing the Pontifical Biblical Commission, the commentary on *Inter Insigniores* said the New Testament did "not on its own enable us to give an account of certain sacraments, and especially of the structure of the sacrament of order" (§41). That is, scripture alone could not support a male-only priesthood. "We cannot omit the study of tradition: it is the Church [hierarchy] that scrutinizes the Lord's thought by reading scripture, and it is the Church that gives witness to the correctness of its interpretation" (§42). Unless the value of "unwritten traditions" is admitted, "it is sometimes difficult to discover in scripture entirely explicit indications of Christ's will" (§59).

At this point, the commentary addressed the authenticity of Paul's writings where *Inter Insigniores* had left off, actually expanding the content of the original declaration.

> It can be questioned whether two of Paul's most famous texts on women are authentic or should rather be seen as interpolations, perhaps even relatively late ones. The first is 1 Cor. 14:34–35: "The women should keep silence in the churches. For they are not permitted to speak, but should be subordinate as even the law says." These two verses, apart from being missing in some important manuscripts and not being found quoted before the end of the second century, present stylistic peculiarities foreign to Paul. The other text is 1 Tim. 2:11–14: "I do not allow a woman to teach or to exercise authority over men." The Pauline authenticity of this text is often

questioned, although the arguments are weaker. However, *it is of little importance whether these texts are authentic or not: theologians have made abundant use of them to explain that women cannot receive either the power of magisterium or that of jurisdiction.* But there are other Pauline texts of unquestioned authenticity that affirm that *"the head of the woman is the man"* (§§63–65).[247]

This remarkable passage not only contradicted Vatican II's rejection of "subordinationism" by restating the male's headship over the female, it also placed scripture in the service of tradition, making "abundant use" of a perhaps inauthentic text to explain why women could not receive the "power of magisterium." The anonymous author's scriptural claims (but not the ideas they represented) were abandoned in later documents, although the selective use of scripture generally would be maintained.

The Sixth Sacrament: "Orders" Is Not for Women

According to *Inter Insigniores,* until the 1960s the practice of male priesthood had constituted "an unbroken tradition throughout the history of the Church" (§39). Since it had "enjoyed peaceful and universal acceptance," Rome had not needed "to formulate a principle which was not attacked, or to defend a law which was not challenged" (§§12–13). But by the mid-1970s, Rome was feeling the pressure to provide concrete teachings against women priests. The CDF commentary quoted Bonaventure[248] as saying that the male priesthood was due "not so much to a decision by the Church" as to the fact that the sacrament was not for women (§34). The reality was, however, that it was precisely the church hierarchy that had decided "the fact" that this sacrament was not for women.

The commentary acknowledged "a long way to go before all the inequalities of which women are still the victims are eliminated, not only in the field of public professional and intellectual life, but even within the family" (§111). In this document, some Catholics sensed the possibility that the Vatican's interest in furthering women's cultural advancement was at least partly motivated by Rome's growing need to deflect attention away from its own unreformed practice of sex discrimination. Not only was the commentary silent about discrimination within the church itself, but even more tellingly it concluded with a call to end the ordination controversy altogether so that "the pastors and faithful of the Church" would no longer be "distracted" by the issue (§109).

Immediately following publication of this commentary, however, twenty-three theologians at the Jesuit School of Theology in Berkeley, California, one of six pontifical faculties in the United States, penned an open letter to the local apostolic delegate, a papal representative responsible for overseeing (and reporting to the pope about) church affairs within his territory. The priests' letter was particularly concerned with the commentary's claim that what the church had never done, the church could never do in the future.

"To say that we have never ordained women in the past and therefore cannot do so now is to ignore the fact that the issue has never arisen in precisely these contemporary terms and within the new realization of women's place in the world," the theologians wrote. The Vatican's position could not be sustained by "the evidence and the arguments alleged in its support." Indeed, Rome's position threatened a "serious injustice" arising from the exclusion of "an entire class of Catholics" from priesthood "on principle *even from the possibility that Christ might call them.*"[249] The Jesuits' letter was firm, direct, and very public: "Roman congregations have made serious mistakes in the past whose harm to the church we continue to experience centuries afterwards. We believe that we may well be on a similar path again."[250]

•   •   •

On November 20, 1887, during a pilgrimage to Rome with her father and younger sister, fourteen-year-old Thérèse was part of a group from her hometown of Lisieux to be granted a general audience with Pope Leo XIII. Her request for admission to the convent at Carmel having been rejected by the local Carmelite Father Superior and the bishop, she had formulated a plan to pursue the "Yes" upon which she had set her heart.

Leo XIII was wearing a cassock and white cape during the papal audience, she later wrote. Pilgrims passed, kissing the pope's foot and then his hand, as was the custom. As her turn to speak to the pontiff drew near, the vicar general of Lisieux "announced in a loud voice that he absolutely forbade anyone to address the holy father."[251] When the pontiff extended his hand for her kiss, Thérèse looked anxiously at her sister Céline, who whispered: "Speak up!" Thérèse did, announcing to the pontiff that she wanted to enter Carmel at age fifteen (which had never before been allowed). Stunned, the pope looked to the vicar general, standing nearby, who more fully explained Thérèse's request. Somewhat condescendingly, it seemed, the pope told her that if God willed she would enter the convent. Feeling crushed, yet reluctant to leave, Thérèse had to be carried out by two guards and the vicar general.[252]

Part III

POPE JOHN PAUL II

Chapter 9

One Step Forward, Two Steps Back

THE CODE OF CANON LAW
Pontifical Commission for the Revision of the Code
November 27, 1983

The 1983 Code of Canon Law[253] was considered to be the last document to emerge from Vatican II. The official collection of ecclesiastical law for Roman Catholics — commissioned by John XXIII and promulgated by John Paul II — it contained 2,414 canons (rules) for the administration of the church.

Published eighteen years after the close of Vatican II, the Code reflected the egalitarian spirit of that council while maintaining the male-only priesthood (canon 1024). It also continued to ban women from the nonordained ministries of lector and altar server, while still providing for the "installation" of lay men to these ministries (canon 230:1).[254] However, in a qualified accommodation to the West, where women were already serving as lectors (without formal installation), the Code allowed lay "persons" to "fulfill the function" (but *not* the formal ministry) of lectors and altar servers "by temporary deputation" according to the "necessity of the Church" and when qualified ministers (males) were "lacking" (canon 230:2–3). In other words, as Rosie the Riveter helped build airplanes until the soldiers returned from World War II, women could "supply some of the same services"[255] of these ministries for the duration of ecclesiastical need.

This provision puzzled canon lawyers and editors of the 1983 Code, who wrote that "the restriction of installation in these ministries to men" was "questioned throughout the process for revising the Code" because the ministries of lector and altar server were "truly lay ministries" and the restriction to males appeared to be an "unwarranted discrimination."

> What would be the impact on the community if some [males] who provide these ministries were to be installed but others [females], equally qualified and experienced, were to be denied installation merely on the basis of sex? It would seem to belie the provisions of canon 208 on the equality of the baptized.[256]

These remarks, of course, could also apply to denying ordination to women.

More boldly, the new Code said that "a dearth of priests" could allow a local bishop to decide that pastoral care of the parish could be entrusted to a "person who is not a priest" (canon 517:2). Sociologist Ruth Wallace identified this canon as a "Pandora's box for the church, because the wording of this new law opened the door for female leadership on the parish level, and consequently created a new role for women in the Catholic church."[257]

Canon 1024, however, reproduced the 1917 Code (canon 968:1), stating the prime requisite for valid orders: "Only a baptized male [*vir*] validly receives sacred ordination."[258] Retention of this brief statement was "sustained without discussion" among the Code's editors, who explained that its inclusion had been determined by the papal climate beginning with Paul VI. In a brief commentary, however, they wrote: "Although the interpretation of this canon is traditional and clear, the literature on this canon during the revision process exceeds the total amount of literature on all the other canons on orders."[259] The inclusion of that remark conveyed that the canon was not nearly as persuasive as it was intended or believed to be.

Roots and Reforms

In 1970, German theologian Ida Raming published a study of the canonical exclusion of women from priesthood. She traced this exclusion back to the massive codification of church law by a Camaldolese monk, Gratian, in the twelfth century, and then to his sources — the Bible, church fathers, and the early councils. Three years later, Jesuit theologian Haye van der Meer wrote:

> A number of things become clear in [Raming's] analysis: a large part of Gratian's work in this area was based on earlier forged documents (the pseudo-isidorian decretals),[260] on documents that were erroneously thought to be conciliar decrees (*Statuta Ecclesiae Antiqua*), and serious misreadings or misunderstandings of other documents; at the base of Gratian's work in this area was his conviction of the decided metaphysical and moral inferiority of women and their consequent "status subjectionis."[261]

Women have seldom fared well in canon law. In 1917, canon 93 stated that a wife necessarily shared the domicile of her husband, just like "the insane that of his guardian," and "the minor that of the person in whose charge he is." Canon 1264 said that nuns, assuming they had permission from the local bishop "to sing in their own church," were to sing from "a place where they cannot be seen by the people."[262] This segregation was pursuant to a "thorough reform" of church music by Pope Pius X, in which women were "not to have a part in the strictly liturgical chants of the sacred liturgy."[263] In 1903, Pius X wrote that because women were "incapable" they could not be admitted to the choir. "If high voices, such as treble and alto, are wanted, these parts must be sung by boys, according to the ancient custom of the church."[264] Indeed, canon 1262:1 decreed that men were to be separated from the women altogether during worship, "in keeping with the ancient discipline."[265]

The 1917 list of activities barred to women was largely a product of its time, and many of the outmoded restrictions were relaxed (although not altogether abolished) in the 1983 text. Hence, while 1983 canon 230 excluded women from "installation" as lector or altar server, it provided for the "temporary deputation" of "lay persons" to "fulfill the function of lector."[266] Little more than a decade later, the Vatican lifted the ban against females serving on the altar (with the permission of local bishops).[267]

Compared to 1917, the 1983 Code referred to women more as adults than in their familiar roles as dependent creatures. Further, it signaled a time, between two papal statements against women priests — Pope Paul VI's *Inter Insigniores* ("Declaration on the Admission of Women to the Ministerial Priesthood," 1976) and John Paul II's *Ordinatio Sacerdotalis* ("On Reserving Priestly Ordination to Men Alone," 1994) — when Catholics enjoyed relatively open reflection and discussion of an inclusive priesthood. An example of this openness was a statement to the 1983 World Synod of Bishops by Archbishop L. A. Vachon of Quebec on behalf of the Canadian Conference of Catholic Bishops:

> Since John XXIII's recognition, in Section I of *Pacem in Terris*, and since Vatican II issued *Gaudium et Spes*, a number of episcopates [bodies of bishops] have acted unceasingly to sensitize public opinion to the difficult — and in fact oppressive — cultural condition of women. But these appeals of the Church to the world for the advancement of the status of women are on the point of losing all impact *unless the recognition of women as full members becomes simultaneously a reality within the Church itself.*[268]

The Canadian bishops had articulated what was rarely uttered by church leaders: working for women's *cultural* advancement meant little without a corresponding attention to women's roles in the *church*. They challenged themselves to recognize their own "male appropriation of Church institutions" that caused a "cultural deformation" of the church.[269]

• • •

Despite the earthly rules against it, God willed that Thérèse enter the convent at Carmel at age fifteen. Thanks to the intercession of the vicar general of Lisieux, who had overheard her plea to the pontiff the year before, Thérèse was admitted to Carmel of Lisieux on April 9, 1888. The Father Superior of the Carmelites, displeased that his earlier "No" to Thérèse had been overruled by the bishop following her trip to Rome, addressed the assembled nuns upon her arrival: "I present to you this child of fifteen, whose entry you have desired. I trust that she will not disappoint your hopes, but I remind you that if it turns out otherwise, the responsibility will be yours alone."[270]

Nine months after her entry into Carmel, Thérèse's older sisters, Pauline and Marie, who were already Carmelite nuns, witnessed their little sister's acceptance as a novice when she took the white veil.

Within the close confines of Carmel, however, spiritual and temporal maturity was not always encouraged or even possible. In addition to being vowed to obedience to their Reverend Mother, the cloistered nuns of Lisieux necessarily served as "spiritual mothers" to each other. Having lost her own mother at age four, and having been unceasingly doted upon by her father and sisters at home, Thérèse often impressed the nuns not as "motherly" at all but rather as a religious and spiritual know-it-all who was sharp and defensive toward others and who thought she had, as one biographer put it, "a hot line to Jesus."[271]

The nuns weren't without grounds for their impression of Thérèse, who according to an early biographer was "eager, intelligent, headstrong, and almost unbelievably stubborn," and who displayed "a rapacity, an egoism, a spirit of conquest"[272] uncommon in a woman.

→ Chapter 10 ←

An Element of Grave Difficulty

Anglican-Roman Catholic Relations

LETTER OF POPE JOHN PAUL II
TO ARCHBISHOP ROBERT RUNCIE
December 20, 1984

LETTER OF ARCHBISHOP RUNCIE
TO POPE JOHN PAUL II
December 11, 1985

LETTER OF ARCHBISHOP RUNCIE
TO CARDINAL JAN WILLEBRANDS
December 18, 1985

LETTER OF CARDINAL WILLEBRANDS
TO ARCHBISHOP RUNCIE
June 17, 1986

Following Vatican II (1962–65), most analyses of male priesthood were grounded in three sources — (1) the council's call for increased lay participation; (2) the secular women's movement; and (3) the opening of clerical ranks to women in other Christian denominations.

By the mid-1980s, the ecumenical aspect of the priesthood issue was becoming openly apparent, and the Vatican found itself increasingly isolated. Women's ordinations in Protestant churches, in which pastoral ministry was not sacramental (claiming no apostolic succession), posed no real problem for Rome. But when women were ordained into the Episcopal and Anglican denominations, which have specific ministerial priesthood, "the issue was raised within the context of eucharistic ministry," said religious studies professor Mary Jo Weaver, "and so moved Roman officials to react vigorously against it."[273]

This was important because, as sociologist Mark Chaves pointed out, exclusion of women from priesthood revealed a denomination's social priorities. A church's insistence on a male priesthood had more to do with external pressures than internal problems, and ecumenical considerations were often included as "reasons against ordaining women."[274]

A Serious Obstacle

In 1974 in Philadelphia, a group of retired Episcopal bishops[275] conferred priestly ordination on eleven women, qualified in every category except sex. These "irregular" Episcopal ordinations sent a powerful message to Anglican and Roman Catholic leadership that not all Christian women could be counted on to silently acquiesce to church laws they believed to be unjust. Following the Congregation for the Doctrine of the Faith's 1976 release of *Inter Insigniores*, the National Consultation of the Episcopal and Roman Catholic Churches in the U.S.A. issued a report on the role of women in both churches, recommending a study of "the still deeply divisive questions raised around the ordination of women."[276]

Correspondence between Britain's archbishop of Canterbury Donald Coggan and Pope Paul VI in the 1970s acknowledged the serious obstacle that women's ordination posed to relations between the Anglican Communion and the Roman Catholic Church. The issue was placed on the agenda of the first Anglican-Roman Catholic International Commission (ARCIC I), which met from 1970 to 1981 and issued its final report in 1982.[277] After a second commission (ARCIC II) was established to continue dialogue, Pope John Paul II in 1984 issued a letter to archbishop of Canterbury Robert Runcie. Saying that Rome must "base frank and constructive dialogue upon clarity regarding her own positions,"[278] the Anglican Communion's recent support for women's ordination prompted John Paul II "with all brotherly frankness" to reaffirm the Vatican's unflinching position:

> It was with profound sadness that Pope Paul VI contemplated a step which he saw as introducing into our dialogue "an element of grave difficulty," even "a threat." Since that time we have celebrated together the progress towards reconciliation between our two Communions. But in those same years the increase in the number of Anglican Churches which admit, or are preparing to admit, women to priestly ordination constitutes, in the eyes of the Catholic Church, an increasingly serious obstacle to that progress.[279]

The implication was clear: the Anglicans had introduced a "serious obstacle" forcing the Vatican to adopt an isolationist stance, one of what Chaves characterized as "the many instances of Roman Catholic spokesmen pointing out to other denominations the negative consequences for future union if a denomination were to ordain women."[280] The pope concluded his letter to Runcie with no reference to further dialogue.

Runcie answered one year later, explaining that the process of collegiality had slowed his response time.

> The receipt of your letter of December last year on this question therefore prompted me to [undertake] confidential consultation with the [leaders] of the autonomous provinces of the Anglican Communion throughout the world. They also judged your letter to be of great importance and by various means themselves sought the counsel of their own Provinces. Accordingly it is only now that I am able to make a substantive reply to your letter in the light of the responses I have received from the different parts of the Anglican Communion.[281]

Runcie's pointed and detailed reference to his consultation with the world's Anglican leaders could not have failed to catch the attention of John Paul II, who was beginning to suffer criticism for not consulting his own bishops, a neglect that would become more pronounced and public in coming years.

Acknowledging that "Anglican opinion is itself divided," Runcie explained that churches within the Communion had "serious doctrinal reasons" for ordaining women and he stressed "the urgent need for a joint study on the question of the ordination of women to the ministerial priesthood." A continuing dialogue was the path to "mature trust" between the churches.[282]

One week after sending his letter to the pope, Runcie sent a letter to Cardinal Jan Willebrands, president of the Vatican Secretariat for Promoting Christian Unity, expressing hope that the letter would help the Vatican interpret the "actions of the Churches of the Anglican Communion more intelligibly and sympathetically." John Paul II's letter to Runcie had merely referred the Anglican archbishop to *Inter Insigniores* ("On Reserving Priestly Ordination to Men Alone," 1976) for church teaching on the issue, but Runcie's letter to Willebrands carefully and substantially outlined the Anglican position:[283]

- scripture and tradition offered *no fundamental objections* to the ordination of women to ministerial priesthood;

- exclusion of women from priestly ministry *could not be shown* to be of divine law;

- it was insufficient simply to state there were no fundamental reasons against women's ordination; it also was necessary to demonstrate *compelling doctrinal reasons* for such a significant theological development;

- the most substantial doctrine that *justified* women's ordination also *demanded* it: in the Christian order of salvation, Jesus assumed human flesh so that all people might be redeemed, or in words common to both churches, "As he came to share in our humanity, so we may share in the Redemption he won for us on the Cross"; and

- the ministerial priesthood, "commissioned by the Church in ordination to represent the priestly nature of the whole body" of believers in sacramental relationship to Christ should "be opened to women in order the more perfectly to represent Christ's inclusive High Priesthood"; the representational nature of *priesthood was "actually weakened by a solely male priesthood"* specifically because it was *not* inclusive of all Christians.

Runcie said the two churches were indeed at a difficult place, but it was precisely "at such difficult times" that dialogue was essential. The International Commission's mandate to study "all that hinders the mutual recognition of the ministries of our Communions" could not be fulfilled without Vatican cooperation.[284]

Unsatisfactory Arguments

In June 1986, Cardinal Jan Willebrands responded to the Anglican archbishop's letter and affirmed the need for further study, but he reminded Runcie that the principal reason put forth by *Inter Insigniores* for banning women's ordination was the same tradition shared by the Anglican Communion, which, as "part of the whole Catholic [universal] Church," could not undertake "so radical a departure from Tradition independently of the Roman Catholic and the Orthodox Churches." Willebrands said he did not intend "to deal in detail with this question" in his letter, but he wished "to indicate why" the Anglican archbishop's arguments were unsatisfactory. Saying the context for discussion was "sacramental theology and the tradition of the Church," Willebrands made the following points:[285]

- women's ordination was a question of sacramental ordination relevant only to Christians sharing an understanding of sacramental ministry; further, sacramental ministry must be understood in its "appropriate context" of theology: *only a male priesthood could make the "once-for-all sacrifice of Christ [a] present reality"*;
- the Old Testament envisioned Israel as the bride of Yahweh, and Paul in the New Testament called the church the "bride of Christ"; the church understood itself "in terms of this feminine imagery and symbolism as the Body which received the Word of God"; Christ, on the other hand, was the *"Head of the Body,"* and it was "through the head that the whole Body is redeemed"; and
- Christ took on human nature to redeem all humanity, but Christ was male, and his *maleness was "an inherent feature"* of salvation, in which the priest represented "Christ in his saving relationship with his Body the Church."

In simpler language, (1) sacramental ordination required maleness, (2) biblical nuptial imagery (priest/bridegroom/head and church/bride/body) was to be interpreted literally, and (3) Christ's maleness required a male priesthood.

Although Willebrands did not address Runcie's detailed arguments, he said there was a "serious question" as to whether the Anglican leader's arguments possessed "an adequate or proper understanding" of "salvation as revealed in the Scriptures and mediated and preached in the Church." In closing, he said that Runcie could not provide sufficient reasons for the "radical innovation of ordaining women to the priesthood," but that the topic would, "of course, continue to be a matter of discussion."[286] His prediction would go unfulfilled, at least by Rome.

Important Differences

In contrast, the 1988 Lambeth Conference found the ARCIC I report "consonant in substance with the faith of Anglicans" and "a sufficient basis for taking the next step forward towards the reconciliation of our churches grounded in agreement in faith."[287] But the issue of women priests clearly had emerged as a major stumbling block to ecumenical relations, evidenced by the pope's reaffirmation that year of the male-only priesthood.[288]

In 1991, the Congregation for the Doctrine of the Faith and the Pontifical Council for Promoting Christian Unity issued a joint response to the ARCIC I report. The Vatican stressed that the report neglected "important differences regarding essential matters of Catholic doctrine," including the nature of male-only priesthood.[289] Despite the ARCIC's decade of work, the result was unacceptable to Rome. Responding candidly to this concern, the new archbishop of Canterbury, George L. Carey, wrote that rather than searching for common ground, "the question to our two communions appears to have been understood instead as asking: Is the Final Report identical with the teachings of the Roman Catholic Church?"[290]

In 1992, the Church of England formally approved women's ordination, placing even more public pressure on Rome to update its teaching on ordination.

• • •

Life at Carmel was challenging. Fifteen-year-old Thérèse had been strictly sheltered, and pampered, at home. Now, in the convent, she sometimes found it difficult to get along with the other, more mature nuns. Not long after her entry, she enjoyed a revelation of great spiritual and practical merit — Jesus' commandment to love one's neighbor as oneself. Jesus had loved his disciples "not for their natural qualities" but because he wanted "to see them near him in the kingdom" of heaven. This new understanding showed her that "true charity" consisted in tolerating "all one's neighbor's faults, never being surprised by his weakness, and being inspired by the least of his virtues." The real meaning of this commandment, she said, was that it was Jesus' will "to love in me all those whom You command me to love."[291]

The idea that God wished to love in her all those people whom she was called to love was revolutionary for Thérèse, who had never succeeded at forging successful relationships outside her own family. But, if she could love her neighbors so that God could love them in her, the task was suddenly no longer impossible.

⇻ Chapter 11 ⇺

Motherhood in a Manly Way

"HOLY THURSDAY LETTER TO PRIESTS"
Pope John Paul II
March 25, 1988

By the late 1980s, after a decade of systematically deflecting calls for women's ordination, Pope John Paul II appeared to be strategically transferring women's traditional roles to the clergy, encouraging priests to act as both father *and* mother to their flocks. In his "Holy Thursday Letter to Priests,"[292] he followed tradition in calling the church "a virgin who keeps whole and pure the fidelity she has pledged to her Spouse." In scripture, the faithful could find "the truth about the Church's motherhood." But in this letter, he introduced an innovative concept by suggesting that this motherhood become a greater part of priestly consciousness. "If each [priest] lives the equivalent of this spiritual motherhood in a manly way, namely, as a 'spiritual fatherhood,' then Mary, as a 'figure' of the Church, has a part to play in this experience of ours." Moreover, this manly expression of motherhood was "inscribed at the very center" of priestly service.[293]

Actually, "priest as mother" was not a new idea, although it had not previously been clearly referred to as such. In 1977, responding to *Inter Insigniores* ("Declaration on the Admission of Women to the Ministerial Priesthood," 1976), Hans Urs von Balthasar, whose writings influenced the theology of John Paul II, wrote that to priests, "Jesus granted a participation in his precise Messianic functions [of] representing God and his definitive work of salvation." This service required "the *transmission* of God's gifts," a talent that was not "possessed *by* himself, or even only essentially *in* himself." A priest, by his sacred office, was a vessel *through whom* was transmitted God's gift. In other words, as priest, a man could function as a woman, like Mary, through whom flowed the gift of God.[294]

John Paul II (and Balthasar) asked priests to assume a complicated persona. He said the analogy between Mary and church, both "called mother and virgin," had a "special eloquence" for priests, who were called to "renounce fatherhood 'according to the flesh' in order that there may grow and develop in us fatherhood 'according to the Spirit.'" This fatherhood in the spirit included the "maternal characteristics"[295] of docility and receptivity. This letter provided another occasion for the world's theologians and bishops to put their skills to the task of second-guessing the pope — in this case discerning the "maternal characteristics"

74

of "spiritual fatherhood." Likewise, they struggled to respond to the pontiff's call for priests to pursue their role as spiritual fathers *and* mothers in order to "discover in a new way the question of the dignity and vocation of *women*."[296] With priests assuming the roles of male *and* female, the question of women's participation in the church was murkier than ever.

In a final note, John Paul II told the priests: "Let us also give thanks to Mary for the indescribable gift of the priesthood.... [Let] us give thanks together with Mary, the Mother of priests." Devotion to Mary as the "mother of priests" was a signature of John Paul II's pontificate, and his passion for (some would say fixation on) Mary — mother and virgin — seemed to suggest a strong motivator for his unyielding insistence that women's roles were found in motherhood and virginity. Further, his intense focus on maternity would repeatedly manifest itself as a spiritual goal of men's priesthood.

• • •

Thérèse had an abiding devotion to the Blessed Mother. Like Mary, she wanted to be a mother — a "mother of souls." For a half-century after her death, Thérèse was portrayed as a typical, nineteenth-century "plaster-cast saint," without blemish, without flesh and blood. But in the mid-twentieth century, scholars began recovering the real Thérèse, discovering that sharing with and caring about others was not always her strong suit. She wrote candidly: "Talking to other people bored me, even when we spoke about religion."[297] In fact, she saw Carmel as a desert where God wanted her to hide herself. As a child, she had shared her longing to enter Carmel with the prioress, who responded that "nine-year-old postulants were not received" and Thérèse would have to wait until she was sixteen.[298] But Thérèse was not good at waiting, and at an early age she displayed a strong sense of what she wanted.

When she was four, Thérèse's sister Léonie, having outgrown her dolls, held up a basket filled with doll clothes and ribbons. She told Thérèse and another sister to take whatever they wanted. The other sister chose some silk braid. Thérèse thought for a moment, then stretched out her hands and declared: "I choose everything!"

Throughout her life, Thérèse wanted to "choose everything." She did want to be the "mother of souls." She also wanted to be "a priest, an apostle, a doctor of the Church, a martyr." Most of all, she wanted to become a saint, a goal that God led her to understand she would reach: "The glory I was to win would never be seen during my lifetime. My glory would consist in becoming a great saint."[299]

❧ Chapter 12 ❧

Woman

Always the Bride

MULIERIS DIGNITATEM
("On the Dignity and Vocation of Women")
Pope John Paul II
August 15, 1988

Pope John Paul II wrote this apostolic letter, *Mulieris Dignitatem* ("On the Dignity and Vocation of Women"), in response to the 1987 World Synod of Catholic Bishops, which highlighted the role of women in the church. That meeting again revealed that women's concerns about their roles in the church were not limited to Catholics in the United States or even in the West, but constituted a worldwide issue.[300] Accordingly, *Mulieris Dignitatem* made a broad sweep of church teachings about women.[301]

In this document, John Paul II made perhaps the strongest statement yet on the worth of women. Referencing Ephesians 5:22–23, he said that out of reverence to Christ, the exhortation "Wives, be subject to your husbands" was to be carried out not as subjection of wife to husband but as "mutual subjection" of spouses to each other. Yet he could not escape his conviction that women's worth lay in the roles of virgin and mother, after the example of Mary, the mother of Jesus. Motherhood and virginity were "two dimensions of women's vocation."[302] The exclusion of women from priesthood could no longer be on account of their inferiority, as Aquinas and others had taught, but because of their *differentness* from men, for which Christ himself excluded them from priesthood.

This logic was unacceptable to many Catholics. Gail Grossman Freyne, a women's studies researcher at University College Dublin, wrote: "Women do not ask for, they do not want, a 'special nature' if this nature excludes them from the possibility of full participation in the life of the church."[303]

Apostles as Priests

John Paul II said that Jesus freely chose and established the apostles as priests; hence, Jesus' exclusion of women from the Twelve determined their "unsuitability" for priesthood. But according to all four gospels, women *were* apostles, a class of followers (including Paul and Mary of Magdala) not limited to the Twelve. In the New Testament, women were not marginal figures in the Christian community but rather "exercised leadership as apostles, prophets, and missionaries."[304] Thus, *all of the Twelve were apostles, but not all apostles belonged to the Twelve.* Yet here the pope virtually conflated the terms "apostles" and "the Twelve."

Nevertheless, according to John Paul II, Jesus intended to establish a sacramental priesthood with the Twelve.[305] "*In calling only men as his apostles,* Christ acted *in a completely free and sovereign manner.*" The assumption that he called only men to the Twelve "in order to conform" to his culture did not "correspond to Christ's way of acting," which was countercultural.[306] The pope's assertion at least logically implied that Christ's exclusion of Gentiles from the Twelve would likewise bind Rome to ordain only Jews. Did Christ's ethnic Jewishness, so crucial to the story of Christianity itself, belong to a lower order than his sex? If the clergy were to physically represent Christ, could the faithful see the dusky-skinned, dark-haired, Jewish Christ in a milky-skinned, red-haired, Irish priest?

In *Mulieris Dignitatem,* Pope John Paul II was keenly interested in an apostolic priesthood "destined to last in endless succession throughout history." Ironically, his call in a later document, *Pastores Dabo Vobis* ("I Will Give You Shepherds," 1992), to discern the needs of the priesthood "in the third millennium" could have served well as a call *for* women's ordination:

> The life and ministry of the priest must also adapt to every era and circumstance of life. [We] must therefore seek to be as open as possible to light from on high from the Holy Spirit, in order to discover the tendencies of contemporary society, recognize the deepest spiritual needs, determine the most important concrete tasks and the pastoral methods to adopt, and thus respond adequately to human expectations.[307]

"Christian Anthropology"

"Christian anthropology" — according to the Vatican — is a creation-based understanding of divinely assigned sex roles in church, society, and the family. The notion had been articulated in *Gaudium et Spes* ("The Church in the Modern World," 1965):

> Adam, the first man, was a type of him who was to come, Christ the Lord. [Christ] who is the "image of the invisible God" is himself the perfect man who has restored in the children of Adam that likeness to God which had been disfigured ever since the first sin.[308]

Eve was absent from this equation because she was not the "type" (sex) of Jesus. This Christian (or "theological") anthropology would provide the basis for much of John Paul II's later writings on women's ordination.

The pope presented his ideas in two fundamental but broad categories: anthropology and biblical history, interconnecting both with the "bridegroom"/"bride" symbolism that Paul VI had presented so forcefully in *Inter Insigniores.* According to John Paul II in *Mulieris Dignitatem,* the image in Ephesians (5:25–32)[309] of Christ as bridegroom expressed the "nuptial analogy":

... the truth about the Church as the bride of Christ, and also indicates how this truth *is rooted in the biblical reality of the creation of the human being as male and female.* In the Church every human being — male and female — is the "Bride," in that he or she accepts the gift of the love of Christ the Redeemer, and seeks to respond to it with the gift of his or her own person.[310]

This literal application of the nuptial analogy stressed that both women *and* men were the "bride" (church). "In this way, being the 'bride,' and thus the 'feminine' element" was a "symbol of *all* that is 'human,' according to the words of Paul: 'There is neither male nor female; for you are all *one* in Christ Jesus.' "[311] As "bride," or church, males were "all that is human" — male *and* female. But only men could be "bridegroom" (Christ), because the role could be filled only by a male. This duality echoed Augustine and centuries of dualist thinking: males were complete beings unto themselves, but by themselves women were incomplete.

The "great mystery" — in which the bride/church responded to the "gift of love" from the bridegroom/priest — defined the holiness to which the church's "hierarchical structure is totally ordered." That is, the bridegroom (Jesus/priest) both *offered* and *was* the gift; the bride (church), being female, was to *receive* and *respond* to the bridegroom.

In this hierarchy, wrote John Paul II, *"it is precisely 'the woman,' Mary of Nazareth, who is the 'figure' of the Church"*[312] — female and passive (receiver). The man, Jesus, was the figure of the priest, male and active (giver). For this reason, the Catholic Church could never be called "he." The (active) priest was to the (receptive) church what the bridegroom was to the bride, putting the spiritual community in a literal relationship with biology. The pope did not address the prickly logical consequence of Jesus being a "bridegroom" to his mother, a "bride."

This concretization of the bridegroom/bride metaphor contained an internal contradiction that critics were quick to point out, as did religion writer Peter Steinfels:

Complementarity of the sexes ... might be said to *require* both men and women as priests rather than limit priesthood to one sex. [Instead] of delineating male-female difference, spousal imagery might simply stress an intimacy, union, and interdependence in divine-human love that would be incongruous with excluding one sex from priesthood.[313]

According to the concept of complementarity, if men could be both bridegroom (priest) *and* bride (church member), then women should be both bride *and* bridegroom. Anything less would break apart the complementarity between male and female. That is, with the altar as an axis for the law of complementarity, Rome violated that law by putting males on *both* sides of the altar. In its insistence upon natural law and heterosexual complementarity within a "nuptial" arrangement, the Vatican had also created and maintained a homosexual one. The only way around this state of affairs was to declare the church, including its male members, to be a woman.

At the heart of this difficulty, wrote theologian Richard Viladesau, was the fact that the pope's argument attempted to draw specific, concrete conclusions from a mélange of metaphors. "When any single metaphor becomes so dominant as to be exclusive," he said, there is a risk of "absolutizing certain aspects" of the human-divine relationship, in which case "the transcendence of God is compromised by anthropomorphism," or assigning human shape and characteristics to the divine. Once it was acknowledged that "the spousal analogy is simply a metaphor," and not the only possible one, the rationale lost its force: "Why should *this* metaphor, in which there is a sexual element, be determinative for office in the church."[314]

Two weeks after releasing *Mulieris Dignitatem*, John Paul II told a group of U.S. bishops that "in dealing with the specific rights of women as women, it was necessary to return again and again to the immutable basis of Christian anthropology" found in the story of Adam and Eve. "Whatever violates the complementarity of women and men," he said, "offends the dignity of both women and men."[315] He frequently referred to Eve as having been created from Adam as a "helpmate" for him, according to the second creation story found in Genesis 2:18–25, in which woman was created from man's rib because the man was lonely. The pope virtually ignored Genesis 1:26–27, in which the two sexes were created together in God's image. In *Mulieris Dignitatem*, he maintained that true Christian feminism (which he did not define) derived from both accounts, in which there was no essential contradiction, although his teaching on ordination pointed virtually exclusively to the "rib" account.

John Paul II wrote that woman formed "a life's companion with whom . . . the man can unite himself,"[316] clearly indicating his conviction that woman's role was defined by her relationship to man. Further, he observed that woman was "the only creature on earth which God willed for its own sake."[317] This enigmatic claim echoed and was explained by Hans Urs von Balthasar, who said woman "has nothing to represent which she is not herself, while the male must represent the Origin of all life, which he can never be."[318] That is, gender difference

> . . . assigns to the woman, not representation, but being; and to the man the task to represent, making him more, and at the same time less, than himself. As far as he is more, he is the "head" of the woman, and in the Christian context he is mediator of God's gifts. As far as he is less, however, he is dependent on the woman as nurturing shelter and model of completion.[319]

Balthasar believed that any discussion of essential gender differences would have to "center on Christ as a male" and in the context of the eucharist, where Christ — complete as an individual beyond any sexual connotation — made himself into "God's seed." In other words, the male priest ("complete as individual") transcended his gender ("sexual connotation") and became the child ("seed") of God. Only a male priesthood could participate "in this all-sexuality-transcending male fertility," a concept Balthasar admitted was "very difficult to formulate" and could only be "hinted at." If this truth *could* be "fully brought to light," however, "the previously latent inferiority of the man in relation to the woman [could] be somehow overcome."

This was an astounding claim to make in the late twentieth century: the male priest could somehow transcend his sex and overcome his inability to be a woman,

"the privileged place where God is able and willing to be received into this world."
Balthasar ended his lengthy reflection with a remarkable conclusion about male
priesthood: "What little we are able to catch and form into stammering words,
shows us that this tradition is justified and *immune to the changes of time and opinion*
(including opinions about the proper role of the sexes)."[320]

In *Mulieris Dignitatem*, John Paul II further wrote that God was spirit and
possessed "no property typical of the body, neither 'feminine' nor 'masculine.'"
According to biblical revelation, "while man's 'likeness' to God is true, the *'non-
likeness'* which separates the whole of creation from the Creator is *still more
essentially true*."[321] It is difficult to reconcile this statement with his conviction that maleness-as-likeness to Jesus was more essential to priesthood than
humanness-as-likeness.

Virgin-Mother-Spouse

Near the end of the document, the pope returned to the familiar theme of
women's special character: "If the human being is entrusted by God to women in
a particular way, does not this mean that *Christ looks to them for the accomplishment
of the 'royal priesthood'* which is the treasure he has given to every individual?"[322]
That is, women's special role was to produce ("accomplish") the priesthood of
believers — the church. This role of motherhood was clear:

> This eternal *truth about the human being*, man and woman — a truth which is im-
> mutably fixed in human experience — *at the same time constitutes the mystery which
> only in "the Incarnate Word takes on light* . . . (since) Christ fully reveals man to himself
> and makes his supreme calling clear," as the [Second Vatican] Council teaches. In
> this "revealing of man to himself," do we not need to find a special place for that
> "woman" who was the mother of Christ? Cannot the *"message" of Christ* . . . say much
> to the church and to humanity about the dignity of women and their vocation?[323]

This passage revealed John Paul II's insistence upon gender-exclusive language.
He defined "human being" as "man and woman." But immediately he said Jesus
revealed "man to himself" and made man's "supreme calling clear." Meanwhile,
"we" (men?) needed to find a place for the mother of Christ as manifested in
Catholic women and "their" vocation. This we-them language marked all of John
Paul II's writings concerning women, as it did the popes before him.

In terms of women's vocation, Mary provided the model for "two particular dimensions of the fulfillment of the female personality" — virginity and
motherhood.[324] She was the paradigm for the "mystery of 'woman': virgin-mother-
spouse,"[325] in which women could discover their own "supreme vocation."[326] John
Paul II offered no complementary vocation for men.

• • •

*None of the Martin daughters — Marie, Pauline, Léonie, Céline, or Thérèse — had
chosen marriage or motherhood. They had been raised in a religion, and a family, in
which religious life was considered superior to the married state. Thérèse, especially,
had a "unique" vocation, hardly one that other women shared, at least openly. Always*

candid, she wrote in her autobiography: "It should be enough for me, Jesus, to be Your spouse, to be a Carmelite and, by union with You, to be the mother of souls. Yet I long for other vocations: I want to be a warrior, a priest, an apostle, a doctor of the Church, a martyr."[327]

After her death, a biographer would call her a "warrior" of souls. A pope would call her an "apostle." Another pope would declare her a Doctor of the Church. And because she would die an agonizing death, she would be called a martyr. Among the five vocations for which Thérèse so earnestly prayed, the only one refused her was priesthood.

Chapter 13

A Theology of the Body

CHRISTIFIDELES LAICI
("On the Vocation and Mission of the Lay Faithful
in the Church and in the World")
Pope John Paul II
December 30, 1988

In the 1988 apostolic exhortation *Christifideles Laici* ("On the Vocation and Mission of the Lay Faithful"), Pope John Paul II repeated many of his assertions in *Mulieris Dignitatem* ("On the Dignity and Vocation of Women," 1988). He stressed that "when confronted with the various forms of discrimination and marginalization to which women are subjected simply because they are women," there was an "urgency to defend and to promote the personal dignity of women, and consequently her [*sic*] equality with man." He continued his call for the full recognition of women's dignity in the church, but he again reminded the faithful that women had "their own specific vocation"[328] — as virgin, mother, and wife. He mentioned no corresponding roles for men.

It was becoming increasingly clear that, in the Roman Catholic Church, women's "equality" with men held the same coded significance as the "separate but equal" catchphrase had for racially segregated schools in the pre–civil rights American South — always separate, never equal. Sister Christine Schenk, director of FutureChurch, an organization calling for women's equality in the church, summed up many Catholics' response to the pope's continuing claim that men and women were equal in the church: " 'Equality' seems to mean that male Catholics are equally entitled to make the rules and female Catholics are equally entitled to obey them."[329]

In *Christifideles Laici,* John Paul II said that if anyone had the task of advancing women's dignity in the church, it was "women themselves who must recognize their responsibility as leading characters." This must be "the first step taken to promote the full participation of women in Church life."[330] Predictably, this "full participation" did not include priestly ministry. Repeating his now-familiar call for women to extend their domestic arts to the public sphere, the pope wrote that although women were not called to ministerial priesthood, their often "lowly and hidden" work could "humanize" social relations.[331] Accordingly, women's "rightful presence" in the church required

82

...accurate consideration of the anthropological foundation for masculinity and femininity with the intent of clarifying *woman's personal identity in relation to man,* that is, a diversity yet mutual complementarity, not only as it concerns roles to be held and functions to be performed, but also, and more deeply, as it concerns her make-up and meaning as a person.[332]

In these few words, the pope revealed what was perhaps his fundamental belief about women: an "accurate" understanding of anthropology would reveal not only a woman's gender roles and functions "in relation to man" but also her very "make-up and *meaning as a person.*"

Mary Jo Weaver questioned the pope's application of mutual complementarity. "If women are not inferior to men," she asked, "then why does complementarity function to treat them as if they were?"[333]

Repeating what he had said in *Mulieris Dignitatem,* John Paul II said that any reflection on women's human dignity must take place within the context of the church, using the traditional "theology of the body" to understand the "anthropological and theological foundation of women's dignity as a person."[334] In other words, women's dignity was to be found in their biology. The pope called on every woman to use gifts that were "properly hers," especially the "gift" that was her "very dignity as a person" and therefore "connected with her vocation as a woman" — as virgin and mother — because the world needed her "irreplaceable and customary contributions" in these roles.[335]

An Unacceptable Omission

Women's "customary contributions" were only a part (albeit the larger part) of the pontiff's concerns. The attention being given to women was causing problems, he said, because "many voices" were raising the "fear that excessive insistence given to the status and role of women would lead to an unacceptable omission, regarding men."[336] He did not cite the sources of those voices, or the specific nature of their concerns, but in 1995 Gerald Brown, president of the Conference of Major Superiors of Men in the United States, issued a statement concerning the Vatican's neglect of men and their issues. "One would hope that maleness would be more than the remainder of what is left over after all the dimensions of femininity have been articulated," he said. Brown proposed a dialogue on men's concerns in order to "lessen the distortion that inevitably comes from constant reference to the gifts of women without reference to the giftedness of men." What John Paul II had done for women, Brown said, "needs to be done for men as well."[337]

Educator Regina Coll had written in 1982 that men often felt "left out, somewhat alien to the discussion" of women's issues, and to such men the language sounded foreign, the images appeared strange, and the symbols and metaphors were uncomfortable.[338] The irony of these concerns was that they so closely resembled women's experience of feeling left out of a church operated solely by men for two millennia. While seemingly oblivious to this paradox, John Paul II's statement — and Brown's ironic complaint that men deserved the same treatment

from John Paul II as women received — afforded a rare and candid acknowledgment that a discussion weighted in favor of one sex over the other could be
perceived as an "unacceptable" omission.

Theologian Thomas H. Groome provided an example of this type of exclusion.
He recalled one day as a student arriving at class to find the female students
meeting alone with the professor and refusing to allow male students into class:

> Never before had I felt so victimized and excluded. I felt that my rights as a student
> had been violated as had the academic freedom of the theological enterprise, since
> this enterprise should include all perspectives in its quest for truth. Only on later
> reflection did I come to image how women must feel about two thousand years of
> such exclusion.[339]

The concern that women's ascendancy might be accomplished at the expense
of men's status had been articulated as early as 1979 by theologian Elisabeth
Schüssler Fiorenza, in the context of a sacramental church:

> The sacraments, as rituals of birthing and nurturing, appear to imitate the *female*
> power of giving birth and of nurturing the growth of life. One would think that,
> therefore, *women* would be the ideal administrators of the sacrament. Yet there
> appears to exist a deep fear in men that women's powers would become so over-
> whelming if they were admitted to the priesthood and the sacramental ritual, that
> men would be relegated to insignificance. The demand of women to be admitted to
> the sacramental priesthood is, therefore, often not perceived as a genuine desire of
> women to live their Christian vocation and to serve the people of God, but as an
> attempt completely to "overtake" the church.[340]

The pope indeed wished to avoid an "unacceptable omission" of men. In *Christifideles Laici,* he called for "the coordinated presence of both men and women" in
the church,[341] but this presence came with the customary qualification: women
could not fulfill the "proper function of the ministerial priesthood." That function could only be found "in the expressed will of Christ [who] called only
men to be his apostles," which could be "understood from the rapport between
Christ, the Spouse, and his Bride, the Church." Again, a literal application of the
"bride"/"bridegroom" metaphor had determined a hierarchy in which all Christians were the "bride" of Christ "equally capable of receiving the outpouring of
divine truth and love in the Holy Spirit."[342] Only men, however, could act in the
person of Christ, the "bridegroom." Richard Viladesau posed a question:

> The notion of "representation" needs close examination and clarification. In ex-
> actly what sense does a priest in fact "represent" God or Christ, and precisely *as*
> "bridegroom"? . . . Could not the reasoning in fact be reversed: the priest "repre-
> sents" the church and acts "in persona ecclesiae" [in the role of the church]; the
> church is female, and the bride of Christ; therefore, the priest ought to be female?[343]

John Paul II pointed out that in the realm of ministerial priesthood, he was
speaking "in the area of function, not of dignity and holiness." The church hierarchy was "totally ordered to the holiness of Christ's members."[344] That is, all
Christians were holy. But since men and women each had their own distinct

"function" and "customary contribution" to offer, the male hierarchy did not diminish women's holiness by banning them from priesthood.

The ideas in *Christifideles Laici* were not new; in fact, most could be found in *Mulieris Dignitatem*. But a harbinger of things to come in the 1990s was to be found in the document's carefully constricted articulation of the "theology of the body," the "Christian anthropology" of which John Paul II so often spoke. As complicated as it would become, this anthropology had one simple message: women could not be priests because they were not male.

• • •

Thérèse had grown up knowing a woman's place, watching her mother bear nine children. She herself repeatedly stated her wish to remain lowly and hidden. In a book described as "a revised translation of the definitive Carmelite edition of her autobiography," Reverend Thomas N. Taylor wrote that during her "earthly career," Thérèse "desired to remain forgotten and unknown. Equally passionate was her desire to bestow on her divine Spouse all the confidence and affection of which her childlike heart was capable."[345]

According to one of her more scholarly biographers, Monica Furlong, the real Thérèse was "quirkier and more subversive," a side of her that was universally neglected:

> *So firmly is this side of her character ignored that it is possible to feel that what appeals to many in Thérèse is that she can be molded in fantasy to an image many priests have preferred for women — sexless, obedient, gentle, and good — the model of "safety."*[346]

Furlong's strong claim was supported in particular by Thérèse's own writing and in general by the church's long history of portraying female saints as impassive, obedient, and long-suffering. In fact, Thérèse was both long-suffering and ambitious. The young woman who so consistently claimed a desire to remain lowly and hidden also deeply mourned her stillborn vocation to priesthood: "If only I were a priest! How lovingly, Jesus, would I hold You in my hands when my words had brought You down from heaven and how lovingly would I give you to the faithful."[347] *Since she could not be a priest, however, she would spend her short life praying for priests.*

In the effort to record Thérèse's life, to canonize her a saint, and to declare her a Doctor of the Church, priests were especially ardent supporters. At her funeral, October 4, 1897, it was reported, "there gathered in the chapel of our Carmel a goodly company of priests — an honor most assuredly due to one who had so earnestly prayed for those called to that sacred office."[348]

❯❯ Chapter 14 ❮❮

Pleasing No One

"PARTNERS IN THE MYSTERY OF REDEMPTION"
National Conference of Catholic Bishops (U.S.A.)
March 23, 1988

**" 'ONE IN CHRIST JESUS': TOWARD A PASTORAL RESPONSE TO
THE CONCERNS OF WOMEN FOR THE CHURCH & SOCIETY"**
National Conference of Catholic Bishops (U.S.A.)
December 17, 1992

In 1972, the United States Catholic bishops formed a committee to explore ways to implement Vatican II's call to address the concerns of women. In 1983, the National Conference of Catholic Bishops (NCCB) formed the Ad Hoc Committee for a Pastoral Response to Women's Concerns. In preparation for a pastoral letter on this topic, a drafting committee of bishops began a pioneering series of "listening sessions" to hear the concerns of American Catholic women.[349] The committee heard from women and men in a hundred dioceses, sixty college campuses, and forty-five military bases, totaling some seventy-five thousand responses.[350] The committee's 246-paragraph draft, "Partners in the Mystery of Redemption," was intended to report the results of "extensive consultations with women, to reflect on this input in the light of our Christian heritage, and to offer responses and recommendations" for "ongoing dialogue and appropriate action."[351] In this spirit, the bishops disseminated the document for the purpose of eliciting further responses from Catholics.

Perhaps the document's most striking claim was the bishops' assertion that sexism in any form was a "moral and social evil."[352] Responding to what they had heard, the bishops said they did not want to ignore the "genuine aspirations of women to be included more in the church's liturgical, administrative and pastoral life." They described the church as a community of disciples endowed with unique gifts, and they appeared to outline arguments against the male-only priesthood: "Baptism configures women and men to Christ, making them members of his body and therefore his image and presence in this world."[353] While this claim seemed to contradict Rome's teaching that women did not bear the "image" of Christ, the bishops immediately repeated Rome's claim that women's "genuine" aspirations and "unique" gifts implied a distinctive nature and function but did not qualify them for ordination. Increasingly, however, women claimed that this thinking reflected the hierarchy's tradition of treating women as quasi-adolescents unequipped to assume a full role in the church.[354]

The bishops recommended further study to deepen "understanding of the relationship of [women's ordination] to Christian anthropology, the sacrament of holy orders and ministry in the church." As usual, however, such study was intended not to broaden the horizons of knowledge and understanding but to place "in the proper light the church's consistent practice" of a male-only priesthood.[355]

The American bishops, in their attempt to conciliate the various factions involved, had toed the Vatican line while showing intense sympathy for Catholic women. Predictably, their letter was harshly criticized by the Vatican and other defenders of the male-only priesthood. Nevertheless, Bishop P. Francis Murphy of Baltimore released a statement saying he had long "felt the profound pain of women over their exclusion from the sacrament of Holy Orders," and he called for "a new dialogue and study on women's ordination among the bishops."[356]

"One in Christ Jesus"

In 1990, after assessing feedback from parishes across the country, the American bishops released a second draft of their pastoral letter, now entitled " 'One in Christ Jesus': A Pastoral Response to the Concerns of Women for Church and Society."[357] Another clumsy if well-intended attempt at compromise, this second draft drew criticism from both the Vatican *and* women's groups. The draft boldly addressed the depth of sexism in the church and all forms of violence against women, but it was confusing and often contradictory. On the one hand, it rejected subordinationism, the traditional assumption that women were incomplete without men. On the other, it upheld metaphors of the male priest as "bridegroom" of the church, "shepherd" of the flock, and "head" of the mystical body — roles that the New Testament used for Christ alone and that Rome used for males alone.

The eight-hundred-member Leadership Conference of Women Religious (LCWR) said the new draft was "a distinct improvement over the first," especially because it addressed the "sin of sexism" and took the insights of women seriously. But the LCWR charged the bishops with assigning stereotypical functions and resorting to language of complementarity to keep women in biologically determined spiritual roles. The document's "pervasive contradiction" was its claim that gender equality was foundational even while sex differences justified inequalities within the church.[358]

For the LCWR, the phrase "equal in dignity" posed a particularly thorny problem: did equal dignity imply equal rights and responsibilities currently lacking for Catholic women? Further, the uneven application of "complementarity" continued to "introduce a basis for distinction [that was] unacceptable in the context."[359] This was "nowhere more evident" than in the document's repetition from *Inter Insigniores*: "the church, in fidelity to the example of the Lord, does not consider herself authorized to admit women to priestly ordination."[360] The

LCWR issued a statement saying the bishops should not adopt the draft pastoral letter.[361]

The American bishops continued working on the document despite widespread criticism of a process that included listening to women while excluding them from the writing process. A third unsuccessful draft was likewise rejected, but the bishops continued on their perilous course. While they were a good deal more sympathetic to women's ordination (and women in general) than was John Paul II, the bishops were not without their own passionate traditionalists. In an oft-quoted statement, Auxiliary Bishop Austin Vaughan of New York declared: "In the year 2000, 20,000, or 2,000,000, there will still be a Catholic church and it will still have an all-male clergy. A woman priest is as impossible as for me to have a baby."[362]

Then, on November 11, 1992, after years of debate, the Church of England (Anglican) formally approved women's ordination. This and other external pressures for Catholic women's ordination prompted the November 18 release of the American Catholic bishops' fourth and final draft document, "'One in Christ Jesus': Toward a Pastoral Response to the Concerns of Women for Church and Society."[363] The title of this draft was noticeably changed from that of the second letter. "A Pastoral Response" (1990) now became "*Toward* a Pastoral Response," as if, in the process of listening to women, the bishops had learned that a single document might not represent an altogether complete response to the needs and concerns of Catholic women.

In this fourth draft, the bishops stated their support for gender equality and promised to act against sex discrimination, to study inclusive language, and to establish a commission for women in each U.S. diocese, among other things. They called for across-the-board measures "to provide teaching and formation fully consistent with Scripture and the Church's tradition on the equality and dignity of women in the training of all persons involved in lay or ordained ministries."[364] Again, in their zeal, the bishops had struggled to please both supporters and opponents of women's ordination. The effort failed, and the NCCB did not adopt the letter. Religious studies scholar Catherine Wessinger wrote that the defeat of the pastoral letter was seen as a victory by both groups. Ordination supporters knew "the pope would not permit the bishops to follow through logically on the implications for the Roman Catholic Church of their unequivocal statement in the first draft that 'sexism is a sin.'" Ordination opponents also saw the letter's defeat as a victory, because they believed that the "bishops had no business writing a pastoral letter on women when the pope had already done so."[365]

Two American groups, the Women's Ordination Conference and Call to Action, had strongly urged that the pastoral letter project be scuttled. Their sentiments found agreement among twenty-four Catholic reform groups, which issued a joint statement saying that reconsidering the document at new hearings on women's concerns could "avert disaster" by preventing the "alienation of a major segment of Catholic women and a good number of Catholic men." Publishing the document as is, they said, could only "represent a major embarrassment for the

U.S. Church."[366] The bishops followed this advice, and their decision proved politically astute. Standing between Rome and American Catholics, they had faced a lose-lose position; worse, unbeknownst to the bishops, John Paul II was about to unleash his most powerful ruling yet against women's ordination, an order the world's bishops would be charged with enforcing.

• • •

Thérèse experienced a long period of trying and failing beginning in 1889, when her father suffered a series of strokes that damaged his brain. His personality changed. He hallucinated. At one point, he grabbed for his gun as if going into battle. It became clear to his daughters that he would have to be institutionalized. He was taken to an asylum for the insane, where he stayed for three years.[367]

During this time, Thérèse experienced a spiritual dryness, complaining that Christ was not "doing much to keep the conversation going."[368] *In fact, after so much prayer and effort, Thérèse's spiritual life seemed stalled:*

> *It seems that the darkness, borrowing the voice of sinners, says mockingly to me: "You are dreaming about the light, about a country fragrant with sweetest perfumes; you are dreaming about the eternal possession of the creator of all these marvels; you believe that one day you will walk out of this fog which surrounds you! Dream on, dream on; rejoice in death which will not give you what you hope for, but even deeper night, the night of nothingness."*[369]

Even in ordinary circumstances, Thérèse experienced difficulty with meditation and prayer. She did not "hunt through books" for prayers, because "there are so many of them that I get a headache." When she felt so "spiritually barren" that she could not summon "a single worthwhile thought," she would say an Our Father or Hail Mary. Otherwise, she behaved like a child "who cannot read: I tell God very simply what I want and He always understands."[370]

⇒ Chapter 15 ⇐

The Ordination of Women
Is Not Possible

CATECHISM OF THE CATHOLIC CHURCH
United States Catholic Conference
1994 (English Edition)

At this point, we momentarily leave the realm of Vatican proclamations and commentaries and enter the dominion of the catechism (Gr. *catechesis,* "oral instruction"), a compilation of Roman Catholic teachings. The first catechism written in the United States, published in 1891 by the Third Plenary Council in Baltimore, was a collection of doctrines and church laws known as the "Baltimore Catechism" to generations of school children (and their parents who drilled them in its teachings). In 1985, the Roman Synod ordered a new catechism to be written for Catholics worldwide.

Preserving Masculine Language

The English edition of the *Catechism of the Catholic Church*[371] was delayed for two years over a struggle between Rome and the American bishops, whose attempt to infuse the catechism with gender-inclusive language ultimately was quashed. This situation was not without irony. Peter Steinfels explained that the prologue to the long-delayed, Vatican-approved edition was "practically a parody" of the language dispute itself.[372] This was painfully apparent in the first half of the catechism's opening paragraph:

> God, infinitely perfect and blessed in himself, in a plan of sheer goodness freely created man to make him share in his own blessed life. For this reason, at every time and in every place, God draws close to man. He calls man to seek him, to know him, to love him with all his strength.[373]

Steinfels, noting what his sixth-grade teacher, Sister Mary Jerome, "would have underlined in red as pronouns with confusing antecedents," rewrote the passage to make his point:

> God...freely created man to make *him* [man] share in *his* [God's] own blessed life. For this reason...God draws close to man. *He* [God] calls *him* [man] to seek *him* [God], to know *him* [God], to love *him* [God], with all *his* [man's] strength.[374]

Such was the Vatican's corrective to the American bishops' effort to use inclusive language. As Steinfels pointed out, the use of "He" for God, or the use of the abstract "man" in the Psalms, did not really offend most women. It was when masculine pronouns were "brandished like battle flags, as in the *Catechism of the Catholic Church*," or when inclusive language could be "so easily adopted" but wasn't, that it seemed to be "nothing less than a deliberate slap in the face."[375]

On a related note, a seemingly minor but in fact common and revealing Vatican tradition referred to males in terms of their ordination status, and to females in terms of their sexual status, even though priests and nuns both took celibacy vows. For example, in spring 2004, Pope John Paul II beatified one man and three women: Luigi Talamoni, "priest, founder"; Matilde del Sagrado Corazón Tellez Robles, "virgin, foundress"; Piedad de la Cruz Real, "virgin, foundress"; and Maria Candida dell'Eucaristia, "virgin, nun."[376] In the official roster of saints, women have always filled the ranks as virgins before anything else, while men have not been listed according to their celibacy record. Three weeks later, the pope made several appeals for the use of "positive" language to promote "ideals and noble initiatives in an attractive way."[377]

Just before the annual U.S. bishops' meeting in Washington, D.C., in 1994, Archbishop William Keeler of Baltimore, president of the National Conference of Catholic Bishops (NCCB), confirmed that the Congregation for the Doctrine of the Faith (CDF) had withdrawn approval of the New Revised Standard Version (NRSV) of the Bible for liturgical and teaching use. The original approval, by the Congregation for Divine Worship and the Sacraments, had followed the American bishops' 1991 approval of 195 to 24. In addition, the Vatican revoked its 1992 confirmation of the American bishops' approval of the New American Bible (NAB). The NCCB had sponsored the NAB translation, and Pope Paul VI had called it a "notable achievement." The reason given for Rome's delayed disapproval of the NRSV and NAB was the moderate use of gender-inclusive language, the same reason given for the delay of the English translation of the catechism. Biblical scholars later learned that the information contained in Keeler's eleventh-hour announcement had actually been given to him in a letter from the Vatican — five months earlier.[378]

Less than three years later, in 1997, eleven men met in Rome to revise the American lectionary, a book of scripture readings for use during mass. Of the group's members, chosen by the pope, only one held a graduate degree in scripture studies. In 1990, the NCCB had approved guidelines for an inclusive-language lectionary, but in the mid-1990s the CDF secretly issued norms for the translation of American liturgical documents. In 1997 the Vatican, having revamped texts earlier approved by the American bishops, presented U.S. Catholics with their new lectionary, which *retained* "many of the most controversial uses of masculine vocabulary."[379]

In 2001, the Congregation for Divine Worship and the Discipline of the Sacraments issued *Liturgiam Authenticam* ("Authentic Liturgy"), guidelines for translating liturgical texts. This document called for the literal translation of ancient Latin words without regard for context or comprehensibility to modern ears.

Not surprisingly, Rome composed and issued the guidelines without consultation of the world's bishops or even all the members of the issuing congregation.[380]

New Catechism, Old Priesthood

The new catechism retained the teaching on priesthood:

> "Only a baptized man (*vir*) validly receives sacred ordination."[381] The Lord Jesus chose men (*viri*) to form the college of the twelve apostles, and the apostles did the same when they chose collaborators to succeed them in their ministry. The college of bishops, with whom the priests are united in the priesthood, makes the college of the twelve an ever-present and ever-active reality until Christ's return. The Church recognizes herself to be bound by this choice made by the Lord himself. For this reason the ordination of women is not possible.[382]

This paragraph asserted that Jesus Christ both organized and classified the Twelve into a "college" (a hierarchical organization) of twelve apostles with the intent of binding a future church to this system; in turn, the apostles formed a "college" of bishops to succeed them.

Concurrent with this unhistoric account was the unqualified definition of "apostle" as a member of the "college of the Twelve" rather than in the more traditional meaning of the Greek *apostoloi,* a postresurrectional designation as traveling emissaries. Under the catechism's definition, for example, Paul could not be considered an apostle because he did not belong to the "college of the Twelve."

Fifteen years earlier, a U.S. bishops' executive committee had written that the New Testament, while not decisive by itself, pointed "toward the admission of women to priestly ministry."[383] The circle of apostles, they said, was wider than the "Twelve" and the designation could "neither be conferred nor handed on by successors." Hence, the claim that Jesus intended to provide an exclusive model of priesthood open only to men could not be sustained "on either logical or historical grounds."

Nevertheless, the revised catechism repeated an unrevised theme:

> The saving mission entrusted by the Father to his incarnate Son was committed to the apostles and through them to their successors: they receive the Spirit of Jesus to act in his name and in his person. The ordained minister is the sacramental bond that ties the liturgical action to what the apostles said and did and, through them, to the words and actions of Christ.[384]

The teaching that the priest acted in "the name" and "the person" of Jesus Christ had been treated thoroughly in *Inter Insigniores* ("Declaration on the Admission of Women to the Ministerial Priesthood," 1976), and here the catechism closed the circle of the "saving mission" of Christ around and through the apostles to their successors.

In the same year, 1992, John Paul II insisted anew that the priest must physically resemble Christ in order to act "in the person" of Christ. In his apostolic exhortation, *Pastores Dabo Vobis* ("I Will Give You Shepherds"), he wrote:

Certainly there is an essential aspect of the priest that does not change: the priest of tomorrow, no less than the priest of today, must resemble Christ. When Jesus lived on this earth, he manifested in himself the definitive role of the priest establishing a ministerial priesthood with which the apostles were the first to be invested.[385]

This statement made four claims:

- resemblance to Christ was *essential* to priesthood;
- Jesus modeled the "*definitive* role" of earthly priesthood;
- Jesus *established* the earthly priesthood; and
- the apostles were "*invested*" with this priesthood.

The pope's insistence that Jesus established an earthly, male-only priesthood assumed that Jesus foresaw and willed the development of a permanent, institutional, hierarchical church.

• • •

"One of the principal duties of the saints throughout the ages is to incarnate anew, to dress in contemporary clothes, such ancient truths as are likely to be overlooked because of the appearance they have worn too long," wrote Henri Ghéon, one of Thérèse's early biographers, for whom Thérèse at first held no attraction. Indeed, some of her most ardent followers started out disliking both her spiritual and literary style. "The tinseled and sugary manifestations of devotion" to the "little saint" had repelled Ghéon. "There were too many roses, too many flowers." The Carmelite monastery showed a "crushing excess of ornament, as useless as it is bad," and the shrine to Thérèse was a "masterpiece of hideousness and stupidity." It was "showy, clumsy, quite without beauty," with a "dressed-up" saint in a "gold and crystal cage," the whole thing "idealized beyond words." Ghéon, who developed a genuine devotion to Thérèse, opened his 1934 biography by pointing out this "stumbling block" to persons, like himself, unable to abide highly wrought and outdated frippery. Thérèse's spiritual home, as Carmel developed after her death, "would be laughable, if one could find the heart to laugh."[386] But the overlays of piety and complexity added after her death had put great distance between who she really was and what she had been made to become — an icon of womanhood existing only in the minds of saint-makers. She was, in fact, a young woman who followed her calling the only way she was allowed to and the best way she knew how.

→ Chapter 16 ←

No Authority Whatsoever

ORDINATIO SACERDOTALIS
("On Reserving Priestly Ordination to Men Alone")*
Pope John Paul II
May 30, 1994

By 1994, Pope John Paul II was displaying increasing frustration with the call for women's ordination. Jesuit scholar Thomas J. Reese recounted a papal lunch with a group of U.S. bishops, when the question of women's ordination came up: the pope "pounded on the table for emphasis."[387] Having addressed the increasingly prickly issue of women's ordination via pontifical commission, Vatican declaration, canon law, apostolic constitution, apostolic letter, and the universal catechism, he now was going to take even more rigorous measures to deflect growing pressure to ordain women.

Vatican observer Peter Hebblethwaite described John Paul II's intention for *Ordinatio Sacerdotalis* ("On Reserving Priestly Ordination to Men Alone"), released days after the pope's seventy-fourth birthday: "Before it was too late, he produced this brief five-page letter designed to commit the Church definitively" to the male-only priesthood. An "act of authority born of irritation," the letter's message was "clear, peremptory, brutal and decisive."[388]

Weeks before issuing *Ordinatio Sacerdotalis*, the pope (via the Congregation for Divine Worship and the Sacraments) issued a communication to the world's bishops' conferences regarding the "authentic interpretation" of canon 230:2 allowing females to serve mass "by temporary deputation" for the duration of need.[389] (Males served mass by being formally "installed" to the ministry of acolyte, or altar server.) This letter explained that in June 1992, the Pontifical Council for the Interpretation of Legislative Texts had examined a *dubium,* a question, about whether the role of altar server could be included in the "temporary deputation" functions open to females. The council returned an affirmative answer, which John Paul II confirmed. In the letter, Cardinal Antonio Ortas (the congregation's prefect) clarified "certain aspects" of the canon's "authentic interpretation." In brief, he said that deciding whether to allow females on the altar was up to the local bishop, who should remember that it would "always be very appropriate

---

*The document is included in the appendix, p. 211.

to follow the noble tradition of having boys serve at the altar," a practice that provided "a reassuring development of priestly vocations." Because altar boys provided a pool of potential priests, "the obligation to support such groups of altar boys will always continue." However, if a local bishop "for particular reasons" wished to allow girls to serve mass, his decision "must be clearly explained to the faithful." Above all, it "must be clearly understood" that this service was only to be carried out *ex temporanea deputatione* (by temporary deputation).[390]

In 2001, the Congregation for Divine Worship and the Sacraments again stressed that authorizing females to serve at the altar could not in any way "exclude men or, in particular, boys from service at the altar, nor require that priests of the diocese would make use of female altar servers." The congregation emphasized that "non-ordained faithful do not have a right to service at the altar" but can only be "admitted to such service by the Sacred Pastor." Again, it was important not to overstress the presence of females at the altar, because the "obligation to support groups of altar boys" was paramount "due to the well known assistance that such programs have provided since time immemorial in encouraging future priestly vocations."[391] For this and other reasons, John Paul II's formal (if limited) acceptance of girls in altar service posed an enigma that is worth exploring a bit further before entering discussion of *Ordinatio Sacerdotalis*.

A few years earlier, in 1988, Jesuit theologian Joseph Fessio had written a lucid if overblown defense of male-only altar service, in which he articulated the familiar Vatican position. He argued that the altar was a sacred place, the eucharist a sacred act, and the priest a sacred person, and the altar boy became "the hands of the priest." If a girl were to take this role, she would cause a "serious disharmony with the very nature and character of the *whole order of grace and redemption*" and would even confuse the "symbolic character of men and women."[392]

There was a "logical connection and progression from altar boy [to] the priesthood," Fessio wrote. "If women are admitted to these offices, then it may give them the false hope of becoming priests." Indeed, he called such a move "unfair" to girls, whose hopes for ordination would be raised by dressing "in the garments of the priest," causing "an identity problem for the girl herself and for the faithful who see her on the altar vested as a priest."[393] Indeed, Paul VI in *Inter Insigniores* had made just this point referring to women priests, in whom "it would be difficult to see" the image of Christ (§45).

In the case of priests, religious studies professor Kelley Raab raised a question not often seen in discussions of Roman Catholic women priests, but a question that nonetheless underlay any consideration of the issue:

> While the Catholic male priest, a celibate, has traditionally been viewed as asexual, the [Episcopal] woman priest is automatically seen as a sexual being, forcing the issue of sexuality into the theological arena.... When only men could be clergy, one never thought about the priest's gender. Now that both sexes are represented, it has dawned on parishioners that most clergy are male, as opposed to neuter.... Pandora's Box would indeed be opened if Catholic women were ordained

to the priesthood. Many conflicting and controversial views on sexuality would surface, and additional discussions on the issue would be critical.[394]

Fessio's complaint that anyone seeing a girl on the altar would suffer "an identity problem" was not his biggest concern. Assuming that boys would not want to do something that girls could do, he warned that if Rome allowed altar girls, "many young boys" would not want to be altar boys, causing "a decline in vocations to the priesthood." Worse, the presence of altar girls would cause the "inevitable perception" that the "first step toward women's ordination" had been achieved. And, altar girls would have a "negative influence" on the "majority of Catholic women who support the Church's teaching on the roles for men and women." Worst of all, altar girls would cause "demoralization of the faithful laity and priests." Of the various negative implications, one specter in particular haunted Fessio: "Giving in on [altar girls would] be seen by the feminists, and rightly, as a sign of *weakness* on the part of the Pope and the Catholic church."[395]

Without naming Fessio (instead referring to him as a priest "with strong con-nections to Cardinal Ratzinger"), Richard McBrien later outlined Fessio's major objections to allowing girls to serve on the altar:

- women would be frustrated by the "false hope of ordination";

- priestly vocations would decline because "boys would no longer want to take a job that girls were allowed to do";

- girls would incur "an identity problem" and "the faithful would be confused";

- faithful Catholics "would be demoralized";

- feminists would be "emboldened to seek even greater victories."[396]

Thus would Rome cause for itself, said Fessio, "a situation similar to that which Pope Paul VI faced with his 1968 document, *Humanae Vitae*" ("On the Regulation of Birth"),[397] an unyielding reiteration of church teaching against contraception that Catholics widely rejected. In this regard, Fessio was right. Pope John Paul II's 1994 consent for girls to serve on the altar contributed to a climate in which his teaching on male priesthood would be increasingly rejected by Roman Catholics.

Always his own man, John Paul II on March 15, 1994, not only changed church discipline to allow females to serve mass but also as lectors, eucharistic ministers, and religious educators. (In many places, women were already serving in these roles.) On May 30, he issued *Ordinatio Sacerdotalis* ("On Reserving Priestly Ordi-nation to Men Alone"), a major apostolic letter insisting that women could not be priests. This combination of decisions might seem odd, but in reality it was strate-gic. New Testament scholar Luke Timothy Johnson pointed out that parishioners were "so pleased to see (and to be)" in these new (but still nonordained) roles that they did not yet "appreciate how such accommodation simply continues with slight variations the traditional exploitation of women under male leadership."[398] While many Catholics might shrink from the charge of "exploitation," Johnson's conclusion was inescapable.

From Tradition to Authority

In *Ordinatio Sacerdotalis* ("On Reserving Priestly Ordination to Men Alone"),[399] John Paul II offered no new scriptural or theological arguments against, nor did he respond to, a quarter century of arguments for the ordination of women. Addressed to the world's bishops, who knew little or nothing of its contents prior to its publication,[400] the document reiterated the pope's long-held conviction that a male priesthood was rooted in Christ's example of choosing only males to the Twelve. While *Ordinatio Sacerdotalis* offered no new teaching, it introduced a significant switch in strategy for the pope, who now argued much less from Christ's example and much more from papal authority.[401]

This change in direction had been building for some time. In his 1993 encyclical, *Veritatis Splendor* ("Splendor of Truth"), the pope had charged that church teaching risked "being distorted or denied" because of "numerous doubts and objections" among Catholics. This problem was no longer a matter of limited or occasional dissent, but an "overall and systematic calling into question of traditional moral doctrine." Opposition could "not be seen as a legitimate expression either of Christian freedom or of the diversity of the Spirit's gifts." To deal with dissenters, bishops needed recourse to "appropriate measures," provided by the pope, to guard the faithful "from every doctrine and theory" contrary to church teaching.[402]

John Paul II's expanding use of papal power had an equal and opposite reaction among the world's bishops, who logically surrendered some of their local authority to an ever more centralizing force in Rome. This process, which grew throughout John Paul's papacy, violated the Vatican II teaching of "subsidiarity," which held that a higher authority should not usurp power from a lower authority in matters belonging to the lower authority's jurisdiction. Hence, when John Paul II announced new rules as well as the punishments for violating them, without any prior consultation with (or even notification of) the world's bishops, he eroded the bishops' authority accordingly. Further, as the pope acted more and more independently, the concept of collegiality (the professional relationships among bishops as colleagues) likewise wore away, because decision-making was being reserved by the pope, for the pope.

But losing their episcopal authority by degrees was not something bishops could openly discuss, a scenario that was bound to cause friction. Mary Louise Hartman, president of the Association for the Rights of Catholics in the Church, recalled the story of one bishop at the 2001 Bishops' Synod in Rome. During his speech, the bishop paused and shouted at John Paul II: "Look at me when I am speaking to you!" Hartman pointed to the "recurring statements by bishops lamenting the lack of Vatican respect" for the local authority and suggested that the outspoken bishop would not have spoken to the pope "in such a manner unless he knew that he was giving voice to the thoughts of other bishops."[403]

In late spring 1994, the pope signed *Ordinatio Sacerdotalis*, decisively manifesting his resolve to silence calls for women's ordination through an unparalleled show of papal force.[404] Released on Pentecost Sunday, which celebrates the coming of the Holy Spirit and the giving of spiritual gifts to all baptized Christians, *Ordinatio Sacerdotalis* asserted that, because of what Christ did not do or say, the church had "no authority whatsoever" to ordain women.

John Paul II restated his concern with "theological anthropology,"[405] an understanding of female and male bodies as created according to divine intent for specified roles. He recalled Paul VI's 1977 claim that "the real reason" for banning women's ordination was that, "in giving the Church her fundamental constitution, her theological anthropology — thereafter always followed by the Church's tradition — Christ established things in this way" (§5).[406] As a defense of male-only priesthood, the concept of theological (or Christian) anthropology had been systematically developed only after Vatican II, with the writings of Paul VI, Hans Urs von Balthasar, and Pope John Paul II, who again stressed the concept in a 1993 address to the U.S. bishops:

> The equality of the baptized, which is one of the great affirmations of Christianity, exists in a differentiated body, in which men and women have roles which are not merely functional but are deeply rooted in Christian anthropology and sacramentology.[407]

This statement said that according to Christian (or theological) anthropology, women and men were created to assume "differentiated" *sacramental roles*. This explained why the church provided seven sacraments for men, but only six for women.

Inter Insigniores ("Declaration on the Admission of Women to the Ministerial Priesthood," 1976) had emphasized that Christ's role "must be taken by a man" — not from any "personal superiority" of males but "from a difference of fact on the level of functions and service" (§53). *Ordinatio Sacerdotalis* now said that the twelve men whom Christ made "the foundation" of the church "did not in fact receive only a function" (§8), but rather illustrated the "theological anthropology" of the "fundamental constitution" for the church established by Christ (§5). That is, the maleness of the Twelve showed the importance of maleness in the church's hierarchical organization.

Writing "in order that all doubt may be removed regarding a matter [pertaining] to the church's divine constitution itself," John Paul II declared, "the Church has no authority whatsoever to confer priestly ordination on women," a judgment "to be definitively held by all the church's faithful." This paragraph contained four distinct claims:

- priesthood belonged to the church's divinely mandated organization;

- priesthood was reserved to males alone;

- the pope could not change this reality; and

- this judgment was to be "definitively held" by all Catholics (§13).

In a fourteen-paragraph document, John Paul II had bound Roman Catholics to a teaching that even many of the world's bishops questioned.

"Receive" vs. "Confer"

Theologians around the world replied swiftly, saying John Paul II's loosely connected appeals to scripture, tradition, and theology could not hold up to critical analysis. Elizabeth Johnson recalled the "Declaration on Religious Liberty"[408] of Vatican II, which said that a teaching can impose itself on the mind only by the force of its own truth:

> If a declared teaching or practice continuously jars our mind as missing the mark, as in the present case, it is our responsibility to explore and express the reasons why. This resistance is not to be equated with disloyalty or rebellion, let alone lack of faith, but with a form of loyalty and service.[409]

When *Ordinatio Sacerdotalis* was issued in 1994, the Vatican had been jarring Catholic minds for two decades with its reasons for a male-only priesthood, and many Catholics had been critically analyzing those reasons. Each time scholars and supporters of women's ordination moved closer to revealing the flaws of a particular argument, Rome seemed to move away from that argument toward another one.

Most noteworthy was Rome's history-making abandonment — via *Inter Insigniores* (1976) and again in *Ordinatio Sacerdotalis* (1994) — of the long-held argument of Aquinas that women were biologically flawed, irrational, and logically subject to the authority of men hence unqualified to *receive* the sacrament of ordination. *Inter Insigniores* had argued that since women could not stand in the role of Christ, because they were not male, the church could not *admit* them as priests. In *Ordinatio Sacerdotalis,* Pope John Paul II stressed that because Christ had excluded women from the Twelve, Rome could not *confer* ordination upon them.

By progressing from women being unable to "receive" ordination to Rome being unable to "admit" or "confer" ordination, Paul VI and John Paul II rejected the biological inferiority of women in name, but they kept women subordinate in fact by employing new justifications for a male-only priesthood. Among other things, *Ordinatio Sacerdotalis* proclaimed that the real problem was that the church could not confer ordination on women without renouncing its mission of imitating Christ, a claim that would become John Paul II's rationale of choice.

Like his predecessor Paul VI, John Paul II praised "the dignity of women and their vocation." Women were "the holy martyrs, virgins, and the mothers [who] bravely bore witness to their faith and passed on the Church's faith and tradition by bringing up their children in the spirit of the Gospel" (§10). His emphasis on motherhood created a female analogy to the male priest's fatherhood as transmitter of divine gifts, a theme he amplified in the 1980s. According to Hans Urs von Balthasar, a theologian whose thought greatly influenced the pontiff, the priest transmitted divine gifts by making himself a "simple instrument of transmission."[410] According to Catholic teaching, priests and laity shared this task of transmitting divine gifts, but in radically different ways: priests by being ordained and celibate, and women by marrying and having children.

Archbishop William Keeler of Baltimore, then-president of the National Conference of Catholic Bishops, said *Ordinatio Sacerdotalis* affirmed that a "diversity of roles" emphasized the "equal dignity of both women and men," and the Vatican would "not accept an understanding of equality which ignores the unique roles and gifts of women and men."[411]

Education and Opportunities

But this "uniqueness" was crumbling in the face of a changing culture and practical needs. The reality was that the vast majority of priestless parishes in the United States and elsewhere were being "pastored" by women who functioned "as priest in almost every sense."[412] By the early 1990s, some 85 percent of new parish ministers in the United States were women.[413] Baltimore's auxiliary bishop Francis Murphy pointed out that when women taught, they were seen as teaching for the church; when they conducted communion services, they were seen as celebrating a liturgy. Even though their titles might be "pastoral associate" or "parish administrator," to parishioners they were "pastors."[414] But, only 25 percent of all top diocesan administrative positions were held by women.[415] Jesuit Thomas P. Sweetser, codirector of the Parish Evaluation Project (surveying tens of thousands of registered parishioners in the United States), said in 1994 that to ask women to fulfill the responsibilities of priesthood and not ordain them was "morally wrong and discriminatory."[416]

And, statistically, disingenuous. Vatican observer Thomas Reese in 1998 wrote that "alienation among lay Catholics often increases as they become more active in their parishes as volunteer ministers, religious educators, or social ministers," and that the "growing alienation of educated Catholic women" was especially critical for the future church because women traditionally passed the faith to future generations.[417]

But as students in Catholic institutions of higher education, women were increasingly visible. By 1980, according to political scientist Mary F. Katzenstein, 94 percent of American sisters had bachelor's degrees; further, over 40 percent had at least a master's degree, a percentage much higher than for priests.[418] A 1994 study of Catholic graduate ministry education in the United States showed an enrollment of 2,915 (male) seminarians and 1,860 lay men — for a total of 4,775 men — and 4,140 women.[419] While these numbers appeared to suggest that men still outnumbered women in ministry education, the reality was that, aside from the male-only seminarian group (with their tuition largely subsidized by their dioceses or religious orders), 69 percent of the 6,000 lay persons enrolled were women.

By the late-1990s, more than 80 percent of all parish administrators in the United States were women,[420] and women held 47 percent of the nation's diocesan administrative and professional positions.[421] Some of these women, not fully understanding the relationship of authority to ordination, mistook their limited access to ministry for full participation in the church. Others did not. Catholic Church historian R. Scott Appleby reported that many women working in parishes and dioceses felt "isolated by their lack of status within the institutional church," and that "in most dioceses, parish administrators," primarily female, were "not regularly included in presbyteral conferences and pastoral planning meetings."[422] Francis Bernard O'Connor wrote that American women had indeed entered circles of parish leadership, but they were less likely than men to be found in the "inner" circles. This scenario, often described as catching crumbs from the clerical table, excluded women from "helping to shape the church's mission, its teaching, its law, its liturgy. After the decisions are made, women are granted their 'appropriate' role. Women do not even have a voice in defining what is appropriate for *them.*"[423] It was perhaps this last exclusion that rankled Catholic women most of all. O'Connor cited a Gallup poll showing 94 percent of the respondents saying that equal decision-making opportunities were "integral to full participation" in the church. Throughout the history of Catholicism, women have had no voice in the making of church policy, "yet they are expected to obey all the laws of the church made by men."[424]

Pope John Paul II's ongoing campaign to staunch ever-growing support of women's ordination was having the opposite effect. Growing support for women priests prompted theologians to turn their attention to the doctrine of reception and assent, a venerable but perennially neglected prerequisite for valid teaching.

Reception and Assent

Dissent from official church teaching has existed as long as there has been a church, evidenced by the tension between authority and prophecy that quickens both testaments of the Bible. Long, embittered debates texture the history of Christianity — the nature of Jesus Christ (man, god, or both?), the sexual status of priests (married or celibate?), and papal infallibility (justifiable or not?), to name just three. But one safety valve the church has always enjoyed (whether it wanted to or not) has been a system of checks and balances called "reception and assent" of its doctrines.

Often called simply "reception," this doctrine asserts that, "for a law or rule to be an effective guide for the believing community it must be accepted by that community."[425] That is, a doctrine must be "*received* by the Church at large and *accepted* as an accurate, appropriate, and unerring expression of its faith."[426] This doctrine dates back to the twelfth century and states that a law is confirmed when it is approved by the practices of those who use it. Canon lawyer Ladislas Örsy explained that when a law is made known to a people, "mere insistence on obedience cannot be enough. Precisely to obey well, an intelligent person ought [to be able to] grasp the value toward which his or her action is directed; if not, he or she is not obedient, but is acting as a mindless automaton."[427]

Pope Paul VI affirmed the doctrine of reception and assent in his 1965 "Declaration on Religious Freedom," saying that truth was to be sought in a "manner proper to the dignity of the human person" engaging in free inquiry, communication, and dialogue. When persons discovered a truth, it was "by a personal assent" they were to adhere to it.[428]

This had not always been the case. Quoting Pope Pius IX, Leonard Swidler explained: "In 1864, Pope Pius IX in his 'Syllabus of Errors' condemned *that erroneous opinion most pernicious to the Catholic Church* . . . namely, that liberty of conscience and of worship is the right of every human being."[429] Vatican II (1962–65) did much to overturn this condemnation of freedom of conscience. The contemporary doctrine of reception gives Catholics the right to act on an "informed conscience" (canon 748:1) that has been educated in faith and morals. Hence, they possess the right and the duty to accept or reject the religious laws that govern them.

In 1968, the doctrine of reception and assent handed Rome one of its biggest failures with Pope Paul VI's encyclical *Humanae Vitae* (literally "Human Life," known as "On the Regulation of Birth"), which strongly reasserted that only natural birth control (known as the "rhythm method") was morally acceptable.[430] The encyclical taught the opposite of a conclusion reached earlier by a commission established by Pope John XXIII in 1963 and continued by Paul VI. The Papal Birth Control Commission issued its majority report saying that "condemnation of a couple to a long and often heroic abstinence as the means to regulate conception cannot be founded on the truth."[431] Profoundly unsettled, Paul VI disbanded the commission and issued *Humanae Vitae,* barring Catholics from using contraception. His argument was that biology ipso facto determined morality.

In a world standing on the threshold of spectacular advances in biotechnology that could save and improve lives in ways heretofore undreamed of, the argument that women should surrender themselves and their families to the dictates of biology was unpersuasive, especially in the West. While opposition to birth control was "a veritable badge of tribal membership" and "a touchstone of loyalty to the Church"[432] for some, most Catholics refused to implement *Humanae Vitae,* hence refusing to confirm the law.

A decade after *Humanae Vitae,* Jesuit sociologist Joseph Fichter wrote:

> What seems to be happening now is that more and more Catholics are simply disregarding the official pronouncements of the church hierarchy. They are not in revolt. They are not openly disrespectful of the prelates, but they are simply no longer impressed by the need of attending to directives and prohibitions.[433]

Yet it would be a safe bet to say that most lay Catholics knew little or nothing about the doctrine of reception and assent. The result, according to Reverend James R. Roberts of Vancouver, was that Catholics lacked "a vigorous reception of papal and other authoritative church teaching documents [whose] fate seems too often to entail simply either swift praising acceptance on the part of some or equally swift dismissal on the part of others."[434] The result was a loss of two-way communication and informed participation in the church.

The doctrine of reception's provision for rejecting a law never implied the right to question a ruler's authority or the conditions under which a rule is promulgated. That is, popular rejection of the male priesthood could not entail a denial of the pope's authority or his legal right to make such a ruling. Nevertheless, Rome often viewed such rejection not only as an affront to papal authority but also to Catholicism — indeed Christianity — itself. In 1993, the year he wrote *Veritatis*

Splendor ("Splendor of Truth"), in which he warned that moral doctrine was suffering widespread challenges, John Paul II told U.S. bishops that some Catholic women were failing "to distinguish between women's human and civil rights in society and their ministries and functions in the church." Worse, the church itself was "in danger of being undermined."[435]

Erosion of Authority

As John Paul II was writing *Ordinatio Sacerdotalis* in 1994, fewer than 20 percent of American Roman Catholics were following Rome's teaching on birth control,[436] and the fate of Pope Paul VI's 1965 *Humanae Vitae* still haunted Vatican halls. The failure of another papal document would reach far beyond the lack of the document's reception to the erosion of the magisterial authority. Indeed, the Papal Birth Control Commission's minority report (of the commission's 5 percent who condemned contraception) had warned: "If the Church could err, the authority of the ordinary magisterium in moral matters would be thrown into question."[437]

And that is what happened. As Peter Steinfels explained, "the papacy's stand on contraception appeared to do much more than leave huge percentages of Catholics unconvinced. It opened up all sorts of questions ... about the church's whole approach to morals, and about church authority generally."[438] Thomas Reese wrote that the "magisterium's failure to convince significant numbers of the clergy or the faithful of its teaching on birth control, divorce, sexual ethics, and a male celibate priesthood [had] undermined its credibility on other issues."[439]

John Wright wrote that the church was "a society of human beings called together by God" that existed through the "good will and faith" of its members whose attitudes and responses could not "be compelled." Wright recalled the experience of Pope Pius XII, whose *Mystici Corporis Christi* ("The Mystical Body of Christ," 1940) claimed that different religions could not live "in the one body" or in "its one divine Spirit" (non-Catholics could not be saved). When that document failed to convince Roman Catholics, he wrote *Humani Generis* (lit., "The Human Race," but known as "Concerning Some False Opinions Which Threaten to Undermine the Foundations of Catholic Doctrine," 1950), insisting that when popes "purposely pass judgment" on an issue, it could "no longer be regarded as a question freely debated." He then scolded theologians for treating the question of non-Catholic Christians as if it were still open to debate. But little more than a decade later, Vatican II's 1964 "Decree on Ecumenism" strongly rebuffed Pius XII's claim that non-Catholics could not "live in the body" of Christ.[440]

Paul VI's *Humanae Vitae* had failed to convince Catholics that using contraceptives was morally wrong, and the document later would serve as a template of sorts for the experience of John Paul II's *Ordinatio Sacerdotalis*. Constructed atop a foundation of what had *not* been said or done in scripture, what had *not* been treated in traditional theology, and what had *not* satisfactorily addressed the needs of contemporary Catholics, *Ordinatio Sacerdotalis* failed to convince Catholics that ordaining women was impossible. In fact, wrote Reese, the "Vatican's attempt to silence the debate over women's ordination has only succeeded in angering more women."[441]

Strategically, the immediacy of this widespread rejection of *Ordinatio Sacerdotalis* was important. Augustine in the fourth century had said that church laws are subject to judgment when they are first promulgated, but after they are firmly in place decisions are made in accordance with them.[442] In other words, it is easier to dislodge a brand-new law than a firmly entrenched one. When *Ordinatio Sacerdotalis* was issued in 1994, the male-only priesthood certainly was entrenched as a tradition, but it had no real history as a *legal* force. The widespread rejection of *Ordinatio Sacerdotalis* was a rebuff of the still-developing legal aspect of this issue. Rosemary Radford Ruether pointed out that John Paul II's teaching on women's ordination enjoyed no broad consensus either within or outside Catholicism:

> Not only have most Protestant churches, including the Anglican Communion, carefully examined this ban and rejected it on scriptural, theological, and moral grounds, but also a large number of theologians, many priests and bishops, and close to a majority of Catholics are questioning such a ban.[443]

A Continuing Strain

Rome's relations with the Anglican Communion had long been strained by the issue, which had been aggravated by the priestly ordination of thirty-two Anglican women just months before the release of *Ordinatio Sacerdotalis*.[444] American theologian Richard Gaillardetz wrote that *Ordinatio Sacerdotalis* was "no doubt intended as a formal Catholic response to the Anglican Communion's admission of women to the priesthood and [was] apparently a continuation of a papal program intent on restoring the clear lines of orthodoxy."[445]

Five days after the release of *Ordinatio Sacerdotalis*, an editorial in a highly respected British Catholic weekly said:

> [It] sometimes seems that the Catholic authorities do not understand how this language of centralizing control and imposed authority, which has become characteristic of the present Roman tone, is heard inside and outside the Church, and what sort of impression it gives.[446]

High ecumenical stakes were very much at play in the women's ordination debate. The editor of *Ecumenical Trends* wrote that *Ordinatio Sacerdotalis* would "have a chilling effect on some aspects of ecumenism," in part because the statement contained an "implied harsh judgment" on churches that ordained women. The statement, "coupled with the insistence on non-inclusive language" in the 1994 English translation of the new catechism, seemed to teach that males were "*the* normative human creatures," reinforcing the idea that women were inferior. Overall, the Vatican's actions seemed to "indicate that no further ecumenical progress [would] be possible between Anglicans and Roman Catholics during this pope's reign."[447]

To Be "Definitively" Held

Ordinatio Sacerdotalis offered no new reasons why women could not be ordained, but it did establish a new claim about the way Catholics were to *receive* this teaching. John Paul II proclaimed that the teaching was to be held "definitively," a term that confused many theologians and other scholars. Until the publication of *Ordinatio Sacerdotalis*, popes not formally speaking *ex cathedra* ("from the chair" of Peter, in Rome) were said to speak "authoritatively" but "non-definitively," meaning that the case was not closed. Francis Sullivan, a Jesuit theologian and authority on magisterial teaching authority, addressed the pope's new and unorthodox requirement that Catholics hold the teaching "definitively":

> [*Ordinatio Sacerdotalis*] even says: "No one, not even the supreme authority in the Church, can fail to accept this teaching without contradicting the will and example of Christ himself." This last statement would rule out the possibility that even a future pope or ecumenical council could reverse the judgment being taught in this papal letter. One does not find, even in the documents of the Second Vatican Council, any comparable claim to the definitive character of its teaching. [It] would be a very small step, from saying that this papal teaching is definitive and irreformable, to claiming that it is infallible. I am surprised that until now I have not seen any statement to that effect.[448]

Shortly after the release of *Ordinatio Sacerdotalis*, the Belgian bishops' Commission on Woman and the Church released a document, widely circulated among women's ordination supporters in the West, arguing that the discussion must continue and reach into "a pastoral level and in the policymaking" of the church community. "The credibility of the Church's attitude" depended upon "a commitment to a true partnership of men and women."[449] The Belgian bishops declared:

- a sacramental relationship arose not from any "natural resemblance in sex" but rather through liturgy and ritual; the ordination of women would allow them, "just as much as their male colleagues," to act in the person of Christ;

- given the reality of John Paul II's claim in *Mulieris Dignitatem* ("On the Dignity and Vocation of Women," 1988) that God's fatherhood possessed no gender, and that both women and men were created in God's image, one could not "really make the manhood of Jesus Christ a necessary factor" of God's Word made flesh;

- the "bridegroom" and "bride" metaphor used to describe the relationship between Jesus and church could not be anything more than metaphor, and metaphor could not indicate a "real femininity of the Church or a necessary maleness of Christ"; further, in the discussion of women's ordination, Jesus' maleness was being "exaggerated beyond reason";

- the determination of a "distinct vocation for women" by an all-male, clerical leadership reflected "discriminatory thinking of the past";

- the objection in *Ordinatio Sacerdotalis* that the church was "not a democracy" was "out of order" because, "why could a woman not exercise an equal ministry" in a "non-democratic system?"

- the papal objection that ordination was not a question of power but of service was likewise beside the point, because the real question being raised was: "Why exclude women from this task of service?"

- the power of ecclesial decision-making was "tied to the sacrament of ordination," a relationship that needed to be questioned;[450] and

- the characterization of a priestly vocation in women as being a "purely subjective desire" was not borne out by experience, because there was no possibility of "letting this personal vocation grow out into a truly ecclesial vocation as happens in the case of men."

Peter Hebblethwaite wrote that *Ordinatio Sacerdotalis* was "an act of the monarchical, or even imperial, papacy produced without serious consultation on its contents" and that it "relied upon obedience rather than persuasion, disciplinary measures rather than explanation." An example of these "disciplinary measures" could be seen the next year in the case of Mercy Sister Carmel McEnroy. A professor of systematic theology at St. Meinrad School of Theology in Indiana, McEnroy had explored the experiences of female auditors at Vatican II in *Guests in Their Own House: The Women of Vatican II*.[451] In 1995, she was terminated for signing a statement supporting women's ordination. Treating persons with questions as "dissidents," Hebblethwaite said, seemed "to threaten a witch-hunt" and "reanimated discussion more than it closed it down."[452] This had been the case with virtually every Vatican pronouncement on the issue for the previous twenty years. According to Jane Redmont and others, Vatican statements against women's ordination "consistently and paradoxically bolster support for the issue."[453]

The statistics agreed. A 1977 Gallup poll showed that 36 percent of respondents supported women's ordination; by 1993, that number had grown to 64 percent.[454] (Among American Catholics under age thirty-five in 1992, it was 80 percent.[455]) Remarkably, when the *New York Times* reported in mid-1992 that two-thirds of American Catholics favored women's ordination, it added that this was "an increase of 20 percentage points over just seven years ago."[456] Although widely traveled and media savvy, John Paul II apparently issued *Ordinatio Sacerdotalis* on the assumption that shutting down the discussion would remove the issue of women's ordination from the agendas of women's groups around the world. If that was the plan, it didn't succeed, at least among the laity.

It did succeed among (or perhaps accommodated) young male seminarians, who through the 1990s were increasingly conservative. A study of priests by Dean R. Hoge and Jacqueline E. Wenger showed that among a range of issues, priests were most likely to choose the answer "I don't want it discussed" in response to the ordination of women. Hoge wrote that the issue, among others, was a threat to some priests, who might fear they would "lose something precious to them" in a climate of open discussion. All of the "I don't want it discussed" topics pertained "to gender, sexual orientation, and celibacy." Priests in their fifties and older wanted to discuss these questions, but priests under age forty-five were most likely to respond, "I don't want it discussed."[457]

What the younger priests *did* want discussed were working conditions and standardization of salaries, as well as a return to a culture in which a priest was "an icon" and "mystical presence." Their responses showed a concern with separating priesthood from laity and with "adopting practices even from the Middle Ages," including a return to "special vestments [and] Latin prayers." They were less enthusiastic than older priests about "working with lay ministers as equals."

More Papal Authority, More Catholic Dissent

Ordinatio Sacerdotalis presented no new historical, scriptural, or theological justifications for the church's male priesthood; its real innovation was the pope's surprisingly strong assertion of authority. Bishop Michael Kenny of Juneau, Alaska, wrote that *Ordinatio Sacerdotalis* was much more about authority than about ordination, which raised a question: "How can the church present itself to the world as the most just of all societies when its major decisions will continue to rest with men alone?"[458]

Not only for the pope but also for the women's ordination movement, 1994 was an *annus horribilis*. The Vatican had (1) revoked its approval of the gender-inclusive New Revised Standard Version of the Bible, (2) issued the English-language edition of the catechism, purged of inclusive language, and (3) issued *Ordinatio Sacerdotalis*. Vatican sails were intercepting the winds of change and steering the church away from adaptation to the modern world.

• • •

When a young Thérèse had approached Pope Leo XIII to ask his permission to enter the convent at age fifteen, she had come away crushed at his seemingly patronizing response that the answer was up to God. Later that evening, she posted a letter to her sister Pauline at Carmel:

> *The Pope is so old that you would think he was dead. . . . He can say almost nothing. It was M. Révérony who spoke . . . Pauline, I cannot tell you what I felt. I was completely crushed. I felt abandoned, and so far away, so far. I could cry writing this letter, my heart is so sad.*[459]

⇥ Chapter 17 ⇤

Obedience, American Style

"STRENGTHENING THE BONDS OF PEACE"*
United States Catholic Conference
November 1994

One of the more remarkable responses to *Ordinatio Sacerdotalis* from church leaders came from the U.S. bishops. Individually and corporately, the American bishops had tried for years to address the concerns of Roman Catholic women. Their four-draft pastoral letter on the topic had ultimately failed in 1992, but now, reflecting on Pope John Paul II's decision to ban discussion of women's ordination, the bishops had their say — in what appeared to be coded language — in "Strengthening the Bonds of Peace."[460]

First, the American bishops declared that *Ordinatio Sacerdotalis* was a "clear reaffirmation of Catholic teaching as a pastoral service to the whole Church," a teaching they acknowledged should be "definitively held by all the faithful" as directed by the pope (§1). From there, however, the bishops responded to the papal demand for silence by issuing multiple calls for dialogue.

Peace, Justice, and Dialogue

"Peace," they wrote, comes about when Christians "respect the dignity of each person, when we welcome the gifts and competencies of all people, when we respect differences, and when we work together to build the reign of God" (§4). In pursuit of peace, as Pope Paul VI had taught, it was first necessary to *work for justice.* Second, it was necessary to *let the past go,* so that it could "not continue to hold people hostage." The bishops' third requirement for peace, however, seemed to contradict John Paul II's orders to end the public debate over women's ordination.

> Honest, sustained dialogue is indispensable for bringing about genuine peace. We believe this same kind of dialogue is necessary in the Church. We offer this message, then, as one moment in a *developing dialogue,* with the hope that all women and men of the Church will receive it as such and continue as participants in what can be a *sacred conversation* for all of us (§5).[461]

---

*The document is included in the appendix, p. 214.

The bishops did not set boundaries for this "sacred conversation," and their characterization of the dialogue as a "developing" one strongly implied that the subject of women's ordination was not closed at all. Their call for "honest, sustained" dialogue seemed to invite just the kind of conversation John Paul II had tried to end. Tellingly, they turned not to John Paul II but to his predecessor, Pope Paul VI, for guidance on the dialogue they sought.

> As characteristics for that dialogue we draw on the wisdom of Pope Paul VI. In his first encyclical, *Ecclesiam Suam* ["On the Church"], he said that dialogue, which he spoke of as spiritual communication, is marked by: (1) clear, understandable language; (2) meekness, a virtue that makes our dialogue peaceful and patient; (3) trust between speaker and the listener; and (4) sensitivity to the situation and needs of the hearer. (§6)

In the context of dialogue in contemporary America on the issue of women's ordination, these four points raised questions as well as possibilities.

- *Clear, understandable language.* Rome's teaching on women's ordination (including that of Paul VI, although to a greater degree that of John Paul II) was anything but clear or understandable, as evidenced by the need for commentaries and official letters to clarify major Vatican documents. If these documents were so complex and oblique that bishops and theologians had difficulty unraveling their meaning, it was unlikely that they could facilitate "spiritual communication" among Catholics.

- *Meekness.* The world's bishops (with inspiring exceptions) and the post–Vatican II popes had not been known for this character trait. The American bishops, for instance, had repeatedly refused to meet with representatives of the Women's Ordination Conference and others regarding dialogue on the issue. In order for meekness to make dialogue "peaceful and patient," there first had to be dialogue.

- *Trust.* This quality was perhaps unwittingly the most ill-fitting within the context of the bishops' call for honest, sustained dialogue, because in this case the speaker-listener relationship was secondary to the authority-subordinate relationship. That is, the risk of trust would have been relatively small for the bishops, whose role in the hierarchy-laity relationship would weight them more heavily as speakers than listeners. Conversely, the issue of trust for lay persons would be much greater, insofar as they were on the subordinate end of the relationship and bound, one could say helplessly, to the declarations of the hierarchy. For supporters of women's ordination, the subordination of women to an all-male hierarchy meant that even when the clergy kept the doors of dialogue open, they could be trusted to keep their ranks closed to women.

- *Sensitivity to the situation and needs of the hearer.* In this context, the call for sensitivity to the hearer was perhaps the most intriguing of the four characteristics of dialogue. It called for sensitivity *by* the speaker *for* the hearer. A lay person's sensitivity to a bishop might include remembering that even if a bishop supported women priests he was banned from saying so. However, the same bishop's sensitivity to a lay person could not include telling the truth about his own support for women priests, but only a bureaucratic defense of the male priesthood.

The bishops said they were "strengthened" by the teaching in *Ordinatio Sacerdotalis*, and they declared a need to look at "alternative ways" in which women could "exercise leadership" (§8) and have a "voice in the governance" in the church (§12). This could be done in two ways: consulting and cooperating. Consultation was already occurring in the church, they said, carefully pointing out that "final decision-making rests with the pastor" (§14). On the other hand, cooperation entailed "cooperating in the exercise of power in accord with the norm of canon law" (§15), which gives the "power of governance" to priests.[462]

Nevertheless, the bishops wrote that church leaders should "model the truth," which would require "rejecting authoritarian conduct" and inviting the "collaboration of women and men as equal partners" (§17). The important truth for the equal partners to remember, however, was that, whether "consulting" or "cooperating," final decision-making authority was with the pastor, who could not be a woman. Hence, women could have no real decision-making authority.

Equality

Obliquely connected to the issue of authority was a section called "Equality," which attempted to explain the inequality of the "equal partners." To do this, the bishops vascillated between two concepts of gender relations — complementarity (one sex completes the other) and mutuality (both sexes work in harmony). In theory and in practice, these two concepts functioned differently. In the church, "mutuality" was not often mentioned in official documents, and "complementarity" usually meant that women were completed by men.

In this section, the bishops wrote that marriage and family life applied to a larger expression of church life, which they called the "domestic church." They turned away from gender complementarity for a moment and discussed a "practice of mutuality, a sharing of power and exercising of responsibility" (§21), although they did not offer concrete examples. In the next paragraph, they reverted to the more familiar "complementarity," saying that in the "domestic Church" the pastor had the authority, but the lay man or woman might have a particular competence that "complements the pastor's" (§22). It was necessary for the bishops to turn to the idea of "complementarity" here, because "mutuality" would have suggested that the pastor and the lay person were *mutually responsible* for decision-making, which could not be the case. This scenario revealed a practical application of complementarity: the male priest (acting *in persona Christi*) was the active agent ("bridegroom"), and church members (with Mary as their model) were the passive agent ("bride").

The bishops acknowledged that the institutional church was guilty of sexism and domination of women. "A Church that is deepening its consciousness of itself, that is trying to project the image of Christ to the world" would understand the "need for ongoing, prayerful reflection in this area" (§30). The bishops did not elaborate on the clause "trying to project the image of Christ to the world," but in light of church teaching that women could not image Christ, the bishops' wording could hardly have been accidental (although possibly the phrase "trying to project the image of Christ" literally meant one thing to some bishops and something else to others).

The bishops also urged adoption of more inclusive language in teaching and religious materials and in hymns, revealing some dogged determination on their part, in view of the pope's rejection of an inclusive English-language catechism (1994) and the rancorous clash over the failed effort to produce an inclusive-language lectionary of scripture readings for mass. Indeed, it is still common in Catholic churches to recite, in the Nicene creed, that Jesus was born "for us *men* and for our salvation," even though the exclusionary word "men" is clearly unnecessary for content or meaning.

Like their failed pastoral letter on women's concerns, the bishops' document was a mixed bag. While they pledged support for the teaching in *Ordinatio Sacerdotalis*, as they were required to do, they also made some plainly courageous statements, which, if read between the fine lines, revealed a national bishops' conference not so solidly in support of the male-only clergy.

Nevertheless, the bottom line remained the same: women could not be ordained.

• • •

Obedience was the "prime and absolute rule" of Thérèse's religious life. When she first entered the convent at Carmel in 1888, Thérèse never encountered her prioress "without being reprimanded for something." At fifteen, she was much younger than the other nuns, and she felt singled out for undeserved disciplinary actions. "I was scolded nearly all the time during the hour I spent with her whenever — which was not often — she gave me spiritual direction."[463] *Even several years later, wracked by tuberculosis, she obeyed her superior's order not to tell her own blood sisters in the cloister, who did not learn of it until Thérèse was dying.*[464] *She always obeyed her superiors, no matter how much harm it caused.*

Chapter 18

The Bride of Christ
and Mother of Believers

"LETTER TO WOMEN"
Pope John Paul II
June 29, 1995

"JESUITS AND THE SITUATION OF WOMEN
IN CHURCH AND CIVIL SOCIETY"*
Society of Jesus
September 27, 1995

Saying he wanted to reflect "with" women on their condition, Pope John Paul II was the first pontiff to write that the church possibly had been complicit in the oppression of women, and if blame for this "belonged to not just a few members of the Church," he was "truly sorry."[465] Tellingly, however, the pontiff's "Letter to Women" gave no evidence that he had reflected "with" women at all; the tone of his letter suggested he had written "to" them, revealing anew his lack of practical connection to women. This was concisely stated by Jane Redmont, who said that the papal document, "though it may be a step forward, heartfelt and sincere, continues to reflect the isolation in which John Paul lives, particularly his isolation from women in the worlds of work and pastoral practice."[466] From that isolation, the pope had rejected dialogue and collegiality in favor of monologue and unquestioning compliance.

On the threshold of the twenty-first century, John Paul II continued speaking of women in traditional, even medieval ways. This static perspective showed itself in particularly sharp relief in his "Letter to Women,"[467] written for the United Nations Fourth World Conference on Women, held in Beijing during the summer of 1995.

The "Genius" of Women

Objecting to growing criticism that the Vatican's ban against women's ordination was discriminatory and unjust, the pope offered Mary the mother of God as the ultimate example of fidelity to "the role of women":

*The document is included in the appendix, p. 220.

> A *certain diversity of roles* is in no way prejudicial to women, provided that this diversity is not the result of an arbitrary imposition, but is rather an expression of what is specific to being male and female. This issue also has a particular application within the Church. If Christ — by his free and sovereign choice, clearly attested to by the Gospel and by the Church's constant Tradition — entrusted only to men the task of being an *"icon" of his countenance as "shepherd" and "bridegroom" of the Church through the exercise of the ministerial priesthood,* this in no way detracts from the role of women.[468]

But in the eyes of growing numbers of Catholics, the male-only priesthood *did* detract from the role of women, who were increasingly unwilling to limit their spiritual lives to Mary's triple role of virgin, bride, and mother. The pope, however, sanctified only those three functions in Roman Catholic women:

> In fact, there is present in the "womanhood" of a woman...a highly significant "iconic character" which finds its full realization in Mary and which also aptly expresses the very essence of the Church as a community consecrated with the integrity of a *"virgin"* heart to become the *"bride"* of Christ and *"mother"* of believers.[469]

This juxtaposition of virgin, bride, and mother — set in quotation marks and italics — was a familiar but uncommonly condensed statement of the pope's convictions. Clearly, women's sex roles, which the pope always placed in relation to males, determined their roles in the church.[470]

Human nature was determined first by sex and next by intellect. In his opening paragraphs, the pope purposefully revealed this view when he thanked women according to six groups, in order: mothers, wives, daughters, and sisters, women who work, consecrated women, and every woman, "for the simple fact of being a *woman.*"[471] (Nowhere had the pope addressed men in thanks for being a *man.*) The next year, addressing a general audience, he spoke of Old Testament women solely and glaringly in terms of their marital status, concluding: "Although [Wisdom] literature frequently alludes to woman's defects, it perceives in her a hidden treasure: 'He who finds a wife finds a good thing'" (Prov. 18:22).

Nevertheless, the pope pointed to the "urgent need to achieve *real equality* in nearly every area: equal pay for equal work, protection for working mothers, fairness in career advancements, equality of spouses with regard to family rights and the recognition of everything that is part of the rights and duties of citizens in a democratic State."[472] This "universal recognition of the dignity of women" required a clear grasp of gender roles resulting from the "ultimate *anthropological basis* of the dignity of women, making it evident as a part of God's plan for humanity." That is, women's roles were determined by their biology (their ability to bear children), the God-given foundation of their dignity.

Further, women and men were "complementary *not only from the physical and psychological points of view, but also from the ontological,*"[473] from the very essence of their categories of female and male. According to John Paul II, ontological complementarity — the natural and mutual dependence of male and female — was foundational and unchangeable. However, women had a "special genius" rooted in their biology that men did not share. "Genius" was a word John Paul II used numerous times in this letter and elsewhere. In 1995, the U.S. bishops published a compilation of papal statements entitled, *Pope John Paul II on the Genius of Women*,[474] a collection of papal statements for the 1995 United Nations Conference on Women in Beijing. Its first footnote stated: "The phrase 'the genius of women' appears frequently in the writings of Pope John Paul II. Although the word *genius* has several meanings, the pope uses it to connote an essential nature or spirit."

The "several meanings" actually illuminated the pope's chosen definition. The English word came from the Latin *genius*, meaning a guardian spirit, particularly of a person's intellect and natural inclination. According to ancient Roman belief, a guardian spirit (also called "genie") was assigned to a baby at birth. *Genius* also was rooted in *geno* and *gignere* — to produce or give birth. Hence, the pope's frequent allusion to the "genius of women" was something essentially biological. John Paul II would make this clear in his 1996 apostolic exhortation *Vita Consecrata* ("On the Consecrated Life"), when he said the church's devotion to her spouse, Christ, had a "particular meaning for women," who found therein "their feminine identity and as it were discover the special genius of their relationship with the Lord."[475]

By 1995, the repetition of this phrase — genius of women — was attracting the attention of theologians and others. Jane Redmont wrote:

> Mary, the pope writes, continues to be the highest expression of "the feminine genius." Or is she, as we were also taught, the highest expression of the human genius? [If] there is a feminine genius, then surely there is a masculine genius, and I should like to know what it is, how and where it is incarnate and whether one genius is more permeated with the divine than the other.[476]

One important aspect of women's genius, according to John Paul II, could be found in Genesis 2:18–25, where God made a "helper" for the male. The pope said this concept of helper was not a function but rather a mode of *"being"* in which women were "called to *give to men.*"[477] He said the church had many reasons for hoping the United Nations Conference in Beijing would bring out the *"full truth about women"* with "necessary emphasis" on the *"genius of women"*[478] — their ability to be fit helpers for men.

In his 1995 "Letter to Women," John Paul II sent out an appeal for governments and institutions to ensure that "the dignity of womanhood" be given full respect:

> I cannot fail to express my admiration for those women of good will who have devoted their lives to defending the dignity of womanhood by fighting for their basic social, economic and political rights, demonstrating courageous initiative at a time when this was considered extremely inappropriate, the sign of a lack of femininity, a manifestation of exhibitionism, and even a sin![479]

On the global level, this plea for institutional respect for women's dignity surpassed any papal statement in church history. The "Letter to Women" was unprecedented in its apology for and rejection of sexism, even extending its call to equality for children. Earlier that year, the pope had called discrimination against girls an "intolerable" custom that would impair their development. If "girls are looked down upon or regarded as inferior, their sense of dignity will be gravely impaired and their healthy development inevitably compromised. Discrimination in childhood will have lifelong effects and will prevent women from fully taking part in the life of society."[480]

At the same time, this document ignored the expanding scope of pontifical disregard for the status of women and girls *inside* the church. Such compartmentalizing was becoming more common in the thinking of John Paul II. Millions of women around the world were trying to send the message that full recognition of women's dignity required their full participation in the church, but to no avail. Gail Grossman Freyne maintained that John Paul II's claims of women's dignity rang hollow, "when women are to be forever excluded from full authority within the Church for no other reason than for being women." And, echoing the sentiments of many regarding the pope's apology for church discrimination against women, she asked, "Does not the repentance of sin require a firm purpose of amendment?"[481]

The Society of Jesus: Urgency in the Challenge

In September 1995, just three months after John Paul II released his "Letter to Women," the Thirty-fourth General Congregation of the Society of Jesus (Jesuits) publicized "Jesuits and the Situation of Women in Church and Civil Society."[482] This document said the unjust treatment of women had a "universal dimension" involving "men and women everywhere." Unlike the pope, who concentrated his teaching of gender complementarity on the "rib" creation story in Genesis 2:18–25, the Jesuits focused on the creation account in Genesis 1:26–27, in which God created woman and man simultaneously in the divine image, and on Jesus' relationship of mutuality with women. "The original plan of God was for a loving relationship of respect, mutuality, and equality between men and women" and there was "an urgency in the challenge to translate theory into practice not only [in the world] but also within the Church itself."[483]

Also unlike John Paul II, who frequently and unhesitatingly spoke on behalf of women, the Jesuits wrote: "We do not pretend or claim to speak for women. However, we do speak out of what we have learned from women about ourselves and our relationship with them."[484] Their claim to have learned from women contrasted sharply with the attitude of John Paul II, who in his writings to and about women was more prone to say what women could learn from him.

The Jesuits said they had been part of a church tradition that had sometimes offended women, and "like many men, we have a tendency to convince ourselves that there is no problem."[485] Claiming responsibility for change, the Jesuits challenged themselves to live and work "with the tension involved in being faithful to the teachings of the Church and to the signs of the times" and to help bring about "respectful reconciliation" between women and men in a world in which "there is neither Jew nor Greek, there is neither slave nor free, there is neither male nor female, for you are all one in Christ Jesus" (Gal. 3:28).[486]

Rome had spoken for decades about the need for the *outside world* to respect women, but the Jesuits held up a mirror and found a starting place within the tradition of the church itself, which had been "complicit in a form of clericalism" that "reinforced male domination with an ostensibly divine sanction." The Jesuits wished to "react personally and collectively" to change the situation, vowing "to listen carefully and courageously to the experience of women," which "more than anything else will bring about change."[487]

• • •

During meditation hour in the convent, Thérèse frequently found herself sitting near a nun "who never stopped fidgeting, with either her rosary or something else." The sound sorely irritated Thérèse, who wanted "to turn and stare at her until she stopped her noise." Given Thérèse's personality, it would have been a hole-boring stare. Instead, she endured the nun's noise patiently, "first, for the love of God and, secondly, so as not to upset her." After allowing the noise to disturb her for a time, Thérèse found a way out of her dilemma: "Instead of trying not to hear it — which was impossible — I strove to listen to it carefully as if it were a first-class concert, and my meditation, which was not the prayer of quiet, was spent in offering this concert to Jesus."[488]

Chapter 19

The Inadmissibility of Women

RESPONSUM AD DUBIUM
REGARDING ORDINATIO SACERDOTALIS
("Response to a Question regarding *Ordinatio Sacerdotalis*")*
Congregation for the Doctrine of the Faith
October 28, 1995

"TRADITION AND
THE ORDINATION OF WOMEN"
Catholic Theological Society of America
June 6, 1997

Reacting to criticisms of Pope John Paul II's 1994 *Ordinatio Sacerdotalis* ("On Reserving Priestly Ordination to Men Alone"), the Congregation for the Doctrine of the Faith (CDF) promulgated this *Responsum ad Dubium* ("Response to a Question").[489] In a cover letter to the world's bishops' conferences, CDF prefect Cardinal Joseph Ratzinger said that "a number of problematic and negative statements about [*Ordinatio Sacerdotalis*] by certain theologians, organizations of priests and religious, as well as some associations of laypeople" had "attempted to cast doubt on the definitive character of the Letter's teaching on the inadmissibility of women to the ministerial priesthood." In light of such widespread dissent, especially among priests and theologians, it was necessary to issue the *Responsum*, which the pope approved and ordered to be published.[490]

Infallibility

Before exploring the *Responsum*, which made a highly controversial claim to infallibility, it will be helpful to look at the complex role of infallibility. Broadly, in matters of faith and morals the church considers itself to be free from error. There are five sources of this "inerrancy" — God's omniscience, humankind's pre-Fall knowledge, Christ's divine knowledge, scripture, and the church's infallible teaching. The last of these, infallibility, derives from God's revelation and keeps the church from error in matters of faith and morals.

---

*The document is included in the appendix, p. 225.

117

The notion of infallibility emerged in the Middle Ages with a Franciscan who sought to protect Pope Nicholas III's recognition of the Franciscan order, but it was condemned by John XXII in 1324 as "the work of the devil."[491] As a method of protecting papal teachings from being overturned by later popes, infallibility assumed practical significance during a fifteenth-century schism when three duly elected popes fought each other for the papal throne. To unravel this chaos, the Council of Constance (1414–18) declared that an ecumenical council (worldwide meeting of bishops) derived its authority not from the pope but from Christ. Claiming conciliar primacy, the Council of Constance forced the three popes to resign and went about the work of getting the institutional church back on course. Papal power soon reasserted itself, but the idea of infallibility would lay more or less dormant until the nineteenth century.

The controversy running through the infallibility debate was that one pope's infallible teaching could not be overturned by a later pope, who would be bound to a perhaps inauspicious teaching. Nevertheless, when the unification of Italy resulted in the Vatican's loss of the papal states and political power, Vatican I (1869–70) responded by defining the doctrine of papal infallibility. Amid much acrimonious debate among bishops and cardinals, the pope was given absolute authority over the church.

The document *Pastor Aeternus* ("On the Magisterial Infallibility of the Roman Pontiff," 1870) defined papal primacy. According to "tradition received from the beginning," it was "divinely revealed" that by virtue of his apostolic authority the pope could define a doctrine of "faith or morals which must be held by the universal Church." Such a doctrine was "irreformable" in and of itself (*ex sese*), "not from the consent of the Church."[492] The document also distinguished between a doctrine that must be "held" (*tenenda*) and one that must be "believed" (*credenda*). The former doctrine could be changed; the latter could not. Theologian John T. Ford pointed out that Vatican I did not restrict infallibility to matters of faith and belief but allowed the possibility that infallibility might extend to a "doctrine that must be *held*," even though that teaching was not, strictly speaking, a matter of divine revelation,[493] and even though many Roman Catholics might not believe it. The distinction between *credenda* and *tenenda* only enlarged the debate over infallibility that had been simmering for centuries, and it continues to this day.

The first exercise of papal infallibility had actually occurred in 1854, sixteen years before Vatican I defined the doctrine. Pope Pius IX sent letters to the world's bishops asking their thoughts on the infallible nature of the Immaculate Conception (of Mary by her mother). With their enthusiastic consent, he declared the doctrine. The only other exercise of papal infallibility came in 1950, when Pope Pius XII undertook a worldwide consultation of Catholics, who endorsed the infallibility of the Assumption of Mary (into heaven). Both these doctrines were promulgated after worldwide consultation. Today, Rome's only two valid declarations of infallible teaching concern women, and the only known invalid declaration of infallibility likewise concerns women.

Who Is Infallible?

The doctrine of infallibility falls into three categories:

- the *extraordinary magisterium* — when the pope (extraordinary) teaches (magisterium) *ex cathedra* ("from the chair" of Peter) in matters of faith and morals;

- *an ecumenical council,* requiring papal confirmation; and

- the *ordinary, universal magisterium* — when bishops (ordinaries) from their home countries or in an ecumenical council (universal), teach definitively in union with the pope (collectively, the magisterium).

The interpretation of infallibility presented in the 1995 *Responsum ad Dubium* ("Response to a Question") caused global confusion among Roman Catholics because (according to canon 749:3) any infallible doctrine must be "manifestly" established — that is, it must be shown that *"not only the pope but the whole body of Catholic bishops"* proposed the same doctrine that Catholics were "obliged to hold in a definitive way."[494] But since the world's bishops had been neither consulted nor given the opportunity even to read *Ordinatio Sacerdotalis* before its publication, any collegial decision-making by pope and bishops was virtually impossible; hence, the teaching could not be "manifestly" (or even implicitly) established. And, since *Ordinatio Sacerdotalis* had conveyed John Paul II's adamant opposition to women's ordination, it was difficult to envision how dissenting bishops could have said anything at all.

Three decades earlier, Walter Abbott, the Jesuit editor of the documents of Vatican II, had articulated a quite different view contained in a footnote to *Lumen Gentium* ("Dogmatic Constitution on the Church," 1964):

> To the difficulty sometimes raised, "What if the Pope were to define something to which the rest of the episcopal college or the faithful did not agree?" [*Lumen Gentium*] replies that the case is a purely imaginary one, since one and the same Holy Spirit directs the Pope, the college of bishops, and the whole body of the faithful. In practice, the Pope always consults the other bishops and the faithful before making a doctrinal decision, but the validity of his action does not legally depend upon any kind of ratification by them.[495]

In his 1994 *Ordinatio Sacerdotalis,* the reality was that the pope *had* defined something to which bishops and faithful did not agree, and that the pope had *not* consulted the bishops (much less the faithful) before making a doctrinal decision. Francis Sullivan, a widely acknowledged expert on infallibility, said that the pope could have claimed infallibility using his *ex cathedra* authority, which would have closed "the last chink for disagreement."[496] However, that had *not* been done, leaving the world's Catholics to wonder not only about the status of women's ordination, but also what was, and was not, infallible teaching. While the "validity of his action" may not have legally depended upon "any ratification" by bishops and faithful, actions by the Congregation for the Doctrine of the Faith (CDF) and its prefect, Cardinal Joseph Ratzinger, were far less clear-cut.

Responsum ad Dubium

In his cover letter to the *Responsum,* Ratzinger said that negative reactions to *Ordinatio Sacerdotalis* ("On Reserving the Priesthood to Men Alone," 1994) had "attempted to cast doubt on the definitive character of the letter's teaching," and had "questioned whether this teaching belonged to the deposit of the faith," forcing the CDF to issue the *Responsum.*[497] Faithful Roman Catholics who "had suffered the agitation of doubt" on this issue could, thanks to *Ordinatio Sacerdotalis,* find "serenity again."

One of the more perplexing aspects of the *Responsum* was the Vatican's apparent failure to learn from the mistakes of its earlier public pronouncements against women's ordination, which routinely had the effect of increasing the issue's acceptance among Catholics. Predictably, the *Responsum* did not quell the debate at all, but only spawned more resistance by claiming that the teachings in *Ordinatio Sacerdotalis* belonged to the *depositum fidei* ("deposit of faith," the sum of revelation and apostolic tradition). In fact, however, *Ordinatio Sacerdotalis* had said nothing at all about the male priesthood belonging to the deposit of faith. According to systematic theologian Richard Gaillardetz, an authority on the magisterium, Ratzinger soon issued a clarification saying that the *Responsum* did not intend to say that this teaching was a *part of* the deposit of faith but rather that it *pertained to* the deposit of faith, an ambiguity caused in part by "poor English translations of the Latin."[498] But this clarification was not widely published, and it did not prevent wide publication of his claim that the teaching *did* belong to the deposit of faith.

Joseph Komonchak, a theologian and key historian of Vatican II, explained another peculiarity. Precisely in order to highlight its claim concerning the deposit of faith, the CDF appended a second paragraph to the *Responsum,* explaining the first paragraph's claim that the doctrine *did* in fact "belong to" the deposit of faith. Moreover, it was "only in this explanatory [second] paragraph" that the word "infallibly" occurred.[499]

The *depositum fidei* confusion notwithstanding, the *Responsum* claimed that the teaching against women priests had been "set forth infallibly by the ordinary and universal magisterium," requiring "definitive assent" from the faithful (§3). This remarkable claim of infallibility had appeared nowhere in *Ordinatio Sacerdotalis,* opening up a new debate about the boundaries of infallibility itself: could an administrative curial congregation (the CDF) declare a teaching "infallible" *when the pope had not?*

An editorial in *The Tablet* (London) now articulated what was being discussed by Catholics of every stripe. The *Responsum* had been an "unexpected and unprecedented reinforcement" of a doctrine that had already been declared "definitive" and "to be held always, everywhere and by all." This fortification suggested:

> The Vatican sees the slowly increasing level of controversy over the possibility of women priests as a threat to unity within the communion of the Catholic faith that has to be countered forcefully. That in turn suggests that the arguments so far

adduced have not, by themselves, carried the day. In the thinking of the Vatican, therefore, those arguments had to be buttressed by a further use of authority.[500]

The *Responsum's* switch from reason to authority (like that of *Ordinatio Sacerdotalis* before it) was especially evident one week after the document's 1995 release, when John Paul II delivered a "strongly worded" statement to the CDF, warning that dissenters were contributing to the loss of an "authentic concept of authority" and threatening to form a "countermagisterium."[501] Then in 1996, the pope specifically said that theologians who questioned church teaching threatened to form such a "countermagisterium." He noted a "widespread misunderstanding of the meaning and role of the church's magisterium." This misunderstanding was "at the root of the criticisms and protests regarding its pronouncements."[502] That is, Catholics' failure or inability to understand the nature of hierarchical teaching authority was the problem.

What John Paul II called "misunderstanding," however, was widely perceived by others as informed decision-making. A recent study had shown that American Catholics were, if not forming a "countermagisterium," at least making up their own minds on controversial teachings. Only 26 percent believed that acceptance of papal infallibility was necessary to be a good Catholic, and an overwhelming 90 percent believed that one could dissent from Vatican teaching and remain a good Catholic.[503]

Vatican observer Thomas Reese suggested that, in general, the "heart of the Vatican's failure to convince" was the "belief that the word of a teacher must be accepted simply because of his authority and not because of his arguments."[504] That is, based on the traditional teaching model as practiced in Italy, students were expected to listen, memorize, and repeat back to the teacher his own words. Canon lawyer Ladislas Örsy further explained that the church's legal traditions developed during an age when educated men made laws for uneducated masses, and in such times "it may have been right to stress obedience to the law and to assume that the members of the community had little capacity to contribute" to the lawmaking process. Laws, he said, "should bring stability to the social body, yet they should evolve with the same body." Both stability and progress were needed, and the right balance was "somewhere between the two."[505]

Ordinatio Sacerdotalis and, even more, its *Responsum* showed a determination to avoid balance or conciliation. Accordingly, reaction against the *Responsum* was immediate and widespread. The lesson to be learned, said one newspaper editorial, was that "people cannot be ordered to stop asking questions about belief. What Rome has failed to comprehend at great loss to the entire church is that believers deepen their faith by questioning."[506]

In Rome, however, Vatican Radio quoted Ratzinger as saying that *Ordinatio Sacerdotalis* called Roman Catholics to follow the hierarchy's definitions of the faith, and "whoever does not do so obviously separates himself [sic] from the faith of the church."[507]

Christine Schenk, director of FutureChurch, pointed out that Ratzinger's statement was issued on the eve of "the presentation of 1.8 million signatures from

German Catholics (and five hundred thousand from Austrian Catholics collected earlier that year with permission from local bishops) asking that ordination be opened to married people and women," and that the German media interpreted Ratzinger's statement as a "preemptive strike" to the press conference announcing the signatures.[508]

Confusing the Experts

Lay Catholics weren't the only ones troubled by the *Responsum*. A close inspection of the terse, 150-word document revealed five specific claims that caused unprecedented confusion among the world's bishops and theologians.

• The teaching against women's ordination required *definitive assent*. The National Coalition of American Nuns reminded Catholics that teachings considered infallible were "those which have been accepted as true by the entire community of the faithful," and that infallibility should not be used "as a tool to settle a disputed opinion or to cut off discussion" of an issue.[509] Such a move, said Gail Grossman Freyne, forced women to choose "between the scandal of speaking out against the perceived injustice and the scandal of remaining silent."[510]

• The teaching was founded on the *written word* of God. Vatican-trained theologian Richard McBrien asked how it was possible to make this assertion when in 1976 the Pontifical Biblical Commission had concluded that nothing in scripture prohibited the ordination of women. "To say the teaching is founded on the word of God is just simply wrong," he said.[511] Joseph Komonchak explained that John Paul II had said merely that the doctrine was "maintained by the constant and universal tradition of the church and firmly taught by the magisterium in recent documents," and that the CDF had gone beyond the pope's original document when it added the reference to scripture.[512]

• From the beginning, the teaching of a male priesthood had been constantly preserved and applied in *church tradition*. Systematic theologian John Wright pointed out that this document "neither claimed to be infallible itself, nor did it attach infallibility directly to [*Ordinatio Sacerdotalis*]. Rather it appealed to the constant, universal teaching of the Church's magisterium as teaching this infallibly." Yet the *Responsum* offered no evidence that this was the case. *Inter Insigniores* ("Declaration on the Admission of Women to the Ministerial Priesthood," 1976) was the only place where the CDF had "attempted to offer some evidence for constant, universal, and hence infallible, teaching."[513] Cambridge divinity professor Nicholas Lash wrote that far from being "from the beginning constantly preserved and applied," the question whether the "representation of Christ" required maleness "was never even *asked* until about halfway through the [twentieth] century." On the "rare occasions" when the question did arise, it was always answered according to a teaching that actually *had* been constantly preserved and applied: "namely, that women cannot be ordained to apostolic office because they are inferior to men." Since Vatican II had officially set aside the church's centuries-old tradition of women's inherent inferiority, there now was "no traditional teaching on the matter," because the question *as it was now raised* was "a new question."[514]

• The teaching was to be held always and everywhere as *belonging to the deposit of faith*. As has been stated above, Ratzinger was quoted to have denied, retracted, or at least qualified this claim. Even so, an editorialist for *The Tablet* wrote, "within the deposit of faith though they may be, questions about the limits of the Church's jurisdiction over the sacraments are definitely technical, second-order questions. They cannot be treated as if they were crucial to the Gospel message."[515]

• The teaching was *set forth infallibly by the ordinary and universal magisterium*. The claim meant that the teaching had been declared over the centuries by the world's bishops in union with the pope. But Francis Sullivan, echoing other theologians, said that to his knowledge the *Responsum ad Dubium* was "the first official document of the Roman magisterium that ever declared that a specific doctrine was taught infallibly" in this manner. He reiterated that canon 749:3 required that the *fact* of any doctrine being infallibly defined must first be "clearly established." When the claim of infallibility came from a doctrine taught by the ordinary universal magisterium, it meant that "not only the pope, but the whole body of Catholic bishops" had always and everywhere proposed the same doctrine.[516] But there was no available evidence to establish this as fact. To the contrary, the male-only priesthood in no way appeared to enjoy the universal and constant teaching of the world's bishops;[517] rather, the teaching arose only from the pope himself. Ratzinger would later acknowledge that this actually had been the case:

> In the technical language one should say: here we have an act of the ordinary Magisterium of the Supreme Pontiff, an act therefore which is not a solemn definition ex cathedra, even though in terms of content a doctrine is presented which is to be considered definitive.[518]

In response, the National Conference of Catholic Bishops (NCCB) issued a set of briefing questions and statements to prepare American bishops for questions by the media. It said the *Responsum* did "not say anything new." The teaching had been "set forth infallibly" and *Ordinatio Sacerdotalis* had "identified a teaching of the ordinary magisterium as an instance of an infallible teaching, rather than issue a formally infallible pronouncement of this teaching." This remarkable statement claimed that the male priesthood had been "set forth" but not "formally pronounced" infallible, and that it was an "instance" of infallible teaching. Confusion reigned supreme.

Further, the American bishops asserted that the teaching *did* "belong to the deposit of faith," although, they conceded, the CDF had not explained "*how* this teaching pertains to the deposit of faith." Further, the CDF had left "to the bishops and to theologians the task of making this connection clear."[519] As it turned out, most bishops and theologians were, in large number, no clearer on this than anyone else.

What a Pope Can Do

Joan Chittister captured the reaction of many Catholics to the *Responsum* and Ratzinger's clarifications of it: "Has there been a palace coup and someone forgot to tell us about it? Is the pope's name John Paul II or Joseph Ratzinger?"[520] Bishop Francis Murphy of Baltimore cited "Vatican scuttlebutt" that suggested it was not Ratzinger who had inspired the use of "infallible" but rather the pope, whose use of the concept Ratzinger may have prevented in the past. Murphy concluded that theologians "would be well advised to await the arrival of a pontiff as strong-willed and as theologically competent as Wojtyla [John Paul II's surname] to discover whether 'what a pope can do a pope can undo.' "[521] American theologian Anthony Padovano pointed out that another pope could open ordination to women "by being very nuanced and subtle about it." Dominican theologian Edward Schillebeeckx of the Netherlands said it was "totally impossible, dogmatically" for the male-only priesthood to be a matter of infallibility. It was "a matter of church order, and church order can never be a matter of infallibility."[522] Responding to this state of affairs, canon law historian Charles Donahue Jr. wrote a wryly succinct analysis:

> The distinction between the proposition that the church cannot change its practice with regard to the ordination of women and the proposition that it cannot change its views on what it can change with regard to its practices with regard to the ordination of women is a fine one, but it is one that must be maintained. Otherwise, we will end up with a barefoot boy with shoes on, a non-infallible proposition that cannot be changed.[523]

Infallibility notwithstanding, the *Responsum* finished what *Ordinatio Sacerdotalis* had begun — the turn from concern with scripture, tradition, and church teaching, to the final word of Vatican authority: *Roma locuta, causa finita.* Rome has spoken, case closed. Failing to persuade with its arguments, Rome had used its authority to silence dissenters. It appeared an act of desperation, and to no avail. Two years following the *Responsum,* according to Thomas Reese, "the numbers of theologians investigated, silenced, or removed from office [was] at an all-time high," and the relationship between theologians and the papacy was worse than at any time "since the Reformation." If this breach continued, the church would be "incapable of creatively responding to new needs and new opportunities, instead repeating old formulas that do not address new questions and ideas."[524]

Not the Last Word

Theologians, lay persons, women religious, bishops, priests — Catholics of all stripes strongly criticized the CDF's claim that the teaching was infallible. Most widespread was the complaint that doctrinal infallibility had been declared invalidly (by a curial congregation, with no lawful power to declare a teaching infallible) by means of a nonauthoritative instrument (a *responsum,* with no canonical teaching authority).

Elizabeth Johnson called the *Responsum* "a statement of a Vatican congregation, no more, no less." The CDF's use of "infallibility" had made it "clear that Rome is determined to close the question of women's ordination as it is maturing in the church." The Vatican's recourse to "sheer power" had resulted from women's ordination opponents "losing the argument on the field of reasoning."[525]

Indeed, Vatican observer Peter Steinfels wrote, "To forbid discussion of a church practice is a virtual admission that it cannot withstand scrutiny."[526] Nicholas Lash predicted that the CDF's action would undermine Vatican authority because the attempt to use the doctrine of infallibility "as a blunt instrument to prevent the ripening of a question in the Catholic mind" was a "scandalous abuse of power," the most likely consequence of which would be to further "undermine the very authority which the Pope seeks to sustain."[527]

Joan Chittister articulated questions asked by many Catholics:

> Can an office of the Vatican declare a papal statement infallible? And can they do it ex post facto? Why is it that when bishops all over the world ask for this issue to be discussed, they are simply ignored? When, on the other hand, one of the Vatican congregations addresses the issue unilaterally...the subject is happily opened in order to be closed....I am now more convinced than ever that this subject is not closed, in fact, has not even been opened. It has only been suppressed.[528]

The National Coalition of American Nuns (NCAN) said that the Vatican's teaching against women's ordination could not be infallible because it was "unjust and, therefore, in error." The nuns reaffirmed their call, "first made in 1970, for the ordination of women as priests in the Roman Catholic Church" and for "all Catholics, including priests and bishops, to speak their views publicly and courageously" so that Rome could "receive the sense of the faithful."[529] The Leadership Conference of Women Religious (LCWR) in the United States feared that the CDF's *Responsum*, "rather than engendering a higher degree of faithfulness in communion with the church, [would] instead cause division and disillusionment."[530]

This claim confirmed sociologist Joseph Fichter's 1977 report that American Catholicism was "experiencing adaptation at the grass roots," and "faithful children of the Church" were less and less impressed "by the need of attending to directives and prohibitions" from the Vatican.[531] And theologian Lisa Sowle Cahill asked a pointed question regarding the claims in the *Responsum*: "How are we to know whether we are disputing a teaching just prior to or during an era of change? If unanimity erodes, was the teaching previously infallible, but afterwards not?"[532]

While theologians fashioned responses to the *Responsum*, the world's bishops wondered at John Paul II's insistence that they ensure Catholic compliance with this teaching. Cardinal Ratzinger had told them he was "confident" they would ensure the teaching's "favorable reception" among Catholics, taking particular care that theologians, priests, and vowed religious would not again propose "ambiguous and contrary positions."[533] The assignment given the bishops was especially hefty, insofar as "contrary positions" were becoming more and more popular among all those groups, who were unlikely to give this teaching their "favorable reception." In fact, observed Peter Hebblethwaite following *Ordinatio Sacerdotalis*, the best the bishops could hope to do was "engage in damage control."[534]

Catholic Theological Society of America:
Serious, Widespread Disagreement

Eighteen months after the *Responsum*, the Catholic Theological Society of America (CTSA) issued a committee paper entitled, "Tradition and the Ordination of Women."[535] Saying it would not argue for or against women's ordination, the CTSA questioned "whether the reasons given by [the CDF *Responsum*] justify the assertion that the definitive assent of the faithful" was required for male priesthood.[536] The CTSA's probe showed the untenable nature of the Vatican's position based upon church tradition, gender roles, scripture, theology, and infallibility. In a small group, Bishop Raymond Lucker of New Ulm, Minnesota, was reported to have remarked: "Cardinal Ratzinger has said we have the conclusion, now we need the reasons. When we face that, we realize we have very serious problems. How can we support that which has no reasons?"[537]

The CTSA acknowledged the widespread disagreement among theologians and called for continuing discussion. Noting a shift in the nature of Vatican arguments against women's ordination, the CTSA also pointed out that a teaching by the "ordinary and universal magisterium" required "that the whole body of Catholic bishops is teaching the same doctrine and obliging the faithful to give it their definitive assent." Citing canon 749:3, which stated that no doctrine was to be infallibly defined unless first clearly established, the CTSA wrote that the teaching of a male-only priesthood could not be infallible because the CDF "did not, and indeed could not, appeal either to a consultation of all the bishops or to the common adherence of the Catholic faithful."[538] This was because the sense of the faithful (*sensus fidelium*) and their reception of this teaching had not even been considered.

The CTSA membership approved the committee's paper by a vote of 216 to 22, and the paper's conclusion became a resolution of the CTSA board:

> There are serious doubts regarding the nature of the authority of this teaching and its grounds in tradition. There is serious, widespread disagreement on this question not only among theologians but also within the larger community of the Church.[539]

Reaction from the hierarchy to the theologians' resolution was swift. Bishop James McHugh of Camden, New Jersey, called it "decidedly unhelpful in building up the faith of Catholics." Bishop John Myers of Peoria, Illinois, said it lacked "respect and trust" and would likely "harm the faith of many people."[540] Cardinal Bernard Law of Boston called the CTSA a theological "wasteland" whose study was "a transparent ruse" to challenge church authority; indeed, the CTSA had committed a "dereliction of responsibility" that "was predictable" for American theologians. For "authentic Catholic theologians," Law said, the teaching would be "a given," and the only valid study would be one that was undertaken to "elucidate the teaching."[541]

These bishops' reactions suggested that widespread objection to the male priesthood was becoming more and more problematic for the hierarchy. Perhaps nowhere was this stated more simply or succinctly than by David Knight, a pastoral theologian and parish priest in Memphis, who wrote that when the boundaries of infallibility were not clearly acknowledged by papal spokesmen, "the aura of infallibility tends to seep out and spread a false light of certitude over everything that issues from a Vatican office." This harmed church authority, he said, because, "when people are given the impression that everything is infallible, there comes a point when they conclude that nothing is infallible."[542]

• • •

When confusion got out of hand at Carmel, Thérèse's "little way" of spirituality was a tonic for weary minds. She had a way of seeing salvation in little things, indeed seemingly trifling things. As one of her biographers wrote: "Thérèse took what she knew, and as it happened to be what millions of other people also knew, it supplied a very usefully intelligible link between common humanity and the higher revelation."[543] But that "intelligible link" would be established only through her writing, distributed after her death. In the convent, she was frequently looked down upon by the other, more sophisticated nuns, who did not understand Thérèse's insistence that "complicated methods are no use to simple souls."[544]

The spiritual path was not always clear to Thérèse. In her autobiography, she complained about her recurring "scruples,"[545] which she had absorbed from her mother and father, and she wondered whether she might have been altogether mistaken in her vocation. She did not enjoy any certainty about it, but only an expansive hope. By letting her faith be tempted, she said, God greatly increased her "spirit of faith." This same spirit of faith allowed her to see God's will through the guidance of her superiors. "How happy simple nuns are! The will of their superiors is their only compass and so they are always certain of traveling in the right direction. They can never feel mistaken, even if they are certain their superiors are wrong."[546]

❧ Chapter 20 ❦

Due to God and Neighbor

"FROM INTER INSIGNIORES TO ORDINATIO SACERDOTALIS"
Congregation for the Doctrine of the Faith
and United States Catholic Conference
March 1998

"FROM WORDS TO DEEDS"
United States Catholic Conference
October 1998

"TEN FREQUENTLY ASKED QUESTIONS"
National Conference of Catholic Bishops (U.S.A.)
November 1998

In an effort to fulfill their duty of transmitting and enforcing the teaching on male priesthood, the U.S. bishops published From "Inter Insigniores" to "Ordinatio Sacerdotalis": Documents and Commentaries.[547] Published jointly in the spring of 1998 by the Congregation for the Doctrine of the Faith (CDF) and the American bishops' umbrella organization, the United States Catholic Conference (USCC), this 206-page paperback[548] offered the full texts of both documents, with commentaries and remarks by Vatican curial members as well as conservative theologians and bishops, including a theologian greatly admired by John Paul II, Hans Urs von Balthasar.

Congregation for the Doctrine of the Faith prefect Cardinal Joseph Ratzinger wrote that Pope John Paul II had not proclaimed a new doctrine by banning women priests; rather, he was "simply confirming what the whole Church" had "always known."[549] Six years earlier, in 1992, canon lawyer Ladislas Örsy had addressed the scenario that Ratzinger now described. When interpreting existing laws, Örsy said, if "the fact of evolution is not recognized," or if an evolving interpretation "is disapproved" by people judging it, then administrators and interpreters "will often go to extraordinary (and inordinate) lengths to explain that there is *nothing new* in their interpretation, that they are merely proclaiming a meaning which was there, unchanged, ever since the [original] promulgation" of the law. Eventually, this claim would "bring the law into bad repute and, more seriously, widen the gap between law and life."[550]

128

Ratzinger wrote that priestly ministry had its origins in "the twelve men" appointed to represent Christ as "icons of the Lord." But "anthropological upheavals of our day" along with the idea that "the mystery of origin" constituted "discrimination against half of humanity" had brought into question "the previously undisputed certitude concerning the will of Christ in instituting the Church."[551] In his zeal to defend the male priesthood, Ratzinger used selective history, internal contradiction, and remarkably pejorative language; but, as always, he made his point. The priesthood, he said, began with twelve men who outwardly resembled Christ. Modern society, however, considered women to be equal rather than subordinate to men, and since many Christians were turning attention to the first, more egalitarian creation story (Gen. 1:26–27, in which women and men were created simultaneously) rather than the second, subordinationist story (Gen. 2:18–25, in which Eve was created from Adam's rib to be his helper), the "previously undisputed certitude concerning the will of Christ" was now in question.

Later in 1998, the American bishops published "From Words to Deeds: Continuing Reflections on the Role of Women in the Church,"[552] which made no mention of *Inter Insigniores* or *Ordinatio Sacerdotalis*. It addressed issues of the laity's "gifts" and women's appointments to church leadership positions, saying that lay women and men could "cooperate" (if not share) in the "power of governance." The booklet presented a detailed look at ways in which women could participate in "alternative" leadership roles of church leadership, with practical and pastoral suggestions for implementation.[553]

One month later, the American bishops published a pamphlet called "Ten Frequently Asked Questions about the Reservation of Priestly Ordination to Men," saying "no one could take up the task of being a laborer in the harvest without being sent by the Lord," because the ministerial priesthood was "nothing less than Christ's gift to us, his priestly people."[554] Unlike much Vatican language, words like "laborer" and "harvest" were familiar to the laity, and the bishops could present the teaching of *Ordinatio Sacerdotalis* more easily by using this familiar language to explain:

- no one could take up the task of being a laborer (priest) in the harvest without being called by the Lord;

- the pope had said that women were not called by the Lord;

- hence, women could not be laborers in the harvest.

Public response to this publication was negligible, but the bishops had at least put the issue into a more accessible (if not more persuasive) language to explain what many Catholics complained was inexplicable in any language. The bishops reaffirmed John Paul II's claim that the church had no authority to ordain women and Ratzinger's claim that this teaching was to be held as "belonging to the deposit of faith."[555] Since it had been a year since Ratzinger had reportedly clarified the *Responsum*'s claim that male priesthood belonged to the deposit of faith, the bishops' inclusion of this claim revealed the continuing confusion surrounding it.

Addressing widespread criticism that the male priesthood was unjust, the American bishops wrote: "No one has a right by baptism to ordination."[556] They supported this claim with a logical definition oddly absent from Vatican documents: the catechism's definition of justice as giving what is "due to God and neighbor."[557] Withholding ordination from anyone could not be equated with denying justice ("due to God and neighbor") because no one had a right to ordination in the first place. John Paul II had said many times that the male priesthood was not unjust, but in his major publications he had not explicitly used the catechism's definition of justice to support his claim.

The bishops' three booklets comprised a set of works written for three distinct readerships: *From "Inter Insigniores" to "Ordinatio Sacerdotalis"* for persons with the time, ability, and motivation to read original Vatican texts; "From Words to Deeds" for those in search of ways to expand pastoral duties to include women; and "Ten Frequently Asked Questions" for Catholics in search of brief, official answers. The bishops had fulfilled their duty in a credible, understandable manner, yet support for women's ordination continued to grow.

• • •

Thérèse's first calling was to be a priest, and she prayed unceasingly for priests. She did not underestimate, however, her own power to save souls, a power that was her lifelong concern. In a letter she wrote:

> One day I was pondering over what I could do to save souls; a phrase from the Gospel showed me a clear light; Jesus said to His disciples, pointing to the fields of ripe corn: "Lift up your eyes and see the countries. For they are white already to harvest," and a little later, "The harvest indeed is great, but the laborers are few. Pray ye therefore the Lord of the harvest that He send forth laborers." How mysterious it is! Is not Jesus all powerful? [Why] then does Jesus say: "Pray ye the Lord of the Harvest that He send forth laborers . . . ?" Surely because Jesus has so incomprehensible a love for us, that He wants us to have a share with Him in the salvation of souls. He wants to do nothing without us.[558]

At this point, Thérèse revealed her ongoing search for ways to believe that her call to priesthood could be lived alternatively as a nun:

> Is not the apostolate of prayer lifted higher, so to speak, than the apostolate of preaching? Our mission, as Carmelites, is to form those Gospel laborers; they will save millions of souls, whose mothers we shall be. . . . What have priests that we need envy![559]

Chapter 21

Defending the Faith

AD TUENDAM FIDEM
("To Defend the Faith")
Pope John Paul II
June 30, 1998

"COMMENTARY ON THE PROFESSION OF FAITH'S
CONCLUDING PARAGRAPHS"
Cardinal Joseph Ratzinger
June 30, 1998

In *Ordinatio Sacerdotalis* ("On Reserving Priestly Ordination to Men Alone," 1994), Pope John Paul II had declared the male priesthood to be "definitive" teaching, but its "infallible character" and uncertain entry into the deposit of faith had been declared only in a commentary written by a curial congregation (the CDF) with no authority whatsoever to declare a teaching infallible. Now, *Ad Tuendam Fidem* ("To Defend the Faith") provided bishops with a legal instrument to enforce the teaching's reception by the world's Catholics.

Ad Tuendam Fidem was an apostolic letter, issued *motu proprio* (on the pope's own initiative) "to protect the Catholic faith against errors,"[560] especially from theologians and bishops in the United States and other Western countries who questioned papal teaching. As was becoming the norm, the letter was not made available to bishops in advance of its official release. John Paul II strongly warned the world's Catholic bishops that it was their duty to enforce the teaching, and this time he provided for punishment of Catholics who failed to give full assent to "definitively proposed" teachings. But in order to facilitate this punishment, the pope first needed to make some changes in canon law.

Defending the Faith

First, John Paul II modified canon 1371, which provided for a "just penalty" against anyone who: taught a doctrine condemned by the pope or an ecumenical council; failed to place "divine and catholic faith" in truths contained in the word of God and proposed as divinely revealed; refused to make a retraction after having been warned by Rome or the local bishop; or did not "otherwise comply" with directives from Rome, a bishop, or a religious superior. To put teeth into the "just penalty" clause, the pope amended this canon to reference another, canon 750, which bound all Catholics to the deposit of faith. To canon 750, then, he added a paragraph instituting the penalty against dissenters:

> Each and every proposition stated definitively by the magisterium of the church concerning the doctrine of the faith or morals, that is, each and every proposition required for the sacred preservation and faithful explanation of the same deposit of faith, must also be firmly embraced and maintained; anyone, therefore, who rejects those propositions which are to be held definitively is opposed to the doctrine of the Catholic Church (§11).

This papal amendment of canon law, especially when the Code of Canon Law had undergone major revision only fifteen years earlier, was highly unusual (Francis Sullivan said the pope filled "a loophole" in the law[561]). The pope's actions suggested that his escalating view of orthodoxy was being seriously challenged. Insofar as orthodoxy requires enforcement, it would not be long before Rome would have occasion to use this new provision for punishment.

A brief look at the Vatican's "Profession of Faith" is necessary to understand what John Paul II accomplished nearly a decade later with *Ad Tuendam Fidem.* In 1989, the Congregation for the Doctrine of the Faith had issued a *professio fidei* ("profession of faith") to be made by persons holding certain church teaching and leadership offices. More straightforwardly, this profession of faith was a loyalty oath. Replacing a 1967 profession requiring Catholics to believe only those truths that were "divinely revealed," the 1989 profession greatly broadened the beliefs falling into that category.[562] It outlined three types of church teaching and the response owed to each:

- everything divinely revealed and infallibly taught required an *"assent of faith"*;
- Catholics were to "firmly accept and hold" what was *"definitively proposed"*; and
- noninfallible but "authoritative" teachings required *"submission of intellect and will."*[563]

The 1983 Code of Canon Law had provided penalties for infractions against the first (assent of faith) and third (submission of intellect and will) categories, but it said nothing about the new, "definitively proposed" category. In 1998, *Ad Tuendam Fidem* amended canon law to provide penalties for failing to "firmly accept and hold" any "definitively proposed" teaching.

"Second-Order Truths"

Ad Tuendam Fidem contained the strongest and arguably the most complex language yet used by the pontiff to ensure compliance to Vatican directives. Theologian Richard Gaillardetz argued, with others, that the action reflected "a significant expansion of the category of church teaching that we are calling definitive doctrine." Rather than ground his teaching in solemn definitions made by a pope or a world council, John Paul II had conflated "definitive" teaching and "infallibility," claiming that certain teachings currently being declared "definitive" had "*already been taught infallibly* by the whole college of bishops." That is, the bishops and pope had "been in agreement for a significant period in the history of the Church that these teachings must be held as definitive."[564] This meant that, according to the 1989 profession's new category of truth, the status quo could constitute "definitive" teaching.

Gaillardetz also pointed out that Vatican I and Vatican II had understood the safeguarding of the deposit of faith in narrower terms, as teachings "required" to safeguard the *depositum* and to faithfully expound the teaching. Pope John Paul II and Cardinal Joseph Ratzinger, however, considerably broadened this scope to include teachings that were "merely *connected to divine revelation* by 'logical' or 'historical necessity.'" This greatly expanded the range of definitive doctrine itself, because there were "many teachings which might have a historical or logical connection to revelation" but that were "not, strictly speaking, *necessary for safeguarding revelation.*"[565]

Truths merely "connected" to revelation were called "second-order" (or secondary) truths, which, Ratzinger said, need only be "supportive of the fabric of revelation." In early 1997, in a little-noted news conference later treated in the *National Catholic Reporter,* Ratzinger maintained that claiming women could be ordained was not heresy, because the male-only priesthood *did not belong* to the deposit of faith, but was rather a second-order truth connected to (not required for) the deposit of faith. He said the 1995 *Responsum ad Dubium,* which called the ban on women priests "infallible" teaching, really meant to say that the ban belonged to the "second level" of truth, which he described as a truth "not formally revealed" and not required, but so connected to revelation that to deny a second-order truth would destroy "the fabric of revelation."

Nevertheless, the secondary truth of male priesthood was still infallible. The *National Catholic Reporter* called this a shift away from "revealed, primary truth" toward "the murky, more imponderable and probably more impenetrable fortress of 'secondary truth.'"[566]

A Commentary

Accompanying *Ad Tuendam Fidem* ("To Defend the Faith") was a document entitled, "Commentary on the Profession of Faith's Concluding Paragraphs," by CDF prefect Cardinal Joseph Ratzinger,[567] who was also the president of the Pontifical Biblical Commission and the International Theological Commission, both of which had weekly meetings with CDF officials.[568] In other words, Ratzinger's pronouncements carried much weight. His commentary was many times the length of (and went far beyond) *Ad Tuendam Fidem,* saying that anyone who denied a definitively proposed doctrine would "no longer be in full communion with the Catholic Church."[569]

The "Commentary on the Profession" quoted *Lumen Gentium* ("Dogmatic Constitution on the Church," 1964), saying Catholic bishops were "endowed with the authority of Christ," and that "with the Roman pontiff they exercise supreme and full power over all the church, although this power cannot be exercised without the consent of the Roman pontiff."[570] Scholars acknowledged that while canon law allowed for curial *participation* in papal governance of the church, the pope's teaching authority could not be *delegated* to the curia, an administrative body:

> [The *Suprema potestas* ("supreme power") is] given to the college of bishops and its head, the bishop of Rome. This supreme power and authority to teach the faith resides with the college (and its head) alone. According to Roman Catholic ecclesiology, the Roman curia in general, and the Congregation for the Doctrine of the Faith in particular, plays only an auxiliary role in assisting the bishops in the exercise of this *suprema potestas*. However, the growing proliferation of doctrinal statements, clarifications and instructions issued *to* the bishops *from* the curia risks giving the impression that it is the CDF rather than the college of bishops who is the subject of supreme teaching authority.[571]

This situation recalled Joan Chittister's question in 1995: "Has there been a palace coup and someone forgot to tell us about it? Is the pope's name John Paul II or Joseph Ratzinger?"[572]

Ratzinger now maintained that the 1989 Profession of Faith had been written to "better distinguish the order of the truths to which the believer adheres."[573] To help the faithful better understand "second-order" truths requiring definitive assent, he provided four examples of actions condemned by the church: fornication, prostitution, euthanasia, and women's ordination.[574]

He further explained that for a doctrine to be either believed as divinely revealed or definitively held, it must apply to "an act which is either defining or nondefining."[575] A "defining" act of teaching concerned a truth solemnly defined by an *ex cathedra* pronouncement (of the pope alone). A "nondefining" act concerned a truth taught infallibly by the ordinary universal magisterium (the world's bishops, with the pope). The pope could confirm a nondefining doctrine even without recourse to a solemn definition by declaring explicitly that it belonged to the teaching of the "ordinary and universal magisterium" as a truth divinely revealed or a truth of Catholic doctrine.

> Consequently, when there has not been a judgment on a doctrine in the solemn form of a definition, but this doctrine, belonging to the inheritance of the *depositum fidei*, is taught by the ordinary and universal magisterium, which necessarily includes the pope, such a doctrine is to be understood as having been set forth infallibly. The declaration of confirmation or reaffirmation by the Roman pontiff in this case is not a new dogmatic definition, but a formal attestation of a truth already possessed and infallibly transmitted by the church.[576]

This position especially included Rome's teaching on women's ordination. The claim that a doctrine that belonged to the *depositum fidei* ("deposit of faith") and was taught by the "ordinary and universal magisterium" (the pope and bishops) was *"to be understood as having been set forth infallibly"* carried a footnote that was stated in such densely technical language that it was sure to have a limited audience:

It should be noted that the infallible teaching of the ordinary and universal magisterium is not only set forth with an *explicit declaration* of a doctrine to be believed or held definitively, but is also expressed by a doctrine *implicitly contained* in a practice of the church's faith, derived from revelation or, in any case, necessary for eternal salvation and attested to by the uninterrupted tradition: Such an infallible teaching is thus objectively set forth by the whole episcopal body, understood in a diachronic and not necessarily merely synchronic sense. Furthermore, the intention of the ordinary and universal magisterium to set forth a doctrine as definitive is not generally linked to technical formulations of particular solemnity; it is enough that this be clear *from the tenor of the words used and from their context.*[577]

In this paragraph, the world's bishops, with the pope, objectively set forth infallible doctrine by means of:

- an *explicit* declaration of a doctrine to be definitively held;

- a doctrine *implicit* in church practice derived from revelation or necessary for salvation;

- the *tone and context* of their words.

Finally, this setting forth of doctrine took place according to a "diachronic" perspective allowing multiple phenomena to influence each other while changing over time.

In short, a doctrine — even if only "*implicitly* contained" in tradition — could be declared "definitive" according to the "tenor of the words used" and "their context," and later isolated and declared infallible. This teaching reserved seemingly unlimited power to Rome.

[The] supreme pontiff, while not wishing to proceed to a dogmatic definition, intended to reaffirm that this doctrine [of male-only priesthood] is to be held definitively, since, founded on the written word of God, constantly preserved and applied in the tradition of the church, it has been set forth infallibly by the ordinary and universal magisterium.[578]

This paragraph made four crucial claims:

- the pope did not wish to proceed *to a dogmatic definition*, but the teaching was infallible because it was taught by the world's bishops and the pope;

- the doctrine *was to be held definitively*;

- the teaching was *founded on the written word of God* and *constantly preserved*; and

- the teaching had been *set forth infallibly* by the *ordinary and universal magisterium*.

Despite the facts that the world's theologians questioned the unfolding definition of a "definitively held" doctrine, that the Bible mentioned no ordained priesthood, and that the world's bishops disagreed on the matter, Ratzinger said there was a possibility that "in the future the consciousness of the church might progress to the point where this teaching could be defined as a doctrine to be believed *as divinely revealed.*"[579]

Whirling Away in a Void

After publication of the "Commentary on the Profession of Faith's Concluding Paragraphs," relations grew strained all around. Adding to the tension was the fact that Ratzinger had released this document — which also confirmed the centuries-old Roman Catholic position that Anglican orders are "invalid" — less than three weeks before the Lambeth Conference, the worldwide meeting of Anglican bishops held every ten years in Canterbury. He had given Catholic cardinal Basil Hume of Westminster no advance warning that the document would appear virtually on the doorsteps of the Anglican bishops surrounding him, leaving Hume knowing nothing more about it than his Anglican counterparts.[580]

The relationship between John Paul II and many of the world's bishops grew even more strained as the Vatican continued issuing documents without the bishops' input. It was well known, even among the laity, that priests supporting women's ordination would not be made bishops; in fact, American bishops were to "give proof of [their] pastoral ability and leadership by withdrawing all support from individuals or groups who ... promote the ordination of women to the priesthood."[581] The gap between hierarchy and laity was widening, and papal threats of punishment suggested that Rome was increasingly out of touch with the beliefs and pastoral needs of Catholics in the pews. Papal observer Peter Hebblethwaite commented that despite the "voluminous flow of encyclicals and instructions," the pontificate was "to some extent whirling away in a void, cut off from the real life of the People of God."[582] Ecclesiologist George B. Wilson wrote that the church's traditional "parent-child educational model" ignored the vast changes in global communications that facilitated *"a never-ending worldwide conversation."* Moreover, he said, the laity were perfectly capable of comprehending church teaching that *made sense,* and of recognizing when *it didn't*: "Even the untutored lay person can smell the presence of theological obfuscation in the blah-blahing of ecclesiastical puffballs."[583]

A Burning Issue

During the summer of 1998, Sister Lavinia Byrne, a member of the Institute of the Blessed Virgin Mary (IBVM) in England, learned that thirteen hundred copies of her 1994 book, *Woman at the Altar: The Ordination of Women in the Roman Catholic Church,*[584] had been burned by the Liturgical Press, owned by the Order of St. Benedict at St. John's Abbey in Collegeville, Minnesota.[585] The book had been completed and sent to the publisher months before the release of *Ordinatio Sacerdotalis,* but Byrne had worked with the publisher to include the pope's apostolic letter in the back of her book just before its publication. In her introduction, she wrote:

> I completed this book early in 1994 and it was already being [type]set before the publication of the Apostolic Letter of His Holiness Pope John Paul II on Reserving Priestly Ordination to Men Alone [*Ordinatio Sacerdotalis,* 1994]. In [this] event the publishers have kindly agreed to carry the full text of this letter as an appendix.[586]

Despite this gesture, the Vatican opened an investigation of Byrne and warned Liturgical Press against selling her books, which resulted in the book burning.

The situation took its toll on the nun, who as a regular contributor to BBC Radio 4 told listeners: "You can go to a rape therapist or a grief counselor, but there aren't too many book-burning counselors around."[587] That same year, 1998, Continuum in New York released another edition of the book, whose back cover announced in bold black letters: "Banned by the Vatican." Rome eventually dropped its investigation.

• • •

In 1898, The Story of a Soul *was printed and distributed to Carmelite convents in* Europe. *The nuns of Lisieux, including Thérèse's beloved blood sister, Pauline, had heavily edited the young nun's work, deleting or rewriting passages in order to render the story more suitable for a saint (for they were sure she would be one). Thérèse had written from the confines of her sickbed, where tubercular fits sometimes made it difficult for her to edit her writing for political correctness. One day, surrounded by visitors, Thérèse complained in her journal that the visitors sat around her bed like* "a string of onions."[588] *It was this sort of candid observation that Pauline edited out, inserting flowery phrases that were expected of nineteenth-century nuns.*

The "edited" Thérèse *was sickeningly sweet. Everyone and everything around her was* "little" *and* "darling," *and her sentences fairly gushed off the page. One biographer called this writing,* "... infuriating ... nauseating ... sugary ... namby pamby, silly."[589] *And it was. Adding to the syrupy image were relatives and contemporaries of Thérèse who understandably wished to further the cause of her sainthood, a process that began almost immediately after Thérèse's death. One of her teachers described her as a young girl:*

> Her manners were sweet and amiable, her spirit of devotion very deep, her sense of duty meticulous, her aversion to boisterous games and large crowds very marked.... She was obedient, showing a minute fidelity to the smallest detail of the rules, alarmed with even the semblance of a fault, sometimes to the extent of giving the appearance of being over-scrupulous.[590]

Such language may have appealed to early twentieth-century Catholics, but as the century unfolded Thérèse's flowery prose sounded sadly out of date. In the irony that belongs to authentic spirituality, it was in order to attract a modern generation of readers that Thérèse's original words were restored. The restoration revealed the real Thérèse, whose mother had once said: "She flings herself into the most dreadful rages when things don't go as she wants them. She rolls on the ground as if she's given up hope of anything ever being right again. Sometimes she's so overcome that she chokes."[591]

Whether saintly, sassy, or both, Thérèse was her own person with a vocation from God. Once her autobiography was restored and her own voice allowed to speak, the Catholic world recovered a saint for the twenty-first century, a Doctor of the Church who felt God's call to be a priest, a call denied her because of her sex.

Chapter 22

Father God and Mother Church

"ADDRESS OF THE HOLY FATHER
TO THE GERMAN BISHOPS"*
Pope John Paul II
November 20, 1999

Perhaps nowhere did Pope John Paul II more vehemently assert the ban on women's ordination than in a text written for his address to the German bishops during their 1999 *ad limina* visit,[592] a regular visit to Rome every five years during which bishops deliver detailed reports on their dioceses. The pope's language in this letter was extraordinary for two reasons. First, his customarily even-tempered prose was replaced by strongly defensive language. Second, he took one of his sharpest turns yet to refocus his ongoing attempt to quell the debate on women's ordination.

This time, he included a lesson on the rarely mentioned relationship between "Father God" and "Mother Church." Priests were not only "fathers" of their flocks but also exercised the church's *maternal* authority, submission to which was required for one's salvation:

> *Mater* is also *Magister*; she has the authority to bring up and teach her children, and so lead them to salvation. Mother Church gives birth to her sons and daughters; she nurtures and educates them. She gathers her children together and sends them out, all the while assuring them that they are *safe in her motherly bosom*. At the same time she is saddened by those who have fallen away and holds the door open to reconciliation, which is her constant concern. You Pastors have a particular responsibility in this regard: *as "fathers of your communities," you have the right and duty to exercise the Church's "maternal authority . . ."* (§10). The Church's sons and daughters must respond to her motherly affection with heartfelt obedience. . . . Only those who heed Mother Church obey God the Father. . . . *Whatever forsakes its mother's womb can neither live nor breathe on its own, but loses the possibility of salvation* (§11).[593]

Clerical appropriation of a father's authority was familiar, but assumption of a *mother's* duties was less so. According to this paragraph, priests were both father *and* mother. Priests, the pope wrote, were members of the Body of the Church (the "bride," the "body" of Christ responsible for giving birth to the church) who at *the same time* represented Christ its head (the "bridegroom"). Accordingly,

---

*The document is included in the appendix, p. 226.

priests could exercise the church's "maternal authority" by virtue of their power as "fathers" of their communities, leaving the laity with no authority, real or metaphorical.

Further, obedience to Mother Church was required for salvation. Since priests represented the fatherhood of the Catholic community *and* the church's maternal authority, disobedience would deprive the believer of salvation. On the eve of the twenty-first century, this reservation of *all* the church's active roles and authority to priests alone — at risk of eternal damnation — seemed backward-looking.

Infallible, Definitive, Absolute

John Paul II had often warned against blurring the distinction between laity and clergy, a transgression he charged the German church with making. Now, he let the German bishops know he was watching. "In your land, there is growing discontent with the Church's attitude towards the role of women," he said, adding that in pursuit of women's rights too little consideration was given to the difference between human rights in the world and divine rights in the church — rights that were essentially different. The German bishops had the duty to "encourage that open and clear dialogue in truth and love which Mother Church must foster regarding the future of her daughters." This "dialogue," however, could in fact move in only one direction: John Paul II reminded the bishops that the male priesthood carried "the character of infallibility" and was "to be held definitively and absolutely" by all the faithful, especially the daughters. Then, he leveled a warning: "We should stop at nothing, if necessary, to dispel confusion and correct errors" (§10).

• • •

As novice mistress at Carmel "Thérèse sometimes amused herself by testing the obedience of her nuns with ludicrous orders to see how far she could go without her authority being questioned."[594] *Still, she realized that the virtue of obedience had its limits. Stories about naïve souls unquestioningly following orders were common inside the convent, like the one about the prioress who told a novice to go soak her head in the nearest well and meditate on her sins, and who then had to chase after the girl to keep her from jumping in head first.*

→ Chapter 23 ←

Women's Deeper Nature
Includes Saying "No"

**"MESSAGE OF THE HOLY FATHER TO THE
WORLD UNION OF CATHOLIC WOMEN'S ORGANIZATIONS"***
John Paul II
March 7, 2001

**FIRST INTERNATIONAL CONFERENCE,
WOMEN'S ORDINATION WORLDWIDE**
June 2001

In his 2001 message to the General Assembly of the World Union of Catholic Women's Organizations in Rome,[595] John Paul II strongly reiterated his convictions regarding women's role in the divine plan. Concerned with the implications of women's "deeper nature," he encouraged the delegates to "thank God for all that being a woman signifies in the divine plan, and to ask his help in overcoming the many obstacles which still hinder full recognition of the dignity and mission of women in society and within the ecclesial community." Women had shown "clear-mindedness and courage" to achieve freedom of decision in many public roles, thereby expressing their "characteristic genius" (§2).

Application of the word "genius" to women had become commonplace in John Paul II's documents and speeches, and he used it in this message many times. Neither here nor elsewhere did he ever define exactly what he meant, but in context his allusions to women's "genius" pointed to motherhood and women's ability to domesticate family and society. "In the family and in society you work for the sanctification of the world from within," he said (§5). Exploring the task of domesticity inside and outside the home, the pontiff used numerous evocative words and phrases to describe women's roles according to their feminine "genius," "specific charism," "unique gifts," and "feminine holiness" indispensable to the church:

> In the hierarchy of holiness *it is precisely the "woman,"* Mary of Nazareth, who is the "figure" of the Church. Women who live in holiness are a model of the *"sequela*

---

*The document is included in the appendix, p. 232.

140

Christi" [the following of Christ], an example of how the Bride must respond with love to the love of the Bridegroom (§3).[596]

Through the concept of *sequela Christi* women could "follow" Christ, who was modeled by priests.

Catholic women honored God's name through a "fruitful" role in "transmitting the genuine sense of the faith." The church's presence and action in the new millennium would become manifest in woman's capacity, like that of Mary, to "receive and keep God's word." By virtue of her "specific charism," or divinely endowed capacity, woman was "uniquely gifted" in the task of passing on "the Christian message and mystery in the family and in the world of work, study and leisure" (§4).

Among John Paul II's list of spheres in which women could transmit the Christian message — family, work, study, and leisure — the church again was absent, even as the call for women priests was growing in the United States, Germany, Austria, Brazil, Britain, Ireland, and many other countries. The pope must have known by now that within months a full-fledged and very public (if invalid) ordination would take place on the Danube River that would grab the attention of the world's Catholics.

Women's Ordination Worldwide

Less than four months later, in June 2001, the first international conference of Women's Ordination Worldwide (WOW), held in Dublin, largely dispelled the notion that the women's ordination issue was limited to the United States. Attending were 1,370 participants from Australia, Austria, Denmark, England, France, Germany, Ghana, Holland, Hungary, India, Ireland, Japan, Kenya, Mexico, Pakistan, Portugal, Scotland, South Africa, Spain, Sri Lanka, Switzerland, Uganda, and the United States.[597] The group's mission was to promote "ordination of Roman Catholic women to a renewed priestly ministry in a democratic church, and to stand in solidarity with women who are ordained in the ongoing renewal of the church."[598] The group's use of "renewed," "democratic," and "solidarity," went further than earlier statements by national groups in saying *when* women would be ordained, and *by whom*. Attaining women's ordination *within* the existing Catholic hierarchy was important, but not necessarily first on the agenda.

The hierarchy was paying attention to the preparations for the Dublin conference. Best-selling author and international lecturer Joan Chittister was ordered by the Vatican to refrain from addressing or even attending the conference. Her prioress at Mount Saint Benedict Monastery in Erie, Pennsylvania, Sister Christine Vladimiroff, traveled to Rome to discuss the issue with church officials. Vladimiroff later released a statement explaining why she felt called to refuse the Vatican's order to prohibit Chittister from attending the conference:

> There is a fundamental difference in the understanding of obedience in the monastic tradition and that which is being used by the Vatican. Benedictine authority and

obedience are achieved *through dialogue* between a member and her prioress in a spirit of co-responsibility, *always in the context of community.*[599]

According to Vladimiroff, Chittister's participation was not "a source of scandal to the faithful" as Rome claimed, but rather it was the faithful who were "scandalized when honest attempts to discuss questions of import to the church are forbidden."[600] A Benedictine nun for fifty years and author of more than twenty books, Chittister told the press, "I did not do this in defiance of the church. I did this because the best history of the church is in discussion. *To suppress discussion is a sin against the Holy Spirit.*"[601] Suppression of discussion, she pointed out, had not worked with *Humanae Vitae* ("On the Regulation of Birth," 1968), Pope Paul VI's widely rejected encyclical banning contraception. "What was bad for the church was not discussion but the oppression of ideas, the silencing of people."[602]

In a letter to John Paul II, 127 of the 128 nuns at Mount Saint Benedict signed their support for Chittister. Some did so from wheelchairs. Among the younger nuns, thirty-five signed a statement requesting the Vatican to also give them any punishment meted out to Chittister.[603] This overwhelming support accompanied Chittister to the conference in Dublin, where she (and her Benedictine community) received a sustained standing ovation. She told participants that her fifteen-hundred-year-old religious order had survived world wars, plagues, and persecutions: "We won't let a little letter from Rome get us down."[604]

Notre Dame de Namur Sister Myra Poole of London, a nun for forty-two years and a major organizer for the Women's Ordination Worldwide conference, also received a Vatican order, through her religious superior, to absent herself from the conference under threat of dismissal from her religious order. At first, she withdrew from the conference in obedience, but her conscience won out and she "slipped quietly into the hall towards the end of Saturday afternoon's business [during] a panel discussion with women from developing countries, for whom she had raised the funds to be present."[605]

After the conference, a Vatican spokesman announced that Chittister and Poole would not be punished,[606] a gesture which, like the one following the burning of Lavinia Byrne's book, was surely designed to spare Rome further public scrutiny.

One conference speaker, however, did stay away. The representative of the World Council of Churches (WCC), Aruna Gnanadason, did not attend because, according to conference organizers, the WCC did not want to interfere in the internal affairs of the Roman Catholic Church. However, conference organizer Soline Vatinel told the *Irish Times*, "The unofficial reason was that the Vatican said it would withdraw from commissions involving the WCC if Ms. Gnanadason spoke at the conference."[607]

The international conference yielded eleven resolutions supporting women's ordination, including calls for:

- the pope to revoke the ban on debate;

- the restoration of the diaconate to women, according to the practice in the early church;

- ministers to adapt liturgical language and images to reflect the equal dignity of women and men; and

- member groups to create avenues of financial support for persons losing employment in the church because of their support for the ordination of women.[608]

One resolution narrowly missed the 60 percent approval required by the conference. That resolution would have redirected contributions to Peter's Pence (an annual, worldwide collection for the maintenance of the Vatican) away from Rome to organizations supporting women's ordination. Although approved by a majority of participants, the failure of this resolution suggested the reluctance of many participants to further the cause of women's ordination at the expense of the institutional church, and it hinted at the as yet subterranean fault line separating those who supported enduring fidelity to the church from those increasingly willing to make changes with or without the blessing of Rome.

• • •

Thérèse of Lisieux knew about being told "No." The Carmelite nuns had said "No" when she first asked to join the convent. The Catholic Church said "No" to her desire to be a priest. Even her faith frequently said "No."

As soon as she entered the convent, Thérèse was haunted by the sense of being abandoned by God. There was even a time when she questioned the existence of heaven. An early biographer wrote that she "experienced no ecstasies, raptures, supernatural communications, or interior consolations, but most of the time even had no sense of God's presence."[609]

Another biographer said there was "no originality in her thought, no ambition in her behavior beyond that supreme ambition, astounding in its audacity, its simplicity, and its execution, to add herself to the Communion of Saints." Throughout her physical and emotional suffering, Thérèse discovered a path to God that required nothing more than "doing the tiniest thing right, and doing it for love." It was a vocation that could be realized right here, right now.[610] She had discovered the secret to a successful practice of Christianity: "not to do extraordinary things, but to do ordinary things extraordinarily well."[611]

Perhaps the ordinary thing Thérèse did best was to suffer. A recent biographer, Monica Furlong, remarked on Thérèse's childhood inability to find acceptance among her peers, the very early death of her mother, the entrance of her older sisters into Carmel — repeated experiences of rejection and loss. If suffering was "embraced instead of avoided," however, some of the sting could be taken out of it. Further, if it were true that one's suffering could bring God's love to others by actually bearing the pain in their place ("substitutive suffering"), the "imitation of Jesus bearing the sin and suffering of the world upon the cross" could sanctify the sufferer. At Carmel, where black-painted letters above the doors read, "To suffer and to die,"[612] Thérèse "found a pathway through the insoluble problem of being helpless."[613]

⇒ Chapter 24 ⇐

A Warning, a Decree,
an Excommunication

"WARNING REGARDING THE ATTEMPTED
PRIESTLY ORDINATION OF SOME CATHOLIC WOMEN"
Congregation for the Doctrine of the Faith
July 10, 2002

"DECREE OF EXCOMMUNICATION REGARDING THE ATTEMPTED
PRIESTLY ORDINATION OF SOME CATHOLIC WOMEN"
Congregation for the Doctrine of the Faith
August 5, 2002

"DECREE ON THE ATTEMPTED
PRIESTLY ORDINATION OF SOME CATHOLIC WOMEN"*
Congregation for the Doctrine of the Faith
December 21, 2002

By the turn of the twenty-first century, women's ordination supporters were expressing a new level of frustration that approached rebellion, evidenced by the illegal and very public ordinations of ten Catholic women in three years — one in 2001, seven in 2002, and two in 2003. The circumstances of these ordinations, however, were radically different.

Women Priests: From *Corpus* Christi to *Spiritus* Christi

In 1998, Bishop Matthew Clark directed Corpus Christi parish in Rochester, New York, to suspend its long-standing practice of encouraging broad lay participation in liturgical activities. According to *Time* magazine: "For years the Vatican peppered the Bishop of Rochester with complaints about Corpus Christi and probably made its feelings clear during his official visit to Rome" in 1998. Specifically, Clark asked Mary Ramerman, who had been appointed associate pastor by the pastor, James Callan, to desist from "priestly gestures" on the altar. She refused and was dismissed on October 15, 1998.[614]

---

*The three documents are included in the appendix, pp. 235, 236, and 237.

Eleven days before Christmas that year, in a move later called the "Monday Massacre," Clark fired six staff members with no severance pay or benefits. The following Sunday, mass attendance was down by two-thirds. Many parishioners had already held their own service, collecting more than $30,000 to help the fired employees and their families.[615]

Ramerman, a wife and mother with a master's degree in theology, had been in ministry for a quarter-century. After the bishop ordered her off the altar, she joined many ministers (including the recently removed Callan) and members from Corpus Christi ("Body of Christ") to form a new parish, Spiritus Christi ("Spirit of Christ"). The new parish joined the Ecumenical Catholic Communion (ECC), an international group of independent Catholic faith communities not under papal jurisdiction. The ECC offered the sacraments to all the faithful and extended priestly ordination to women and men, married and celibate.

One ECC member congregation, the Old Catholic Church, broke from Rome in 1889 to protest the First Vatican Council's 1870 declaration of papal infallibility. On November 17, 2001, a bishop of this church, California Bishop Peter Hickman, ordained Mary Ramerman. Roman Catholic bishop Matthew Clark called Ramerman's ordination a "formally schismatic act,"[616] but a long-time supporter of Ramerman, the Women's Ordination Conference, announced enthusiastic support for her ordination, adding that the ordination of Roman Catholic women through the Old Catholic Church, or other Christian communities, was "only a step toward our goal of reshaping and reforming the Roman Catholic Church" in which women could be "ordained to a renewed, and renewing Roman Catholic priestly ministry."[617] On February 22, 2003, Hickman ordained one of Ramerman's colleagues, long-time family minister Denise Donato, one of the Corpus Christi staff fired by Clark.

In August 2003, another woman made priestly vows — South African Dominican Sister Patricia Ann Fresen, a theologian with academic credentials from the Pontifical Institute in Rome and a professor at St. John Vianney Seminary in Pretoria. A nun for forty-four years, she was ordained at the Second European Women's Synod in Barcelona.[618] In a letter to supporters, Fresen explained that when she studied theology in Rome with male seminarians during the 1980s, she had been invited to many of their ordinations, causing "desire and anger" to alternate within her. After feeling called to priesthood for a quarter-century, she decided that the "only way to change an unjust law is to break it. We learned this lesson very well in South Africa during the apartheid years."[619]

The National Coalition of American Nuns (NCAN) wrote Fresen in January 2004, comparing her to Rosa Parks, the black woman whose refusal to give up her bus seat to a white man sparked the 1960s civil rights movement in the American South: "If she complied with the law, she would proclaim her second-class status and lose her self-respect. If she sat where she believed she belonged, she would incur the punishment [meted out to] those who broke the law." Further, the NCAN letter to Fresen said: "You could have chosen to remain in your prestigious and acceptable teaching position within the Church," but instead "you resolved to follow God's call to you."[620]

The ordinations of these three women — Ramerman, Donato, and Fresen — attracted wide attention, enthusiastic support, and bitter condemnation, but they were calm compared to the ordinations of seven women who would grab headlines and Rome's increasingly frustrated attention.

Germany 2002: Seven Women's Ordination

Ordinatio Sacerdotalis ("On Reserving Priestly Ordination to Men Alone," 1994), the *Responsum ad Dubium* ("Response to a Question Regarding *Ordinatio Sacerdotalis*," 1995), and *Ad Tuendam Fidem* ("To Defend the Faith," 1998) had been viewed by many Catholics as advancing the male-only priesthood to the status of "quasi-dogma,"[621] prompting theologians Iris Müller and Ida Raming of Germany to announce that a change in Rome's position was "not to be expected in the foreseeable future."[622]

Saying their call to ordination was rooted in their creation in the image of God and baptism in Jesus Christ, a small group of women from Austria, Germany, and the United States decided to proceed with what they acknowledged would be illegal ordinations.

> The women considered themselves to be "followers of Jesus who himself broke laws that had been installed by the hierarchical religious authorities of his time and religion. [Jesus possessed] the insight that human beings do not exist to abide by norms and laws that lack humanity, but that the laws of religion have to be for the service of humankind."[623]

Women wanting to live out their call to priesthood experienced a "grave conflict of conscience," wrote Müller and Raming. On the one hand, they faced the opposition of church leadership; on the other hand, they felt God's call to priestly service. With change nowhere in sight, the women chose the path of ordination *contra legem* ("against the law"). It was not they who decided to act *contra legem*, the women said; rather, the church leaders' intransigence had forced this act of defiance. Canon 1024, which said only males could be ordained, contained "a heresy that women in the Roman Catholic church are no longer willing to accept."[624]

The seven women were ordained June 29, 2002, aboard a chartered boat on the Danube River at the German-Austrian border.[625] The event attracted worldwide attention, both positive and negative. As had others before him, Italian Cardinal Joachim Meisner compared *a woman wanting to be a priest with a man wanting to give birth.*[626]

Ordaining the women was Argentinean Romulo Antonio Braschi, a Marist priest ordained in 1966 and excommunicated in the 1970s. He claimed to have been consecrated a bishop twice by Argentinean bishops — in 1998 by Bishop Roberto Padin and in 1999 by Bishop Geronimo Jose Podesta, who had been consecrated a bishop by Pope John XXIII and had later married. Podesta had consecrated Braschi (who also had married) "for the purpose of ordaining women to renew the priesthood."[627]

For the Danube ordinations, Braschi stood in at the last moment for the bishop originally scheduled to ordain the women, Dusan Spiner, who was delayed by heavy traffic. Spiner, who had ordained the women as deacons just weeks earlier on Palm Sunday, had been secretly consecrated a bishop in Communist-controlled Czechoslovakia by Bishop Felix Davidek, the same man who had ordained Ludmila Javorova in 1970. At the time of the Danube ordinations, Spiner enjoyed good standing with the Vatican as a practicing priest (although not as bishop). The various bishops' official standing with Rome, however, was irrelevant, because in no case could a bishop, no matter how orthodox his credentials, validly ordain a woman.

The ordination ceremony was attended by Roman Catholic priests, male and female Lutheran ministers, Old Catholic Church priests, and Islamic prayer leaders, all of whom participated in laying hands on the seven women. Also attending was Braschi's wife, "wearing liturgical vestments and carrying a crozier."[628] During the ceremony, Braschi said: "I am catholic but not Roman," and "I am not working in the name of the Roman Catholic Church."[629] Having said that, he ordained seven women:

- Dr. Iris Müller, Dr. Ida Raming, Dr. Gisela Forster, and Pia Brunner of Germany;

- Christine Mayr-Lumetzberger and Sister Adelinde Theresia Roitinger of Austria; and

- Angela White,[630] a pseudonym for Dagmar Braun Celeste of Cleveland, an Austrian by birth, former first lady of Ohio, and former board member of the Women's Ordination Conference.[631]

The Danube ordinations forced supporters of women's ordination to openly consider an issue that formerly had been discussed somewhat quietly. Should women wait to be ordained within the church? Or, in the absence of any sign of change, should women initiate an ordination process themselves? Both strategies had supporters.

The Women's Ordination Conference (WOC) issued press releases stating enthusiastic support for the Danube ordinations. During June, WOC had published an open letter in the *National Catholic Reporter*, sporting hundreds of signatures from across the United States, to Ludmila Javorova. "God's call to prophetic obedience will not be denied," the letter said. "You have gone before us, and . . . many more women will follow."[632] One WOC attendee released a statement concerning the Danube ordinations, saying the "American women present vowed that they will do the same action in the United States in the near future."[633]

Other women's ordination groups, however, including We Are Church in Austria, Church from Below in Germany, the New Wine movement in Britain, and the world's largest website for women's ordination, www.womenpriests.org, argued that women's ordination should take place within mainstream Catholicism. The debate among supporters over whether ordinations should take place immediately outside the church, or later inside the church, continued as Rome geared up for multiple excommunications.

A Warning Ignored

On July 10, 2002, the Congregation for the Doctrine of the Faith (CDF) issued, in several languages, a "Warning Regarding the Attempted Priestly Ordination of Some Catholic Women."[634] In order to "dispel any doubts which may have arisen" concerning the ordinations, Cardinal Ratzinger signed the document restating the claim of *Ordinatio Sacerdotalis* that "the Church has no authority whatsoever to confer priestly ordination on women." For this reason, any such ordination would constitute "the simulation of a sacrament and thus [would be] invalid and null, as well as constituting a grave offense to the divine constitution of the Church" (§2).

The CDF declared that because Braschi belonged to a schismatic religious community, the ordinations were a serious attack on the unity of the church, and such an attack constituted an affront to the "dignity of women," whose specific role in the Church and society was "distinctive and irreplaceable" (§2). The declaration gave "formal warning" that the women would incur excommunication if, within twelve days, they did not "(1) acknowledge the nullity of the 'orders' [ordination] received from a schismatic Bishop in contradiction to the definitive doctrine of the Church and (2) state their repentance and ask forgiveness for the scandal caused to the faithful" (§3).

The Women's Ordination Conference pointed out that the Code of Canon Law detailed "only nine offenses for which excommunication could be imposed — of which a woman receiving priestly ordination was not one."[635]

As promised, Rome issued its "Decree of Excommunication Regarding the Attempted Priestly Ordination of Some Catholic Women." In a one-sentence preface to this brief document, the CDF stated that by virtue of his schism Braschi had already incurred excommunication, and the women were guilty of a "most serious offense" that had "wounded" the church. Hence, they had incurred excommunication "reserved to the Apostolic See, with all the effects established by canon 1331 of the Code of Canon Law" (§§2–3).[636]

The women released a letter dated August 14, 2002, asking that the decree of excommunication be revoked on grounds that they had committed no offense legally punishable by excommunication, and that the male priesthood contradicted the very principles of Catholicism. On September 27, they filed for recourse against the decree, referencing canons §§1732–39.[637]

The CDF notified the women on October 21 that their request would be submitted to the appropriate authority. On December 21, Rome rendered a response in its "Decree on the Attempted Priestly Ordination of Some Catholic Women."[638] The CDF had reached a "collegial decision" to confirm the women's excommunication. Recourse was not possible, because the Decree of Excommunication had been issued by a Vatican agency acting "in the name of the Supreme Pontiff" (§4), against whom there was no recourse.

To "remove any doubt in the matter," the CDF underlined certain points:

- the women's excommunication was not a *latae sententiae* (a penalty incurred automatically at the time of the offense), but rather a *ferendae sententiae* penalty (given only after a warning);[639]

- the women's offense was of "particular gravity," because (1) the ordaining bishop was in schism, making the women "accomplices in schism"; (2) the women "formally and obstinately rejected a doctrine" that John Paul II had "definitively proposed," hence they deserved "a just penalty" pursuant to *Ad Tuendam Fidem*, n. 4; and (3) by denying this doctrine, the women failed "to recognize that the teachings of the Supreme Pontiff on doctrines to be held definitively by all the faithful are irreformable"; and

- the women's "open and divisive disobedience" to the pope and diocesan bishops made excommunication necessary in order "to protect true doctrine, to safeguard the communion and unity of the Church and to guide the consciences of the faithful" (§3).

In response, the excommunicated women charged Rome with making "grave errors" and showing "the spirit of the Inquisition." The male priesthood came not from God but rather had been "imposed upon women by men of the church."[640] The acrimonious connection between the Vatican and the seven women was thus severed. Excommunication of the seven women ordained on the Danube, said Sister Patricia Ann Fresen of South Africa, was "an unjust punishment for breaking an unjust law." Further, it carried a bitter irony. "They do not excommunicate child abusers, mass murderers, hijackers, or people who start wars."[641]

In July 2003 two of the excommunicated women, Christine Mayr-Lumetzberger and Gisela Forster, were consecrated as bishops. According to the Women's Ordination Conference, their consecrations "took place secretly and in the presence of a notary and eye-witnesses." The names of the ordaining bishops were "kept secret in order to avoid severe punishments by the Vatican." Although invalid, the ordinations meant that "apostolic succession [had] been laid into the hands and responsibility of women."[642] The next month, Mayr-Lumetzberger and Forster ordained Fresen to the priesthood.[643] Fresen left her religious order, which did not support her ordination, and began working with Women Priest Movement, a theological formation program in Austria for women wishing to be priests. The program was established by the European We Are Church movement and funded by local parishes.[644]

Power-Hungry Witches

Things were heating up in the United States, as well. A few weeks earlier, attorney Susan Rockwell of Vermont had filed a brief in U.S. District Court against the Diocese of Manchester, Archdiocese of Boston, National Conference of Catholic Bishops, and the Commissioner of the Internal Revenue Service, seeking revocation of the Roman Catholic Church's tax exempt and charitable deduction status for sex discrimination. She vowed to "continue her case, even to the Supreme Court if necessary and possible."[645]

Meanwhile, Rome was no closer to resolving its frustrations with women. *Time* magazine quoted a "Vatican functionary" as characterizing the "bulk" of women active in various forms of church ministry as "power-hungry witches" with "no concern for the church and for souls."[646] The world's ordination groups likewise seemed no closer to securing valid ordination for women. The only reality that remained clear to everyone was that the "problem" wasn't going away.

• • •

When Thérèse died in 1897, few people mourned her passing. Fifty years after her death, however, more than 850 works about her had been published in most of the world's languages.[647] *When Pope John Paul II declared Thérèse of Lisieux a Doctor of the Church in 1997, she became the third woman*[648] *and the youngest of the thirty-three doctors to receive that honor. In declaring her a Doctor of the Church, Pope John Paul II wrote:*

> To everyone Thérèse gives her personal confirmation that the Christian mystery, whose witness and apostle she became by making herself in prayer "the apostle of the apostles," as she boldly calls herself, must be taken literally, with the greatest possible realism, because it has a value for every time and place.[649]

John Paul II may have "literally" called Thérèse an apostle, but like Leo XIII a century earlier he would not have ordained her a priest. After her trip to Rome as a young teen to speak to Leo XIII, Thérèse wrote:

> I cannot understand why women are so easily excommunicated in Italy, for at every moment someone was saying to us: "Don't enter here, Don't enter there, you will be excommunicated." Ah, poor women, how they are misunderstood![650]

Part IV

CHANGE
AND THE
VATICAN

⇒ Chapter 25 ⇐

The Documents in Brief

Various Roman Catholic authorities have tried to explain the hierarchy's exclusion of women from ordained ministry. Yet most of the documents addressing the issue are decidedly inaccessible to most Catholics: the texts are written in densely technical language; they present a maze of arguments drawn from biblical metaphors sometimes taken out of context; they depend upon unevenly applied biological differences and obsolete cultural stereotypes; they are often delivered late to the world's bishops, who are then unable to study the documents in advance of their release to Catholics and the media; and, their general tone is patriarchal and often patronizing, leaving many women's ordination supporters feeling like errant children told to go outside and play while the adults attend to business.

In 1996, Pope John Paul II complained of "widespread misunderstanding" of church authority causing widespread criticism of its documents. He directed church leaders to address this by calling attention to Vatican documents and "their style and language so as to harmonize the solidity and clarity of the doctrine with the pastoral concern to use forms of communication and means of expression that are incisive and effective for the consciousness of contemporary man."[651] His call for church leaders to clear up the "misunderstanding" among Catholics was, like most other documents originating in Rome, puffy. Moreover, his documents concerning women revealed that John Paul II frequently disregarded the very people he wanted to convince. For instance, in his call to show "pastoral concern" by using forms of communication that would reach the "consciousness of contemporary man," he insisted upon using the exclusionary "man" to mean contemporary men and women. Likewise in 1994, Cardinal Joseph Ratzinger had highlighted the "equal dignity of men and women in the order of sanctity," because holiness alone was the "common goal of all *men*."[652] Somewhere between the order of sanctity and the goal of holiness, women got lost.

In response to John Paul II's call to pursue "means of expression that are incisive and effective" in informing the laity, following are thumbnail descriptions of the documents examined in this book.

- "Women in Canon Law" (1975) — The Canon Law Society of America declared the exclusion of women from church decision-making to be a "grave pastoral problem," and that there was *no theological reason why women could not be ordained.*

- "Women in Church and Society" (1975) — The U.S. bishops said there *was theological evidence against ordaining women* and they encouraged discussion as a way of "deepening" Catholics' understanding of this evidence. They prioritized reform of church processes and structures affecting women.

- "Report of the Pontifical Biblical Commission" (1976) — This commission declared that the *New Testament alone was not sufficient to settle the question* of women's ordination. The study was complicated by the fact that the institution of ordained priesthood was postbiblical. (The text is included in the appendix, p. 177.)

- *Inter Insigniores* ("Declaration on the Admission of Women to the Ministerial Priesthood," 1976) — Writing under the aegis of Pope Paul VI in response to ecumenical and internal support for women in the Catholic priesthood, the Congregation for the Doctrine of the Faith declared that *the church had never believed that ordination could be validly conferred upon women.* Christ's incarnation had occurred in a male, which was part of God's plan for salvation. Symbolically, Christ and his male priests were the "bridegroom" ever faithful to their (female and male) "bride," the church, who must show fidelity to the will of her spouse (Jesus). *Inter Insigniores* did not expressly employ the centuries-old subordinationist claim that women could not *receive* ordination because they were inferior to men; instead, it claimed that church tradition did not allow for the valid ordination of women. (The text is included in the appendix, p. 185.)

- "Commentary on the Declaration" (1977) — An anonymous writer for the Congregation for the Doctrine of the Faith asserted that *Inter Insigniores* was necessary because other Christian denominations were ordaining women, and Catholic women also were questioning the male-only priesthood. The commentary went beyond *Inter Insigniores,* saying that *Paul's teaching that men were superior to women was "immutable" church teaching,* an assertion that reverted to the recently discarded teaching on subordinationism. The commentary acknowledged recent scripture scholarship suggesting that the Pauline text commanding women to keep silent in the churches was not authentic, but its authenticity was of "little importance" because theologians already had made "abundant use" of the text. (The text is included in the appendix, p. 196.)

- Canon 1024 (1983) — This canon stated simply that *only a baptized male* could be ordained to the priesthood.

- "Holy Thursday Letter to Priests" (1988) — John Paul II encouraged priests to practice Mary's "spiritual motherhood" in a "manly way" by pursuing its equivalent, "spiritual fatherhood." His expanding use of gender metaphors allowed him to say that *priests could practice spiritual motherhood, but women could not practice spiritual fatherhood.* By extension, this explained why priests were also members of Mother Church (the bride), but women could not represent Christ (the bridegroom).

- *Mulieris Dignitatem* ("On the Dignity and Vocation of Women," 1988) — More than any document before it, Pope John Paul II's apostolic letter acknowledged women's worth. However, the pope again expounded on *female biological functions as they defined women's relationship to men.* These functions, he said, endowed women with a twofold vocation, virginity and motherhood. Women and men were equal but different, and it was women's differentness from men that defined their role in the church.

- *Christifideles Laici* ("On the Vocation and Mission of the Lay Faithful in the Church and in the World," 1988) — John Paul II again explored the biological foundations of "woman's dignity" and the gifts "proper" to women. His language was strikingly more gender inclusive than in past documents, although his teaching was not. *Women's personal identity in relation to men determined their place in the church and even their "make-up and meaning"* as persons. He employed traditional imagery of women as social housekeepers whose "customary contributions" as wives and mothers qualified them to serve as guardians of the "moral dimension of culture."

- "Partners in the Mystery of Redemption" (1988) — After listening to the concerns of some seventy-five thousand women, the U.S. bishops wrote that both *women and men were "configured to Christ" by virtue of baptism,* a claim that potentially threatened church teaching on a male priesthood. This first-draft pastoral letter was soundly criticized by the Vatican.

- "One in Christ Jesus" (1992) — The fourth and last draft of the U.S. bishops' letter said that *women and men were equal in dignity, but the church was not authorized to ordain women.* Widely criticized by conservatives and liberals alike, the letter was never adopted by the National Conference of Catholic Bishops.

- *Catechism of the Catholic Church* (1994) — The catechism repeated canon 1024's *limitation of priesthood to baptized males.* The English edition was delayed for two years while Rome recast inclusive language in traditional male terms.

- *Ordinatio Sacerdotalis* ("On Reserving Priestly Ordination to Men Alone," 1994) — John Paul II added *no new arguments* to the debate. Notably, he diverged from Paul VI by avoiding any description of priesthood in terms of "function" or "power," two concepts then in use to criticize the male priesthood. The priesthood was about neither of those things, but rather about the grace to serve the church, grace given by God to males through holy orders. By declaring that the church had *"no authority whatsoever to confer priestly ordination on women,"* and by ordering this *teaching to be "definitively held"* by all Catholics, the pope moved the issue from the realm of debate to papal authority. (The text is included in the appendix, p. 211.)

- "Strengthening the Bonds of Peace" (1994) — The U.S. bishops confirmed and commented on the teaching of *Ordinatio Sacerdotalis.* Then they called for adoption of inclusive language in religious materials and an *"honest, sustained" dialogue* between the laity and bishops. (The text is included in the appendix, p. 214.)

- "Letter to Women" (1995) — John Paul II denied that the ban on women's ordination constituted an injustice. The *ban was based on "essential dimensions"* of sex modeled by Mary the mother of Jesus and by Peter the apostle. Accordingly, gender roles in the church were forever fixed.

- "Jesuits and the Situation of Women in Church and Civil Society" (1995) — The Jesuits acknowledged their own participation in the church hierarchy's unjust treatment of women, and they *resolved to help bring about "respectful reconciliation" with women.* (The text is included in the appendix, p. 220.)

- *Responsum ad Dubium* ("Response to a Question Regarding *Ordinatio Sacerdotalis,*" 1995) — The Congregation for the Doctrine of the Faith declared that the teaching against women's ordination in *Ordinatio Sacerdotalis* was *not only "definitive"* but now *also "infallible"* because it had been taught by the "ordinary universal magisterium" (the world's bishops, including the pope), a claim that had never before been used to declare a doctrine infallible. Theologians adjudged this claim of infallibility to be invalid on grounds that the infallibility of a teaching, especially one only very questionably linked to matters of faith, could *not* be declared by a curial (advisory and administrative) agency in response to a question. (The text is included in the appendix, p. 225.)

- "Tradition and the Ordination of Women" (1997) — The Catholic Theological Society of America quoted canon 749:3: "No doctrine is understood to be infallibly defined unless this fact is clearly established." *Since the ordination ban had never been established as such, it could not be infallible.*

- *From "Inter Insigniores" to "Ordinatio Sacerdotalis"* (1998) — The United States Catholic Conference collected thirteen commentaries *supporting and explaining the teachings* put forth in these two documents. Of the thirteen essayists, only three were women, two of whom wrote about motherhood.

- "From Words to Deeds: Continuing Reflections on the Role of Women in the Church" (1998) — While acknowledging that there were *"different kinds of gifts"* and "different forms of service," the United States Catholic Conference offered concrete steps to expand women's nonordained roles in the church.

- "Ten Frequently Asked Questions about the Reservation of Priestly Ordination to Men" (1998) — The U.S. bishops invoked the catechism's definition of justice *as that "due to God and neighbor"* to assert that the male priesthood was not unjust because priesthood was not a right due to anyone. This particular definition of justice had not been employed in Rome's documents.

- *Ad Tuendam Fidem* ("To Defend the Faith," 1998) — John Paul II openly and strongly *charged the world's bishops with the duty of securing Catholic assent* to (and meting out punishment for dissent from) "definitive" church teaching. He established *juridical, disciplinary, and penal provisions* in canon law for a "second category" of truths necessary to defend the faith.

- "Commentary on the Profession of Faith's Concluding Paragraphs" (1998) — In the most technically complex language yet used in the pageant of Rome's documents, the Congregation for the Doctrine of the Faith asserted that while there were various levels of church teaching, *all* required assent by the faithful. *Dissenters would "no longer be in full communion* with the Catholic Church."

- "Address of the Holy Father to the German Bishops" (1999) — Pope John Paul II sternly warned the bishops against allowing "any human power to loosen the indissoluble bonds between [them] and the Successor of Peter." He reiterated that Rome had "no authority whatsoever" to ordain women. This teaching was infallible, and it was the bishops' task "to reject contrary opinions." Further, priests were to assume the "maternal" authority of the church, and obedience to that authority was required for salvation. (The text is included in the appendix, p. 226.)

- "Message of the Holy Father to the World Union of Catholic Women's Organizations" (2001) — John Paul II repeated that a female's "specific charism" was motherhood, in which she was "uniquely gifted in the task of passing on the Christian message" and for "the *sanctification of the world from within*" (from the womb or from home). This document once again stressed the pontiff's earlier assertion that women's role was to be found in the domestic sphere. (The text is included in the appendix, p. 232.)

- "Warning Regarding the Attempted Priestly Ordination of Some Catholic Women" (2002) — The Congregation for the Doctrine of the Faith issued this document to "give *direction to the consciences of the Catholic faithful* and dispel any doubts" about the recent ordinations of seven women, which constituted "an affront to the dignity of women." The document gave the women twelve days to acknowledge the nullity of their ordinations and to ask forgiveness. (The text is included in the appendix, p. 235.)

- "Decree of Excommunication Regarding the Attempted Priestly Ordination of Some Catholic Women" (2002) — As promised, the Congregation for the Doctrine of the Faith excommunicated the seven women ordained earlier that year. (The text is included in the appendix, p. 236.)

- "Decree on the Attempted Priestly Ordination of Some Catholic Women" (2002) — The Congregation for the Doctrine of the Faith notified the women that the revocation request they had filed earlier was not valid because the excommunication had been issued in the name of the pope. (The text is included in the appendix, p. 237.)

Sensus Fidelium

Many elements within these documents, all written since Vatican II, already are obsolete. Even as he commissioned *Inter Insigniores* in 1976, Pope Paul VI knew that the question of women's ordination was widespread, and he must have suspected that the issue was unlikely to go away. Further, the male-only priesthood currently lacks extensive reception and assent among Catholics, many of whom do not accept its inflation to the level of doctrine. The *sensus fidelium* ("sense of the faithful") that male priesthood is no longer appropriate continues to manifest the mind and conscience of growing numbers of Catholics. And Rome's continuing intransigence contributes to polarization within the church.

In 1870, Vatican I stated that the pope was not endowed with infallibility in isolation, but rather he *shared it with the people of the church.* In the 1960s, Vatican II strenuously emphasized the "sense of the faithful" and the "assent of the Church" required for valid doctrine.[653] *Lumen Gentium* ("Dogmatic Constitution on the Church," 1964) spoke of the infallibility of the church *as a people,* teaching that "a genuine *ex cathedra* definition could only be received by the Church with the assent of faith." That is, a *genuine* definition of papal infallibility was one that enjoyed the reception and assent of Catholics in the parishes and had no need for ongoing clarifications and commentaries, changes in canon law, or punishment for dialogue. It is specifically the continuing *lack* of reception and assent among Catholics that has occasioned the continuing flow of documents studied here.

It is not possible for an informed conscience to give assent to a teaching while retaining serious doubt whether that teaching is true, or when it is unpersuaded by attempts to stifle questions. Moreover, it is difficult for Catholics to give their assent to teachings explained in serpentine documents whose language and logic proceeds by twists and turns, confusing even the bishops and theologians responsible for teaching them. Having summarized the conclusions of these documents, it is time to reassess their themes.

• • •

Thérèse once told a story that summed up her personality:

> *One day, a horse was standing in front of our garden gate, hindering us from getting through. The others talked to him and tried to make him move. Meanwhile I quietly slipped between his legs. Such is the advantage of being a little one.*[654]

She may have been little, but she was also clever. After photographs of her were restored in the mid-twentieth century (they had been retouched following her death), both child-like simplicity and unmistakable shrewdness radiated from her straightforward, self-assured gaze. Hers were the eyes of someone who was destined for sainthood and knew it.

❧ Chapter 26 ❦

Reexamining
the Vatican's Themes

In 1997, the *National Catholic Reporter* ran a story claiming that in a small group discussion, Bishop Raymond Lucker of New Ulm, Minnesota remarked: "Cardinal Ratzinger has said we have the conclusion, now we need the reasons. When we face that, we realize we have very serious problems. How can we support that which has no reasons?"[655] Following are brief summaries of the Vatican's conclusions about the male-only priesthood, and some Catholic responses to them (in italics).

Creation

Christian anthropology, as taught by the Vatican in the context of priesthood, is a creation-based understanding of divinely assigned sex roles. It teaches that Adam (not Eve) physically resembled the savior who was to come. Scripture traditionally ascribed to Paul codified the inferiority of women. Christian anthropology maintains that the male is qualified to be priest, being sexually modeled after Christ, who is head of the body. The female is only the body.

In this context, Christian anthropology is rooted in the belief that women's spiritual roles are determined by the Genesis 2:18–25 creation story. God said, "It is not good that the man should be alone; I will make him a helper fit as his partner." So God created "every living creature" for the man to name. But the man was still lonely, because among all the animals and birds "there was not found a helper as his partner." So God created woman. The fact that woman was created only after the animals failed to keep the man company is not often included in the teaching of this creation story, or in Christian anthropology, which also depends upon extensions of biblical metaphors and writings ascribed to Paul (which may be inauthentic) to maintain that the head (priest/male) necessarily directs the body (church/male and female).

Complementarity is based upon natural law, in which male and female live in a mutually dependent relationship for the perpetuation of the human race and an efficient division of labor. God created woman and man to be complementary as female and male, a communion of persons in which each can be a helpmate to the other.

Rome takes complementarity beyond its naturally useful or valid bounds by using it unevenly to define men as independent beings while classifying women according to their biology and their relationships to men.

Subordinationism is a concept taught by Aristotle, Augustine, and Aquinas, among many others, that says that women are naturally inferior to men because they are physically "incomplete males" (Aristotle) or because of their secondary status in the "rib" version of creation. Vatican Council II (1962–65) repudiated this teaching, but it is still used to defend the male priesthood.

Complementarity is a positive, organic model for gender relations, but the Vatican's uneven use of the concept in relation to priesthood has caused complementarity to devolve into subordinationism, in which the sexes are in hierarchy: the male priest is head of the female church body (which includes nonordained males). By applying complementarity in this manner, the Vatican is able to denounce subordinationism without abandoning its practice.

"Feminine genius," a favorite phrase of Pope John Paul II, proclaims women's biological capacities and religious roles as the "body" — virgin, wife, and mother.

While his use of this phrase may have been thoroughly sincere, John Paul II's frequent use of it to assign biological roles to women's spiritual lives served as a rigid boundary line for women's religious vocations. Linguistically, "feminine genius" created an alternative (code) phrase for the outmoded and popularly rejected "woman's place."

The Church's Divine Constitution

The church was established by Christ, according to Roman Catholic teaching, hence it must be maintained in accordance with Christ's "positive will." In cases where he was silent (as with priesthood), the hierarchy reserves the right and duty to determine his will.

Since Jesus said nothing about priesthood, the Vatican's arguments against women priests are drawn indirectly from scripture (insufficient to determine priesthood and, in any event, may include inauthentic teachings ascribed to Paul); theology (codified by the Vatican); tradition (the validity of which is determined by the Vatican), and church teaching (promulgated by the Vatican). The official arguments for a male priesthood do not depend upon the stated teaching of Jesus or even consistently logical assumptions about his ministry.

The college of twelve apostles comprises Jewish men called by Christ (Luke 6:13) to sit on heavenly thrones and judge the Twelve Tribes of Israel (Matt. 19:28). Jesus charged these men with carrying the gospel ("good news") to the world. Peter defined an apostle as one who witnessed the resurrection (Acts 1:21–22). According to church teaching, these twelve apostles were entrusted with the founding and nurturing of the church and succession of apostolic leadership. Apostolic succession is grounded in a biblical interpretation that says the Twelve understood themselves to be a priesthood, and their successors immediately organized a church with bishops and a pope serving in Rome. Because these apostles were male, it was Jesus' will that priests must be male.

As the evangelist Matthew points out, Jesus chose twelve men to extend and carry on his work. Neither history nor broader biblical interpretations, however, bears out the claim that priesthood or the papacy emerged immediately after Christ's following, or that Christ intended for priesthood to be open to some Christians but closed to others.

Concerning the Twelve, others witnessed the resurrection and spread the gospel, and the apostle most responsible for founding the church, Paul, never saw or met the earthly Jesus.

A priest is a vehicle of salvation, because through ordination he has been given the ministry of Peter, and he exercises the "maternal authority" of "Mother Church," obedience to which is required for salvation. Only men may exercise this maternal authority.

Pope John Paul II caused chagrin in the theological world when he claimed that obedience to the magisterium was required for salvation. Further, bishops have not widely repeated the pope's assertion that only men can represent the church's female authority, at least not in those words.

Tradition

Church fathers (early teachers of the faith) clearly taught that women were not to be priests. To do this, they employed sexist and even misogynist language, but, according to Vatican thinking, that did not affect their pastoral practice or teachings.

Very few church fathers (and usually the same ones) are quoted by Rome to defend the male priesthood. For some reason, Rome repeatedly quotes men who call women the devil's gateway, the portal of evil, vile creatures, and other pejorative terms, while claiming that their appalling views of women in no way affected their Christian ministry. This posture is reminiscent of the man who robbed an elderly woman on the street but first wrapped a towel around his gun so it wouldn't frighten her.

The Deposit of Faith is the entire collection of revealed teachings and church tradition whose protection and promulgation is reserved to the magisterium. Cardinal Joseph Ratzinger taught that the male-only priesthood belonged to the deposit of faith.

At present, many theologians, bishops, and other Catholics widely reject the suggestion that the male priesthood belongs to the deposit of faith. It is difficult to see how maleness could be considered such bedrock teaching.

Scripture

Scripture alone is not sufficient to show that only males can be priests. In recent years, scholars have suggested that certain misogynist writings ascribed to Paul are not authentic. But even if some texts are not genuine, the Vatican says, the fact that they have been used for so long to justify the male priesthood makes their authenticity irrelevant.

Alternatively stated: the Bible's ultimate veracity is not important as long as scripture passages allow the church to defend a crumbling tradition.

Metaphors and Images

The nuptial analogy is an extension of images from the Song of Songs in which the lover is Jesus and the beloved is the church. Jesus is male, the church female.

Since priests represent Christ, only males can be priests, who represent Christ. Further, they embody "spiritual fatherhood" as well as "maternal authority." Hence, priests have both male and female roles to play: male as person, female as church member. Women have nothing to represent which they are not, hence they are always only female.

What is less often seen are the logical consequences of concretizing this metaphor, which was taken out of context from the Song of Songs and never meant to address priesthood, regardless of sex. One consequence is the relationship of Jesus to his mother in this metaphor: he is "bridegroom" and she is "bride." Another logical consequence is that it distorts sexuality, or at least allows males to be spiritually bisexual when they stand on both sides of the altar, the nuptial axis of Christ and church.

In persona Christi describes the priest's cultic function. He stands in the person and the role of Christ. Maleness is required for this role. Otherwise, the priest could not be recognized as Christ and would confuse the faithful.

The in persona Christi *argument for priesthood reveals a limited image of Jesus and reduces him to a sexual unit.*

Church-as-woman has Mary the mother of Jesus as its model and norm. The church, like Mary, is passive and receptive to God's Word.

Mary has always provided the church with the model of "feminine holiness," and all that it implies. But Pope John Paul II's fascination with Mary and her sexual status drove his insistence that she was the sole model for a women's biological vocation as virgin, wife, and mother. When he spoke of Mary's "fiat" (her reception of God's seed in her virgin womb) as a model for women's vocation, missing was the very element that made her fiat so sacred: she freely chose her vocation because God offered it to her. But the church teaches that God does not offer priesthood to women. The irony of this teaching is that God chose a woman to physically give birth to Jesus, but not to spiritually represent him.

Sacrament of Holy Orders

The church has no authority to change the substance of a sacrament; hence holy orders must remain closed to women. There will always be seven sacraments for men and six for women.

A sacrament is a gift of grace from God for the building up of the church. The restriction of holy orders is not building up the church; rather it is harming the church. A sacrament works through the rite itself — ex opere operato — "from the work worked." If a duly ordained priest embezzles half a million dollars from his parish while carrying on his sacramental duties, the sacraments he performs are no less valid because he is an embezzler. If he were a holy nun, however, the same sacraments would be worthless.

Authority

The magisterium comprises the teaching authority of the church that determines and enforces church law. According to certain procedures, the church teaches "infallibly" and pronounces teachings to be "definitively held." All decision-making power ultimately is tied to ordination, as the priestly hierarchy alone has the right to authenticate a man's call to priesthood.

As a basis of a male priesthood at the turn of the twenty-first century, Rome has moved from a claim of tradition to the use of authority. The nature and extent of "definitively held" and "infallible" teachings have recently stimulated much controversy, as the Vatican has seemed to use both in innovative and unpredictable ways, including a claim of infallibility by a Vatican administrative body for a document that was only an answer to a question.

Discipline and punishment are necessary to preserve the deposit of faith and to fight heresy. These tools include silencing of unorthodox clerics and theologians, and excommunicating Catholics charged with heresy.

These forms of punishment are like squeezing a water balloon: with every squeeze, the water bubbles up in another direction. Aside from contradicting the very nature of religious liberty and freedom of conscience, both of which the church defends, in the Internet age silencing solves nothing, and excommunication sends the message that the Vatican is responding to a serious threat. It is well known that priests who support women's ordination are not made bishops, and bishops brave enough to speak out can count on a telephone call, a formal letter, or even a visit from a papal representative. Nevertheless, because this teaching lacks reception and assent by millions of Catholics, the Vatican has retreated to an old tradition: "Roma locuta, causa finita" — *Rome has spoken, the case is closed.*

Modern World

Women's progress in society prompts the church to examine women's roles more closely and to encourage their accomplishments in society. But women's rights in society are not the same as those in the church, where their participation is divinely restricted.

As theologians, sociologists, and women's studies scholars point out, the refusal to ordain women to the priesthood serves as an alternative culture within the church and an effective barrier against the modern world, including the secular and women's ordination movements. In effect, this creates a dualism for Catholic women, for whom daily life and spiritual life are lived according to two different sets of rules.

The priesthood has two roles to play. Priests are both father and mother, priest and church, head and body, male and female. They must be effective models of each role in relation to its place in the earthly hierarchy, which mirrors the heavenly hierarchy.

As it is evolving, the priesthood is reflecting the values of Pope John Paul II regarding women. Young priests, many of whom have never experienced any other pope, are more likely than their older colleagues to believe women should not be priests, and more likely to be reticent about working with lay people at all.

Ecumenism is an important element of the ordination issue. Women's ordination poses a serious obstacle to interchurch relations, especially with the Anglican Communion, a sacramental church that ordains women.

As other Christian denominations opened priesthood to women, the Vatican insisted its position was not open to debate, driving a wedge in Rome's relations with those churches, especially the Anglican Communion. Communications between Rome and Canterbury suggest that ecumenical considerations have been of great importance to this issue.

Justice

Priesthood is not a matter of justice, because no one has a "human right" to ordination.

Catholics are not asking for women's "right" to priesthood, but only the same consideration that men enjoy: the opportunity to have their call to priesthood tested by the church.

Reception and Assent

Reception and assent of a teaching by the faithful are required for that teaching to be valid. Where there is widespread rejection of a teaching, there cannot be valid doctrine.

For reception and assent to be meaningful, the faithful must have the knowledge necessary for an informed choice and the liberty to publicly explore an issue. When these are denied, reception and assent take on the significance of a rubber stamp. The teaching against women priests does not enjoy reception and assent by the Catholic faithful.

The Vatican's reasons for banning women from priesthood have been credibly questioned by many people over many years. Yet aside from a 1976 pontifical commission established to study scriptural foundations of priesthood — a commission that said there was no reason priests must be male — the hierarchy has made no study of women's ordination other than to seek out more reasons against it. The more reasons it has produced, the more Catholics have called for women priests.

• • •

As Lent drew to a close in 1897, Thérèse's appearance caused concern among the sisters of Carmel. Her face flushed and her energy greatly diminished, she coughed incessantly. Although the prioress had known of her illness for months, no particular care was taken of Thérèse, nor did she do much to take care of herself. She continued with her routine habits — usual fasts, hard work, little sleep. For many months, on orders from her superior, she had kept her illness secret, even from her blood sisters.

After a few months of continued decline, she was ordered to the infirmary, where tuberculosis of the lungs persisted in its attack on the small nun. During her illness, upon orders from the prioress, Thérèse had been writing the story of her life. Although she maintained her strength of attitude, her handwriting deteriorated from the perfect penmanship of a nun to the unintelligible scrawl of a dying woman.

Finally, she could no longer move without help. She endured chills and fever, constant vomiting, labored breathing, and fainting spells. Each night, it took her an hour to undress. Thérèse underwent painful treatments, including "bleeding" by leeches and cauterization with hot irons.[656] Yet according to biographers, Mother Superior would not allow Thérèse (or any of the sisters) to take morphine or any pain relievers, considering them "incompatible with the heroism called for in the life of Carmel." The purpose of weakness was "for divine strength to work in and through it," and Thérèse lived and died through "the power of her powerlessness."[657] On July 30, Thérèse received Extreme Unction (Anointing of the Sick), and on August 19 she received her last communion. At last, after months of excruciating pain, she died on September 30, 1897.

Shortly before her death, Thérèse had overheard a nun say she didn't know how Mother Superior would eulogize Thérèse because, although the little sister was friendly enough, she had "never done anything worth talking about."[658] Indeed, Thérèse had lived a lowly and hidden life, a life of no particular note. But, when her life story circulated among Carmelites everywhere and then the parishes, Carmel of Lisieux was flooded with requests for copies of the little book. Moreover, young women began knocking on convent doors, wanting to follow in Thérèse's footsteps. Her story of faith opened a floodgate of religious vocations.[659]

From Subordination to Ordination

When women were first ordained to Episcopal Church priesthood, a young priest was assigned to a small town (as women priests were and still are). As the story goes, the priest invited several parishioners to join her family for their first Thanksgiving dinner in their new home. In the familiar custom, the children were seated at the "children's table" near the adults. During dinner, someone asked the children what they wanted to be when they grew up. One little boy said, "I want to be a priest!" The priest's preschool daughter grew agitated, looked at her mother, and asked: "Mommy, can *boys* be priests?" She had never seen a male cleric.

This story suggests a question: Is gender a function of *being* or of *having*? In 1992, Pope John Paul II wrote that the "very meaning" of priesthood was as a "special witness to the primacy of 'being' over 'having.' "[660] Few would propose that "being" (who we are) is on a plane with "possessing" (what we have), but a problem arises when we apply the question of *being* vs. *having* to a sex-specific priesthood.

If priesthood is a state of *having*, then God divides humanity and calls priests according to the "haves" of maleness. In this case, women are rightly excluded from priesthood because they are irreparably "have-nots." This was Aquinas's argument, supported by Genesis 2:18–25, that males are primary and females secondary.

If, on the other hand, priesthood is a state of *being*, then God calls priests according to their human-beingness. This theology resonates with Genesis 1:26–27, in which each sex is mutually (not exclusively) complementary to the other. But the church tradition excluding women from priesthood suggests that Christ's maleness was more important than his humanity, and that a sex-based priesthood requires privileging one sex over the other.

Cardinal Joseph Ratzinger said in 1994 that "being taken into the sacrament of [orders] is a renunciation of oneself in order to serve Jesus Christ."[661] Yet Ratzinger was a formidable foe of women's ordination. His claim that holy orders was a "renunciation of oneself in order to serve Jesus" was hard to reconcile with his adamant assertions that priests must be male.

Even the staunch defender of male priesthood Hans Urs von Balthasar wrote the following about his departure, at age forty-four, from the Jesuits (although not the priesthood):

> I took this step, for both sides a very grave one, after a long testing of the certainty I had reached through prayer that I was being called by God to certain definite tasks

in the Church.... So, for me, the step taken means an application of Christian obedience to God, who at any time has the right to call a man not only out of his physical home ... but also from his chosen spiritual home in a religious order, so that he can use him for purposes within the Church.[662]

Balthasar, whose prodigious writing revealed a genius for theology, frequently found himself taking different roads, and while he vigorously defended the Vatican's ban on women priests, it is difficult to imagine that he would have faulted anyone for applying "Christian obedience of God," who at any time might call a woman in order to use her for the church.

Elizabeth Johnson highlighted the importance of asking whether our image of God truly reflects our own contemporary human experience: "If the idea of God does not keep pace with developing reality, the power of experience pulls people on and the god dies, fading from memory." Can the Christian God "take account of, illumine, and integrate" contemporary women's experiences? "This is an absolutely critical question."[663]

Lost Voices

As younger men, the church leaders most responsible for contemporary teaching on ordination — Pope Paul VI and Pope John Paul II — appeared to be far less rigid in their theology, with a sense of the hope and promise of the future.

Paul VI wrote in 1966: "Doctrinal dialogue should be initiated with courage and sincerity, with the greatest of freedom," recognizing the truth everywhere, *"even if the truth demolishes one so that one is forced to reconsider one's own position,"* because the "liberty of the participants must be ensured by law and reverenced in practice."[664]

As archbishop of Krakow in 1969, Karol Wojtyla once encouraged responsible dissent in the church: "Conformity means death for any community. A loyal opposition is a necessity in any community." Later, as Pope John Paul II, and even as he was silencing numerous theologians, he asked: *"What should one say of the practice of combating or silencing those who do not share the same views?"*[665]

The documents studied here reveal two popes — Paul VI and John Paul II — strong in their beliefs, dedicated to the church, and intent upon keeping women out of the priesthood. They answered impassioned calls for change by nailing their thesis to the twenty-first-century church door: Women need not apply.

Two Stories of Faith

Being locked out is a theme many Catholic women have grown weary of seeing, hearing, and feeling. It is not the value of tradition they reject, but rather the scandal of its abuse. This dilemma was explored by a lay woman, Rose Hoover:

As a Southerner, reverence for tradition is part of my inheritance. I cherish the traditions of my ancestors, of my region, and especially of my church. Far from alienating me, an appeal to tradition tends to warm my heart. On the other hand, since I am all too aware, again as a Southerner, of the damage wreaked by the misuse of tradition, I have begun to ponder the meaning and nature of tradition and to look critically at its role in the Christian life. What is it that makes a traditional practice honorable...not to mention valid, for a Christian? Is it the fact that we have always done it that way? Or is something more required?...My forebears ingested racism with their mothers' milk, though they would not have thought of themselves as racists. They regarded a hierarchy of the races as God's will. They would never have joined the Ku Klux Klan or consciously harmed a person of any race. They were kind in the way they knew how to be kind. In their hearts they believed they were living in the way God had ordained for them — yet what unspeakable damage their convictions about race inflicted on generation unto generation![666]

Quite a different (and neglected) tradition was established by Jesus' practice of empowering women. Genesis 16–21 tells the story of Hagar, the Egyptian handmaid of Sarah, wife of Abraham. Believing herself to be barren, Sarah arranged for Hagar to be Abraham's concubine in order to produce an heir. Hagar gave birth to a son, Ishmael. Later, when Sarah by the grace of God gave birth to a son, Isaac, she caused Abraham to banish Hagar and Ishmael into the desert. When it looked as if Ishmael would die of exposure, an angel of God told Hagar that her son would become the father of a great nation. At that moment, God opened Hagar's eyes (Gen. 21:19) and she saw the water well, where she filled her container to the brim.

This story points to something important. It does not say that God gave Hagar water because she had *a right* to the water, or even that she *asked for* it. God *called* her to the life-giving water. "God opened Hagar's eyes" and she took the water God had provided for her.

Hagar has inspired many women to "keep the faith" through the long desert days of the women's ordination movement, faith that God will in fact appear in their midst to reward their longsuffering with a deep well of renewing water. But for other Catholic women, the call to priesthood feels like a stillborn baby, a love that cannot live yet never dies. Some are silent, some speak out. Too many leave the church, too few remain.

Gail Grossman Freyne explained why she stayed: "I am not a heretic. Maybe I am an apostate. More likely, a schismatic. Does the label matter? Whatever they name me, the clear intention is that it will never be *priest*."[667] But labels have a way of becoming history's most surprising moments, such as the time an uneducated, blue-collar worker from a dusty little town, accused by the local law of being a troublemaker, turned out to be the messiah. Just as he was always renewing the people around him, the Roman Catholic Church is *ecclesia semper reformanda*, a church always reforming itself. Sometimes, the renewal process can be slow and tedious. But it always happens.

A crucial element of this self-reformation is a perspective of doctrine as unfolding rather than static. Nineteenth-century cardinal John Henry Newman eloquently traced the progression of a "great idea":

Its beginnings are no measure of its capabilities, nor of its scope. At first no one knows what it is, or what it is worth. It remains perhaps for a time quiescent; it tries, as it were, its limbs, and proves the ground under it, and feels its way. From time to time it makes [experiments] which fail, and are in consequence abandoned. It seems in suspense [as to] which way to go; it wavers, and at length strikes out in one definite direction. In time it enters upon strange territory; points of controversy alter their bearing; parties rise and fall around it; dangers and hopes appear in new relations; and old principles reappear under new forms. It changes with them in order to remain the same. In a higher world it is otherwise, but here below to live is to change, and to be perfect is to have changed often.[668]

More than a century later, Ladislas Örsy wrote that an understanding of Christian doctrine develops as the believer's spiritual horizon expands through knowledge and faith. Echoing Augustine, this widely recognized canon lawyer said that "once a concept is firmly circumscribed by law there is little room for evolution." Even further, when the law is believed to be "the will of the legislator" — such as a pastor, bishop, or pope — *any* critical assessment of the law "can be seen as undue criticism of the personal judgment of the legislator."[669] As we have seen, valid criticism of the male priesthood is often perceived as undue criticism of the pope, indeed of Catholicism itself. Such is the wage of prophecy.

Yet, as theologian Anthony Padovano pointed out, Jesus was a reformer who "insisted that people were more important than the Sabbath, that forgiveness mattered more than worship, that compassion was the essence of discipleship." Ministry according to Jesus "was service and not dominion." Hence, he got into trouble. Jesus dedicated himself to *service*, but he was not *subservient*. "Had he been more conventional and obedient, more orthodox and subservient, more compliant and submissive, he would not have been crucified. It is as simple and awful as that."[670] In short, Jesus could have avoided a lot of trouble by acting like a woman.

When women began abandoning *subservience* to the law to pursue *service* to God's people they got into trouble, but not from Jesus. In the Gospel of Luke (10:38–42), when two sisters welcomed Jesus to their home, one sister (Martha) went about her housework, while the other sister (Mary) left her women's work to sit, in the manner of a rabbinical student, at the feet of the master. When Martha complained that Mary was shirking the housework, Jesus replied that Mary had chosen the better course, and it *would not be denied her.*

In the institutional Roman Catholic Church, "woman's work" includes keeping quiet. During mass, women cannot read the gospel, cannot preach, cannot offer the prayer of sacrifice that transforms bread and wine into the body and blood of Christ. Yet women freely sit at the feet of the master, because it is not Jesus who silences them. Only the Vatican silences women.

From Jewish tradition there is the voice of a sage who warned against making a definitive decision on a complex issue if the evidence to support the decision was not clear. When the leaders of the Sanhedrin were concerned about the Christian apostles and their efforts to evangelize the Jews, a Pharisee and legal expert named Gamaliel counseled:

I tell you, keep away from these people and let them alone; because if this plan or this undertaking is of human origin, it will fail; but if it is of God, you will not be able to overthrow them — in that case you may even be found fighting against God! (Acts 5:38–39)

What Happens Next?

In the early twenty-first century, the Roman Catholic Church appears to be walking forward while looking backward, a sure way to lose the path. Meanwhile, Catholicism is losing many of its best and brightest members, who feel forced out of their own spiritual home to seek belonging elsewhere. "The alienation is so intense," historian Jay Dolan wrote, "that many women leave the church, while others just drop out, joining one of the largest religious communities in the United States, the 20 million Catholics who do not belong to a parish."[671]

Twenty years ago, Rosemary Radford Ruether conducted an informal survey that showed "it was fairly common for Catholic women who obtained M. Div. [Master of Divinity] degrees to switch to a Protestant denomination to become ordained ministers."[672] Certainly today, Episcopalians and Lutherans, among others, are familiar with former Catholic women who are now their priests, ministers, and seminarians. In 1994, Jane Redmont astutely observed: "Disaffection and leaving. Disaffection and staying. Either way, Christian unity is affected."[673] Mostly, Roman Catholicism is affected.

Relations with the world's non-Catholic Christians suffer, too. British Broadcasting Corporation's Radio 4 commentator Libby Purves once said that the longer a church denies the strengths of the society it lives in, "the weaker that church grows."[674] Surely, the converse is also true. The longer a church denies the strengths of its own faithful, the weaker it grows. Sister Francis Bernard O'Connor in 1993 explained in bluntly practical terms that in the United States "slaves were freed, not because slavery was a demeaning, degrading and inhuman institution, but rather to save the union. If the unity of the church is to be preserved, women must also be given freedom from oppression."[675] The comparison to slavery was only part of O'Connor's argument. While valid, utilitarianism by itself cannot suffice to support women's ordination.

To remain true to the meaning of priesthood, women must be ordained for the *same reasons men are ordained.* Any attempt to deploy women to serve as priests "for the duration" of a sex scandal or clergy shortage would only devalue the call to priesthood and confirm what the magisterium already teaches: women are defined in their relation to (the needs of) men.[676] In the future, as Richard McBrien pointed out, the church will have to be as concerned with right practice as with right belief: "The call of women to 'practice' the Gospel is no less urgent than it is for men. And the call of the Church to 'practice' the Gospel toward women is no less urgent for men than it is for women themselves."[677]

Today, with growing numbers of women's ordination groups around the world, the idea of ordaining Catholic women seems less radical than it did just a few decades ago. This has doubtless been brought about in part by the worsening priest shortage[678] and the sex abuse scandal involving priests in the West. Neither of these realities, however, can provide a valid or even workable reason for the ordination of Catholic women.[679] To remain true to priestly charism (divinely bestowed fitness for ministry), women must be ordained not for politics but for priesthood: to serve the People of God by teaching, sanctifying, and governing.

Diffusing the Demand

In a scenario he doubts is the "most likely or most logical," Vatican observer Peter Steinfels addressed the prospect that the demand for women's ordination arises from the concern that without ordination women will remain powerless and unable to use their spiritual gifts in the church. In such a case, he said, Rome could enhance and permanently (not just in the absence of priests) employ women in administrative, theological, and liturgical roles, including preaching, as well as increase their numbers in meaningful decision-making capacities ("with women among the cardinals heading Vatican offices and electing popes"). In this scenario, Catholics might conclude that the male priesthood was merely a "symbolic division of labor" rather than a genuine attempt to preserve a male monopoly of power based upon belief in women's inferiority.[680] In other words, placing nonordained women in high places might appear to be consistent with the church's professed commitment to women's equality with men while defusing the demand for women's ordination.

In early 2004, Pope John Paul II appointed women for the first time to the International Theological Commission — theologians Barbara Hallensleben, a German, and Sister Sara Butler, an American member of the Missionary Servants of the Most Blessed Trinity. Butler was known for having "switched her views on the ordination of women in mid-career,"[681] which, intended or not, had the effect of clearing the way for her high-level Vatican appointment. On the same day, the pope appointed the first woman to one of the ten pontifical academies when he named Harvard law professor and longtime conservative Vatican advisor Mary Ann Glendon president of the Pontifical Academy of Social Sciences. These announcements were made on United Nations International Women's Day, but the Vatican "promptly denied the appointments had anything to do with their gender."[682]

In light of Steinfels's theoretical scenario, it was unclear whether these prestigious appointments were a sincere move to bring women's voices into the hierarchy or an attempt to quell the growing voices for women's ordination — or perhaps a mixture of both. At the very least, the appointments marked the first time that curial administrators experienced working with women of the same professional rank.

Controlling Beliefs

Mary Katzenstein outlined three controls over heterodoxy[683] — opinions and beliefs that sometimes question established doctrine. The Vatican has used each of these.

Punitive controls include transferring or denying promotions to clergy and church workers who question church authority, silencing theologians, and excommunicating believers.

Institutional controls include setting up counterorganizations to weaken institutions where resistance is housed. For instance, the Council of Major Superiors of Women Religious in the U.S.A. was established to weaken the more liberal Leadership Conference of Women Religious.

Discursive controls include official interpretative responses to challenges, such as the Vatican's replacement of inclusive language with male-oriented language in the English edition of the catechism. Other examples are the use of labels such as "extreme" and "leftist," and replacing offensive language, such as "woman's place" with innovative phraseology, such as "feminine genius."

Punitive, institutional, and discursive controls on beliefs and persons questioning traditional Roman Catholic practice and teaching on male priesthood are painfully evident throughout this book.

Having surveyed numerous Vatican documents and Catholic responses to them, as well as the recent invalid ordinations of women, I wish to pose a question: *Will Rome strategically consent to ordain women in order to exercise control over them?* Will Rome ordain women in order to bring them into orthodoxy and thus circumvent the kind of popular rejection of male-only priesthood as Catholics handed the church's teaching on birth control? The Vatican may have no way of dealing with what people do in their bedrooms, but there's a great deal to be done about what Catholics do on the altar.

Five Minutes

Rosemary Jantzen Doherty of Cedar, Michigan, wrote that because she had listened to homilies for at least two thousand hours of her life, it was only appropriate that the clergy listen to her for five minutes:

> I would like to suggest to you, priests and bishops, that you use your imaginations to picture a church with gender roles reversed. You remain a male in the church where women have the power and authority. You are denied one of the sacraments. You are excluded by the language from most of the readings you hear when you attend Mass. Moral issues are defined by women.[684]

Doherty also explained why she stayed in the Catholic Church:

> Why have I remained a member of the church? Because I believe the Eucharist is the Body of Christ; because Christ did not ever demean women; he treated them with respect and generosity; he did not exclude them from being disciples. He had been born a human, to a woman; and the most momentous of all events, his resurrection, he announced first to a woman.[685]

Jesus spent his ministry correcting the images of God held by the priests and scribes of Jerusalem. He knew that when values no longer serve a culture, the foundation of law collapses, and the law eventually collapses as well. Jesus redefined and enlivened the old law, freeing his followers from meaningless legal formulas. As Denise Carmody wrote, Jesus treated men and women simply as individuals who needed his help, or as co-workers, or friends. He offered women "no separate but equal way of works"; he compiled "no segregating list of feminine virtues."[686] The Vatican's exclusion of women from priesthood is an old custom (and not-so-old law) that is out of sync with a developing understanding of what it means to follow Christ, not mechanically mimicking what has been done in the past but rather living the gospel in our own day.

Matthew's gospel reveals that Peter had trouble understanding Jesus' teachings (15:15); he tried to walk on water but nearly drowned for lack of faith (14:28); when Jesus was arrested, Peter lagged behind and even sat with the guards to see how things would to turn out (26:58); and when a girl recognized him as a disciple of Christ, Peter denied even knowing him (26:69–75). Despite these human shortcomings, Jesus called him "Peter" (Gr. *Petros*), "the rock" (Gr. *petra*) upon which Jesus would build the church. Jesus said nothing about, and provided no model for, an ordained priesthood, but he gave Peter the "keys of the kingdom," saying "whatever you bind on earth will be bound in heaven, and whatever you loose on earth will be loosed in heaven" (16:18–19). According to the church's teaching of apostolic succession by which popes derive their authority from Peter (who derived his from Christ), the pope has the power to "bind" the priesthood to beneficiaries of an accident of birth: maleness. But, *the pope likewise has the authority to "loose" the priesthood from this constriction.*

Roman Catholic tradition like most of human history is one of deep misogyny. That is a historical fact. The statements studied here were all products of their time. Just as we cannot *judge* old actions by new insights, we should not *bind* our present actions to outdated ideas. Likewise, just as illiterate masses needed a certain kind of leadership in the Dark Ages, Roman Catholics today need a twenty-first century church. In his famous *Pange Lingua,* Thomas Aquinas wrote that Jesus obeyed the Law's directions, even as the Old Law ended. The Old Law and New Law are not different statutes but only different applications of the *same law* adapted to different needs. When church leaders find the courage, with Jesus, to say, "This tradition no longer serves the people of God and should be transformed," the old law itself will become a witness to change.

An Unexamined God

For most of us, talking to God involves asking questions, and the answers we reach depend upon the questions we ask. What would happen if we *changed the questions*? Instead of asking why *Rome* excludes women from priesthood, what if we asked: "Why does Rome teach that *God* excludes women from priesthood?" What reason does *God* have for commanding that only men can celebrate eucharist? Why does *God*, who has no gender, determine that only a male can hear the confession of a woman? Why does *God* decree that only a male should baptize the baby of a woman? Why does *God* design a woman to have one "spiritual" sex (as a "bride") but a man to have two such sexes (as "bride" *and* "bridegroom")? Why does *God* give seven sacraments for a man but only *six* for a woman? Why does God insist that a woman can *bear the Word of God* in her womb but *cannot proclaim that Word* in the Roman Catholic community?

Asking old questions in new ways can lead to new answers. As lay Catholics grow in faith and knowledge we can expand our horizon and take a fresh look at familiar beliefs, raise new questions, listen to the Spirit, and discover new answers. If we are to believe that we are all one in Christ Jesus, and if we are to follow Christ according to his call and our own gifts, we can only conclude that the priesthood is not about sex, it is about souls.

• • •

During the Great Depression of the 1930s, Catholic Worker cofounder and social justice activist Dorothy Day remembered her first attempt to read Thérèse's autobiography: "I dutifully read The Story of a Soul *and am ashamed to confess that I found it colorless, monotonous, too small in fact for my notice." She dismissed the book as "pious pap" that insulted her intelligence.*[687]

Then, however, she discovered that Thérèse's manuscript in fact had been edited after her death by the nuns at Carmel. As scholars retranslated the writings they recovered the authentic Thérèse — fiery, determined, devoted to the Bible, dedicated to Teresa of Avila and to John of the Cross, and always the dogged practitioner of a "little way" of spiritual childhood, of trust and absolute self-surrender to God. Also restored were the old photos that had been doctored by her Carmelite sisters to make her look more saintly according to nineteenth-century standards: gone now was the soft-edged, doe-eyed face, and in its place was a broad, firm chin and probing eyes. The "Little Flower" was a woman of robust faith and a genuine vocation to priesthood.

Thérèse of Lisieux described perfection as "doing His will, in being that which He wants us to be."[688] *More than a century later, her call lives on.*

APPENDIX

➤ Document 1 ◀

Report of the Pontifical Biblical Commission

July 1976

1. The Pontifical Biblical Commission was asked to study the role of women in the Bible in the course of research being carried out to determine the place that can be given to women today in the church.

2. The question for which an answer is especially sought is whether or not women can be ordained to the priestly ministry (especially as ministers of the eucharist and as leaders of the Christian community).

3. 1. In general the role of women does not constitute the principal subject of biblical texts. One has to rely often on information given here and there. The situation of women in the biblical era was probably more or less favorable judging from the limited data that we have at our disposal.

4. 2. The question asked touches on the priesthood, the celebrant of the eucharist and the leader of the local community. This is a way of looking at things which is somewhat foreign to the Bible.

5. (A) Surely the New Testament speaks of the Christian people as a priestly people (1 Pet. 2:5, 9; Apoc. 1:6; 5:10). It describes that certain members of this people accomplish a priestly and sacrificial ministry (1 Pet. 2:5, 12; Rom. 12:1, 15:16; Phil. 2:17). However it never uses the technical term *hiereus* for the Christian ministry. *A fortiori* it never places *hiereus* in relationship with the eucharist.

6. (B) The New Testament says very little on the subject of the ministry of the eucharist. Luke 22:19 orders the apostles to celebrate the eucharist in memory of Jesus (cf. 1 Cor. 11:24). Acts 20:11 shows also that Paul broke the bread (see also Acts 27:35).

7. (C) The pastoral epistles which give us the most detailed picture of the leaders of the local community (*episkopos* and *presbyteroi*) never attribute to them a eucharistic function.

8. 3. Beyond these difficulties resulting from a study of the biblical data from the perspective of a later conception of the eucharistic priesthood, it is necessary to keep in mind that this conception itself is now placed in question as one can see in the more recent declarations of the magisterium which broaden the concept of priesthood beyond that of eucharistic ministry.

Part I
Woman's Place in the Family

1. "In the Beginning"

9. In Genesis, the "beginning" serves less to present the beginning of history than the fundamental plan of God for mankind. In Genesis 1, man and woman are called together to be the image of God (Gen. 1:26f) on equal terms and in a community of life. It is in common that they receive rule over the world. Their vocation gives a new meaning to the sexuality that man possesses as the animals do.

10. In Gen. 2, man and woman are placed on equal terms: woman is for man a "helper who is his partner" (2:18), and by community in love they become "the two of them one body" (2: 24). This union includes the vocation of the couple to fruitfulness but it is not reduced to that.

11. Between this ideal and the historical reality of the human race, sin has introduced a considerable gap. The couple's existence is wounded in its very foundation: love is degraded by covetousness and domination (3:16). The woman endures pains in her condition as mother which nevertheless put her closely in contact with the mystery of life. The social degradation of her condition is also related to this wound, manifested by polygamy (cf. Gen. 4), divorce, slavery, etc. She is nevertheless the depository of a promise of salvation made to her descendants.

12. It is noteworthy that the ideal of Gen. 1 and 2 remained present in the thought of Israel like a horizon of hope; it is found again explicitly in the book of Tobias.

2. The Symbolism of the Sexes in the Old Testament

13. The Old Testament excluded the sexual symbolism used in Eastern mythologies, in relation to the fertility cults: there is no sexuality in the God of Israel. But very early, the biblical tradition borrowed traits from the family structure to trace pictures of God the Father. Then also it had recourse to the image of the spouse to work out a very lofty concept of the God of the covenant.

14. In correlation with these two fundamental images, the prophets gave value to the dignity of women by representing the people of God with the help of feminine symbols of the wife (in relation to God) and of the mother (in relation to the human partners of the covenant, men and women). These symbols were used particularly to evoke in advance the eschatological covenant in which God is to realize his plan in its fullness.

3. The Teachings of Jesus

15. Considering the social and cultural milieu in which Jesus lived, his teaching and behavior with regard to women are striking in their newness. We leave aside here his behavior (cf. the following reports). Questioned about divorce by the Pharisees (Mark 10:1–12), Jesus moves away from the rabbinic casuistry that, on the basis of Deut. 24:1, discriminated between the respective rights of men and women.

16. Reminding the Pharisees of the original plan of God (Gen. 1:27 and 2:24), he shows his intention of establishing here below a state of things that realizes the

plan fully; the reign of God, inaugurated by his preaching and his presence, brings with it a full restoration of feminine dignity. But it brings also a surpassing of the ancient juridical structures in which repudiation showed the failure of marriage "by reason of the hardness of hearts." It is in this perspective that the practice of celibacy "for the sake of the kingdom of God" (Matt. 19: 12), for himself and for those "to whom it is given" (19:11) is understood. His attitude toward women should be examined from that point of departure.

17. Thus Jesus inaugurates in the framework of the present world the order of things that constitutes the final horizon of the kingdom of God: that order will result, in "a new heaven and a new earth," in a state in which the risen will no longer need to exercise their sexuality (Matt. 21:31). Consequently, to represent the joy of the kingdom of heaven, Jesus can properly use the image of the virgins called to the wedding feast of the bridegroom (Matt. 25:1–10).

4. From the Mother of Jesus to the Church

18. Considering the historical existence of Jesus, son of God sent into the world (Gal. 4:4 etc.), one might take a look at his beginnings.

19. The evangelists, Matthew and especially Luke, have made clear the irreplaceable role of his mother Mary. The values proper to femininity that the Old Testament presented are recapitulated in her, so that she accomplishes her unique role in the plan of God. But in the very accomplishment of this maternal role, she anticipates the reality of the new covenant of which her son will be the mediator. In fact she is the first one called to a faith that concerns her son (Luke 1:42) and to an obedience in which she "listens to the word of God and puts it into practice" (Luke 11:28, cf. 1:38).

20. Moreover, the Spirit who brings about in her the conception of Jesus (Luke 1:35, Matt. 1:18) will make a new people spring up in history on the day of Pentecost (Acts 2). Her historic role is therefore linked to a resumption of the feminine symbolism used to evoke the new people: from then on, the church is "our mother" (Gal. 4:20). At the end of time, it will be the "spouse of the Lamb" (Apoc. 21). It is by reason of this relationship between Mary, concrete woman, and the church, symbolic woman, that in Apoc. 12 the new humanity rescued from the power of sin and death can be presented as giving birth to Christ, her first born (Apoc. 12:4–15), expecting to have as posterity "those who keep the word of God and have the testimony of Jesus."

5. Woman in the Church

21. Nuptial symbolism is specifically taken up again by St. Paul to evoke the mystery of Christ and his church (Eph. 5:22–33). But it is first of all the relationship between Christ and the church, his body, which casts light on the reality forming the basis for Paul's approach.

22. Despite an institutional framework which implies the submission of women to their husbands (cf. Eph. 5:22; Col. 3:18; 1 Pet. 3:1), Paul reverses the perspective to emphasize their mutual submission (Eph. 5:21) and love (5:25, 33) for which Christ's love is the source and model: charity (cf. 1 Cor. 13) becomes the measure of conjugal love. It is through it that the "original perfection" (that is to say the fullness of the plan of God for the human couple) can be attained (cf. Eph. 5:31 citing Gen. 2:24). That supposes between man and woman not only an equality of rights and duties explicitly affirmed (1 Cor.

7:3–4), but also an equality in adoptive sonship (Gal. 3:28, 2 Cor. 6:18) and in the reception of the Spirit who brings about participation in the life of the church (cf. Acts 2:17–18).

23. Marriage, having thus received its full meaning, thanks to its symbolic relationship with the mystery of Christ and the church (Eph. 5:32), can regain also its indissoluble solidity (1 Cor. 7:10–12; cf. Luke 16:18).

24. At the heart of a sinful world, maternity has a saving value (1 Tim. 2:15). Outside conjugal life, the church grants a place of honor to consecrated widowhood (1 Tim. 5:3) and it recognizes in virginity the possible meaning of eschatological witness (1 Cor. 7:25–26) and of a more complete freedom to consecrate oneself to "the business of the Lord" (1 Cor. 7:32ff.). Such is the background against which theological reflection on the place and function of women in society and in the church takes place.

PART II
The Social Condition of Woman
According to Biblical Revelation

25. I. The Bible, especially the New Testament, teaches very clearly the equality of man and woman in the spiritual domain (relationships with God) and in the moral area (relationships with other human beings). But the problem of the social condition of woman is a sociological problem that must be treated as such:

26. 1. In terms of the laws of sociology: physical and psychosomatic data of feminine behavior in an earthly society;

27. 2. In terms of the history of the societies in which the people of God lived during and after the composition of the Bible;

28. 3. In terms of the laws of the church of Christ, his body, whose members live an ecclesial life under the direction of a magisterium instituted by Christ, while belonging to other societies and states.

29. II. The biblical experience shows that the social condition of woman has varied, but not in a linear manner as if there were continual progress. Ancient Egypt experienced a real flourishing of woman before the existence of Israel. The Israelite woman experienced a certain flourishing under the monarchy, then her condition became subordinate once more. In the time of Christ the status of woman appears, in Jewish society, inferior to what it is in Greco-Roman society where their lack of legal status is in the process of disappearing and in which "women handle their business themselves" (Gaius).

30. In relation to his contemporaries, Christ has a very original attitude with regard to woman which gives renewed value to her situation.

31. III. Christian society is established on a basis other than that of Jewish society. It is founded on the cornerstone of the risen Christ and is built upon Peter in collegiality with the twelve. According to the witness of the New Testament, especially the Pauline epistles, women are associated with the different charismatic ministries (diaconies) of the church (1 Cor. 12:4; 1 Tim. 3:11, cf. 8): prophecy, service, probably even apostolate...without, nevertheless, being of the twelve. They have a place in the liturgy at least as prophetesses

(1 Cor. 11:4). But according to the Pauline corpus (1 Cor. 14:33–35; cf. 1 Tim. 2:6–15) an apostle such as Paul can withdraw the word from them.

32. This Christian society lives not only on the government of the twelve who are called apostles in Luke and elsewhere in the New Testament, but also on the liturgical sacramental life in which Christ communicates his spirit as high priest no longer according to Aaron but according to Melchisedech, king and priest (Heb. 8; cf. Ps. 110).

33. Sociologically speaking, in Jewish society, therefore for Christians until the break, the consecrated priesthood of Aaron (Lev. 9) assured an authentic liturgical and sacrificial life in the temple of stone. But Christ is the true high priest and the true temple (John 2:21). He was consecrated and sent (*hagiazein, apostellein*) by the Father (John 10:26), and he consecrates himself in order to consecrate the apostles in the truth that he himself is (John 17:17. 19). It is a fundamental characteristic of the society that is the church in the midst of other societies, that it dispenses eternal life through its own liturgy.

34. IV. The problem is to know whether in Christian society ruled by the apostles — the twelve, Paul, Titus, Timothy — and by their successors (bishops, presbyters, *higoumenes*) women can be called to participate in this liturgical ministry and in the direction of local communities, as the queens of the Old Testament, especially widows, were called to participate in the royal functions of anointed kings. In fact in the New Testament no text formally supports this hypothesis, even though one may note the role of widows in the pastoral epistles (1 Tim. 5) and what Luke says of Anna in the Temple (*latreuein*). This study is no longer a matter of sociology, but of the labors of our third section (condition of woman in cult).

PART III
Ecclesial Condition of Woman

Old Testament

35. In the Old Testament, the Yahwist religion was not reserved to men alone, as is said elsewhere. Women as well as men could have sacrifices offered, participate in worship. Nevertheless, contrary to the customs of the contemporary pagan peoples, the worship of the second temple was exclusively reserved to men of the tribe of Levi (not only the function of priests, but also that of cantor, porter, etc.).

36. Moreover, there are women who bore the name of prophetess (Maria, Deborah, Huldam, Noiada), while not playing the role of the great prophets. Other women exercised an important function for the salvation of the people of God at critical moments of this people's history (for example, Judith, Esther) (cf. section 2).

37. (Amendment of Father Wanbacq) "In the Old Testament, the Yahwist religion was not a religion in which women were excluded, as is sometimes held. Women as well as men could participate in worship. Contrary to the usages of the contemporary pagan peoples, the official exercise of the temple worship was reserved to men, in the second temple to those of the tribe of Levi."

The Gospels

38. In striking contrast to the contemporary usages of the Jewish world, we see Jesus surrounding himself with women who follow him and serve him (Luke 8:2–3). Mary of Bethany is even described as the exemplary disciple "listening to the word" (Luke 10:38–42). It is the women who are charged with announcing the resurrection "to the apostles and to Peter" (Mark 16:7).

39. The fourth gospel stresses this role of witness attributed to women: the Samaritan woman, whose mere conversation with Jesus had astonished the apostles, goes carrying her witness to Jesus to her fellow citizens. After the resurrection, the evangelist emphasizes the role of Mary Magdalene, whom tradition will call "the apostle of the apostles."

Acts and Paul

40. As Christianity spread, women took a notable part. That again distinguished the new religion sharply from contemporary Judaism.

41. Some women collaborated in the properly apostolic work. This is shown at numerous points in the Acts and the epistles. We shall limit ourselves to a few of them.

42. In the establishment of local communities, they are not content with offering their houses for meetings, as Lydia (Acts 16:14–15), the mother of Mark (Acts 12:12), Prisca (Rom. 16:5), but, according to Phil. 4:2, for example, Evodia and Syntyche are explicitly associated with "Clement and the other collaborators of Paul" in the community. Of the 27 persons thanked or greeted by Paul in the last chapter of the Epistle to the Romans, nine or perhaps 10 are women. In the case of several of them, Paul insists on specifying that they have tired themselves for the community, using a Greek verb (*kopian*) most often used for the work of evangelization properly so called.

43. The case of Prisca and her husband, Aquila, whom Paul calls "his collaborators in Christ" and of whom he says that "to them are indebted not only himself but all the churches of the Gentiles" (Rom. 16:3–4), shows us concretely an example of this "collaboration": their role in the story of Appollo is well known (Acts 18:24–28).

44. Paul mentions explicitly a woman as "deacon" (*diaconos*) of the church of Cenchrees, who "was also" he says, "for many Christians and for himself, a protectress" (Rom. 16:1–2). In the pastoral epistles, the women indicated after the bishops and the deacons probably had a status of *diaconos* (1 Tim. 3:11). Also notable is the case of Junias or Junio, placed in the rank of the apostles (Rom. 16:7), with regard to whom one or another raises the question of whether it is a man.

Part IV
Reply to the Question about the Eventual Ordination of Women to the Priesthood

1. The Ministry of Leadership According to Jesus and the Apostolic Church

45. In establishing the kingdom of God, Jesus, during his ministry, chose a group of 12 men who, after the fashion of the 12 patriarchs of the Old Testament,

would be the leaders of the renewed people of God (Mark 3:14–19); these men whom he destined to "sit upon twelve thrones judging the twelve tribes of Israel" (Matt. 19:28) were first sent to "proclaim that the kingdom of heaven is at hand" (Matt. 10:7).

46. After his death and resurrection, Christ confided to his apostles the mission of evangelizing all nations (Matt. 28:19, Mark 16:5). These men would become his witnesses, beginning at Jerusalem and reaching to the ends of the earth (Acts 1:8, Luke 24:47). "As my Father sent me," he told them, "I also send you" (John 20:21).

47. Upon leaving the earth to return to his Father, he also delegated to a group of men whom he had chosen the responsibility to develop the kingdom of God and the authority to govern the church. The apostolic group thus established by the Lord appeared thus, by the testimony of the New Testament, as the basis of a community which has continued the work of Christ, charged to communicate to humanity the fruits of his salvation.

48. As a matter of fact, we see in the Acts of the Apostles and the epistles that the first communities were always directed by men exercising the apostolic power.

49. The Acts of the Apostles shows that the first Christian community of Jerusalem knew only one ministry of leadership, which was that of the apostles: this was the *urministerioum* from which all the others derived. It seems that, very early, the Greek community received its own structure, presided over by the college of seven (Acts 6:5). A little later there was a question for the Jewish group about a college of presbyters (ibid. 11:30). The church at Antioch was presided over by a group of "five prophets and teachers" (ibid. 13:1). At the end of their first missionary journey, Paul and Barnabas installed presbyters in the newly founded churches (ibid. 14:23).

50. There were also presbyters at Ephesus (ibid., 20:17), to whom were given the name of bishop (ibid. 20:28).

51. The epistles confirm the same picture: There are *proistamenoi* in 1 Thess. 5:12 (cf. 1 Tim. 5:17 *"hoi kalos proestotes presbyteroi"*), of Christian *presbyteroi* (1 Tim 5:1, 2, 17, 19; Titus 1:5; James 5:4; 1 Pet. 5:1, 5), of *episkopoi,* of *hegoumenoi* (Heb. 13:7, 13, 24; cf. Luke 22:26).

52. 1 Cor. 16:16 recommends "submission" to Christians regarding those of the "house of Stephanas" who were sent for the service of the saints.

53. Whatever this last designation may be (verse 17 speaks of Stephanas, Fortunatus and Achaikos), all that we can know of those who held a role of leadership in the communities leads to the conclusion that this role was always held by men (in conformity with the Jewish custom). (N.B. The *"presbytides"* mentioned in Titus 2:3 were elderly women, and not priestesses).

54. The masculine character of the hierarchical order which has structured the church since its beginning thus seems attested to by scripture in an undeniable way. Must we conclude that this rule must be valid forever in the church?

55. We must however recall that according to the gospels, the Acts and St. Paul, certain women made a positive collaboration in service to the Christian communities.

56. Yet one question must still always be asked: What is the normative value which should be accorded to the practice of the Christian communities of the first centuries?

2. *The Ministry of Leadership and the Sacramental Economy*

57. One of the essential elements of the church's life is the sacramental economy which gives the life of Christ to the faithful. The administration of this economy has been entrusted to the church for which the hierarchy is responsible.

58. Thus the question is raised by the relationship between the sacramental economy and the hierarchy.

59. In the New Testament the primordial role of the leaders of the communities seems always to lie in the field of preaching and teaching. These are the people who have the responsibility of keeping the communities in line with the faith of the apostles.

60. No text defines their charge in terms of a special power permitting them to carry out the eucharistic rite or to reconcile sinners.

61. But given the relationship between the sacramental economy and the hierarchy, the administration of the sacraments should not be exercised independently of this hierarchy. It is therefore within the duties of the leadership of the community that we must consider the issue of eucharistic and penitential ministry.

62. In fact there is no proof that these ministries were entrusted to women at the time of the New Testament. Two texts (1 Cor. 14:33–35 and 1 Tim. 2:11–15) forbid women to speak and to teach in assemblies. However, without mentioning doubts raised by some about their Pauline authenticity, it is possible that they refer only to certain concrete situations and abuses. It is possible that certain other situations call on the church to assign to women the role of teaching which these two passages deny them and which constitute a function belonging to the leadership.

63. Is it possible that certain circumstances can come about which call on the church to entrust in the same way to certain women some sacramental ministries?

64. This has been the case with baptism which, though entrusted to the apostles (Matt. 28:19 and Mark 16:15ff), can be administered by others as well. We know that at least later, it will be entrusted also to women.

65. Is it possible that we will come to this even with the ministry of eucharist and reconciliation which manifest eminently the service of the priesthood of Christ carried out by the leaders of the community?

66. It does not seem that the New Testament by itself alone will permit us to settle in a clear way and once and for all the problem of the possible accession of women to the presbyterate.

67. However, some think that in the scriptures there are sufficient indications to exclude this possibility, considering that the sacraments of eucharist and reconciliation have a special link with the person of Christ and therefore with the male hierarchy, as borne out by the New Testament.

68. Others, on the contrary, wonder if the church hierarchy, entrusted with the sacramental economy, would be able to entrust the ministries of eucharist and reconciliation to women in light of circumstances, without going against Christ's original intentions.

Inter Insigniores

("Declaration on the Admission of Women
to the Ministerial Priesthood")

Congregation for the Doctrine of the Faith

October 15, 1976

Introduction: The Role of Women
in Modern Society and the Church

1. Among the characteristics that mark our present age, Pope John XXIII indicated, in his encyclical *Pacem in Terris* of April 11, 1963, "the part that women are now taking in public life.... This is a development that is perhaps of swifter growth among Christian nations, but it is also happening extensively, if more slowly, among nations that are heirs to different traditions and imbued with a different culture."

2. Along the same lines, the Second Vatican Council, enumerating in its pastoral constitution *Gaudium et Spes* the forms of discrimination touching upon the basic rights of the person which must be overcome and eliminated as being contrary to God's plan, gives first place to discrimination based upon sex. The resulting equality will secure the building up of a world that is not leveled out and uniform but harmonious and unified, if men and women contribute to it their own resources and dynamism, as Pope Paul VI recently stated.

3. In the life of the Church herself, as history shows us, women have played a decisive role and accomplished tasks of outstanding value. One has only to think of the foundresses of the great religious families, such as St. Clare and St. Teresa of Avila. The latter, moreover, and St. Catherine of Siena have left writings so rich in spiritual doctrine that Pope Paul VI has included them among the doctors of the Church. Nor could one forget the great number of women who have consecrated themselves to the Lord for the exercise of charity or for the missions, and the Christian wives who have had a profound influence on their families, particularly for the passing on of the faith to their children.

4. But our age gives rise to increased demands: "Since in our time women have an ever more active share in the whole life of society, it is very important that they participate more widely also in the various sectors of the Church's apostolate." This charge of the Second Vatican Council has already set in motion the whole

process of change now taking place: these various experiences of course need to come to maturity.

5. But as Pope Paul VI also remarked, a very large number of Christian communities are already benefiting from the apostolic commitment of women. Some of these women are called to take part in councils set up for pastoral reflection, at the diocesan or parish level; and the Apostolic See has brought women into some of its working bodies.

6. For some years now various Christian communities stemming from the sixteenth century Reformation or of later origin have been admitting women to the pastoral office on a par with men. This initiative has led to petitions and writings by members of these communities and similar groups, directed towards making this admission a general thing; it has also led to contrary reactions.

7. This therefore constitutes an ecumenical problem, and the Catholic Church must make her thinking known on it, all the more because in various sectors of opinion the question has been asked whether she too could not modify her discipline and admit women to priestly ordination.

8. A number of Catholic theologians have even posed this question publicly, evoking studies not only in the sphere of exegesis, patrology, and church history but also in the field of the history of institutions and customs, of sociology, and of psychology. The various arguments capable of clarifying this important problem have been submitted to a critical examination. As we are dealing with a debate that classical theology scarcely touched upon, the current argumentation runs the risk of neglecting essential elements.

9. For these reasons, in execution of a mandate received from the Holy Father and echoing the declaration which he himself made in his letter of November 30, 1975, the Sacred Congregation for the Doctrine of the Faith judges it necessary to recall that the Church, in fidelity to the example of the Lord, does not consider herself authorized to admit women to priestly ordination. The sacred congregation deems it opportune at the present juncture to explain this position of the Church. It is a position that will perhaps cause pain but whose positive value will become apparent in the long run, since it can be of help in deepening understanding of the respective roles of men and of women.

I. The Church's Constant Tradition

10. The Catholic Church has never felt that priestly or episcopal ordination can be validly conferred on women. A few heretical sects in the first centuries, especially Gnostic ones, entrusted the exercise of the priestly ministry to women: this innovation was immediately noted and condemned by the fathers, who considered it as unacceptable in the Church. It is true that in the writings of the fathers one will find the undeniable influence of prejudices unfavorable to women, but nevertheless, it should be noted that these prejudices had hardly any influence on their pastoral activity, and still less on their spiritual direction.

11. But over and above considerations inspired by the spirit of the times, one finds expressed — especially in the canonical documents of the Antiochian and Egyptian traditions — this essential reason, namely, that by calling only men to the priestly order and ministry in its true sense, the Church intends

to remain faithful to the type of ordained ministry willed by the Lord Jesus Christ and carefully maintained by the apostles.

12. The same conviction animates medieval theology, even if the scholastic doctors, in their desire to clarify by reason the data of faith, often present arguments on this point that modern thought would have difficulty in admitting or would even rightly reject. Since that period and up to our own time, it can be said that the question has not been raised again, for the practice has enjoyed peaceful and universal acceptance.

13. The Church's tradition in the matter has thus been so firm in the course of the centuries that the magisterium has not felt the need to intervene in order to formulate a principle which was not attacked, or to defend a law which was not challenged. But each time that this tradition had the occasion to manifest itself, it witnessed to the Church's desire to conform to the model left to her by the Lord.

14. The same tradition has been faithfully safeguarded by the Churches of the East. Their unanimity on this point is all the more remarkable since in many other questions their discipline admits of a great diversity. At the present time these same Churches refuse to associate themselves with requests directed towards securing the accession of women to priestly ordination.

II. The Attitude of Jesus

15. Jesus Christ did not call any woman to become part of the Twelve. If he acted in this way, it was not in order to conform to the customs of his time, for his attitude towards women was quite different from that of his milieu, and he deliberately and courageously broke with it.

16. For example, to the great astonishment of his own disciples Jesus converses publicly with the Samaritan woman (cf. John 4:27); he takes no notice of the state of legal impurity of the woman who had suffered from hemorrhages (cf. Matt. 9:20–22); he allows a sinful woman to approach him in the house of Simon the Pharisee (cf. Luke 7:37ff); and by pardoning the woman taken in adultery, he means to show that one must not be more severe towards the fault of a woman than towards that of a man (cf. John 8:11). He does not hesitate to depart from the Mosaic law in order to affirm the equality of the rights and duties of men and women with regard to the marriage bond (cf. Mark 10:2–11; Matt. 19:3–9).

17. In his itinerant ministry Jesus was accompanied not only by the Twelve but also by a group of women: "Mary, surnamed the Magdalene, from whom seven demons had gone out, Joanna the wife of Herod's steward Chuza, Susanna, and several others who provided for them out of their own resources" (Luke 8:2–3). Contrary to the Jewish mentality, which did not accord great value to the testimony of women, as Jewish law attests, it was nevertheless women who were the first to have the privilege of seeing the risen Lord, and it was they who were charged by Jesus to take the first paschal message to the apostles themselves (cf. Matt. 28:7–10; Luke 24:9–10; John 20:11–18), in order to prepare the latter to become the official witnesses to the resurrection.

18. It is true that these facts do not make the matter immediately obvious. This is no surprise, for the questions that the word of God brings before us go beyond

the obvious. In order to reach the ultimate meaning of the mission of Jesus and the ultimate meaning of scripture, a purely historical exegesis of the texts cannot suffice.

19. But it must be recognized that we have here a number of convergent indications that make all the more remarkable the fact that Jesus did not entrust the apostolic charge to women. Even his mother, who was so closely associated with the mystery of her Son, and whose incomparable role is emphasized by the Gospels of Luke and John, was not invested with the apostolic ministry.

20. This fact was to lead the fathers to present her as the example of Christ's will in this domain; as Pope Innocent III repeated later, at the beginning of the thirteenth century, "Although the Blessed Virgin Mary surpassed in dignity and in excellence all the apostles, nevertheless it was not to her but to them that the Lord entrusted the keys of the kingdom of heaven."

III. The Practice of the Apostles

21. The apostolic community remained faithful to the attitude of Jesus towards women. Although Mary occupied a privileged place in the little circle of those gathered in the upper room after the Lord's ascension (cf. Acts 1:14), it was not she who was called to enter the college of the Twelve at the time of the election that resulted in the choice of Matthias: those who were put forward were two disciples whom the Gospels do not even mention.

22. On the day of Pentecost, the Holy Spirit filled them all, men and women (cf. Acts 2:1, 1:14), yet the proclamation of the fulfillment of the prophecies in Jesus was made only by "Peter and the eleven" (Acts 2:14).

23. When they and Paul went beyond the confines of the Jewish world, the preaching of the Gospel and the Christian life in the Greco-Roman civilization impelled them to break with Mosaic practices, sometimes regretfully. They could therefore have envisaged conferring ordination on women, if they had not been convinced of their duty of fidelity to the Lord on this point.

24. In the Hellenistic world, the cult of a number of pagan divinities was entrusted to priestesses. In fact the Greeks did not share the ideas of the Jews: although their philosophers taught the inferiority of women, historians nevertheless emphasize the existence of a certain movement for the advancement of women during the imperial period.

25. In fact we know from the book of the Acts and from the Letter of St. Paul that certain women worked with the apostle for the Gospel (cf. Rom. 16:3–12; Phil. 4:3). St. Paul lists their names with gratitude in the final salutations of the letters. Some of them often exercised an important influence on conversions: Priscilla, Lydia, and others; especially Priscilla, who took it on herself to complete the instruction of Apollos (cf. Acts 18:26); Phoebe, in the service of the Church of Cenchreae (cf. Rom. 16:1). All these facts manifest within the apostolic Church a considerable evolution vis-à-vis the customs of Judaism. Nevertheless at no time was there a question of conferring ordination on these women.

26. In the Pauline letters, exegetes of authority have noted a difference between two formulas used by the apostle: he writes indiscriminately "my fellow workers" (Rom. 16:3; Phil. 4:2–3) when referring to men and women helping him

in his apostolate in one way or another; but he reserves the title "God's fellow workers" (1 Cor 3:9; cf. 1 Thess. 3:2) to Apollos, Timothy, and himself, thus designated because they are directly set apart for the apostolic ministry and the preaching of the word of God. In spite of the so important role played by women on the day of the resurrection, their collaboration was not extended by St. Paul to the official and public proclamation of the message, since this proclamation belongs exclusively to the apostolic mission.

IV. Permanent Value of the Attitude of Jesus and the Apostles

27. Could the Church today depart from this attitude of Jesus and the apostles, which has been considered as normative by the whole of tradition up to our own day? Various arguments have been put forward in favor of a positive reply to this question, and these must now be examined.

28. It has been claimed in particular that the attitude of Jesus and the apostles is explained by the influence of their milieu and their times. It is said that, if Jesus did not entrust to women and not even to his mother a ministry assimilating them to the Twelve, this was because historical circumstances did not permit him to do so.

29. No one however has ever proved — and it is clearly impossible to prove — that this attitude is inspired only by social and cultural reasons. As we have seen, an examination of the Gospels shows on the contrary that Jesus broke with the prejudices of his time, by widely contravening the discriminations practiced with regard to women. One therefore cannot maintain that, by not calling women to enter the group of the apostles, Jesus was simply letting himself be guided by reasons of expediency.

30. For all the more reason, social and cultural conditioning did not hold back the apostles working in the Greek milieu, where the same forms of discrimination did not exist.

31. Another objection is based upon the transitory character that one claims to see today in some of the prescriptions of St. Paul concerning women, and upon the difficulties that some aspects of his teaching raise in this regard. But it must be noted that these ordinances, probably inspired by the customs of the period, concern scarcely more than disciplinary practices of minor importance, such as the obligation imposed upon women to wear a veil on the head (1 Cor. 11:2–16); such requirements no longer have a normative value.

32. However, the apostle's forbidding of women "to speak" in the assemblies (cf. 1 Cor. 14:34–35; 1 Tim. 2:12) is of a different nature, and exegetes define its meaning in this way: Paul in no way opposes the right, which he elsewhere recognizes as possessed by women, to prophesy in the assembly (cf. 1 Cor. 11:5); the prohibition solely concerns the official function of teaching in the Christian assembly. For St. Paul this prescription [*sic*] is bound up with the divine plan of creation (cf. 1 Cor. 11:7; Gen. 2:18–24): it would be difficult to see in it the expression of a cultural fact.

33. Nor should it be forgotten that we owe to St. Paul one of the most vigorous texts in the New Testament on the fundamental equality of men and women, as children of God in Christ (cf. Gal. 3:28). Therefore there is no reason

for accusing him of prejudices against women, when we note the trust that he shows towards them and the collaboration that he asks of them in his apostolate.

34. But over and above these objections taken from the history of apostolic times, those who support the legitimacy of change in the matter turn to the Church's practice in her sacramental discipline. It has been noted, in our day especially, to what extent the Church is conscious of possessing a certain power over the sacraments, even though they were instituted by Christ. She has used this power down the centuries in order to determine their signs and the conditions of their administration: recent decisions of Popes Pius XII and Paul VI are proof of this.

35. However, it must be emphasized that this power, which is a real one, has definite limits. As Pope Pius XII recalled: "The Church has no power over the substance of the sacraments, that is to say, over what Christ the Lord, as the sources of revelation bear witness, determined should be maintained in the sacramental sign." This was already the teaching of the Council of Trent, which declared: "In the Church there has always existed this power, that in the administration of the sacraments, provided that their substance remains unaltered, she can lay down or modify what she considers more fitting either for the benefit of those who receive them or for respect towards those same sacraments, according to varying circumstances, time or places."

36. Moreover, it must not be forgotten that the sacramental signs are not conventional ones. Not only is it true that, in many respects, they are natural signs because they respond to the deep symbolism of actions and things, but they are more than this: they are principally meant to link the person of every period to the supreme event of the history of salvation, in order to enable that person to understand, through all the Bible's wealth of pedagogy and symbolism, what grace they signify and produce.

37. For example, the sacrament of the eucharist is not only a fraternal meal, but at the same time the memorial that makes present and actual Christ's sacrifice and his offering by the Church. Again, the priestly ministry is not just a pastoral service; it ensures the continuity of the functions entrusted by Christ to the apostles and the continuity of the powers related to those functions. Adaptation to civilizations and times therefore cannot abolish, on essential points, the sacramental reference to constitutive events of Christianity and to Christ himself.

38. In the final analysis it is the Church, through the voice of her magisterium, that, in these various domains, decides what can change and what must remain immutable. When she judges that she cannot accept certain changes, it is because she knows that she is bound by Christ's manner of acting. Her attitude, despite appearances, is therefore not one of archaism but of fidelity: it can be truly understood only in this light. The Church makes pronouncements in virtue of the Lord's promise and the presence of the Holy Spirit, in order to proclaim better the mystery of Christ and to safeguard and manifest the whole of its rich content.

39. This practice of the Church therefore has a normative character: in the fact of conferring priestly ordination only on men, it is a question of an unbroken tradition throughout the history of the Church, universal in the East and in the West, and alert to repress abuses immediately. This norm, based on Christ's

example, has been and is still observed because it is considered to conform to God's plan for his Church.

V. The Ministerial Priesthood in the Light of the Mystery of Christ

40. Having recalled the Church's norm and the basis thereof, it seems useful and opportune to illustrate this norm by showing the profound fittingness that theological reflection discovers between the proper nature of the sacrament of order, with its specific reference to the mystery of Christ, and the fact that only men have been called to receive priestly ordination. It is not a question here of bringing forward a demonstrative argument, but of clarifying this teaching by the analogy of faith.

41. The Church's constant teaching, repeated and clarified by the Second Vatican Council and again recalled by the 1971 Synod of Bishops and by the Sacred Congregation for the Doctrine of the Faith in its declaration of June 24, 1973, declares that the bishop or the priest, in the exercise of his ministry, does not act in his own name, *in persona propria*: he represents Christ, who acts through him: "the priest truly acts in the place of Christ," as St. Cyprian already wrote in the third century.

42. It is this ability to represent Christ that St. Paul considered as characteristic of his apostolic function (cf. 2 Cor. 5:20; Gal. 4:14). The supreme expression of this representation is found in the altogether special form it assumes in the celebration of the eucharist, which is the source and center of the Church's unity, the sacrificial meal in which the people of God are associated in the sacrifice of Christ: the priest, who alone has the power to perform it, then acts not only through the effective power conferred on him by Christ, but in *persona Christi*, taking the role of Christ, to the point of being his very image, when he pronounces the words of consecration.

43. The Christian priesthood is therefore of a sacramental nature: the priest is a sign, the supernatural effectiveness of which comes from the ordination received, but a sign that must be perceptible and which the faithful must be able to recognize with ease.

44. The whole sacramental economy is in fact based upon natural signs, on symbols imprinted upon the human psychology: "Sacramental signs," says St. Thomas, "represent what they signify by natural resemblance."

45. The same natural resemblance is required for persons as for things: when Christ's role in the eucharist is to be expressed sacramentally, there would not be this "natural resemblance" which must exist between Christ and his minister if the role of Christ were not taken by a man: in such a case it would be difficult to see in the minister the image of Christ. For Christ himself was and remains a man.

46. Christ is of course the firstborn of all humanity, of women as well as men: the unity which he re-established after sin is such that there are no more distinctions between Jew and Greek, slave and free, male and female, but all are one in Christ Jesus (cf. Gal. 3:28). Nevertheless, the incarnation of the word took place according to the male sex: this is indeed a question of fact, and this fact, while not implying an alleged natural superiority of man over woman, cannot

be disassociated from the economy of salvation: it is, indeed, in harmony with the entirety of God's plan as God himself has revealed it, and of which the mystery of the covenant is the nucleus.

47. For the salvation offered by God to men and women, the union with him to which they are called — in short, the covenant — took on, from the Old Testament prophets onwards, the privileged form of a nuptial mystery: for God the chosen people is seen as his ardently loved spouse.

48. Both Jewish and Christian traditions have discovered the depth of this intimacy of love by reading and rereading the Song of Songs; the divine bridegroom will remain faithful even when the bride betrays his love, when Israel is unfaithful to God (cf. Hos. 1–3; Jer. 2).

49. When the "fullness of time" (Gal. 4:4) comes, the Word, the Son of God, takes on flesh in order to establish and seal the new and eternal covenant in his blood, which will be shed for many so that sins may be forgiven. His death will gather together again the scattered children of God; from his pierced side will be born the Church, as Eve was born from Adam's side.

50. At that time there is fully and eternally accomplished the nuptial mystery proclaimed and hymned in the Old Testament: Christ is the bridegroom; the Church is his bride, whom he loves because he has gained her by his blood and made her glorious, holy and without blemish, and henceforth he is inseparable from her.

51. This nuptial theme, which is developed from the Letters of St. Paul onwards (cf. 2 Cor. 11:2; Eph. 5:22–23) to the writings of St. John (cf. especially John 3:29; Rev. 19:7, 9), is present also in the synoptic Gospels: the bridegroom's friends must not fast as long as he is with them (cf. Mark 2:19); the kingdom of heaven is like a king who gave a feast for his son's wedding (cf. Matt. 22:1–14).

52. It is through this scriptural language, all interwoven with symbols and which expresses and affects man and woman in their profound identity, that there is revealed to us the mystery of God and Christ, a mystery which of itself is unfathomable.

53. That is why we can never ignore the fact that Christ is a man. And therefore, unless one is to disregard the importance of this symbolism for the economy of revelation, it must be admitted that, in actions which demand the character of ordination and in which Christ himself, the author of the covenant, the bridegroom and head of the Church, is represented, exercising his ministry of salvation — which is in the highest degree the case of the eucharist — his role (this is the original sense of the word *persona)* must be taken by a man. This does not stem from any personal superiority of the latter in the order of values, from a difference of fact on the level of functions and service.

54. Could one say that, since Christ is now in the heavenly condition, from now on it is a matter of indifference whether he be represented by a man or by a woman, since, "at the resurrection men and women do not marry" (Matt. 22:30)? But this text does not mean that the distinction between man and woman, insofar as it determines the identity proper to the person, is suppressed in the glorified state; what holds for us holds also for Christ.

55. It is indeed evident that in human beings the difference of sex exercises an important influence, much deeper than, for example, ethnic differences: the

latter do not affect the human person as intimately as the difference of sex, which is directly ordained both for the communion of persons and for the generation of human beings. In biblical revelation this difference is the effect of God's will from the beginning: "male and female he created them" (Gen. 1:27).

56. However, it will perhaps be further objected that the priest, especially when he presides at the liturgical and sacramental functions, equally represents the Church: he acts in her name with "the intention of doing what she does." In this sense, the theologians of the Middle Ages said that the minister also acts *in persona Ecclesiae,* that is to say, in the name of the whole Church and in order to represent her. And in fact, leaving aside the question of the participation of the faithful in a liturgical action, it is indeed in the name of the whole Church that the action is celebrated by the priest: he prays in the name of all, and in the Mass he offers the sacrifice of the whole Church.

57. In the new Passover, the Church, under visible signs, immolates Christ through the ministry of the priest. And so, it is asserted, since the priest also represents the Church, would it not be possible to think that this representation could be carried out by a woman, according to the symbolism already explained?

58. It is true that the priest represents the Church, which is the body of Christ. But if he does so, it is precisely because he first represents Christ himself, who is the head and shepherd of the Church. The Second Vatican Council used this phrase to make more precise and to complete the expression *in persona Christi.* It is in this quality that the priest presides over the Christian assembly and celebrates the eucharistic sacrifice "in which the whole Church offers and is herself wholly offered."

59. If one does justice to these reflections, one will better understand how well-founded is the basis of the Church's practice; and one will conclude that the controversies raised in our days over the ordination of women are for all Christians a pressing invitation to meditate on the mystery of the Church, to study in greater detail the meaning of the episcopate and the priesthood, and to rediscover the real and preeminent place of the priest in the community of the baptized, of which he indeed forms part but from which he is distinguished because, in the actions that call for the character of ordination, for the community he is — with all the effectiveness proper to the sacraments — the image and symbol of Christ himself who calls, forgives, and accomplishes the sacrifice of the covenant.

VI. The Ministerial Priesthood in the Mystery of the Church

60. It is opportune to recall that problems of sacramental theology, especially when they concern the ministerial priesthood, as is the case here, cannot be solved except in the light of revelation. The human sciences, however valuable their contribution in their own domain, cannot suffice here, for they cannot grasp the realities of faith: the properly supernatural context of these realities is beyond their competence.

61. Thus one must note the extent to which the Church is a society different from other societies, original in her nature and in her structures. The pastoral charge in the Church is normally linked to the sacrament of order: it is not a simple

government, comparable to the modes of authority found in states. It is not granted by people's spontaneous choice: even when it involves designation through election, it is the laying on of hands and the prayer of the successors of the apostles that guarantee God's choice; and it is the Holy Spirit, given by ordination, who grants participation in the ruling power of the supreme pastor, Christ (cf. Acts 20:28). It is a charge of service and love: "If you love me, feed my sheep" (cf. John 21:15–17).

62. For this reason one cannot see how it is possible to propose the admission of women to the priesthood in virtue of the equality of rights of the human person, an equality which holds good also for Christians. To this end use is sometimes made of the text quoted above, from the Letter to the Galatians (3:28), which says that in Christ there is no longer any distinction between men and women. But this passage does not concern ministries: it only affirms the universal calling to divine filiation, which is the same for all.

63. Moreover, and above all, to consider the ministerial priesthood as a human right would be to misjudge its nature completely: baptism does not confer any personal title to public ministry in the Church. The priesthood is not conferred for the honor or advantage of the recipient, but for the service of God and the Church; it is the object of a specific and totally gratuitous vocation: "You did not choose me, no, I chose you; and I commissioned you" (John 15:16; Heb. 5:4).

64. It is sometimes said and written in books and periodicals that some women feel that they have a vocation to the priesthood. Such an attraction, however noble and understandable, still does not suffice for a genuine vocation. In fact a vocation cannot be reduced to a mere personal attraction, which can remain purely subjective.

65. Since the priesthood is a particular ministry of which the Church has received the charge and the control, authentication by the Church is indispensable here and is a constitutive part of the vocation: Christ chose "those he wanted" (Mark 3:13). On the other hand, there is a universal vocation of all the baptized to the exercise of the royal priesthood by offering their lives to God and by giving witness for his praise.

66. Women who express a desire for the ministerial priesthood are doubtless motivated by the desire to serve Christ and the Church. And it is not surprising that, at a time when they are becoming more aware of the discriminations to which they have been subject, they should desire the ministerial priesthood itself.

67. But it must not be forgotten that the priesthood does not form part of the rights of the individual, but stems from the economy of the mystery of Christ and the Church. The priestly office cannot become the goal of social advancement; no merely human progress of society or of the individual can of itself give access to it: it is of another order.

68. It therefore remains for us to meditate more deeply on the nature of the real equality of the baptized which is one of the great affirmations of Christianity: equality is in no way identity, for the Church is a differentiated body, in which each individual has his or her role. The roles are distinct, and must not be confused; they do not favor the superiority of some vis-à-vis the others, nor do they provide an excuse for jealousy; the only better gift, which can and

must be desired, is love (cf. 1 Cor. 12–13). The greatest in the kingdom of heaven are not the ministers but the saints.

69. The Church desires that Christian women should become fully aware of the greatness of their mission: today their role is of capital importance, both for the renewal and humanization of society and for the rediscovery by believers of the true face of the Church.

70. *His Holiness, Pope Paul VI, during the audience granted to the undersigned prefect of the Sacred Congregation on October 15, 1976, approved this declaration, confirmed it, and ordered its publication.*

Given in Rome, Sacred Congregation for the Doctrine of the Faith
October 15, 1976, the feast of St. Teresa of Avila
Cardinal Francis Seper, Prefect, Congregation for the Doctrine of the Faith

A Commentary on the Declaration

Prepared by an Expert Theologian at the Request of the Congregation for the Doctrine of the Faith

January 27, 1977

Circumstances and Origins of the Declaration

1. The question of the admission of women to the ministerial priesthood seems to have arisen in a general way about 1958, after the decision by the Swedish Lutheran Church in September of that year to admit women to the pastoral office. This caused a sensation and occasioned numerous commentaries.

2. Even for the communities stemming from the sixteenth century Reformation it was an innovation: one may recall, for example, how strongly the *Confessio Fidei Scotiae* of 1560 accused the Roman Church of making improper concessions to women in the field of ministry. But the Swedish initiative gradually gained ground among the Reformed Churches, particularly in France, where various national synods adopted similar decisions.

3. In reality, the admission of women to the pastoral office seemed to raise no strictly theological problem, in that these communities had rejected the sacrament of order at the time of their separation from the Roman Church.

4. But a new and much more serious situation was created when ordinations of women were carried out within communities that considered that they preserved the apostolic succession of order: in 1971 and 1973 the Anglican bishop of Hong Kong ordained three women with the agreement of his synod; in July 1974 at Philadelphia there was the ordination in the Episcopal Church of eleven women — an ordination afterwards declared invalid by the House of Bishops.

5. Later on, in June 1975, the General Synod of the Anglican Church in Canada, meeting in Quebec, approved the principle of the accession of women to the priesthood; and this was followed in July by the General Synod of the Church of England: Dr. Coggan, Archbishop of Canterbury, frankly informed Pope Paul VI "of the slow but steady growth of a consensus of opinion within the Anglican Communion that there are no fundamental objections in principle to the ordination of women to the priesthood."

6. These are only general principles, but they might quickly be followed by practice, and this would bring a new and serious element into the dialogue with the Roman Catholic Church on the nature of the ministry. It has provoked a warning, first by the archbishop for the Orthodox in Great Britain, Athenagoras of

Thyateira, and then, more recently, by Pope Paul VI himself in two letters to the Archbishop of Canterbury.

7. Furthermore, the ecumenical sectors brought the question to the notice of all the Christian denominations, forcing them to examine their positions of principle, especially on the occasion of the Assembly of the World Council of Churches at Nairobi in December 1975.

8. A completely different event has made the question even more topical: this was the organization under United Nations auspices of International Women's Year in 1975. The Holy See took part in it with a Committee for International Women's Year, which included some members of the Commission for the Study of the Role of Women in Society and the Church, which had already been set up in 1973.

9. Ensuring respect for and fostering the respective rights and duties of men and women leads to reflection on participation by women in the life of society on the one hand, and in the life and mission of the Church on the other. Now, the Second Vatican Council has already set forth the task: "Since in our times women have an ever more active share in the whole life of society, it is very important that they participate more widely also in the various fields of the Church's apostolate." How far can this participation go?

10. It is understandable that these questions have aroused even in Catholic quarters intense studies, indeed passionate ones: doctoral theses, articles in reviews, even pamphlets, propounding or refuting in turn the biblical, historical, and canonical data and appealing to the human sciences of sociology, psychology, and the history of institutions and customs.

11. Certain famous people have not hesitated to take sides boldly, judging that there was "no basic theological objection to the possibility of women priests." A number of groups have been formed with a view to upholding this claim, and they have sometimes done this with insistence, as did the conference held in Detroit (U.S.A.) in November 1975 under the title "Women in Future Priesthood Now: A Call for Action."

12. The magisterium has thus been obliged to intervene in a question being posed in so lively a fashion within the Catholic Church and having important implications from the ecumenical point of view.

13. Archbishop Bernardin of Cincinnati, president of the U.S. National Conference of Catholic Bishops, declared on October 7, 1975, that he found himself "obliged to restate the Church's teaching that women are not to be ordained to the priesthood"; church leaders, he said, should "not seem to encourage unreasonable hopes and expectations even by their silence."

14. Pope Paul VI himself had already recalled the same teaching. He did so at first in parenthetical fashion, especially in his address on April 18, 1975, to the members of the Study Commission on the Role of Women in Society and in the Church and the Committee for the Celebration of International Women's Year: "Although women do not receive the call to the apostolate of the Twelve and therefore to the ordained ministries, they are nonetheless invited to follow Christ as disciples and co-workers.... We cannot change what our Lord did, nor his call to women."

15. Later he had to make an express pronouncement in his exchange of letters with Dr. Coggan, Archbishop of Canterbury: "Your Grace is of course well

aware of the Catholic Church's position on this question. She holds that it is not admissible to ordain women to the priesthood, for very fundamental reasons."

16. It is at his order that the Sacred Congregation for the Doctrine of the Faith has examined the question in its entirety. The question has been complicated by the fact that on the one hand arguments adduced in the past in favor of the traditional teaching are scarcely defensible today, and on the other hand the reasons given by those who demand the ordination of women must be evaluated.

17. To avoid the rather negative character that must mark the conclusions of such a study, one could have thought of inserting it into a more general presentation of the question of the advancement of women. But the time is not ripe for such a comprehensive exposition, because of the research and work in progress on all sides.

18. It was difficult to leave unanswered any longer a precise question that is being posed nearly everywhere and that is polarizing attention to the detriment of more urgent endeavors that should be fostered. In fact, apart from its nonacceptance of the ordination of women, the document points to positive matters: a deeper understanding of the Church's teaching and of the ministerial priesthood, a call to spiritual progress, an invitation to take on the urgent apostolic tasks of today.

19. The bishops, to whom the document is primarily addressed, have the mission of explaining it to their people with the pastoral feeling that is theirs and with the knowledge they have of the milieu in which they exercise their ministry.

20. The declaration begins by presenting the Church's teaching on the question. This in fact has to be the point of departure. We shall see later how necessary it is to follow faithfully the method of using *loci theologici.*

The Tradition

21. It is an undeniable fact, as the declaration notes, that the constant tradition of the Catholic Church has excluded women from the episcopate and the priesthood. So constant has it been that there has been no need for an intervention by a solemn decision of the magisterium.

22. "The same tradition," the document stresses, "has been faithfully safeguarded by the Churches of the East. Their unanimity on this point is all the more remarkable since in many other questions their discipline admits of a great diversity. At the present time these same Churches refuse to associate themselves with requests directed towards securing the accession of women to priestly ordination."

23. Only within some heretical sects of the early centuries, principally Gnostic ones, do we find attempts to have the priestly ministry exercised by women. It must be further noted that these are very sporadic occurrences and are moreover associated with rather questionable practices.

24. We know of them only through the severe disapproval with which they are noted by St. Irenaeus in his *Adversus Haereses,* Tertullian in *De Praescriptione Haereticorum,* Firmilian of Caesarea in a letter to St. Cyprian, Origen

in a commentary on the First Letter to the Corinthians, and especially by St. Epiphanius in his *Panarion.*

25. How are we to interpret the constant and universal practice of the Church? A theologian is certain that what the Church does she can in fact do, since she has the assistance of the Holy Spirit. This is a classical argument found again and again in St. Thomas with regard to the sacraments.

26. But what the Church has never done — is this any proof that she cannot do it in the future? Does the negative fact thus noted indicate a norm, or is it to be explained by historical and by social and cultural circumstances? In the present case, is an explanation to be found in the position of women in ancient and medieval society and in a certain idea of male superiority stemming from that society's culture?

27. It is because of this transitory cultural element that some arguments adduced on this subject in the past are scarcely defensible today. The most famous is the one summarized by St. Thomas Aquinas: *quia mulier est in statu subiectionis.* In St. Thomas' thought, however, this assertion is not merely the expression of a philosophical concept, since he interprets it in the light of the accounts in the first chapters of Genesis and the teaching of the First Letter to Timothy (2:12–14).

28. A similar formula is found earlier in the *Decretum* of Gratian, but Gratian, who was quoting the Carolingian Capitularies and the false Decretals, was trying rather to justify with Old Testament prescriptions the prohibition — already formulated by the ancient Church — of women from entering the sanctuary and serving at the altar.

29. The polemical arguments of recent years have often recalled and commented on the texts that develop these arguments. They have also used them to accuse the fathers of the Church of misogyny. It is true that we find in the fathers' writings the undeniable influence of prejudices against women. But it must be carefully noted that these passages had very little influence on their pastoral activity, still less on their spiritual direction, as we can see by glancing through their correspondence that has come down to us.

30. Above all it would be a serious mistake to think that such considerations provide the only or the most decisive reasons against the ordination of women in the thought of the fathers, of the medieval writers, and of the theologians of the classical period. In the midst of and going beyond speculation, more and more clear expression was being given to the Church's awareness that in reserving priestly ordination and ministry to men she was obeying a tradition received from Christ and the apostles and by which she felt herself bound.

31. This is what had been expressed in the form of an apocryphal literature by the ancient documents of church discipline from Syria, such as the *Didascalia Apostolorum* (middle of the third century) and the apostolic constitutions (end of the fourth or beginning of the fifth century), and by the Egyptian collection of twenty pseudoapostolic canons that was included in the compilation of the Alexandrian *Synodos* and translated into many languages.

32. St. John Chrysostom, for his part, when commenting on chapter 21 of John, understood well that women's exclusion from the pastoral office entrusted to Peter was not based on any natural incapacity, since, as he remarks, "even the majority of men have been excluded by Jesus from this immense task."

33. From the moment that the teaching on the sacraments is systematically pre-
    sented in the schools of theology and canon law, writers begin to deal *ex
    professo* with the nature and value of the tradition that reserved ordination
    to men. The canonists base their case on the principle formulated by Pope
    Innocent III in a letter of December 11, 1210, to the bishops of Palencia and
    Burgos, a letter that was included in the collection of Decretals: "Although the
    Blessed Virgin Mary was of higher dignity and excellence than all the apostles,
    it was to them, not her, that the Lord entrusted the keys of the kingdom of
    heaven." This text became a *locus communis* for the *glossatores*.

34. As for the theologians, the following are some significant texts: St. Bonaven-
    ture: "Our position is this: it is due not so much to a decision by the Church
    as to the fact that the sacrament of order is not for them. In this sacrament
    the person ordained is a sign of Christ the mediator."

35. Richard of Middleton, a Franciscan of the second half of the thirteenth century:
    "The reason is that the power of the sacraments comes from their institution.
    But Christ instituted this sacrament for conferral on men only, not women."

36. John Duns Scotus: "It must not be considered to have been determined by
    the Church. It comes from Christ. The Church would not have presumed to
    deprive the female sex, for no fault of its own, of an act that might licitly have
    pertained to it." Durandus of Saint-Pourcain: "...the male sex is of necessity
    for the sacrament. The principal cause of this is Christ's institution.... Christ
    ordained only men...not even his mother.... It must therefore be held that
    women cannot be ordained, because of Christ's institution."

37. So it is no surprise that until the modern period the theologians and canonists
    who dealt with the question have been almost unanimous in considering this
    exclusion as absolute and having a divine origin. The theological notes they
    apply to the affirmation vary from "theologically certain" (*theologice certa*)
    to, at times, "proximate to faith" (*fidei proxima*) or even "doctrine of the
    faith" (*doctrina fidei*). Apparently, then, until recent decades no theologian or
    canonist considered that it was a matter of a simple law of the Church.

38. In some writers of the Middle Ages however there was a certain hesitancy,
    reported by St. Bonaventure without adopting it himself and noted also by
    Joannes Teutonicus in his gloss on *Caus.* 27, q. 1, c. 23. This hesitancy
    stemmed from the knowledge that in the past there had been deaconesses: had
    they received true sacramental ordination? This problem has been brought up
    again very recently.

39. It was by no means unknown to the seventeenth and eighteenth century theo-
    logians, who had an excellent knowledge of this history of literature. In any
    case, it is a question that must be taken up fully by direct study of the texts,
    without preconceived ideas; hence the Sacred Congregation for the Doctrine
    of the Faith has judged that it should be kept for the future and not touched
    upon in the present document.

The Attitude of Christ

40. In the light of tradition, then, it seems that the essential reason moving the
    Church to call only men to the sacrament of order and to the strictly priestly
    ministry is her intention to remain faithful to the type of ordained ministry

willed by the Lord Jesus Christ and carefully maintained by the apostles. It is therefore no surprise that in the controversy there has been a careful examination of the facts and texts of the New Testament, in which tradition has seen an example establishing a norm.

41. This brings us to a fundamental observation: we must not expect the New Testament on its own to resolve in a clear fashion the question of the possibility of women acceding to the priesthood, in the same way that it does not on its own enable us to give an account of certain sacraments, and especially of the structure of the sacrament of order.

42. Keeping to the sacred text alone and to the points of the history of Christian origins that can be obtained by analyzing that text by itself would be to go back four centuries and find oneself once more amid the controversies of the Reformation. We cannot omit the study of tradition: it is the Church that scrutinizes the Lord's thought by reading scripture, and it is the Church that gives witness to the correctness of its interpretation.

43. It is tradition that has unceasingly set forth as an expression of Christ's will the fact that he chose only men to form the group of the Twelve. There is no disputing this fact, but can it be proved with absolute certainty that it was a question of a deliberate decision by Christ?

44. It is understandable that the partisans of a change in discipline bring all their efforts to bear against the significance of this fact. In particular, they object that, if Christ did not bring women into the group of the Twelve, it was because the prejudices of his time did not allow him to: it would have been an imprudence that would have compromised his work irreparably.

45. However, it has to be recognized that Jesus did not shrink from other "imprudences," which did in fact stir up the hostility of his fellow citizens against him, especially his freedom with regard to the rabbinical interpretations of the Sabbath. With regard to women his attitude was a complete innovation: all the commentators recognize that he went against many prejudices, and the facts that are noted add up to an impressive total.

46. For this reason greater stress is laid today on another objection: if Jesus chose only men to form the group of the Twelve, it was because he intended them to be a symbol representing the ancestors of the tribes of Israel ("You who have followed me will also sit on Twelve thrones and judge the tribes of Israel": Matt. 19:28; cf. Luke 22:30); and this special motive, it is added, obviously referred only to the Twelve and would be no proof that the apostolic ministry should thereafter always be reserved to men. It is not a convincing argument.

47. We may note in the first place how little importance was given to this symbolism: Mark and John do not mention it. And in Matthew and Luke this phrase of Jesus about the twelve tribes of Israel is not put in the context of the call of the Twelve (Matt. 10:1–4) but at a relatively late stage of Jesus' public life, when the apostles have long since been given their "constitution": they have been called by Jesus, have worked with him and been sent on missions.

48. Furthermore, the symbolism of Matt. 19:28 and Luke 22:30 is not as certain as is claimed: the number could designate simply the whole of Israel. Finally, these two texts deal only with a particular aspect of the mission of the Twelve: Jesus is promising them that they will take part in the eschatological judgment. Therefore the essential meaning of their being chosen is not to be sought in

this symbolism but in the totality of the mission given them by Jesus: "he appointed twelve; they were to be his companions and to be sent out to preach" (Mark 3:14).

49. As Jesus before them, the Twelve were above all to preach the good news (Mark 3:14, 6:12). Their mission in Galilee (Mark 6:7-13) was to become the model of the universal mission (Mark 12:10; cf. Matt. 28:16–20). Within the messianic people the Twelve represent Jesus. That is the real reason why it is fitting that the apostles should be men: they act in the name of Christ and must continue his work.

50. It has been described above how Pope Innocent III saw a witness to Christ's intentions in the fact that Christ did not communicate to his mother, in spite of her eminent dignity, the powers which he gave to the apostles.

51. This is one of the arguments most frequently repeated by tradition: from as early as the third century the fathers present Mary as the example of the will of Jesus in this matter. It is an argument still particularly dear to Eastern Christians today. Nevertheless it is vigorously rejected by all those who plead in favor of the ordination of women.

52. Mary's divine motherhood, the manner in which she was associated with the redeeming work of her Son, they say, put her in an altogether exceptional and unique position; and it would not even be fair to her to compare her with the apostles and to argue from the fact that she was not ranked among them.

53. In point of fact these assertions do have the advantage of making us understand that there are different functions within the Church: the equality of Christians is in harmony with the complementary nature of their tasks, and the sacramental ministry is not the only rank of greatness, nor is it necessarily the highest: it is a form of service of the kingdom. The Virgin Mary does not need the increase in "dignity" that was once attributed to her by the authors of those speculations on the priesthood of Mary that formed a deviant tendency which was soon discredited.

The Practice of the Apostles

54. The text of the declaration stresses the fact that, in spite of the privileged place Mary had in the upper room after the ascension, she was not designated for entry into the college of the Twelve at the time of the election of Matthias. The same holds for Mary Magdalene and the other women who nevertheless had been the first to bring news of the resurrection.

55. It is true that the Jewish mentality did not accord great value to the witness of women, as is shown by Jewish law. But one must also note that the Acts of the Apostles and the Letters of St. Paul stress the role of women in evangelization and in instructing individual converts.

56. The apostles were led to take a revolutionary decision when they had to go beyond the circle of a Jewish community and undertake the evangelization of the Gentiles. The break with Mosaic observances was not made without discord. Paul had no scruples about choosing one of his collaborators, Titus, from among the Gentile converts (Gal. 2:3).

57. The most spectacular expression of the change that the good news made on the mentality of the first Christians is to be found precisely in the Letter of the

Galatians: "For as many of you as were baptized in Christ have put on Christ. There is neither Jew nor Greek, there is neither slave nor free, there is neither male nor female; for you are all one in Christ Jesus" (Gal. 3:27–28).

58. In spite of this, the apostles did not entrust to women the strictly apostolic ministry, although Hellenistic civilization did not have the same prejudices against them as did Judaism. It is rather a ministry which is of another order, as may perhaps also be gathered from Paul's vocabulary, in which a difference seems to be implied between "my fellow workers" (*synergoi mou*) and "God's fellow workers" (*Theou synergoi*).

59. It must be repeated that the texts of the New Testament, even on such important points as the sacraments, do not always give all the light that one would wish to find in them. Unless the value of unwritten traditions is admitted, it is sometimes difficult to discover in scripture entirely explicit indications of Christ's will. But in view of the attitude of Jesus and the practice of the apostles as seen in the Gospels, the Acts, and the letters, the Church has not held that she is authorized to admit women to priestly ordination.

Permanent Value of This Practice

60. It is the permanency of this negative decision that is objected to by those who would have the legitimacy of ordaining women admitted. These objections employ arguments of great variety.

61. The most classic ones seek a basis in historical circumstances. We have already seen what is to be thought of the view that Jesus' attitude was inspired solely by prudence, because he did not want to risk compromising his work by going against social prejudices. It is claimed that the same prudence was forced upon the apostles.

62. On this point too it is clear from the history of the apostolic period that there is no foundation for this explanation. However, in the case of the apostles, should one not take into account the way in which they themselves shared these prejudices? Thus St. Paul has been accused of misogyny and in his letters are found texts on the inferiority of women that are the subject of controversy among exegetes and theologians today.

63. It can be questioned whether two of Paul's most famous texts on women are authentic or should rather be seen as interpolations, perhaps even relatively late ones. The first is 1 Cor. 14:34–35: "The women should keep silence in the churches. For they are not permitted to speak, but should be subordinate as even the law says." These two verses, apart from being missing in some important manuscripts and not being found quoted before the end of the second century, present stylistic peculiarities foreign to Paul. The other text is 1 Tim. 2:11–14: "I do not allow a woman to teach or to exercise authority over men." The Pauline authenticity of this text is often questioned, although the arguments are weaker.

64. However, it is of little importance whether these texts are authentic or not: theologians have made abundant use of them to explain that women cannot receive either the power of magisterium or that of jurisdiction. It was especially the text of 1 Timothy that provided St. Thomas with the proof that woman is in a state of submission or service, since (as the text explains) woman was created after man and was the person first responsible for original sin.

65. But there are other Pauline texts of unquestioned authenticity that affirm that "the head of the woman is the man" (1 Cor. 11:3; cf. 8–12; Eph. 5:22, 24). It may be asked whether this view of man, which is in line with that of the books of the Old Testament, is not at the basis of Paul's conviction and the Church's tradition that women cannot receive the ministry.

66. Now this is a view that modern society rejects absolutely, and many present-day theologians would shrink from adopting it without qualifying it. We may note however that Paul does not take his stand on a philosophical level but on that of biblical history: when he describes, in relation to marriage, the symbolism of love, he does not see man's superiority as domination but as a gift demanding sacrifice, in the image of Christ.

67. On the other hand there are prescriptions in Paul's writings that are unanimously admitted to have been transitory, such as the obligation he imposed on women to wear a veil (1 Cor. 11:2–16). It is true that these are obviously disciplinary practices of minor importance, perhaps inspired by the customs of the time. But then there arises the more basic questions: since the Church has later been able to abandon prescriptions contained in the New Testament, why should it not be the same with the exclusion of women from ordination?

68. Here we meet once again the essential principle that it is the Church herself that, in the different sectors of her life, ensures discernment between what can change and what must remain immutable. As the declaration specifies, "When she judges that she cannot accept certain changes, it is because she knows that she is bound by Christ's manner of acting. Her attitude, despite appearances, is therefore not one of archaism but of fidelity: it can be truly understood only in this light. The Church makes pronouncements in virtue of the Lord's promise and the presence of the Holy Spirit, in order to proclaim better the mystery of Christ and to safeguard and manifest the whole if its rich content."

69. Many of the questions confronting the Church as a result of the numerous arguments put forward in favor of the ordination of women must be considered in the light of this principle. An example is the following question dealt with by the declaration: why will the Church not change her discipline, since she is aware of having a certain power over the sacraments, even though they were instituted by Christ, in order to determine the sign or to fix the conditions for their administration? This faculty remains limited, as was recalled by Pius XII, echoing the Council of Trent: the Council has no power over the substance of the sacraments. It is the Church herself that must distinguish what forms part of the "substance of the sacraments" and what she can determine or modify if circumstances should so suggest.

70. On this point, furthermore, we must remember, as the declaration reminds us, that the sacraments and the Church herself are closely tied to history, since Christianity is the result of an event: the coming of the Son of God into time and to a country, and his death on the cross under Pontius Pilate outside the walls of Jerusalem. The sacraments are a memorial of saving events. For this reason their signs are linked to those very events They are relative to one civilization, one culture, although destined to be reproduced everywhere until the end of time.

71. Hence historical choices have taken place by which the Church is bound, even if speaking absolutely and on a speculative level other choices could be imagined. This, for instance, is the case with bread and wine as matter for the

eucharist, for the Mass is not just a fraternal meal but the renewal of the Lord's supper and the memorial of his passion and thus linked with something done in history.

72. It has likewise been remarked that in the course of time the Church has agreed to confer on women certain truly ministerial functions that antiquity refused to give them in the very name of the example and will of Christ. The functions spoken of are above all the administration of baptism, teaching, and certain forms of ecclesiastical jurisdiction. As regards baptism, however, not even deaconesses in the Syriac-speaking East were permitted to administer it, and its solemn administration is still a hierarchical act reserved to bishop, priest, and, in accessory fashion, deacon. When urgently required, baptism can be conferred not only by Christians but even by unbaptized people whether men or women.

73. Its validity therefore does not require the baptismal character, still less that of ordination. This point is affirmed by practice and by theologians. It is an example of this necessary discernment in the Church's teaching and practice, a discernment whose only guarantee is the Church herself.

74. As regards teaching, a classical distinction has to be made, from Paul's letters onwards. There are forms of teaching or edification that lay people can carry out and in this case St. Paul expressly mentions women. These forms include the charisms of "prophecy" (1 Cor. 11:15).

75. In this sense there was no obstacle to giving the title of doctor to Teresa of Avila and Catherine of Siena, as it was given to illustrious fathers such as Albert the Great or St. Laurence of Brindisi. Quite a different matter is the official and hierarchical function of teaching the revealed message, a function that presupposes the mission received from Christ by the apostles and transmitted by them to their successors.

76. Examples of participation by women in ecclesiastical jurisdiction are found in the Middle Ages: some abbesses (not abbesses in general, as is sometimes said in popularizing articles) performed acts normally reserved to bishops, such as the nomination of parish priests or confessors. These customs have been more or less reproved by the Holy See at different periods: the letter of Pope Innocent III quoted earlier was intended as a reprimand to the Abbess of Las Huelgas.

77. But we must not forget that feudal lords arrogated to themselves similar rights. Canonists also admitted the possibility of separating jurisdiction from order. The Second Vatican Council has tried to determine better the relationship between the two; the Council's doctrinal vision will doubtless have effects on discipline.

78. In a more general way, attempts are being made, especially in Anglican circles, to broaden the debate in the following way: is the Church perhaps bound to scripture and tradition as an absolute, when the Church is a people making its pilgrim way and should listen to what the Spirit is saying? Or else a distinction is made between essential points on which unanimity is needed and questions of discipline admitting of diversity: and if the conclusion reached is that the ordination of women belongs to those secondary matters, it would not harm progress toward the union of the Churches.

79. Here again it is the Church that decides by her practice and magisterium what requires unanimity, and distinguishes it from acceptable or desirable pluralism. The question of the ordination of women impinges too directly on the nature of the ministerial priesthood for one to agree that it should be resolved within the framework of legitimate pluralism between Churches. That is the whole meaning of the letter of Pope Paul VI to the Archbishop of Canterbury.

The Ministerial Priesthood
in the Light of the Mystery of Christ

80. In the declaration a very clear distinction will be seen between the document's affirmation of the datum (the teaching it proposes with authority in the preceding paragraphs) and the theological reflection that then follows. By this reflection the Sacred Congregation for the Doctrine of the Faith endeavors "to illustrate this norm by showing the profound fittingness" to be found "between the proper nature of the sacrament of order, with its specific reference to the mystery of Christ, and the fact that only men have been called to receive priestly ordination."

81. In itself such a quest is not without risk. However, it does not involve the magisterium. It is well known that in solemn teaching infallibility affects the doctrinal affirmation, not the arguments intended to explain it. Thus the doctrinal chapters of the Council of Trent contain certain processes of reasoning that today no longer seem to hold.

82. But this risk has never stopped the magisterium from endeavoring at all times to clarify doctrine by analogies of faith. Today especially, and more than ever, it is impossible to be content with making statements, with appealing to the intellectual docility of Christians: faith seeks understanding, and tries to distinguish the grounds for and the coherence of what it is taught.

83. We have already discarded a fair number of explanations given by medieval theologians. The defect common to these explanations is that they claimed to find their basis in an inferiority of women vis-à-vis men; they deduced from the teaching of scripture that woman was "in a state of submission," of subjection, and was incapable of exercising functions of government.

84. It is very enlightening to note that the communities springing from the Reformation which have had no difficulty in giving women access to the pastoral office are first and foremost those that have rejected the Catholic doctrine on the sacrament of order and profess that the pastor is only one baptized person among others, even if the charge given has been the object of a consecration.

85. The declaration therefore suggests that it is by analyzing the nature of order and its character that we will find the explanation of the exclusive call of men to the priesthood and episcopate. This analysis can be outlined in three propositions: (1) in administering the sacraments that demand the character of ordination the priest does not act in his own name (*in personal propria*), but in the person of Christ (*in persona Christi*); (2) this formula, as understood by tradition, implies that the priest is a sign in the sense in which this term is understood in sacramental theology; (3) it is precisely because the priest is a sign of Christ the savior that he must be a man and not a woman.

86. That the priest performs the eucharist and reconciles sinners in the name and place of Christ is affirmed repeatedly by the magisterium and constantly taught by fathers and theologians. It would not appear to serve any useful purpose to give a multitude of quotations to show this. It is the totality of the priestly ministry that St. Paul says is exercised in the place of Christ. "We are acting as ambassadors on behalf of Christ, God, as it were, appealing through us" — in fact this text from 2 Corinthians has in mind the ministry of reconciliation (5:18–20) — "you have received me as an angel of God, even as Christ Jesus" (Gal. 4:14).

87. Similarly St. Cyprian echoes St. Paul: "The priest truly acts in the place of Christ." But theological reflection and the Church's life have been led to distinguish the more or less close links between the various acts in the exercise of the ministry and the character of ordination and to specify which require this character for validity.

88. Saying "in the name and place of Christ" is not however enough to express completely the nature of the bond between the minister and Christ as understood by tradition. The formula *in persona Christi* in fact suggests a meaning that brings it close to the Greek expression *mimema Christou*. The word *persona* means a part played in the ancient theater, a part identified by a particular mask. The priest takes the part of Christ, lending him his voice and gestures.

89. St. Thomas expresses this concept exactly: "The priest enacts the image of Christ, in whose person and by whose power he pronounces the words of consecration." The priest is thus truly a sign in the sacramental sense of the word. It would be a very elementary view of the sacraments if the notion of sign were kept only for material elements.

90. Each sacrament fulfills the notion in a different way. The text of St. Bonaventure already mentioned affirms this very clearly: "the person ordained is a sign of Christ the mediator."

91. Although St. Thomas gave as the reason for excluding women the much discussed one of the state of subjection (*status subiectionis*), he nevertheless took as his starting point the principle that "sacramental signs represent what they signify by a natural resemblance," in other words the need for that "natural resemblance" between Christ and the person who is his sign. And, still on the same point, St. Thomas recalls: "Since a sacrament is a sign, what is done in the sacrament requires not only the reality but also a sign of the reality."

92. It would not accord with "natural resemblance," with that obvious "meaningfulness," if the memorial of the supper were to be carried out by a woman; for it is not just the recitation involving the gestures and words of Christ, but an action, and the sign is efficacious because Christ is present in the minister who consecrates the eucharist as is taught by the Second Vatican Council, following the encyclical *Mediator Dei*.

93. It is understandable that those favoring the ordination of women have made various attempts to deny the value of this reasoning. It has obviously been impossible and even unnecessary for the declaration to consider in detail all the difficulties that could be raised in this regard. Some of them however are of interest in that they occasion a deeper theological understanding of traditional principles.

94. Let us look at the objection sometimes raised that it is ordination — the character — not maleness, that makes the priest Christ's representative. Obviously it is the character, received by ordination, that enables the priest to consecrate the eucharist and reconcile penitents. But the character is spiritual and invisible (*res et sacramentum*). On the level of the sign (*sacramentum tantum*) the priest must both have received the laying on of hands and take the part of Christ. It is here that St. Thomas and St. Bonaventure require that the sign should have natural meaningfulness.

95. In various fairly recent publications attempts have been made to reduce the importance of the formula *in persona Christi* by insisting rather on the formula *in persona Ecclesiae*. For it is another great principle of the theology of the sacraments and liturgy that the priest presides over the liturgy in the name of the Church, and must have the intention of "doing what the Church does."

96. Could one say that the priest does not represent Christ, because he first represents the Church by the fact of his ordination? The declaration's reply to this objection is that, quite on the contrary, the priest represents the Church precisely because he first represents Christ himself, who is the head and shepherd of the Church. It indicates several texts of the Second Vatican Council that clearly express this teaching.

97. Here there may well be in fact one of the crucial points of the question, one of the important aspects of the theology of the Church and priesthood underlying the debate on the ordination of women. When the priest presides over the assembly, it is not the assembly that has chosen or designated him for this role. The Church is not a spontaneous gathering. As its name of *ecclesia* indicates, it is an assembly that is convoked. It is Christ who calls it together. He is the head of the Church, and the priest presides "in the person of Christ the head" (*in persona Christi capitis*).

98. That is why the declaration rightly concludes "that the controversies raised in our days over the ordination of women are for all Christians a pressing invitation to meditate on the mystery of the Church, to study in great detail the meaning of the episcopate and the priesthood, and to rediscover the real and preeminent place of the priest in the community of the baptized, of which he indeed forms part but from which he is distinguished because, in the actions that call for the character of ordination, for the community he is — with all the effectiveness proper to the sacraments — the image and symbol of Christ himself who calls, forgives, and accomplishes the sacrifice of the covenant."

99. However, the objectors continue: it would indeed be important that Christ should be represented by a man if the maleness of Christ played an essential part in the economy of salvation. But, they say, one cannot accord gender a special place in the hypostatic union: what is essential is the human nature — no more — assumed by the word, not the incidental characteristics such as the sex or even the race which he assumed. If the Church admits that men of all races can validly represent Christ why should she deny women this ability to represent him?

100. We must first of all reply, in the words of the declaration, that ethnic differences "do not affect the human person as intimately as the difference of sex." On this point biblical teaching agrees with modern psychology. The difference between the sexes however is something willed by God from the beginning, according to the account in Genesis (which is also quoted in the Gospel), and

is directed both to communion between persons and to the begetting of human beings. And it must be affirmed first and foremost that the fact that Christ is a man and not a woman is neither incidental nor unimportant in relation to the economy of salvation.

101. In what sense? Not of course in the material sense, as has sometimes been suggested in polemics in order to discredit it, but because the whole economy of salvation has been revealed to us through essential symbols from which it cannot be separated, and without which we would be unable to understand God's design. Christ is the new Adam. God's covenant with men is presented in the Old Testament as a nuptial mystery, the definitive reality of which is Christ's sacrifice on the cross.

102. The declaration briefly presents the stages marking the progressive development of this biblical theme, the subject of many exegetical and theological studies. Christ is the bridegroom of the Church, whom he won for himself with his blood, and the salvation brought by him is the new covenant: by using this language, revelation shows why the incarnation took place according to the male gender, and makes it impossible to ignore this historical reality. For this reason, only a man can take the part of Christ, be a sign of his presence, in a word "represent" him (that is, be an effective sign of his presence) in the essential acts of the covenant.

103. Could one do without this biblical symbolism when transmitting the message, in contemplating the mystery and in liturgical life? To ask this, as has been done in certain recent studies, is to call into question the whole structure of revelation and to reject the value of scripture. It will be said, for example, that "in every period the ecclesial community appeals to the authority it has received from its founder in order to choose the images enabling it to receive God's revelation." This is perhaps to fail even more profoundly to appreciate the human value of the nuptial theme in the revelation of God's love.

The Ministerial Priesthood
in the Mystery of the Church

104. It is also striking to note the extent to which the questions raised in the controversy over the ordination of women are bound up with a certain theology of the Church. We do not of course mean to dwell on the excessive formulas which nonetheless sometimes find a place in theological reviews. An example is the supposition that the primitive Church was based on the charisms possessed by both women and men. Another is the claim that "the Gospels also present women as ministers of unction." On the other hand, we have already come across the question of the pluralism that can be admitted in unity and seen what is limits are.

105. The proposal that women should be admitted to the priesthood because they have gained leadership in many fields of modern life today seems to ignore the fact that the Church is not a society like the rest. In the Church, authority or power is of a very different nature, linked as it normally is with the sacrament, as is underlined in the declaration. Disregard of this fact is indeed a temptation that has threatened ecclesiological research at all periods: every time that an attempt is made to solve the Church's problems by comparison with those of

states, or to define the Church's structure by political categories, the inevitable result is an impasse.

106. The declaration also points out the defect in the argument that seeks to base the demand that the priesthood be conferred on women on the text Galatians 3:28, which states that in Christ there is no longer any distinction between man and woman. For St. Paul this is the effect of baptism. The baptismal catechesis of the fathers often stressed it. But absolute equality in baptismal life is quite a different thing from the structure of the ordained ministry. This latter is the object of a vocation within the Church, not a right inherent in the person.

107. A vocation within the Church does not consist solely or primarily in the fact that one manifests the desire for a mission or feels attracted by an inner compulsion. Even if this spontaneous step is made and even if one believes one has heard as it were a call in the depths of one's soul, the vocation is authentic only from the moment that it is authenticated by the external call of the Church. The Holy Office recalled this truth in its 1912 letter to the bishop of Aire to put an end to the Lahitton controversy. Christ chose "those he wanted" (Mark 3:13).

108. Since the ministerial priesthood is something to which the Lord calls expressly and gratuitously, it cannot be claimed as a right, any more by men than by women. Archbishop Bernardin's declaration of October 1975 contained the sound judgment: "It would be a mistake . . . to reduce the question of the ordination of women to one of injustice, as is done at times. It would be correct to do this only if ordination were a God-given right of every individual; only if somehow one's human potential could not be fulfilled without it. In fact, however, no one, male or female, can claim a 'right' to ordination. And, since the episcopal and priestly office is basically a ministry of service, ordination in no way 'completes' one's humanity."

109. The declaration of the Sacred Congregation for the Doctrine of the Faith ends by suggesting that efforts in two directions should be fostered, efforts from which the pastors and faithful of the Church would perhaps be distracted if this controversy over women's ordination were prolonged.

110. One direction is in the doctrinal and spiritual order: awareness of the diversity of roles in the Church, in which equality is not identity, should lead us — as St. Paul exhorts us — to strive after the one gift that can and should be striven after, namely love (1 Cor. 12–13). "The greatest in the kingdom of heaven are not the ministers but the saints," says the declaration. This expression deserves to be taken as a motto.

111. The other direction for our efforts is in the apostolic and social order. We have a long way to go before people become fully aware of the greatness of women's mission in the Church and society, "both for the renewal and humanization of society and for the rediscovery by believers of the true countenance of the Church." Unfortunately we also still have a long way to go before all the inequalities of which women are still the victims are eliminated, not only in the field of public professional and intellectual life, but even within the family.

Ordinatio Sacerdotalis

("On Reserving Priestly Ordination to Men Alone")

Pope John Paul II

May 30, 1994

Venerable brothers in the episcopate:

1. 1. Priestly ordination, which hands on the office entrusted by Christ to his apostles of teaching, sanctifying, and governing the faithful, has in the Catholic Church from the beginning always been reserved to men alone. This tradition has also been faithfully maintained by the Oriental churches.

2. When the question of the ordination of women arose in the Anglican Communion, Pope Paul VI, out of fidelity to his office of safeguarding the apostolic tradition, and also with a view to removing a new obstacle placed in the way of Christian unity, reminded Anglicans of the position of the Catholic Church:

3. "She holds that it is not admissible to ordain women to the priesthood, for very fundamental reasons. These reasons include the example recorded in the sacred scriptures of Christ choosing his apostles only from among men; the constant practice of the Church, which has imitated Christ in choosing only men; and her living teaching authority which has consistently held that the exclusion of women from the priesthood is in accordance with God's plan for his Church."

4. But since the question had also become the subject of debate among theologians and in certain Catholic circles, Paul VI directed the Congregation for the Doctrine of the Faith to set forth and expound the teaching of the Church on this matter. This was done through the declaration *Inter Insigniores,* which the supreme pontiff approved and ordered to be published.

5. 2. The declaration recalls and explains the fundamental reasons for this teaching, reasons expounded by Paul VI, and concludes that the Church "does not consider herself authorized to admit women to priestly ordination." To these fundamental reasons the document adds other theological reasons which illustrate the appropriateness of the divine provision, and it also shows clearly that Christ's way of acting did not proceed from sociological or cultural motives peculiar to his time. As Paul VI later explained: "The real reason is

that, in giving the Church her fundamental constitution, her theological anthropology — thereafter always followed by the Church's tradition — Christ
established things in this way."

6. In the apostolic letter *Mulieris Dignitatem,* I myself wrote in this regard:

7. "In calling only men as his apostles, Christ acted in a completely free and
sovereign manner. In doing so, he exercised the same freedom with which,
in all his behavior, he emphasized the dignity and the vocation of women,
without conforming to the prevailing customs and to the tradition sanctioned
by the legislation of the time."

8. In fact, the Gospels and the Acts of the Apostles attest that this call was
made in accordance with God's eternal plan: Christ chose those whom he
willed (cf. Mark 3:13–14; John 6:70), and he did so in union with the Father,
"through the Holy Spirit" (Acts 1:2), after having spent the night in prayer (cf.
Luke 6:12). Therefore, in granting admission to the ministerial priesthood, the
Church has always acknowledged as a perennial norm her Lord's way of acting in choosing the twelve men whom he made the foundation of his Church
(cf. Rev. 21:14). These men did not in fact receive only a function which could
thereafter be exercised by any member of the Church; rather they were specifically and intimately associated in the mission of the incarnate Word himself
(cf. Matt. 10:1, 7–8; 28:16–20; Mark 3:13–16; 16:14–15). The apostles did
the same when they chose fellow workers who would succeed them in their
ministry. Also included in this choice were those who, throughout the time of
the Church, would carry on the apostles' mission of representing Christ the
Lord and Redeemer.

9. 3. Furthermore, the fact that the Blessed Virgin Mary, mother of God and
mother of the Church, received neither the mission proper to the apostles nor
the ministerial priesthood clearly shows that the nonadmission of women to
priestly ordination cannot mean that women are of lesser dignity nor can it be
construed as discrimination against them. Rather, it is to be seen as the faithful
observance of a plan to be ascribed to the wisdom of the Lord of the universe.

10. The presence and the role of women in the life and mission of the Church,
although not linked to the ministerial priesthood, remain absolutely necessary
and irreplaceable. As the declaration *Inter Insigniores* points out, "the Church
desires that Christian women should become fully aware of the greatness of
their mission: Today their role is of capital importance both for the renewal
and humanization of society and for the rediscovery by believers of the true
face of the Church." The New Testament and the whole history of the Church
give ample evidence of the presence in the Church of women, true disciples,
witnesses to Christ in the family and in society, as well as in total consecration
to the service of God and of the Gospel. "By defending the dignity of women
and their vocation, the church has shown honor and gratitude for those women
who — faithful to the Gospel — have shared in every age in the apostolic
mission of the whole people of God. They are the holy martyrs, virgins, and
the mothers of families, who bravely bore witness to their faith and passed on
the Church's faith and tradition by bringing up their children in the spirit of
the Gospel."

11. Moreover, it is to the holiness of the faithful that the hierarchical structure of
the Church is totally ordered. For this reason, the declaration *Inter Insigniores*
recalls: "The only better gift, which can and must be desired, is love (cf. 1 Cor.

12 and 13). The greatest in the kingdom of heaven are not the ministers but the saints."

12. Although the teaching that priestly ordination is to be reserved to men alone has been preserved by the constant and universal tradition of the Church and firmly taught by the magisterium in its more recent documents, at the present time in some places it is nonetheless considered still open to debate, or the Church's judgment that women are not to be admitted to ordination is considered to have a merely disciplinary force.

13. Wherefore, in order that all doubt may be removed regarding a matter of great importance, a matter which pertains to the Church's divine constitution itself, in virtue of my ministry of confirming the brethren (cf. Luke 22:32) I declare that the Church has no authority whatsoever to confer priestly ordination on women and that this judgment is to be definitively held by all the Church's faithful.

14. Invoking an abundance of divine assistance upon you, venerable brothers, and upon all the faithful, I impart my apostolic blessing.

May 22, the solemnity of Pentecost, in the year 1994,
the 16th of my pontificate.
JOHN PAUL II

Strengthening the Bonds of Peace

A Pastoral Reflection on Women
in the Church and in Society

United States Conference of Catholic Bishops

November 1994

1. Earlier this year the Holy Father issued the apostolic letter, *Ordinatio Sacerdotalis*, reaffirming the teaching and practice that priestly ordination is restricted to men. We bishops recognize this clear reaffirmation of Catholic teaching as a pastoral service to the whole Church, and we accept that it be definitively held by all the faithful.[1] This letter also reiterated the "necessary and irreplaceable" role of women in the Church.

2. Some people received the letter with joy and peace. Others found acceptance difficult. We encourage all our brothers and sisters, through prayer, study, and dialogue, to accept and seek to understand more fully the teaching that *Ordinatio Sacerdotalis* reaffirms.

3. This brief reflection reaches out to all. It is an invitation to strengthen the bonds of peace and cultivate the unity that the Spirit gives (Eph. 4:3). For certainly all can agree that peace is a blessing we long for — peace in our hearts, in our homes, in our Church, and in our world.

4. Peace, we know, is more than the absence of conflict. Peace comes about when we, as members of Christ's Church, respect the dignity of each person, when we welcome the gifts and competencies of all people, when we respect differences, and when we work together to build the reign of God. We will work to bring about this peaceful climate where we can assess and respond to challenges of all kinds.

5. We can begin by embracing three principles. First, in the words of Pope Paul VI, "if you want peace, work for justice."[2] Second, peacemaking needs to focus on the present and future. We know that people have suffered greatly in the past — for example, from racism and sexism — but we know that these evils must not continue to hold people hostage. As Christians, we look toward the future. Third, in the world at large we have seen that honest, open, sustained dialogue is indispensable for bringing about genuine peace. We believe this same kind of dialogue is necessary in the Church. We offer this message, then, as one moment in a developing dialogue, with the hope that all women and men of the Church will receive it as such and continue as participants in what can be a sacred conversation for all of us.

6. As characteristics for that dialogue we draw on the wisdom of Pope Paul VI. In his first encyclical, *Ecclesiam Suam,* he said that dialogue, which he spoke of as spiritual communication, is marked by: (1) clear, understandable language; (2) meekness, a virtue that makes our dialogue peaceful and patient; (3) trust between speaker and the listener; and (4) sensitivity to the situation and needs of the hearer.[3]

7. With Pope Paul VI's words in mind, we consider these points: leadership in the Church, equality of women and men, and diversity of gifts. Confident that the Holy Spirit will guide us in the way of peace and justice, we invite all women and men in the Church to join in this dialogue.

Leadership

8. Strengthened by the teaching reaffirmed in *Ordinatio Sacerdotalis,* we need to look at alternative ways in which women can exercise leadership in the Church. We welcome this leadership, which in some ways is already a reality, and we commit ourselves to enhancing the participation of women in every possible aspect of church life. We are especially concerned that women from different ethnic groups be drawn more fully into this participation.

9. Today, throughout the world, women hold positions of exacting leadership, as heads of government, judges, research doctors, symphony conductors, and business executives. They serve as presidents at Catholic colleges and universities, and as administrators and faculty members at Catholic colleges and seminaries. They are also chief executives of Catholic hospitals and executive directors of Catholic Charities. An increasing number of Catholic theologians are women. Some women serve the diocesan churches as school superintendents and chancellors, as archivists and members of marriage tribunals. More and more women have responsible national positions in the Catholic Church.

10. Locally, we can see in our parishes the scope of women's leadership: in various liturgical ministries, including altar servers and proclaiming the Word before the assembly; in pastoral ministry and administration; in religious education and teaching in schools; in peace and justice activities; in outreach to the homebound and the hospitalized. One recent study shows that 85 percent of nonordained ministerial positions in parishes are now held by women.[4]

11. We know that women's gifts have tremendously improved the quality of parish ministry. Looking to the future, we especially want to encourage women to pursue studies in Scripture, theology, and canon law, not only that the Church may benefit from their skills in these areas, but that they, themselves, may benefit from their own scholarly efforts.

12. An important issue for women is how to have a voice in the governance of the Church to which they belong and which they serve with love and generosity. This can be achieved in at least two ways that are consistent with church teaching: through consultation and through cooperation in the exercise of authority.[5]

13. As recently as July 1994, Pope John Paul II reiterated the need for the consultative expertise of women, saying, "Qualified women can make a great contribution of wisdom and moderation, courage and dedication, spirituality and fervor for the good of the Church."[6] We need to seek ways to honor this

call at every level of the Church, from the parish to the diocese to the national offices that are involved in drafting official church documents for our conference of bishops. As a specific example of this consultative role, we cite the participation of women in the development of pastoral and missionary statements, as called for in the apostolic exhortation on the laity, *Christifideles Laici* (#51).

14. Consultation is already occurring in a number of ways, of course. Parish and diocesan pastoral and finance councils are vehicles for engaging the gifts of lay women and men as important decisions are crafted. While final decision-making rests with the pastor, the *Code of Canon Law* urges consultation even in areas not strictly required. We encourage such consultation. We note, too, that commissions on women, now present in many dioceses, allow for women's concerns to be expressed and their expertise to be utilized.

15. Second, the *Code of Canon Law,* while situating the foundation of jurisdiction in the sacrament of Holy Orders, nevertheless allows for the possibility of lay women and men cooperating in the exercise of this power in accord with the norm of law (canon 129). This may be a graced moment in the life of the Church that enables us to take a fresh and deeper look at the relationship between jurisdiction and ordained ministry, and thus gain a better understanding of legislative, executive, and judicial acts within the Church.[7] We strongly urge that the studies which are underway on this issue be pursued; and we urge canonists to make widely known the provisions in the *Code of Canon Law* for the participation of women in the life and mission of the Church.[8]

16. Change occurs through knowledge and understanding. While not all change is progress, a thoroughly informed laity can only benefit the Church as it seeks to promote dialogue inside and outside the Church. To enhance the dialogue, we invite ecclesiologists and other theologians to join with us to explore new and creative ways in which women can participate in church leadership.

17. Leadership involves servanthood; we learn this from the example of the head of the Church, Jesus Christ. What does it mean for leaders — ordained and lay — to model this truth? Obviously, it will mean rejecting authoritarian conduct. But it will also mean giving time and energy to fostering community life where men and women are called forth and accepted as vital collaborators in the work of evangelization, social justice, teaching, administration, and governance. The collaboration of women and men as equal partners in this servant leadership is a "sign of that interpersonal communion of love which constitutes the mystical, intimate life of God, One in Three."[9]

18. We welcome, too, women's leadership in more traditional areas, e.g., in advocacy for church and societal policies that support just remuneration for women; in establishing a "family wage" to increase the possibility that at least one parent can remain at home during the child's early years; in pro-life efforts that seek justice for the unborn and compassion and assistance for pregnant women in difficult circumstances; in advocating quality child care for employed women; in action to stem the tide of domestic violence against women; in adherence to a family perspective in institutions, programs, and policies of Church and society. Furthermore, we encourage men to join women in these efforts that are needed for strengthening the family, the parish, and the civic community.

19. We pledge our partnership in all these endeavors. In no way should these commitments be construed as "ecclesial political correctness"; they are theologically correct. They are rooted in our baptism and in our understanding of the Holy Spirit who works in the Church to build it up through the gifts of its members.

20. Having looked at women's leadership in the Church, we now turn to two realities that make this leadership possible: the equality of men and women, and the diversity of gifts among God's people.

Equality

21. We reaffirm the fundamental equality of women and men who, created in the image of God, "are called to participate in the same divine beatitude [and]...therefore enjoy an equal dignity."[10] What we said of marriage and family life in our pastoral message *Follow the Way of Love* applies to other expressions of church life as well. In that message we pointed out that equality does not imply sameness in roles or expectations, nor does it mean that two spouses will have identical gifts or character. Rather, they will respect each other's gifts and identity. In this "domestic Church" we see a spirit and practice of mutuality, a sharing of power and exercising of responsibility for a purpose larger than oneself, that is, for God's purpose.

22. The domestic Church reminds us that all women and men must take seriously the need to listen to one another, to try to understand one another, including an appreciation of the different forms of authority. These lessons of the domestic Church, especially concerning relationships, should be reflected in the experience and behavior of the gathered Church. For example, the pastor of a parish has the authority of office, while the lay man or woman will often have a particular competence or knowledge, a specific authority that complements the pastor's. The challenge is for all authority to be exercised for the well-being of the community and the effectiveness of the Church's mission.

23. To meet such a challenge requires a mature spirituality that understands and practices the virtue of humility. We admit that humility is often misunderstood, and we are sensitive to women's concerns that it not be misused to justify the suppression of women's voices. We stress that all of us are called to "be subordinate to one another out of reverence for Christ" (Eph. 5:21). Humility must be practiced mutually by all the faithful, ordained and lay. This mutuality is rooted in an authentic respect for the dignity of each person and our call to belong to one another in the Body of Christ.

24. We can say with certainty that discrimination against women contradicts the will of Christ. We are painfully aware that sexism, defined as "unjust discrimination based on sex,"[11] is still present in some members of the Church. We reject sexism and pledge renewed efforts to guard against it in church teaching and practice. We further reject extreme positions on women's issues that impede dialogue and divide the Church. We commit ourselves to make sure that our words and actions express our belief in the equality of all women and men.

Diversity of Gifts

25. In St. Paul's Letter to the Ephesians we read, "grace was given to each of us according to the measure of Christ's gift...some as apostles, others as prophets, others as evangelists, others as pastors and teachers, to equip the holy ones for the work of ministry, for building up the body of Christ, until we all attain to the unity of faith and knowledge of the Son of God...to the extent of the full stature of Christ" (Eph. 4:7, 11–13).

26. The Church better fulfills its mission when the gifts of all its members are engaged as fully as possible. Women are essential in ministry both within the Church and to the world. The diversity of women's gifts and talents should be celebrated. Different voices, different experiences and perspectives, and different methodologies help the Gospel to be proclaimed and received with freshness. The majority of women exercise their gifts in the home, in the workplace, and in civic leadership. In addition, many are now trained and skilled in spiritual direction, in the leadership of prayer groups, and in the study of Scripture. They are educated and formed for pastoral ministry in parishes. Some are psychologists who are also trained in theology. These gifts are essential in a world where the inner peace of so many has been shattered. Spouses in troubled marriages, families affected by abortion, adult children from dysfunctional families, lonely youth, people of all ages who feel isolated and alienated — all need healing.

27. Countless men and women long for help in the ways of prayer. They seek to be in touch with God in the depths of their souls. We see so many women engaged in meeting these spiritual needs, and we thank God for these gifts to the Church.

28. We are grateful, too, that many women possess leadership and organizational skills that, although often underutilized in the past, are now coming to the fore. We urge pastors to recognize and to continue to call forth the distinct contributions that women can make to the Church and to the world. Diversity of gifts in the service of Christ is not to be feared or suppressed but recognized as a sign of the Church's vitality and ongoing renewal.

Concluding Words: The True Face of the Church

29. In *Ordinatio Sacerdotalis* Pope John Paul II emphasizes that "[the role of women] is of capital importance...for the rediscovery by believers of the true face of the Church."[12] We have seen that the true face of the Church appears only when and if we recognize the equal dignity of men and women and consistently act on that recognition. It is this face, shaped through the centuries, that is visible to the world. From the beginning, women have been essential to this visage: from Mary, the mother of Jesus, and the women of the early Church, through the martyrs, through the doctors of the Church — Saint Teresa of Avila and Saint Catherine of Siena — to the women closer to our own time, such as Saint Elizabeth Seton, Blessed Kateri Tekakwitha, Dorothy Day, Mother Teresa, and Sister Thea Bowman, who have graced the Church in both traditional and new ways.

30. Still, the face of the Church reveals the pain that many women experience. At times this pain results from the flawed behavior of human beings — clergy and

lay — when we attempt to dominate each other. Women also experience pain because of persistent sexism. At times this sexism is unconscious, the result of inadequate reflection. A Church that is deepening its consciousness of itself, that is trying to project the image of Christ to the world, will understand the need for ongoing, prayerful reflection in this area.

31. One example of the need for ongoing reflection concerns the use of language. While inclusive language is becoming a concern in many areas of the world, it has a particular importance in the English-speaking world, especially in North America. Our conference of bishops continues to be engaged in the study of scriptural, doctrinal, and liturgical translations, a highly technical and complex task. Moreover, since the Holy Father has indicated that catechetical and pastoral materials that evolve from the *Catechism of the Catholic Church* could reflect the culture, language, and idiom of a given country, we urge that catechetical and religious materials and hymnals, as well as our daily language and prayer, honor the concerns that shape a more inclusive language, while taking care to ensure that they do not become a source of division, anger, and hurt. This can be accomplished if our conversation within the Church is "full of faith, of charity, of good works, [and is] intimate, and familiar."[13]

32. For many years a dialogue among women and between women and men took place in the Church in the United States, as we tried to write a pastoral letter that would capture the vast range of concerns expressed by women. The pastoral letter was not approved, but the concluding recommendations were sent to the Executive Committee of the National Conference of Catholic Bishops for action by various Conference committees. We bishops pledge ourselves anew, through our committee structure, to continue the dialogue in a spirit of partnership and mutual trust and to implement the recommendations where possible.

33. To be committed to honest dialogue is no easy task. As Pope Paul VI noted, "In the dialogue one discovers how different are the ways which lead to the light of faith, and how it is possible to make them converge on the same goal. Even if these ways are divergent, they can become complementary by forcing our reasoning process out of the worn paths and by obliging it to deepen its research, to find fresh expressions."[14] As we search together for truth, it is critical that we draw upon the insights of contemporary scholarship in a wide variety of disciplines — Scripture, anthropology, history, women's studies, and systematic theology.

34. We pray that others will join us as we listen to one another and learn. For our part we take as our own the words of Pope Paul VI: "The dialogue will make us wise; it will make us teachers."[15] Once again, we urge the Church at all levels to establish structures to hear and respond to the concerns of women.

35. Pope John Paul II has chosen "Women: Educators for Peace" as the theme for the 1995 World Day of Peace, pointing out what women have done, and continue to do, on behalf of peace. While we know that conflict and disagreement often mark the road to peace, we also know that women's energy is a positive force for the good of Church and society. With our Holy Father, we thank God for our sister peacemakers and pray that God will guide us all in the ways of patience, love, unity, justice, and peace.

Notes for this document can be found on pp. 277–278.

Jesuits and the Situation of Women in Church and Civil Society

The Society of Jesus

September 27, 1995

Introduction

1. 361. General Congregation 33 made a brief mention of the "unjust treatment and exploitation of women." It was part of a list of injustices in a context of new needs and situations which Jesuits were called to address in the implementation of our mission. We wish to consider this question more specifically and substantially on this occasion. This is principally because, assisted by the general rise in consciousness concerning this issue, we are more aware than previously that it is indeed a central concern of any contemporary mission which seeks to integrate faith and justice. It has a universal dimension in that it involves men and women everywhere. To an increasing extent it cuts across barriers of class and culture. It is of personal concern to those who work with us in our mission, especially lay and religious women.

The Situation

2. 362. The dominance of men in their relationship with women has found expression in many ways. It has included discrimination against women in educational opportunities, the disproportionate burden they are called upon to bear in family life, paying them a lesser wage for the same work, limiting their access to positions of influence when admitted to public life, and, sadly but only too frequently, outright violence against women themselves. In some parts of the world, this violence still includes female circumcision, dowry deaths, and the murder of unwanted infant girls. Women are commonly treated as objects in advertising and in the media. In extreme cases, for example, in promoting international sex tourism, they are regarded as commodities to be trafficked in.

3. 363. This situation, however, has begun to change, chiefly because of the critical awakening and courageous protest of women themselves. But many men, too, have joined women in rejecting attitudes which offend against the dignity of men and women alike. Nonetheless, we still have with us the legacy of systematic discrimination against women. It is embedded within the economic,

social, political, religious, and even linguistic structures of our societies. It is often part of an even deeper cultural prejudice and stereotype. Many women, indeed, feel that men have been slow to recognize the full humanity of women. They often experience a defensive reaction from men when they draw attention to this blindness.

4. 364. The prejudice against women, to be sure, assumes different forms in different cultures. Sensitivity is needed to avoid using any one simple measurement of what counts as discrimination. But it is nonetheless a universal reality. Further, in many parts of the world, women already cruelly disadvantaged because of war, poverty, migration, or race, often suffer a double disadvantage precisely because they are women. There is a "feminization of poverty" and a distinctive "feminine face of oppression."

The Church Addresses the Situation

5. 365. Church social teaching, especially within the last ten years, has reacted strongly against this continuing discrimination and prejudice. Pope John Paul II in particular has called upon all men and women of goodwill, especially Catholics, to make the essential equality of women a lived reality. This is a genuine "sign of the times." We need to join with interchurch and interreligious groups in order to advance this social transformation.

6. 366. Church teaching certainly promotes the role of women within the family, but it also stresses the need for their contribution in the Church and in public life. It draws upon the text of Genesis which speaks of men and women created in the image of God (1:27) and the prophetic praxis of Jesus in his relationship with women. These sources call us to change our attitudes and work for a change of structures. The original plan of God was for a loving relationship of respect, mutuality, and equality between men and women, and we are called to fulfill this plan. The tone of this ecclesial reflection on Scripture makes it clear that there is an urgency in the challenge to translate theory into practice not only outside but also within the Church itself.

The Role and Responsibility of Jesuits

7. 367. The Society of Jesus accepts this challenge and our responsibility for doing what we can as men and as a male religious order. We do not pretend or claim to speak for women. However, we do speak out of what we have learned from women about ourselves and our relationship with them.

8. 368. In making this response we are being faithful, in the changed consciousness of our times, to our mission: the service of faith, of which the promotion of justice is an absolute requirement. We respond, too, out of the acknowledgement of our own limited but significant influence as Jesuits and as male religious within the Church. We are conscious of the damage to the People of God brought about in some cultures by the alienation of women who no longer feel at home in the Church and who are not able with integrity to transmit Catholic values to their families, friends, and colleagues.

Conversion

9. 369. In response, we Jesuits first ask God for the grace of conversion. We have been part of a civil and ecclesial tradition that has offended against women. And, like many men, we have a tendency to convince ourselves that there is no problem. However unwittingly, we have often contributed to a form of clericalism which has reinforced male domination with an ostensibly divine sanction. By making this declaration we wish to react personally and collectively, and do what we can to change this regrettable situation.

Appreciation

10. 370. We know that the nurturing of our own faith and much of our own ministry would be greatly diminished without the dedication, generosity, and joy that women bring to the schools, parishes, and other fields in which we labor together. This is particularly true of the work of lay and religious women among the urban and rural poor, often in extremely difficult and challenging situations. In addition, many religious congregations of women have adopted the Spiritual Exercises and our Jesuit Constitutions as the basis for their own spirituality and governance, becoming an extended Ignatian family. Religious and lay women have in recent years become expert in giving the Spiritual Exercises. As retreat directors, especially of the Exercises in daily life, they have enriched the Ignatian tradition and our own understanding of ourselves and of our ministry. Many women have helped to reshape our theological tradition in a way that has liberated both men and women. We wish to express our appreciation for this generous contribution of women, and hope that this mutuality in ministry might continue and flourish.

Ways Forward

11. 371. We wish to specify more concretely at least some ways in which Jesuits may better respond to this challenge to our lives and mission. We do not presume that there is any one model of male-female relationship to be recommended, much less imposed, throughout the world or even within a given culture. Rather we note the need for a real delicacy in our response. We must be careful not to interfere in a way that alienates the culture; rather we must endeavor to facilitate a more organic process of change. We should be particularly sensitive to adopt a pedagogy that does not drive a further wedge between men and women who in certain circumstances are already under great pressure from other divisive cultural or socioeconomic forces.

12. 372. In the first place, we invite all Jesuits to listen carefully and courageously to the experience of women. Many women feel that men simply do not listen to them. There is no substitute for such listening. More than anything else it will bring about change. Unless we listen, any action we may take in this area, no matter how well intentioned, is likely to bypass the real concerns of women and to confirm male condescension and reinforce male dominance. Listening, in a spirit of partnership and equality, is the most practical response we can make and is the foundation for our mutual partnership to reform unjust structures.

13. 373. Second, we invite all Jesuits, as individuals and through their institutions, to align themselves in solidarity with women. The practical ways of doing this will vary from place to place and from culture to culture, but many examples come readily to mind:

374. explicit teaching of the essential equality of women and men in Jesuit ministries, especially in schools, colleges and universities

375. support for liberation movements which oppose the exploitation of women and encourage their entry into political and social life

376. specific attention to the phenomenon of violence against women

377. appropriate presence of women in Jesuit ministries and institutions, not excluding the ministry of formation

378. genuine involvement of women in consultation and decision making in our Jesuit ministries

379. respectful cooperation with our female colleagues in shared projects

380. use of appropriately inclusive language in speech and official documents

381. promotion of the education of women and, in particular, the elimination of all forms of illegitimate discrimination between boys and girls in the educational process.

Many of these, we are happy to say, are already being practiced in different parts of the world. We confirm their value, and recommend a more universal implementation as appropriate.

14. 382. It would be idle to pretend that all the answers to the issues surrounding a new, more just relationship between women and men have been found or are satisfactory to all. In particular, it may be anticipated that some other questions about the role of women in civil and ecclesial society will undoubtedly mature over time. Through committed and persevering research, through exposure to different cultures, and through reflection on experience, Jesuits hope to participate in clarifying these questions and in advancing the underlying issues of justice. The change of sensibilities which this involves will inevitably have implications for Church teaching and practice. In this context we ask Jesuits to live, as always, with the tension involved in being faithful to the teachings of the Church while at the same time trying to read accurately the signs of the times.

Conclusion

15. 383. The Society gives thanks for all that has already been achieved through the often costly struggle for a more just relationship between women and men. We thank women for the lead they have given and continue to give. In particular, we thank women religious, with whom we feel a special bond, and who have been pioneers in so many ways in their unique contribution to the mission of faith and justice. We are grateful, too, for what the Society and individual Jesuits have contributed to this new relationship, which is a source of great enrichment for both men and women.

16. 384. Above all we want to commit the Society in a more formal and explicit way to regard this solidarity with women as integral to our mission. In this way we hope that the whole Society will regard this work for reconciliation between women and men in all its forms as integral to its interpretation of Decree 4 of

GC [General Congregation] 32 for our times. We know that a reflective and sustained commitment to bring about this respectful reconciliation can flow only from our God of love and justice, who reconciles all and promises a world in which "there is neither Jew nor Greek, there is neither slave nor free, there is neither male nor female, for you are all one in Christ Jesus" (Gal. 3:28).

❧ Document 7 ❧

Responsum ad Dubium regarding Ordinatio Sacerdotalis

("Response to a Question regarding Ordinatio Sacerdotalis")

Congregation for the Doctrine of the Faith

October 28, 1995

1. *Dubium*: Whether the teaching that the Church has no authority whatsoever to confer priestly ordination on women, which is presented in the apostolic letter *Ordinatio Sacerdotalis* to be held definitively, is to be understood as belonging to the deposit of the faith.

2. *Responsum:* In the affirmative.

3. This teaching requires definitive assent, since, founded on the written word of God and from the beginning constantly preserved and applied in the tradition of the Church, it has been set forth infallibly by the ordinary and universal magisterium (cf. Second Vatican Council, Dogmatic Constitution on the Church *Lumen Gentium*, 25, 2). Thus, in the present circumstances, the Roman pontiff, exercising his proper office of confirming the brethren (cf. Luke 22:32), has handed on this same teaching by a formal declaration, explicitly stating what is to be held always, everywhere, and by all, as belonging to the deposit of the faith.

4. *The Sovereign Pontiff John Paul II, at the audience granted to the undersigned Cardinal Prefect, approved this reply, adopted in the ordinary session of the congregation, and ordered it to be published.*

Rome, Congregation for the Doctrine of the Faith,
Feast of the Apostles SS. Simon and Jude
October 28, 1995
Joseph Cardinal Ratzinger, Prefect,
Congregation for the Doctrine of the Faith

Address of the Holy Father to the German Bishops

Pope John Paul II

November 20, 1999

Your Eminence,
Dear Brothers in the Episcopate!

1. 1. "With the affection of Christ Jesus" (Phil. 1:8), I welcome you, the third group of German Bishops, to this meeting on the occasion of your ad limina visit. I thank the heavenly Father for the commitment we share in spreading the Gospel (cf. Phil. 1:5) and for the communion of faith and love that unites us in serving the People of God. With you I greet the particular Churches over which you preside with great dedication. Prompted by my "anxiety for all the Churches" (2 Cor. 11:28), I ask you to assure the priests, deacons, religious and laity of your Dioceses that the Pope shares their joys and difficulties, and that he prays for their continual growth in grace and holiness of life. In this sense your ad limina visit becomes a spiritual pilgrimage, for you have come not only to fulfill an administrative or juridical obligation of the episcopal office, but also to show authentic brotherhood and solidarity in the love of Christ, the chief Shepherd (cf. 1 Pet. 5:4), who sends his ministers to the Church on her journey through time, "so that, sharing in his power, they might make all peoples his disciples and sanctify and govern them" (*Lumen gentium,* §19).

2. As I did during my two previous meetings with the Bishops of your country, to-day too I would like to develop an essential aspect of the "universal sacrament of salvation" (*Lumen gentium,* §48).

3. My thoughts will focus on a fundamental topic: the Church as mystery. Since in our daily pastoral ministry we must be concerned about so many things in our varied activities, every now and then we need to take a few moments to lift the veil that often blocks our vision and to open our eyes to what is truly essential beneath the surface.

4. 2. I would like to recall an idea expressed by my Predecessor of blessed memory Pope Paul VI in his Encyclical *Ecclesiam suam* regarding the Church and her own awareness of her nature and mission. The invitation he made thirty-five years ago while the Second Vatican Council was in session can serve the Church today as a key to properly understanding the "signs of the time" on the threshold of the third millennium: "In this moment the Church must reflect

on herself to find strength in the knowledge of her place in the divine plan, to find greater light, new energy and more joy in fulfilling her own mission, and to determine the best means for making more immediate, effective and beneficial her contacts with mankind" (ch. I). We should thank God that the Church in our day is also making every effort in the power of the risen Lord to "reveal in the world, faithfully, even though darkly, his mystery until, in the consummation, it shall be manifested in full light" (*Lumen gentium,* §8).

5. We should not forget, of course, that the Church herself, as a "sign and instrument of communion with God and of the unity of all mankind," is a mystery. With good reason the first chapter of the Dogmatic Constitution *Lumen gentium* is entitled "The Mystery of the Church." Therefore, the Church cannot be genuinely renewed, unless our starting-point is her nature as mystery. What the Council had expressly stated was called to mind once again by the Extraordinary Synod of Bishops held twenty years after the close of that ecclesial assembly: "Inasmuch as she is communion* with God, Father, Son and Holy Spirit, the Church is, in Christ, the 'mystery' of the love of God present in human history" (Message, II). This truth should mark the teaching, ministry and pastoral activity of the whole Church. This conviction also forms the basis of all the postconciliar documents of the papal Magisterium, which are meant to foster a renewal in keeping with contemporary needs.

6. 3. It should be noted, moreover, that the same Extraordinary Synod of 1985 felt obliged to raise a warning: the assembled Bishops admitted that "a partial and selective reading of the Council, a one-sided presentation of the Church as a purely institutional structure devoid of her mystery," has led to serious deficiencies particularly in certain lay organizations which "critically consider the Church a mere institution" (Final Document, I, 4). As a result, many claim the right to organize the Church as if she were a multinational corporation and thus subject to a purely human form of authority. In reality, the Church as mystery is not "our" but "his" Church: the People of God, the Body of Christ and the Temple of the Holy Spirit.

7. Dear Brothers in the Episcopate! The Apostle Paul urges us: "Test everything; retain what is good" (1 Thess. 5:21). The Bishop's task is to encourage priests and all those who share responsibility for pastoral care to work towards the spiritual renewal of parishes. Anyone who rushes from one event to another is soon out of breath. In order to prevent spiritual exhaustion, it is more and more necessary to catch one's breath in prayer. For the liveliest parish is not the one with the fullest schedule of events, but the community that concentrates everything it does on its call to live in communion with the Triune God by listening to the word of God and participating in the sacraments. This need has been stressed by many advocates of an ecclesiology of *communio* inspired by the Council's teaching, to which theologians from your country have also rendered great service.

8. 4. We are at the end of the preparation for the Great Jubilee of the Year 2000. This year is dedicated to the first person of the divine Trinity. Reflection on God the Father inevitably leads to the Church, as St. Cyprian summarized in a splendid phrase: "No one can have God as Father who does not have the Church as Mother" (*De ecclesiae catholicae unitate,* §6).

9. This statement, which the Bishop of Carthage felt was necessary after the experiences of Deices' persecutions and the incidents regarding the *lapis,* prompted

the wish "that, if possible, none of the brothers [and sisters] would perish, and that the Mother would joyfully gather to her bosom the one body of a united people" (*De ecclesiae catholicae unitate* §23). We all know the great difference between the message entrusted to the Church and the human frailty of those who preach the Gospel. However history may judge these weaknesses, we should not forget this deficiency. On the contrary, we must do our best to prevent it from harming the spread of the Gospel. For this "Mother Church never ceases to pray, hope and work, and she exhorts her children to purification and renewal so that the sign of Christ may shine more brightly over the face of the Church" (*Lumen gentium*, §15).

10. 5. While the Church shows motherly concern and solidarity for her sons and daughters, at the same time she stands before them. The Mater is also Magister; she has the authority to bring up and teach her children, and so lead them to salvation. Mother Church gives birth to her sons and daughters; she nurtures and educates them. She gathers her children together and sends them out, all the while assuring them that they are safe in her motherly bosom. At the same time she is saddened by those who have fallen away and holds the door open to reconciliation, which is her constant concern. You Pastors have a particular responsibility in this regard: as "fathers of your communities," you have the right and duty to exercise the Church's "maternal authority," as the Second Vatican Council put it so clearly: in their preaching, the Bishops should "proclaim the maternal solicitude of the Church for all people, whether they be Catholics or not, and should be especially solicitous for the poor and weaker brethren.... Since it is the mission of Church to maintain close relations with the society in which she lives, the Bishops should make it their special care to approach people and initiate and promote dialogue with them. These discussions on religious matters should be marked by charity of expression as well as by humility and courtesy, so that the truth may be combined with charity, and understanding with love. The discussions should likewise be characterized by due prudence allied, however, with sincerity, which by promoting friendship is conducive to union of minds" (*Christus Dominus*, §13).

11. 6. The Church's sons and daughters must respond to her motherly affection with heartfelt obedience. At a time when maturity is spoken of so often not only in society but especially in the Church, there is an ever-growing attitude that true freedom can be achieved by "cutting the umbilical cord to the Church." As Bishops, you are trying to correct such erroneous tendencies by clearly and unambiguously preaching and living what was always a rule of life for the great saints: even in personally difficult situations, they never left the bosom of Mother Church. I would like to return to Cyprian's analogy and complete it: only those who heed Mother Church obey God the Father. The Bishop of Carthage developed this idea by pointing out the serious consequences, which are still possible since his time: "Whatever forsakes its mother's womb can neither live nor breathe on its own, but loses the possibility of salvation" (*De ecclesiae catholicae unitate*, §23).

12. 7. These thoughts are not unrealistic. As Shepherds of your flocks in Germany, you too must have experienced, especially in recent years, the great demands that the office of leadership makes on your strength and energy when particular groups try, through concerted action and continuous pressure, to bring about changes in the Church that do not correspond to the will of Jesus Christ. In view of this situation, the Bishop's task is to take the lead, to show the way,

to clarify, calm and always try to bring people together — all this through dialogue. I ask you: do not be discouraged!

13. While listening and reaching out, do not allow any human power to loosen the indissoluble bonds between you and the Successor of Peter!

14. At this point I would like to address a word to the laity. I express my heartfelt appreciation of the countless men and women who faithfully fulfill their call as a chosen race and royal priesthood (cf. 1 Pet. 2:9). In the light of their actions, I likewise point out the attitude that the laity should have towards their Bishops and priests: "To their Pastors they should disclose their needs and desires with that liberty and confidence which befits children of God and brothers of Christ. . . . If the occasion arises, this should be done through the institutions established by the Church for that purpose and always with truth, courage and prudence and with reverence and charity towards those who, by reason of their office, represent the person of Christ" (*Lumen gentium,* §37).

15. Unity with the Bishop is the essential and indispensable attitude of the faithful Catholic, for one cannot claim to be on the Pope's side without also standing by the Bishops in communion with him.

16. Nor can one claim to be with the Bishops without standing by the Head of the College.

17. 8. Venerable Brothers! I greatly appreciate that you are doing everything you can to give your faithful an example of *communio* within the Church. I am indeed aware that your primary concern is to put every pastoral initiative into a framework that is in full agreement with the world's Bishops gathered around the Successor of Peter.

18. Here I am thinking especially of the problem of the defense of life, in which it is essential for all the Bishops of the universal Church to bear unanimous and unambiguous witness. From the letters written by me or at my direction, you can gather how concerned I am about the counseling and aid given to pregnant women. I hope that this significant Church activity in your country will soon be definitively reorganized according to my instructions. I am convinced that Church counseling which is distinguished by its quality will be an eloquent sign for society and an effective way to help women in distress to accept the life they carry in their womb.

19. 9. Speaking of the royal priesthood in connection with the relationship between ordained pastors and the laity, I would like to recall the common priesthood. Thanks be to God that the Second Vatican Council brought this profound truth back to light! In the New Covenant there is only one sacrifice and one priest: Jesus Christ. All the baptized, men and women, have a share in this sacrifice of Christ, for they should "present their bodies as a living sacrifice, holy and acceptable to God" (Rom. 12:1). This participation involves not only the priestly, but also the prophetic and kingly mission of Christ. It expresses, moreover, the Church's organic union with Christ, which the Letter to the Ephesians describes with the image of bridegroom and bride (cf. Eph. 5:21–33).

20. Here we find ourselves at the heart of the paschal mystery, which reveals God's spousal love in all its depth. Christ is the bridegroom because he gave himself: he gave his body and shed his blood for us (cf. Luke 22:19–20). The fact that Jesus "loved to the end" (John 13:1) emphasizes the nuptial meaning of love.

Christ as Redeemer is the bridegroom of the Church. So we should rightly see the Eucharist, in which Christ builds up his Body, the Church, as the sacrament of the bridegroom and his bride.

21. As a consequence, there is a fundamental difference between the common priesthood of all the baptized and the priesthood of the ordained ministers (cf. Interdicasterial Instruction on Certain Questions Regarding the Collaboration of the Non-Ordained Faithful in the Sacred Ministry of Priests). The Church needs ordained priests who in sacramental celebrations act "in persona Christi" and represent Christ the bridegroom in relation to the Church as bride. In other words: the ordained pastors, who are members of the one Body of the Church, represent its head, who is Christ. Therefore, any attempt to clericalize the laity or to laicize the clergy must be rejected. It does not correspond to the mysterious ordering of the Church as willed by her Founder. Nor are tendencies that eliminate the essential difference between clergy and laity of any use in attracting vocations. I ask you, dear Brothers, to keep alive in your parish communities a deep desire for ordained priests. Even a long period of waiting, due to the current shortage of priests, should not lead a community to accept an emergency situation as the rule. Priests and laity need each other. They cannot replace but only complement one another.

22. 10. At this point another observation is particularly useful: in your land, there is growing discontent with the Church's attitude towards the role of women. Unfortunately, not everyone seems to be aware yet that all the statements made about the common priesthood of the baptized apply equally to men and women. Without doubt, the dignity of women is great and must be more and more appreciated! However, too little consideration is given to the difference between the human and civil rights of the person and his rights, duties and related functions in the Church. Precisely for this reason, some time ago, by virtue of my ministry of confirming the brethren, I recalled "that the Church has no authority whatsoever to confer priestly ordination on women and that this judgment is to be definitively held by all the Church's faithful" (*Ordinatio Sacerdotalis,* §4).

23. As the authentic Pastors of your Dioceses, you have the duty to reject contrary opinions put forward by individuals or organizations and to encourage that open and clear dialogue in truth and love which Mother Church must foster regarding the future of her daughters. Do not hesitate, then, to emphasize that the Magisterium of the Church has taken this decision not as an act of her own power, but in the knowledge of her duty to obey the will of the Lord of the Church herself.

24. Therefore, the doctrine that the priesthood is reserved to men possesses, by virtue of the Church's ordinary and universal Magisterium, that character of infallibility which *Lumen gentium* speaks of and to which I gave juridical form in the Motu Proprio *Ad Tuendam Fidem*: When the individual Bishops, "even though dispersed throughout the world but preserving among themselves and with Peter's Successor the bond of communion, agree in their authoritative teaching on matters of faith and morals that a particular teaching is to be held definitively and absolutely, they infallibly proclaim the doctrine of Christ" (*Lumen gentium,* §25; cf. *Ad Tuendam Fidem,* §3).

25. Of course, we should help those who cannot understand or accept the Church's teaching to open their hearts and minds to the challenge that the faith poses

to them. As authentic teachers of the Church who is mother and teacher, it must be one of our highest priorities to help and support the faith of our communities. Therefore, we should stop at nothing, if necessary, to dispel confusion and correct errors. So I invoke the gifts of the Holy Spirit on your efforts to give an authentic character based on Christian doctrine to the role of women — for the renewal of society and for the rediscovery of the Church's true face.

26. 11. Dear Brothers! During this meeting we have considered the Church first and foremost as a mystery. A mystery ultimately escapes the grasp of human reason. Only with the eyes of faith can it be considered lovingly and be understood in depth. The images of the Church as mother and teacher, as bride and body, have always brought us back to Christ, the bridegroom and head of his Church. We feel under particular obligation to him in our pastoral ministry. So the words I have addressed to you at these meetings have been clear and unambiguous. I cannot hide the fact that in recent months I have often felt like the Apostle when he addressed those well-known words to the community in Corinth: "I wrote you out of much affliction and anguish of heart and with many tears, not to cause you pain but to let you know the abundant love that I have for you" (2 Cor. 2:4).

27. Tell your priests, deacons and religious that the Pope is close to them! Assure the men and women, the young and old, the sick and disabled that they can all find refuge in the bosom of Mother Church. With patience, trust and love endeavor to support the local Churches entrusted to each of you and lead them like a bride to the heavenly wedding feast.

28. I ask the Virgin Mary for her protection and call upon her to intercede for you and for everyone entrusted to your pastoral care. What childlike trust is expressed in the words of an old prayer that is widely known in your homeland: Blessed Virgin, God's Mother and mine, let me always be truly thine!

29. May the Apostolic Blessing I cordially give you accompany each and every one of you.

Message of the Holy Father to the World Union of Catholic Women's Organizations

Pope John Paul II

March 7, 2001

To: Mrs. María Eugenia Díaz de Pfennich
President of the World Union of Catholic Women's Organizations

1. With joy I greet the participants in the General Assembly of the World Union of Catholic Women's Organizations, taking place in Rome from March 17 to 21, 2001. Since 1910 your movement has brought Catholic women together from all the continents and from a great variety of backgrounds and cultures. In a spirit of respect for this diversity you now form a large and dynamic family within the Catholic Church. Your meeting at the heart of the universal Church is a special opportunity to reaffirm your identity and to draw on the graces of the Jubilee to open wide to Christ the doors of your hearts and of the homes and communities in which you live, pray and follow the vocation which God has entrusted to each one.

2. At the beginning of a new millennium, the six hundred delegates at this Assembly have the opportunity to thank God for all that being a woman signifies in the divine plan, and to ask his help in overcoming the many obstacles which still hinder full recognition of the dignity and mission of women in society and within the ecclesial community. The journey traveled in the course of the past century has been remarkable. In many countries women today enjoy freedom of movement, of decision and of self-expression, a freedom which they have achieved with clear-mindedness and courage. They express their characteristic genius in many spheres. In today's world there exists a growing awareness of the need to affirm women's dignity. This is no abstract principle for it involves a concerted effort at every level to oppose vigorously "all practices that offend woman's freedom or femininity...so-called 'sexual tourism,' trafficking in young girls, mass sterilization and, in general, every form of violence" (General Audience, November 24, 1999, No. 2). However, women also face many impediments to their genuine fulfillment. The prevailing culture spreads and imposes models of life which are contrary to women's deeper nature. There have been serious aberrations, some arising from individual selfishness and a refusal to love, others from a mentality that stresses each individual's rights to

such an extent that respect for the rights of others is weakened, and particularly those of defenseless unborn children who in many cases are deprived of all legal protection.

3. Your Union exists to help you to acquire a deeper understanding of your mission and to live it to the full. It is present as a voice even in international forums, to insist that every life is a gift of God and deserves to be respected. Working together, you must seek to provide increasing material and moral support to women in difficulty, victims of poverty and violence. Never forget that this important work is rooted in God's love and will bear fruit to the extent that your witness reveals his infinite love for every human person.

4. Feminine holiness, to which each one of you is called, is indispensable to the life of the Church. "The Second Vatican Council, confirming the teaching of the whole of tradition, recalled that in the hierarchy of holiness it is precisely the 'woman,' Mary of Nazareth, who is the 'figure' of the Church. She 'precedes' everyone on the path to holiness" (*Mulieris Dignitatem,* §27). Women who live in holiness are "a model of the 'sequela Christi,' an example of how the Bride must respond with love to the love of the Bridegroom" (ibid., §27).

5. The theme of your Assembly, The Prophetic Mission of Women, should offer an occasion for you to engage in a broad reflection on your commitment. The world and the Church need your specific witness. Christ's prophetic office is shared by the whole People of God and consists above all in listening to God's word and understanding it (cf. *Lumen Gentium,* §12). Catholic women who live by faith and charity and give honor to God's name in prayer and service (cf. ibid.) have always had a supremely fruitful and indispensable role in transmitting the genuine sense of the faith and in applying it to all life's circumstances. Today, at a time of a deep spiritual and cultural crisis, this task has assumed an urgency that cannot be overstated. The Church's presence and action in the new millennium passes by way of woman's capacity to receive and keep God's word. In virtue of her specific charism, woman is uniquely gifted in the task of passing on the Christian message and mystery in the family and in the world of work, study and leisure.

6. The recent Jubilee of the Laity was an opportunity to renew the Second Vatican Council's call to all the lay faithful to proclaim the Good News of Christ by word and witness. In the family and in society you work "for the sanctification of the world from within" (*Lumen Gentium,* §31). Every task, even the most ordinary, provided it is carried out with love, contributes to the sanctification of the world. This is an important truth to recall today, in a world fascinated by success and efficiency, but in which many people have no share in the benefits of global progress and are becoming poorer and more neglected than ever.

7. The Jubilee brought new energies to the whole Church. Let us go forward in hope! (cf. *Novo Millennio ineunte,* §58). Today, as the Church sets out again on her journey to proclaim Christ to the world, she needs women who contemplate the face of Christ, who keep their gaze fixed on him and recognize him in the weakest members of his Body. "Truly, I say to you, as you did it to one of the least of these my brethren, you did it to me" (Matt. 25:40). Keep watch, be an attentive and strong presence, never fail to look to Christ, follow him, keep his word in your hearts. In this way, your hope will not fail; it will spread throughout the world at this promising and challenging time.

8. I once again assure you of my closeness in prayer, confident that this Assembly will be an occasion for you to find fresh energies for your mission. Entrusting all of you to the protection of Mary, Mother of the Redeemer, I cordially impart my Apostolic Blessing.

From the Vatican, March 7, 2001
IOANNES PAULUS II

Warning Regarding
the Attempted Priestly Ordination
of Some Catholic Women

Congregation for the Doctrine of the Faith

July 10, 2002

1. On June 29, 2002, Romulo Antonio Braschi, the founder of a schismatic community, attempted to confer priestly ordination on the following Catholic women: Christine Mayr-Lumetzberger, Adelinde Theresia Roitinger, Gisela Forster, Iris Müller, Ida Raming, Pia Brunner and Angela White.

2. In order to give direction to the consciences of the Catholic faithful and dispel any doubts which may have arisen, the Congregation for the Doctrine of the Faith wishes to recall the teaching of the Apostolic Letter *Ordinatio Sacerdotalis* of Pope John Paul II, which states that "the Church has no authority whatsoever to confer priestly ordination on women and that this judgment is to be definitively held by all the Church's faithful" (n. 4). For this reason, the above-mentioned "priestly ordination" constitutes the simulation of a sacrament and is thus invalid and null, as well as constituting a grave offense to the divine constitution of the Church. Furthermore, because the "ordaining" Bishop belongs to a schismatic community, it is also a serious attack on the unity of the Church. Such an action is an affront to the dignity of women, whose specific role in the Church and society is distinctive and irreplaceable.

3. The present Declaration, recalling the preceding statements of the Bishop of Linz and the Episcopal Conference of Austria and in accordance with canon 1347 §1 of the CIC, gives formal warning to the above-mentioned women that they will incur excommunication reserved to the Holy See if, by July 22, 2002, they do not (1) acknowledge the nullity of the "orders" they have received from a schismatic Bishop in contradiction to the definitive doctrine of the Church and (2) state their repentance and ask forgiveness for the scandal caused to the faithful.

Rome, from the Offices of the
Congregation for the Doctrine of the Faith
July 10, 2002
Joseph Cardinal Ratzinger, Prefect
Tarcisio Bertone, S.D.B., Archbishop Emeritus of Vercelli, Secretary

Decree of Excommunication Regarding the Attempted Priestly Ordination of Some Catholic Women

Congregation for the Doctrine of the Faith

August 5, 2002

Preface to the Decree of Excommunication

1. In order to dispel any doubts about the canonical status of Bishop Romulo Antonio Braschi, who attempted to confer priestly ordination on several Catholic women, the Congregation for the Doctrine of the Faith confirms that, as a schismatic, he has already incurred excommunication reserved to the Apostolic See.

Decree of Excommunication

2. Pursuant to the warning issued by this Congregation on July 10, 2002, and published the following day, because the women Christine Mayr-Lumetzberger, Adelinde Theresia Roitinger, Gisela Forster, Iris Müller, Ida Raming, Pia Brunner and Angela White did not within the period that ended on July 22, 2002, give any indication of amendment or repentance for the most serious offense they had committed, this Dicastery, in keeping with this warning, declares that they have incurred excommunication reserved to the Apostolic See, with all the effects established by canon 1331 of the Code of Canon Law.

3. In having to take this action, the Congregation trusts that, by the grace of the Holy Spirit, the above-mentioned persons may rediscover the path of conversion in order to return to the unity of faith and to communion with the Church, which they have wounded by their actions.

Rome, Congregation for the Doctrine of the Faith
August 5, 2002
Joseph Cardinal Ratzinger
Prefect Tarcisio Bertone, S.D.B., Archbishop of Vercelli, Secretary

➤ Document 12 ◆

Decree on the Attempted Priestly Ordination of Some Catholic Women

Congregation for the Doctrine of the Faith

December 21, 2002

1. On June 29, 2002, Romulo Antonio Braschi, founder of a schismatic community, attempted to ordain the following Catholic women to the priesthood: Christine Mayr-Lumetzberger, Adelinde Roitinger, Gisela Forster, Iris Müller, Ida Raming, Pia Brunner and Dagmar Braun Celeste, who on that occasion identified herself as Angela White.

2. Citing the previous interventions of the Bishop of Linz and of the Austrian Episcopal Conference, the Congregation for the Doctrine of the Faith published a statement on July 10, 2002, warning the above-mentioned persons that they would be punished with excommunication if by July 22, 2002, they had not acknowledged the nullity of their "ordination" and asked forgiveness for the scandal caused to the faithful. As they gave no indication of amendment, this Congregation punished the aforementioned persons with excommunication, reserved to the Apostolic See, in the Decree dated August 5, 2002, expressing the hope that they might be moved to conversion. The Decree also confirmed that the "ordaining" bishop was already excommunicated insofar as he is a schismatic.

3. They subsequently published letters and granted interviews, in which they expressed their conviction regarding the validity of the "ordination" they received, calling for a change of the definitive doctrine according to which ordination to the priesthood is reserved to males, and reaffirming that they celebrate "Mass" and other "sacraments" for small groups. In a letter dated August 14, 2002, they asked that the Decree of Excommunication be revoked, and then, on September 27, 2002, with reference to canons 1732–39 CIC, they made recourse against the Decree. On October 21, 2002, they were informed that their request would be submitted to the competent authority.

4. The request for revocation and the recourse were examined by the Sessione Ordinaria of the Congregation on the 4th and 18th of December 2002. The Members of the Congregation who participated — those resident in Rome — were Cardinals Joseph Ratzinger, Alfonso Lopez Trujillo, Ignace Moussa I. Daoud, Giovanni Battista Re, Francis Arinze, Jozef Tomko, Achille Silvestrini, Jorge Medina Estivez, James Francis Stafford, Zenon Grocholewski, Walter Kasper, Crescenzio Sepe, Mario Francesco Pompedda, and Bishops Tarcisio Bertone, S.D.B., and Rino Fisichella. In the course of these meetings the

Members arrived at the collegial decision to confirm the Decree of Excommunication. In the case under consideration, in fact, hierarchical recourse is not possible, as it concerns a Decree of Excommunication issued by a Dicastery of the Holy See acting in the name of the Supreme Pontiff (cf. can. 360 CIC). So as to remove any doubt in the matter, the Members thought it necessary to underline certain fundamental points.

5. 1. It is necessary above all to state precisely that the case under consideration does not involve a *latae sententiae* penalty, which is incurred *ipso facto* when a delict expressly established by the law is committed. It concerns instead a *ferendae sententiae* penalty, imposed after the guilty party has been duly warned (cf. cann. 1314; 1347:1 CIC). As provided by can. 1319:1 CIC, this Congregation has the power to threaten determinate penalties by precept.

6. 2. The particular gravity of the offenses committed is evident, which can be seen from various aspects.

    (a) There is first of all the issue of schism: the above-mentioned women were "ordained" by a schismatic bishop and — even though not formally adhering to his schism — thereby made themselves accomplices in schism.

    (b) In addition there is the doctrinal aspect, namely, that they formally and obstinately reject a doctrine which the Church has always taught and lived, and which was definitively proposed by Pope John Paul II, namely, "that the Church has no authority whatsoever to confer priestly ordination on women" (Apostolic Letter *Ordinatio Sacerdotalis,* n. 4). The denial of this doctrine is rightly considered the denial of a truth that pertains to the Catholic faith and therefore deserves a just penalty (cf. cann. 750:2; 1372, n. 1 CIC; John Paul II, Apostolic Letter *Motu Proprio Ad Tuendam Fidem,* n. 4A).

    Moreover, by denying this doctrine, the persons in question maintain that the Magisterium of the Roman Pontiff would be binding only if it were based on a decision of the College of Bishops, supported by the *sensus fidelium* and received by the major theologians. In such a way they are at odds with the doctrine on the Magisterium of the Successor of Peter, put forward by both the First and Second Vatican Councils, and they thereby fail to recognize that the teachings of the Supreme Pontiff on doctrines to be held definitively by all the faithful are irreformable.

7. 3. The refusal to comply with the penal precept established by this Congregation is further aggravated by the fact that some of the above-mentioned women have been gathering round them members of the faithful, in open and divisive disobedience to the Roman Pontiff and diocesan bishops. In view of the gravity of this contumacy (cf. can. 1347 CIC), the penalty imposed is not only just, but also necessary, in order to protect true doctrine, to safeguard the communion and unity of the Church and to guide the consciences of the faithful.

8. 4. The above-mentioned Members of the Congregation of the Doctrine of the Faith therefore confirm the Decree of Excommunication issued on August 5, 2002, specifying once again that the attempted priestly ordination of the aforementioned women is null and invalid (cf. can. 1024 CIC) and therefore all those actions proper to the Order of Priesthood performed by them are also null and invalid (cf. cann. 124; 841 CIC). In consequence of the excommunication, they are forbidden to celebrate sacraments or sacramentals, to receive the sacraments and to exercise any function in an ecclesiastical office, ministry or assignment (cf. can. 1331:1 CIC).

9. 5. At the same time, it is hoped that, sustained by the grace of the Holy Spirit, they might discover the path to conversion and so return to the unity of faith and to communion with the Church, a communion broken by their action.

10. The Sovereign Pontiff John Paul II, at the Audience granted to the undersigned Cardinal Prefect on December 20, 2002, approved this Decree, adopted in the *Sessione Ordinaria* of this Congregation, approving at the same time in *forma specifica* n. 4, and ordered its publication.

Rome, Congregation for the Doctrine of the Faith
December 21, 2002
Joseph Cardinal Ratzinger, Prefect
Tarcisio Bertone, S.D.B., Archbishop-elect of Genoa, Secretary

Key Dates

Beginning with Vatican II (1962–65)

1963 Pope John XXIII dies. He is succeeded by Pope Paul VI.

1964 The Southern Baptist Convention (U.S.A.) begins ordaining women when a congregation ordains a woman in the absence of any rule against it.

Upon learning that the absence of women at Vatican II is drawing public criticism, Pope Paul VI invites twenty-two women to observe the proceedings.

1970 The Lutheran Church in America and the American Lutheran Church (now the Evangelical Lutheran Church in America) amend church rules to allow women's ordination.

The National Coalition of American Nuns (U.S.A.) calls for women's ordination.

Ludmila Javorova is ordained a Roman Catholic priest in Communist-controlled Czechoslovakia.

1971 The International Synod of Bishops recommends the creation of a global commission to study Catholic women's ordination. The commission is never established.

1972 Women make up 4.7 percent of seminarians in the United States.

1974 The Leadership Conference of Women Religious (U.S.A.) resolves that all Roman Catholic church ministries should be open to women. Episcopal Church bishops (retired) irregularly ordain eleven women in Philadelphia.

1975 The Canon Law Society of America says there is no reason to bar women from ordination.

Episcopalian bishops irregularly ordain four women, bringing the total to fifteen.

The Women's Ordination Conference organizes and meets in Detroit.

1976 The Pontifical Biblical Commission declares that the Bible cannot be used to justify an all-male priesthood.

The Episcopal Church (U.S.A.) legalizes women's ordination and retroactively validates earlier, irregular ordinations.

The Canadian Anglican Church legalizes women's ordination.

Inter Insigniores declares that Rome "is not authorized" to admit women to priesthood.

1977 In the weeks following *Inter Insigniores,* which formally denied priesthood to women, support for women priests among United States Catholics rises 10 percent.

Women constitute 4 percent of American clergy.

1978 Pope Paul VI dies. He is succeeded by Pope John Paul I, who dies a month later. Pope John Paul II ascends to the papal throne.

1979 Sister Teresa Kane, RSM (U.S.A.), challenges Pope John Paul II to open all church ministries to women. The pope later says he was unable to hear Kane's remarks.

1980 Women make up 15 percent of seminarians in the United States.

1982 The Roman Catholic Church begins ordaining former Episcopal priests. These men, most of whom are married, generally have left the Episcopal Church in protest against women priests in that denomination.

1983 The Canon Law Society of America issues the new Code of Canon Law, which retains the male-only priesthood.

Women-Church gathers in a formation meeting in Chicago.

1984 After twenty years of allowing women's ordination at the local level, the Southern Baptist Convention outlaws women's ordination because it is based upon "modern trends" and "emotional factors."

Anglican–Roman Catholic relations begin to cool as the Anglican Communion moves closer to ordaining women.

1985 Among American Catholics polled, 51 percent of men and 44 percent of women approve of women's ordination.

1988 U.S. bishops release the first draft of their pastoral letter on women, "Partners in the Mystery of Redemption." It is roundly criticized.

Reverend Barbara Harris is ordained suffragan (assistant) bishop in the Episcopal Church.

1990 U.S. bishops release another draft pastoral letter, " 'One in Christ Jesus': A Pastoral Response to the Concerns of Women for Church and Society." It is not adopted.

Approximately 50 percent of United States seminarians are women, up from 4 percent just two decades earlier.

1991 Bishop Kenneth Untener of Saginaw, Michigan, becomes the first American Catholic bishop to publicly call for women's ordination.

Anglican Archbishop of Canterbury George L. Carey responds to Pope John Paul II's escalating condemnation of women's ordination, saying that ecumenical cooperation seems to center on whether joint agreements between the two churches are "identical with the teachings of the Roman Catholic Church."

1992 The Church of England votes to ordain women as priests.

The Anglican churches in Australia and Southern Africa open priesthood to women.

1992 The National Conference of Catholic Bishops (U.S.A.) rejects the fourth and most conservative draft of the bishops' pastoral letter, "One in Christ Jesus': Toward a Pastoral Response to the Concerns of Women for Church and Society."

Although women cannot be ordained, about one-fourth of Roman Catholic seminary students in the United States are female. Two-thirds of American Catholics support women priests.

1993 A survey of American Catholic women shows that 62 percent are willing to withhold financial support to obtain an inclusive church.

1994 The Vatican approves of letting girls serve as altar servers, by temporary deputation from pastors and at the discretion of local bishops.

Pope John Paul II issues *Ordinatio Sacerdotalis,* saying the church has "no authority whatsoever" to ordain women, and that this judgment is to be "definitively held." The issue is no longer to be publicly discussed.

The English edition of the *Catechism of the Catholic Church* is published after a two-year delay to purge the book of gender-inclusive language proposed by the American bishops.

Citing unacceptable inclusive language, the Vatican overturns the American Catholic bishops' adoption of the New Revised Standard Version of the Bible for use in worship and instruction.

The American bishops issue "Strengthening the Bonds of Peace," rejecting "authoritarian conduct" and resolving to continue dialogue with women.

1995 The Society of Jesus adopts "Jesuits and the Situation of Women in Church and Civil Society," calling for Jesuits to "align themselves in solidarity with women."

Pope John Paul II issues his "Letter to Women," apologizing for church complicity in the oppression of the world's women, affirming the equal human dignity of women, and reaffirming divinely mandated role differences for women and men in the church.

The Vatican issues "*Responsum ad Dubium* Regarding *Ordinatio Sacerdotalis,*" saying the teaching in *Ordinatio Sacerdotalis* rested on the "written word of God," was in the church's "constant" tradition, belonged "to the deposit of faith," and was "set forth infallibly."

The Women's Ordination Conference helps found Women's Ordination Worldwide.

1996 The Vatican formally prohibits Czech Ludmila Javorova from exercising priestly functions and orders her to keep silent about the matter.

1997 Pope John Paul II names Saint Thérèse of Lisieux a Doctor of the Church; she is only the third woman to hold this honor.

1998 Pope John Paul II issues *Ad Tuendam Fidem,* saying that persons rejecting "definitively proposed" teachings (such as the male priesthood) would "no longer be in full communion" with the church. He amends canon law to provide for punishment.

1998   Pressured by the Vatican, the Liturgical Press in the United States burns thirteen hundred copies of Sister Lavinia Byrne's book, *Woman at the Altar.*

2000   Women make up more than 80 percent of all parish administrators in the United States.

2001   Long-time lay minister Mary Ramerman is ordained in Spiritus Christi, a large breakaway parish in Rochester, New York.

The first international meeting of Women's Ordination Worldwide is held in Dublin. Sister Joan Chittister and Sister Myra Poole defy Vatican orders to stay away.

2002   Seven Roman Catholic women are ordained by a Catholic priest on the Danube near the Austrian-German border: Iris Müller, Ida Raming, Gisela Forster, Pia Brunner (Germany), Christine Mayr-Lumetzberger, Sister Adelinde Theresia Roitinger (Austria), and Angela White (U.S.A.). Rome declares the ordinations invalid and then excommunicates the women.

2003   Lay minister Denise Donato is ordained in the breakaway Spiritus Christi parish in Rochester, New York.

Two of the women ordained in 2002, Christine Mayr-Lumetzberger and Gisela Forster, are consecrated as bishops.

Sister Patricia Ann Fresen of South Africa is ordained by the newly ordained female bishops.

2004   Pope John Paul II appoints the first female theologians, Barbara Hallensleben and Sister Sara Butler, to the International Theological Commission, and the first woman, law professor Mary Ann Glendon, as president of the Pontifical Academy of Social Sciences.

Notes

Preface

1. Elizabeth A. Johnson, "Response to Rome," *Commonweal* 123, no. 2 (January 26, 1996): 11–12.

2. Dean R. Hoge, *Future of Catholic Leadership: Responses to the Priest Shortage* (Kansas City, Mo.: Sheed & Ward, 1987), 160–61.

3. Betty Bone Schiess, in "Woman Priest," videotape, prod. Joseph Agonito (1986).

Telling the Story of a Soul

4. Nadine Foley, "Woman in Vatican Documents 1960 to the Present," in *Sexism and Church Law*, ed. James A. Coriden (New York: Paulist Press, 1977), 92–95, 106.

5. Ibid.

6. Jay P. Dolan, *In Search of American Catholicism: A History of Religion and Culture in Tension* (New York: Oxford University Press, 2002), 176–77.

7. Thérèse of Lisieux, *The Autobiography of St. Thérèse of Lisieux: The Story of a Soul*, trans. John Beevers (Garden City, N.Y.: Doubleday, 1957), 153. Lisieux is pronounced Lih-*zhoo*.

Chapter 1

8. Contemporary connotations differentiating "gender" (social role assigned to sex) and "sex" (biological designation) are here acknowledged; however, this work uses "gender" and "sex" interchangeably.

9. A basic, informative introduction to women in Christianity may be found in Rosemary Radford Ruether's "Christianity," in *Women in World Religions*, ed. Arvind Sharma (Albany: State University of New York Press, 1987), 207–33.

10. Elisabeth Schüssler Fiorenza, "Women in the Early Christian Movement," in *Womanspirit Rising: A Feminist Reader in Religion*, ed. Carol P. Christ and Judith Plaskow (San Francisco: Harper & Row, 1979), 87, 92.

11. See Gary Macy, "The Ordination of Women in the Early Middle Ages," in *A History of Women and Ordination*, ed. Bernard Cooke and Gary Macy, vol. 1: *The Ordination of Women in Medieval Context* (Lanham, Md.: Scarecrow Press, 2002), chapter 1.

12. See Karen Jo Torjesen's *When Women Were Priests* (San Francisco: HarperCollins, 1994), and "Women's Ordination: The Hidden Tradition," videotape, British Broadcasting Corporation (1992).

13. Bernard Cooke and Gary Macy, eds., *A History of Women and Ordination*, vol. 1: *The Ordination of Women in Medieval Context* (Lanham, Md.: Scarecrow Press, 2002), 11.

14. Ruth A. Wallace, *They Call Her Pastor: A New Role for Catholic Women* (Albany: State University of New York Press, 1992), 4.

15. Aristotle, "On the Generation of Animals" §737a, *The Works of Aristotle, Volume II*, Great Books of the Western World Series 9, ed. Robert Maynard Hutchins (Chicago: William Benton, Encyclopædia Britannica, 1952), 278.

16. Aristotle, "Politics" §1254b, *The Works of Aristotle, Volume II*, Great Books of the Western World Series 9, ed. Robert Maynard Hutchins (Chicago: William Benton, Encyclopædia Britannica, 1952), 448.

17. Augustine, *De Trinitate* 7.7, 10. Quoted in Rosemary Radford Ruether, "Misogynism and Virginal Feminism in the Fathers of the Church," in *Religion and Sexism: Images of Woman in the Jewish and Christian Traditions,* ed. Rosemary Radford Ruether (New York: Simon and Schuster, 1974), 156.

18. Many Christians experience an ambivalent academic and spiritual relationship with Aristotle, Augustine, and Aquinas. I should point out that my disdain for their antiwoman writing is exceeded by profound admiration (indeed awe) for their genius.

19. For a brief but inclusive history of women's exclusion from holy orders, see Katherine Meagher, "Women in Relation to Orders and Jurisdiction," in *Sexism and Church Law: Equal Rights and Affirmative Action,* ed. James A. Coriden (New York: Paulist Press, 1977), 21–42.

20. Heinrich Kramer and James Sprenger, *The Malleus Maleficarum of Heinrich Kramer and James Sprenger,* trans. Montague Summers (New York: Dover Publications, 1971). The 1484 decree of Innocent VIII, *Summis desiderantes affectibus* ("greatly desiring with anxiety"), appeared as the preface to *Malleus Maleficarum.* The introduction to the 1948 edition ranked it "among the most important, wisest, and weightiest books of the world."

21. Kramer and Sprenger, *The Malleus Maleficarum of Heinrich Kramer and James Sprenger,* 173.

22. Ibid., 41–42.

23. This study regrettably excludes issues of women's ordination to the permanent diaconate, which like the priesthood is a male-only institution. See Rome's March 10, 1998, joint declaration, "Basic Norms for the Formation of Permanent Deacons," by the Congregation for Catholic Education, and "Directory for the Ministry and Life of Permanent Deacons," by the Congregation for Clergy, at www.vatican.va/roman_curia/congregations/ccatheduc/. Also see Phyllis Zagano, *Holy Saturday: An Argument for the Restoration of the Female Diaconate in the Catholic Church* (New York: Crossroad, 2000).

24. The obscurity of Vatican language and its effects are not limited to the women's ordination debate. Peter Steinfels wrote that following the early 2001 publication of widespread sex abuse by American priests, Rome issued two statements that "Vatican officials insisted on larding with technical language from church law that was predictably misunderstood and set off more furors." See Peter Steinfels, *A People Adrift: The Crisis of the Roman Catholic Church in America* (New York: Simon & Schuster, 2003), 63.

25. United States Catholic Conference, *From "Inter Insigniores" to "Ordinatio Sacerdotalis"* (Washington, D.C.: United States Catholic Conference, 1998) is an English translation of previously published Vatican documents.

26. Pope John Paul II took this action in his apostolic letter *Ordinatio Sacerdotalis* ("On Reserving Priestly Ordination to Men Alone"), to which we will return.

27. "Czech Priests Defrocked," *Christian Century* 109, no. 17 (May 13, 1992): 513.

28. For an account of Christians living in Communist Czechoslovakia, see Margot Patterson, "Telling the Story of a Brutal Time," *National Catholic Reporter* 38, no. 12 (January 25, 2002), 4–5.

29. "On File," *Origins* 25, no. 34 (February 15, 1996): 570.

30. For an account of the clandestine priesthood in Communist Czechoslovakia, see Miriam Therese Winter, *Out of the Depths: The Story of Ludmila Javorova, Ordained Roman Catholic Priest* (New York: Crossroad, 2001).

31. Ibid., 200.

32. Ibid., 205–6.

33. Ibid., 201.

34. Ibid.

35. "Czech Priests Defrocked," 513.

36. Winter, *Out of the Depths,* 211.

37. Ibid., 240.

38. Henri Ghéon, *The Secret of the Little Flower: St. Thérèse of Lisieux,* trans. Donald Attwater (London: Sheed & Ward, 1934), 207.

39. Ibid., 227.

Chapter 2

40. At the root of this concept is *ordo* ("order"), a term early Christians used to denote the place of the clergy among the faithful. This evolved into the concept of an order for the three degrees of ordination.

41. United States Catholic Conference, *Catechism of the Catholic Church* (Liguori, Mo.: Liguori Publications, 1994), §1538.

42. Richard P. McBrien, *Catholicism,* new edition (New York: HarperCollins, 1994), 869.

43. United States Catholic Conference, *Catechism of the Catholic Church,* §1570, §1256.

44. Richard P. McBrien, "Debate on Women's Ordination Won't Go Away," *Milwaukee Catholic Herald* (December 10, 1998).

45. Quoted in Roger Gryson, *The Ministry of Women in the Early Church,* trans. Jean Laporte and Mary Louise Hall (Collegeville, Minn.: Liturgical Press, 1980), 107.

46. See the National Association of Permanent Diaconate Directors' 1978 resolution requesting Vatican permission to ordain women as deacons in the United States, in "Issues of the Permanent Diaconate," *Origins* 7, no. 39 (March 16, 1978): 624. When Rome declared in 1998 that, by virtue of its share in holy orders (requiring ordination), the diaconate was open to men only, Cardinal Pio Laghi, head of the Congregation for Catholic Education, explained that New Testament women, formerly believed to have served as deacons, were in fact "blessed" rather than "ordained," and that the "sacramental configuration to Christ has always been reserved to men." See "Diaconate Just for Men, Vatican Says," *National Catholic Reporter* 34, no. 20 (March 20, 1998), 8. More realistically, in 1976 theologian Joseph Komonchak theorized that "to say that women may receive the sacramental diaconate is to say that they are capable of receiving the Sacrament of Orders, and, if they can receive it on one level, why may they not receive it on the others?" The sacrament, he said, "is a unity, so that if one may validly receive it in one order, one may validly receive it in any." See Joseph Komonchak, "Theological Questions on the Ordination of Women," in *Women and Catholic Priesthood: An Expanded Vision,* ed. Anne Marie Gardiner (New York: Paulist Press, 1976), 244. This question surely influenced the Vatican's decision.

47. Paula Nesbitt argued that the priest shortage (which first began following Vatican II) "directly contributed to the revival of the ordained permanent diaconate open to married men as an alternative labor supply," a move recognized as yet another "organizational response to pressure by religious and lay women for ordination." See Paula D. Nesbitt, *Feminization of the Clergy in America* (New York: Oxford University Press, 1997), 143. Likewise, many have argued that the lay eucharistic service giving women a sense of participation (if not leadership) allows the hierarchy to evade the ordination issue.

48. United States Catholic Conference, *Catechism of the Catholic Church,* §1569.

49. Canon Law Society of America, *The Code of Canon Law: A Text and Commentary,* ed. James A. Coriden, Donald E. Heintschel, and Thomas J. Green (Mahwah, N.J.: Paulist Press, 1985), canon 1087.

50. Recent scholarly attempts to show that women held priestly office in the early church have produced no firm evidence. See Karen Jo Torjesen's *When Women Were Priests* (San Francisco: HarperCollins, 1994). The book's title (received from its publisher) and selected passages were taken by some commentators as evidence that women were once sacramentally "ordained" to the priesthood, a claim Torjesen did not directly make.

51. McBrien, *Catholicism*, 869.

52. United States Catholic Conference, *Catechism of the Catholic Church*, §1562–68.

53. Canon Law Society of America, *The Code of Canon Law*, canon 835:2.

54. United States Catholic Conference, *Catechism of the Catholic Church*, §1557.

55. Canon Law Society of America, *The Code of Canon Law*, canon 835:1.

56. United States Catholic Conference, *Catechism of the Catholic Church*, §1558.

57. According to *Cassell's Latin Dictionary*, 5th ed. (New York: Macmillan, 1968).

58. McBrien, *Catholicism*, 867.

59. Ibid., 868.

60. Peter Hebblethwaite, *The Next Pope* (San Francisco: HarperSanFrancisco, 1995), 3, 33.

61. See Gary Macy, "The Ordination of Women in the Early Middle Ages," in *A History of Women and Ordination,* ed. Bernard Cooke and Gary Macy, vol. 1: *The Ordination of Women in Medieval Context* (Lanham, Md.: Scarecrow Press, 2002), 2–3.

62. Ibid., ix, 4–5.

63. McBrien, *Catholicism*, 867.

64. Ibid., 800. In brief, a sacrament is a sign that proclaims faith, expresses worship, and reveals Christ's presence in a unified church. We will return to the nature of sacrament in more detail later. McBrien offers a solid overview of sacrament in Part 5.

65. *Codex Iuris Canonici* (The Vatican, 1918), 275. Canon 968:1 reads: "Sacram ordinationem valide recipit solus vir baptizatus..." ("Only a baptized male validly receives sacred ordination").

66. Charles Meyer, *Man of God: A Study of the Priesthood* (Garden City, N.J.: Doubleday, 1974), 49.

67. Pope Pius XII, *Mediator Dei* ("On the Sacred Liturgy"), quoted in *The Christian Faith in the Doctrinal Documents of the Catholic Church,* ed. J. Neuner and J. Dupuis, rev. ed. (New York: Alba House, 1982), 503.

68. *Lumen Gentium* ("Dogmatic Constitution on the Church"), in Walter Abbott, ed., *The Documents of Vatican II* (New York: Herder and Herder, Association Press, 1966), 14–106. See especially §13. Italics added.

69. United States Catholic Conference, *Catechism of the Catholic Church*, §1024, 1577–78. As head of the Interdicasterial Commission for the Catechism of the Catholic Church, Cardinal Joseph Ratzinger issued the *imprimi potest* ("it can be printed") for this publication. Ratzinger was an indefatigable opponent of women priests and a key player in the Vatican's continuing battle to quell support for the movement to ordain women.

70. Divo Barsotti, "Vatican Daily Says No Women Priests," *National Catholic Reporter* 6, no. 14 (February 4, 1970), 3. Italics added.

71. Michael Kenny, "Which Way the Pastoral?" *America* 167, no. 4 (August 15–22, 1992): 76–77.

72. Joseph Fichter, "Restructuring Catholicism," *Sociological Analysis* 38, no. 2 (1977): 162.

73. Barsotti, "Vatican Daily Says No Women Priests," 3.

74. *Lumen Gentium* ("Dogmatic Constitution on the Church"), in Austin Flannery, ed., *Vatican Council II: Constitutions, Decrees, Declarations* (Northport, N.Y.: Costello Publishing Co., 1996), 1–95; §10.

75. Canon Law Society of America, *The Code of Canon Law*, canon 835:4.

76. United States Catholic Conference, *Catechism of the Catholic Church* (Liguori, Mo.: Liguori Publications, 1994), §1547.

77. Congregation for the Clergy, "The Priest: Pastor and Leader of the Parish Community," *Origins* 32, no. 23 (November 14, 2002): 375.

78. See *The Catholic Encyclopedia*, revised and updated edition, ed. Robert C. Broderick (Nashville: Thomas Nelson Publishers, 1987), 492.

79. Congregation for the Clergy, "The Priest: Pastor and Leader of the Parish Community," 378.

80. Ibid., 375.

81. Ibid., 377–78.

82. Canon Law Society of America, *The Code of Canon Law*, canon 1008.

83. Congregation for the Clergy, "The Priest: Pastor and Leader of the Parish Community," 379.

84. The concept of "in the person of Christ" actually appeared in Pope Pius XII's 1947 encyclical, *Mediator Dei*. It was largely overlooked until its revival by Vatican II. For a historical discussion of the nature of priesthood, see David Coffee, "The Common and the Ordained Priesthood," *Theological Studies* 58, no. 2 (June 1997): 209–36.

85. Congregation for the Clergy, "The Priest: Pastor and Leader of the Parish Community," 386.

86. Thérèse of Lisieux, *The Autobiography of St. Thérèse of Lisieux: The Story of a Soul*, trans. John Beevers (Garden City, N.Y.: Doubleday, 1957), 76.

87. Ibid., 91, 153.

Chapter 3

88. Joseph Fichter, "Restructuring Catholicism," *Sociological Analysis* 38, no. 2 (1977): 155.

89. Avery Dulles, "The Church: Introduction," in *The Documents of Vatican II*, ed. Walter Abbott (New York: Herder and Herder, Association Press, 1966), 10–11.

90. Francis Morrisey, "The Juridical Status of Women in Contemporary Ecclesial Law," in *Sexism and Church Law*, ed. James A. Coriden (New York: Paulist Press, 1977), 5.

91. Peter Steinfels, *A People Adrift: The Crisis of the Roman Catholic Church in America* (New York: Simon & Schuster, 2003), 6.

92. See *The Catholic Encyclopedia*, revised and updated edition, ed. Robert C. Broderick (Nashville: Thomas Nelson Publishers, 1987), 28.

93. Ladislas Örsy, *Theology and Canon Law: New Horizons for Legislation and Interpretation* (Collegeville, Minn.: Liturgical Press, 1992), 12.

94. Ibid., 12–13.

95. Ibid., 15.

96. Mary Jo Weaver, *New Catholic Women: A Contemporary Challenge to Traditional Religious Authority* (New York: Harper & Row, 1985), 111.

97. Steinfels, *A People Adrift*, 254.

98. Helen Marie Ciernick, "Cracking the Door: Women at the Second Vatican Council," in *The Annual Publication of the College Theology Society* 40, ed. Mary Ann Hinsdale and Phyllis H. Kaminski (Maryknoll, N.Y.: Orbis Books, 1994), 69.

99. Maureen Fiedler and Linda Rabben, eds., *Rome Has Spoken: A Guide to Forgotten Papal Statements, and How They Have Changed through the Centuries* (New York: Crossroad, 1998), 118. The Catholic women attending that third session were outnumbered by non-Catholic observers. See Austin Flannery, ed., *Vatican Council II: Constitutions, Decrees, Declarations* (Northport, N.Y.: Costello Publishing Co., 1996), xi.

100. Ciernick, "Cracking the Door," 71.

101. Ruth A. Wallace, *They Call Her Pastor: A New Role for Catholic Women* (New York: State University of New York, 1992), 3.

102. Ciernick, "Cracking the Door," 72.

103. This is not to be confused with the third-century heresy, likewise called "subordinationism," that stated that because the Son and Spirit proceed from the Father, they were not fully divine.

104. Rosemary Radford Ruether, "Christianity," in *Women in World Religions*, ed. Arvind Sharma (Albany: State University of New York Press, 1987), 208.

105. Ibid., 209. Italics added.

106. See the "Christianity" section in Denise Lardner Carmody, *Women and World Religions* (Nashville: Abingdon, 1981), 113–36.

107. *Gaudium et Spes* ("On the Church in the Modern World"), in Austin Flannery, ed., *Vatican Council II: Constitutions, Decrees, Declarations* (Northport, N.Y.: Costello Publishing Co., 1996), 163–282, §29.

108. See Timothy E. O'Connell's study of this decree in "Decree on the Ministry and Life of Priests: *Presbyterorum Ordinis*, December 7, 1965," in *Vatican II and Its Documents: An American Reappraisal*, ed. Timothy E. O'Connell, Theology and Life Series 15 (Wilmington, Del.: Michael Glazier, 1986), 197–215.

109. *Presbyterorum Ordinis* ("Decree on the Ministry and Life of Priests"), in Austin Flannery, ed., *Vatican Council II: Constitutions, Decrees, Declarations* (Northport, N.Y.: Costello Publishing Co., 1996), 317–64; §2.

110. R. Scott Appleby, "If the Church Isn't a Democracy, What Is It?" *U.S. Catholic* (May 1996): 13. Appleby recalled that during the council Paul VI established a papal commission to review the church's ban on artificial birth control. When the commission returned its majority report recommending relaxation of the ban, the pontiff disbanded the commission and in 1968 issued *Humanae Vitae* ("Of Human Life"), sternly reinforcing the prohibition. The encyclical was not well received, and many Catholics "began to question any expression of authority exercised in seeming defiance of the consensus of the faithful."

111. Ciernick, "Cracking the Door," 63.

112. Peter Hebblethwaite, *The Next Pope* (San Francisco: HarperSanFrancisco, 1995), 65.

113. Monica Furlong, *Thérèse of Lisieux* (New York: Pantheon, 1987), 62.

Chapter 5

114. *Codex Iuris Canonici* (The Vatican, 1918), 27. Canon 118 reads: "Soli clerici possunt potestatem sive ordinis sive iurisdictionis ecclesiasticae et beneficia ac pensiones ecclesiasticas obtinere" ("Only clerics can obtain the power of either orders or ecclesiastical jurisdiction, and ecclesiastical benefices and pensions").

115. Canon Law Society of America, "Women in Canon Law," *Origins* 5 (November 1975): 260–61.

116. Ibid., 261–62.

117. Ibid., 262.

118. Quoted in Francis Morrisey, "The Juridical Status of Women in Contemporary Ecclesial Law," in *Sexism and Church Law*, ed. James A. Coriden (New York: Paulist Press, 1977), 8.

119. United States Catholic Conference, "Office for Women's Concerns Proposed," *Origins* 5 (November 1975): 397.

120. Ibid., 398.

121. Ibid., 397.

122. United States Catholic Conference, "Identifying Women's Concerns," *Origins* 6, no. 5 (June 24, 1976): 69.

123. Francis Bernard O'Connor, *Like Bread, Their Voices Rise! Global Women Challenge the Church* (Notre Dame, Ind.: Ave Maria Press, 1993), 25, 31.

124. Ibid., 92.

125. Women's Ordination Conference, *New Woman New Church New Priestly Ministry*, ed. Maureen Dwyer (Rochester, N.Y.: Women's Ordination Conference, 1980), Introduction.

126. Mary Daniel Turner, "Synthesis of Ordination Conference," in *Women and Catholic Priesthood: An Expanded Vision*, ed. Anne Marie Gardiner (New York: Paulist Press, 1976), 136.

127. "The WOC Story" (Fairfax, Va.: Women's Ordination Conference, n.d.).

128. Bishop Charles Buswell was a long-time supporter of women's ordination.

129. Mary Fainsod Katzenstein, *Faithful and Fearless: Moving Feminist Protest Inside the Church and Military* (Princeton, N.J.: Princeton University Press, 1998), 114.

130. Richard P. McBrien, "Essays in Theology: The Ordination of Women Movement" (December 8, 1978); http://129.74.54.81/rm/.

131. Personal correspondence with Women's Ordination Conference (Fairfax, Va.), March 2, 2004. The unwritten female-only rule was not limited to WOC's board of directors. In 2003, a website called "CIRCLES: Women's Ongoing Internet Consultation" advertised "vast academic and informational resources" to women who looked forward "to the day when authority and priesthood will be reformed and when women as well as men will enjoy full and equal access to all the ministries." Women were exhorted to join "for a small subscription fee." Men, however, could join only as "guest members." See www.equalrightsforwomen.org/circles/.

132. The LCWR, headquartered in Silver Spring, Maryland, is a support system and corporate voice for leaders of institutes of women religious in the United States.

133. Theresa Kane, "Welcome to Pope John Paul II," October 7, 1979; www.cta-usa.org/foundationdocs/.

134. Women's Ordination Conference, "The WOC Story."

135. See Richard P. McBrien, "Essays in Theology: Sister Theresa Kane and the Pope" (November 2, 1979); http://.129.74.54.81/rm/.

136. Peter Hebblethwaite, *The Next Pope* (San Francisco: HarperSanFrancisco, 1995), 163.

137. John Thavis, "Pope: Reject 'Extreme' Feminism," *National Catholic Reporter* 29, no. 34 (July 16, 1993), 7.

138. This coalition has been called the "Coalition of Women in the Church." See Women's Ordination Conference, "The WOC Story," and "Women of the Church Convergence." Rosemary Radford Ruether, "The Women-Church Movement in Contemporary Christianity," in *Women's Leadership in Marginal Religions: Explorations Outside the Mainstream*, ed. Catherine Wessinger (Urbana: University of Illinois Press, 1993), 199. According to Ruether, the coalition included the National Assembly of Religious Women, the National Coalition of American Nuns, and *Las Hermanas*, among others.

139. The revealing phrase "Women-Church" was first coined by theologian Elisabeth Schüssler Fiorenza: "the *ekklesia gynaikon* or women-church [is] the movement of self-identified women and women-identified men in biblical religion. When as a Christian I use the expression women-church, I do not use it as an exclusionary but as a political-oppositional term to patriarchy," which she defined as a "male pyramid" of "subordinations and exploitations" of women in terms of men's class, race, nationality, and religion. Women-Church operates on this meaning of patriarchy, while the Women's Ordination Conference is more (although not exclusively) concerned with the roles of women within the Roman Catholic Church. See Fiorenza's *Bread Not Stone: The Challenge of Feminist Biblical Interpretation* (Boston: Beacon Press, 1984), Introduction.

140. Katzenstein, *Faithful and Fearless*, 116–17.

141. Ruether, "The Women-Church Movement in Contemporary Christianity," 207–8.

142. Peter Steinfels, *A People Adrift: The Crisis of the Roman Catholic Church in America* (New York: Simon & Schuster, 2003), 281.

143. Ibid., 284.

144. Ruether, "The Women-Church Movement in Contemporary Christianity," 198.

145. Jane Redmont, "The Women's Ordination Movement, Phase Two," *America* (December 9, 1995): 16.

146. Ruth A. Wallace, *They Call Her Pastor: A New Role for Catholic Women* (Albany: State University of New York Press, 1992), 176. The nun's remark described the "recipe" theory of women's rights: take a male-dominated organization, add women, and stir.

147. Questions in a WOC survey revealed the organization's growing intent to broaden the scope of women's church-related concerns. The heading, "Issues Confronting the Church Generally," contained twenty-three questions addressing nine issues — democracy in ecclesial decision-making; birth control, abortion, and sexual activity; justice; married priests and celibacy; homosexuality; AIDS; divorced Catholics; ecumenism; and laity. See Maureen Fiedler and Karen Schwartz, "Benevolent Subversives: A National Study of Roman Catholic Women Called to Priesthood" (Fairfax, Va.: Women's Ordination Conference, 1999), 6–7.

148. "Answers to the Most Asked Questions about the Ordination of Women" (Rochester, N.Y.: Women's Ordination Conference, n.d.).

149. Katzenstein, *Faithful and Fearless*, 109.

150. Margaret Murphy, "Women's Priesthood? Few Women Agree," *National Catholic Reporter* 33, no. 13 (January 31, 1997), 14–15.

151. Ibid.

152. "More Women Opt for 'Ordination-and,'" *National Catholic Reporter* 32, no. 6 (December 1, 1995), 24.

153. Britain was home to the earliest organized women's ordination movement, the Catholic Women's Suffrage Society, founded in London in 1911. The name was changed in 1923 to St. Joan's Social and Political Alliance. In 1954, it became St. Joan's International Alliance.

154. Haye van der Meer, *Women Priests in the Catholic Church? A Theological-Historical Investigation*, trans. Arlene and Leonard Swidler (Philadelphia: Temple University Press, 1973), ix. The person(s) responsible for the change is not named.

155. Thérèse of Lisieux, *The Autobiography of St. Thérèse of Lisieux: The Story of a Soul*, trans. John Beevers (Garden City, N.Y.: Doubleday, 1957), 73.

Chapter 6

156. See the history of the Little Rock Scripture Study Program available online at www.littlerockscripture.org.

157. Pontifical Biblical Commission, "Can Women Be Priests?" *Origins* 6 (July 1, 1976): 92, editorial note.

158. Ibid.

159. Rosemary Radford Ruether refuted the general assumption that Paul was the author of Christian subordination of women. She pointed to recent studies showing that Paul in fact continued most of the assumptions and practices of the early (inclusive) church, and that most of the evidence that women served as local leaders is found in the Pauline letters. See Rosemary Radford Ruether, "Christianity," in *Women in World Religions*, ed. Arvind Sharma (Albany: State University of New York Press, 1987), 212.

160. Lewis M. Hopfe and Mark R. Woodward, *Religions of the World*, 9th ed. (Upper Saddle River, N.J.: Pearson Prentice Hall, 2004), 295, n. 26.

161. National Conference of Catholic Bishops, "Theological Reflections on the Ordination of Women," *Review for Religious* 32, no. 2 (March 1973): 220.

162. See Francis Morrisey, "The Juridical Status of Women in Contemporary Ecclesial Law," in *Sexism and Church Law*, ed. James A. Coriden (New York: Paulist Press, 1977), 13.

163. *Ministeria Quaedam* ("On first tonsure, minor orders, and the subdiaconate"), August 15, 1972, §7. For a related discussion of the provisions of this *motu proprio*, see the Canon Law Society of America, *The Code of Canon Law: A Text and Commentary*, ed. James A. Coriden, Thomas J. Green, Donald E. Heintschel (Mahwah, N.J.: Paulist Press, 1985), 229–30.

164. Catholic Biblical Association of America, "Women and Priestly Ministry: The New Testament Evidence," *Catholic Biblical Quarterly* 41, no. 4 (October 1979): 610.

165. Elisabeth Schüssler Fiorenza, "Women in the Early Christian Movement," in *Womanspirit Rising: A Feminist Reader in Religion*, ed. Carol P. Christ and Judith Plaskow (San Francisco: Harper & Row, 1979), 89–90. Lavinia Byrne further pointed out that Mary, the mother of Jesus, "was at the cross as well as at the cradle." See *Woman at the Altar: The Ordination of Women in the Roman Catholic Church* (New York: Continuum, 1998), 8.

166. See Mark 16:2–8; Luke 24:1–11; Matt. 28:1–10; and John 20:11–18.

167. Catholic Biblical Association of America, "Women and Priestly Ministry," 610.

168. Karl Rahner, "Women and Priesthood," *Concern for the Church*, Theological Investigations 20 (New York: Crossroad, 1986), 40–42.

169. Thérèse of Lisieux, *The Autobiography of St. Thérèse of Lisieux: The Story of a Soul*, trans. John Beevers (Garden City, N.Y.: Doubleday, 1957), 124–26.

170. Ibid., 155.

Chapter 7

171. Congregation for the Doctrine of the Faith, *Inter Insigniores* ("Declaration on the Admission of Women to the Ministerial Priesthood"), *Origins* 6, no. 33 (February 3, 1977): 517–24.

172. United States Catholic Conference, "Office for Women's Concerns Proposed," *Origins* 5 (November 1975): 399.

173. Peter Hebblethwaite, "Women on the Road to Rome," *Pope Paul VI* (Mahwah, N.J.: Paulist Press, 1993), 642.

174. Ibid., 641. This chapter provides an inclusive overview of events leading up to *Inter Insigniores*.

175. Suzanne Radley Hiatt, "Women's Ordination in the Anglican Communion: Can This Church Be Saved?" in *Religious Institutions and Women's Leadership: New Roles Inside the Mainstream*, ed. Catherine Wessinger (Columbia: University of South Carolina Press, 1996), 216–17.

176. This approval, however, was qualified by a "conscience clause" intended to minimize the threat of schism. It stated that "no bishop, priest, or lay person should be coerced or penalized in any manner" for following their convictions. In effect, this clause enabled dioceses to refuse ordination to women. See Paula D. Nesbitt, *Feminization of the Clergy in America* (New York: Oxford University Press, 1997), 38.

177. "On File," *Origins* 6, no. 15 (September 30, 1976): n.p. Surely one of those headaches sprang from the reality that these Episcopalians were providing a model for future Catholic strategy in the United States.

178. Betty Bone Schiess in "Woman Priest," videotape, prod. Joseph Agonito (1986).

179. For a complete account of women's ordination in the Anglican Communion, see Hiatt, "Women's Ordination in the Anglican Communion," 211–27.

180. Ibid., 219.

181. "Letters Exchanged by Pope and Anglican Leader," *Origins* 6, no. 9 (August 12, 1976): 129–33.

182. Pope John XXIII, *Pacem in Terris* ("Peace on Earth"), *The Encyclicals and Other Messages of John XXIII* (Washington, D.C.: TPS Press, 1964), 337.

183. Mark Chaves, *Ordaining Women: Culture and Conflict in Religious Organizations* (Cambridge, Mass.: Harvard University Press, 1999), 33.

184. Ibid.

185. Ibid., 36.

186. National Justice Conference, "Justice in the Church," *Origins* 6, no. 20 (October 4, 1976): 309–13.

187. Karen Bloomquist, "Questioning Lay Ministry," in *Women and Religion: A Reader for the Clergy*, ed. Regina Coll (New York: Paulist Press, 1982), 97–110.

188. While strictly speaking the document was published by the Congregation for the Doctrine of the Faith, it was understood that the sentiments were those of the pontiff.

189. Chaves, *Ordaining Women*, 84, 86.

190. *Sacrosanctum Concilium* ("The Constitution on the Sacred Liturgy"), in Austin Flannery, ed., *Vatican Council II: Constitutions, Decrees, Declarations* (Northport, N.Y.: Costello Publishing Co., 1996), 120–21.

191. Pope Pius XII, *"Mystici Corporis Christi,"* *Four Great Encyclicals of Pope Pius XII* (New York: Paulist Press, 1961), 14, §20.

192. Thomas Aquinas, *Summa Theologiae*, 3, 72, 5. Taken here from Bloomquist, "Questioning Lay Ministry," 99.

193. R. A. Norris Jr., "The Ordination of Women and the 'Maleness' of the Christ," *Living Worship* 13, no. 3 (March 1977): n.p. Also in *Feminine in the Church*, ed. Monica Furlong (London: SPCK, 1984), 83. Italics in the original.

194. For a thoroughly unscholarly but nonetheless instructive editorial on Jesus' omission of a second collection after the Sermon on the Mount, or why men in the Vatican brush their teeth "twice daily in total disregard of the gospel's non-message on the subject," see "Women Priests? Thud! Smash!" in *National Catholic Reporter* 6, no. 14 (February 4, 1970), 10.

195. Haye van der Meer, *Women Priests in the Catholic Church? A Theological-Historical Investigation*, trans. Arlene and Leonard Swidler (Philadelphia: Temple University Press, 1973), chapter 3, "The Church Fathers."

196. Gnosticism was a group of first-century philosophies concerned with personal revelation of truth, rather than faith or grace, as a source of knowledge.

197. Quoted in Karen Jo Torjesen, *When Women Were Priests* (San Francisco: Harper-Collins, 1994), 114.

198. Maureen Fiedler and Linda Rabben, eds., *Rome Has Spoken: A Guide to Forgotten Papal Statements and How They Have Changed through the Centuries* (New York: Crossroad, 1998), 114.

199. Quoted in John H. Wright. "Patristic Testimony on Women's Ordination in *Inter Insigniores*," *Theological Studies* 58, no. 3 (September 1997): 519.

200. Self-castration was perceived by some as an avenue for a Christian man to avoid failing in chastity. For a discussion of the benefits of avoiding women, see Denise Lardner Carmody, subsection entitled "Patristic and Medieval Christianity," *Women and World Religions* (Nashville: Abingdon Press, 1981), 119–28.

201. Torjesen, *When Women Were Priests*, 114.

202. Charles Meyer, *Man of God: A Study of the Priesthood* (Garden City, N.J.: Doubleday, 1974), 72. The Pontifical Biblical Commission had said that the "presbytides"

mentioned in Titus 2:3 were elderly women, not priestesses (§53). However, here Epiphanius was responding to women active as bishops and presbyters among the apocalyptic Montanist sect, which, among other things, proposed human sinfulness beyond forgiveness.

203. Wright, "Patristic Testimony on Women's Ordination in *Inter Insigniores*," 522.

204. van der Meer, *Women Priests in the Catholic Church?* 48. Van der Meer points out that one cannot read such an isolated text as "a valid argument from the Fathers," because "a further reading makes clear that Epiphanius feels there is a necessary close connection between the female priesthood and the adoration of Mary," a heresy against which he is reacting. See p. 7.

205. Italics added.

206. Three years before *Inter Insigniores*, Haye van der Meer highlighted a pattern adopted by three authors writing against women priests. "One notices that these authors at bottom do nothing but ... quote a few Scriptural passages ... quote a few passages from the Fathers and several ancient synods and other documents like the *Didascalia* [and] the *Constitutiones Apostolorum*, [and quote] Thomas Aquinas." See van der Meer, *Women Priests in the Catholic Church?* chapter 3.

207. Roger Gryson, *The Ministry of Women in the Early Church*, trans. Jean Laporte and Mary Louise Hall (Collegeville, Minn.: Liturgical Press, 1980), 37.

208. van der Meer, *Women Priests in the Catholic Church?* 51. Jesuit theologian John H. Wright and theologian Roger Gryson follow R. Hugh Connolly's 1929 translation (*Didascalia Apostolorum*, Oxford): " ... a great peril to her who baptizes and to *him* who is baptized," suggesting that women were not limited to baptizing other women. Italics added. See Wright, "Patristic Testimony on Women's Ordination in *Inter Insigniores*," 523. Also Gryson, *The Ministry of Women in the Early Church*, 38.

209. Wright, "Patristic Testimony on Women's Ordination in *Inter Insigniores*," 524.

210. Gryson, *The Ministry of Women in the Early Church*, 56–57.

211. Quoted in Lavinia Byrne, *Woman at the Altar: The Ordination of Women in the Roman Catholic Church* (New York: Continuum, 1998), 51–52.

212. Mary Ann Rossi, "Priesthood, Precedent, and Prejudice: On Recovering the Women Priests of Early Christianity," *Journal of Feminist Studies in Religion* 7, no. 1 (Spring 1991): 88.

213. Fiedler and Rabben, eds., *Rome Has Spoken*, 116.

214. In 1973, the National Conference of Catholic Bishops in the United States had written that there was "no explicit authoritative teaching concerning the ordination of women that settles the question." This was one of the clearest statements made in the 1970s attesting to the lack of church teaching on the subject. See Committee on Pastoral Research and Practices, National Conference of Catholic Bishops, "Theological Reflections on the Ordination of Women," *Review for Religious* 32, no. 2 (March 1973): 218.

215. Karl Rahner, "Women and Priesthood," *Concern for the Church*, Theological Investigations 20 (New York: Crossroad, 1986), 37–40.

216. The imposition of celibacy for priests occurred in the twelfth century, although at least three more centuries would pass before priestly celibacy was (at least theoretically) universally practiced. Today, married men who are ordained in the Roman Catholic Church after leaving ordained ministry in other denominations, e.g., Lutherans and Episcopalians, are allowed to retain their wives and children.

217. Bernard Leeming, *Principles of Sacramental Theology* (Westminster, Md.: Newman Press, 1960), 426. Leeming points out that the word "institute" has always generated "considerable diversity of interpretation," and even "voluminous discussion." See p. 393.

218. Rahner, "Women and the Priesthood," 43.

219. See *Lumen Gentium*, §10, and *Sacrosanctum Concilium*, §33, in Austin Flannery, ed., *Vatican Council II: Constitutions, Decrees, Declarations* (Northport, N.Y.: Costello Publishing Co., 1996), 14, 129.

220. *Presbyterorum Ordinis* ("Decree on the Ministry and Life of Priests"), in Austin Flannery, ed., *Vatican Council II: Constitutions, Decrees, Declarations* (Northport, N.Y.: Costello Publishing Co., 1996), 317–64; §2.

221. Thomas Newbold, "Symbolism of Sexuality: Person, Ministry and Women Priests," in *Women and Priesthood: Future Directions*, ed. Carroll Stuhlmueller (Collegeville, Minn.: Liturgical Press, 1978), 138–39. Italics in the original.

222. Rose Hoover, "Consider Tradition: A Case for Ordaining Women," *Commonweal* 126, no. 2 (January 29, 1999): 17–20.

223. Richard P. McBrien, *Catholicism*, new edition (New York: HarperCollins, 1994), 482–83.

224. Johnson referenced the Nicene Creed's use of "and he became man," the common English translation of *et homo factus est* ("and he became human"), which uses "man" to include both sexes. But if what Rome really means is *et vir factus est* ("and he became male"), it follows that women are "cut out of the loop of salvation" because "female humanity is not assumed and therefore not saved." See Elizabeth A. Johnson, *She Who Is: The Mystery of God in Feminist Theological Discourse* (New York: Crossroad, 1995), 153.

225. Quoted from *Ein Wort* in Richard Viladesau, "Could Jesus Have Ordained Women? Reflections on *Mulieris Dignitatem*," *Thought* 67, no. 264 (March 1992): 14. Viladesau provides a brief but helpful overview of Balthasar's distinctive influence on John Paul II in *Mulieris Dignitatem*.

226. Hans Urs von Balthasar, "The Uninterrupted Tradition of the Church," *L'Osservatore Romano*, English ed. (February 24, 1977), 6–7.

227. R. A. Norris Jr., "The Ordination of Women and the 'Maleness' of Christ," *Living Worship* 13, no. 3 (March 1977): n.p.

228. Mary Jo Weaver and R. Scott Appleby, *Being Right: Conservative Catholics in America* (Bloomington: Indiana University Press, 1995), 178. Italics added.

229. Pope Paul VI, "Address to the Members of the Study Commission on the Role of Women in Society and in the Church" April 18, 1975, *Acta apostolicae sedis* 67 (1975): 65.

230. Michael V. Fox, "The Song of Solomon," *The Harper Collins Study Bible: New Revised Standard Version* (New York, 1993), 1000–1002.

231. Roland E. Murphy, "Introduction: Canticle of Canticles," in *The New Jerome Biblical Commentary*, ed. Raymond E. Brown, Joseph A. Fitzmyer, and Roland E. Murphy (Englewood Cliffs, N.J.: Prentice-Hall, 1990), 462–63.

232. Sidney Callahan, "The Nuptial Body: One Metaphor among Many," *Commonweal* 123, no. 5 (March 8, 1996): 7–8.

233. Mary Ballou and Nancy W. Gabalac, *A Feminist Position on Mental Health* (Springfield, Ill.: Charles C. Thomas, 1985), 15. This phenomenon was repeated, with a twist, by mid-twentieth century conservative activist Phyllis Schlafly, a lawyer and two-time candidate for United States Congress, who spent the 1970s working to defeat the proposed Equal Rights Amendment for women. A wife and mother, she spent decades on the road telling American women to stay home and mind their families.

234. For the seminal work on the connection between womanhood and the art of domesticity, see Barbara Welter, "The Cult of True Womanhood: 1820–1860," *American Quarterly* 18, no. 2, part 1 (Summer 1966): 151–74.

235. Mary P. Ryan, *Womanhood in America: From Colonial Times to the Present*, 3rd ed. (New York: Franklin Watts, 1983), 210.

236. Joan Chittister, "Pentecost Papacy Would Listen to Women," *National Catholic Reporter* 33, no. 43 (October 10, 1997), 10–11.

237. Leonard Swidler, "Introduction: Roma Locuta, Causa Finita?" in *Women Priests: A Catholic Commentary on the Vatican Declaration,* ed. Leonard Swidler and Arlene Swidler (New York: Paulist Press, 1977), 3.

238. Quoted in "In Context: Declaration on Women in Ministerial Priesthood," *Origins* 6, no. 34 (February 10, 1977): 545–46. Italics added.

239. James Roberts, *Women Priests: Reflections on Papal Teaching and Church Response* (Vancouver, B.C.: Langara College, 1994), 3.

240. V. Sackville-West, *The Eagle and the Dove, A Study in Contrasts: St. Teresa of Avila, St. Thérèse of Lisieux* (Garden City, N.Y.: Doubleday, Doran, 1944), 144–45.

241. Henri Ghéon, *The Secret of the Little Flower: St. Thérèse of Lisieux,* trans. Donald Attwater (London: Sheed & Ward, 1934), 144.

242. Sackville-West, *The Eagle and the Dove,* 144–45.

Chapter 8

243. Congregation for the Doctrine of the Faith, "A Commentary on the Declaration," *Origins* 6, no. 33 (February 3, 177): 524ff.

244. "Congregation for the Doctrine of the Faith"; www.vatican.va.roman_curia/congregations/cfaith.

245. A scholarly reading of this commentary is challenging in part because of its increasingly technical language and in part because its quotes and claims carry no footnotes. It can be found in the United States Catholic Conference, *From "Inter Insigniores" to "Ordinatio Sacerdotalis"* (Washington: United States Catholic Conference, 1998), 55–76.

246. Theologian Yves Congar had earlier raised the question: "From the fact that the church has acted in a certain manner (in the realm of sacramental theology) it can be concluded that she could and can so act. But, from the fact that she has not acted in a certain manner it is not always prudent to conclude that she cannot or will not ever so act." Quoted in Herve-Marie Legrande, "Views on the Ordination of Women," *Origins* 6, no. 29 (January 6, 1977): 465.

247. Italics added.

248. The commentary does not specify which Bonaventure is meant, but the readiest assumption would be the thirteenth-century Doctor of the Church St. Bonaventure, a Franciscan and contemporary of Aquinas. *Inter Insigniores* makes no mention of Bonaventure.

249. James Connor et al., "Letter to the Apostolic Delegate," *Origins* 6, no. 42 (April 7, 1977): 661, 664. Italics added.

250. Ibid., 664.

251. Thomas N. Taylor, *Saint Thérèse of Lisieux, the Little Flower of Jesus* (New York: P. J. Kenedy, 1927), 113–14.

252. Ibid., 114.

Chapter 9

253. Canon Law Society of America, *The Code of Canon Law: A Text and Commentary,* ed. James A. Coriden, Donald E. Heintschel, and Thomas J. Green (Mahwah, N.J.: Paulist Press, 1985).

254. Ibid. The new code retains the traditional provisions of the *General Instruction on the Roman Missal* (no. 70) permitting women to be appointed to "ministries performed *outside* the sanctuary" (emphasis mine), but these provisions "need to be interpreted in keeping with conditions of particular churches." See p. 168. As always, canon law is a sleuth's delight.

255. Canon Law Society of America, *The Code of Canon Law,* 168.

256. Ibid., 168. Canon 208 reads: "In virtue of their rebirth in Christ there exists among all the Christian faithful a true equality with regard to dignity and the activity whereby all cooperate in the building up of the Body of Christ in accord with each one's own condition and function." See p. 139.

257. Ruth A. Wallace, *They Call Her Pastor: A New Role for Catholic Women* (Albany: State University of New York Press, 1992), 7.

258. *Codex Iuris Canonici* (The Vatican, 1918), 275.

259. Canon Law Society of America, *The Code of Canon Law*, 723.

260. The Pseudo-Isidorian Decretals are a ninth-century collection of certain fictitious letters ascribed to early popes.

261. Haye van der Meer, *Women Priests in the Catholic Church? A Theological-Historical Investigation*, trans. Arlene and Leonard Swidler (Philadelphia: Temple University Press, 1973), xxiii.

262. Stanislaus Woywod, *The New Canon Law: A Commentary and Summary of the New Code of Canon Law* (New York: Joseph F. Wagner, 1918), 18, 259.

263. Stanislaus Woywod, *A Practical Commentary on the Code of Canon Law*, vols. 1 and 2 (New York: Joseph F. Wagner, 1952), 2:69.

264. Maureen Fiedler and Linda Rabben, eds., *Rome Has Spoken: A Guide to Forgotten Papal Statements, and How They Have Changed through the Centuries* (New York: Crossroad, 1998), 117.

265. *Codex Iuris Canonici* (The Vatican, 1918), 363. "Optandum ut, congruenter antiquae disciplinae, mulieres in ecclesia separatae sint a viris."

266. Canon Law Society of America, *The Code of Canon Law*, 167. See the complete list of roles barred to women on p. 1152.

267. The process of lifting this ban, either by the "authentic interpretation" or the "correct application" of canon law, continues to cause confusion at the local level, where bishops may ban altar girls in entire dioceses and priests may do the same in parishes. The result is that altars in two churches just blocks apart may have drastically different gender make-up. For an example of institutional confusion, see the Congregation for Divine Worship and the Discipline of the Sacraments, "Concerning the Use of Female Altar Servers (Prot. 2451/00/L)" (July 27, 2001); www.catholicliturgy.com/index.

268. Canadian Conference of Catholic Bishops, "The Status of Women," *The Ecumenist* 22, no. 2 (January–February 1984): 31–32. Italics added.

269. Ibid.

270. V. Sackville-West, *The Eagle and the Dove, A Study in Contrasts: St. Teresa of Avila, St. Thérèse of Lisieux* (Garden City, N.Y.: Doubleday, Doran, 1944), 118–19.

271. Monica Furlong, *Thérèse of Lisieux* (New York: Pantheon, 1987), 82–83.

272. Henri Ghéon, *The Secret of the Little Flower: St. Thérèse of Lisieux,* trans. Donald Attwater (London: Sheed & Ward, 1934), 38, 41.

Chapter 10

273. Mary Jo Weaver, *New Catholic Women: A Contemporary Challenge to Traditional Religious Authority* (New York: Harper & Row, 1985), 111.

274. Mark Chaves, "The Symbolic Significance of Women's Ordination," *Journal of Religion* 77, no. 1 (January 1977): 104. Chaves pointed out that "market forces" (i.e., priestless parishes) determine when women are hired to fill the "functional clergy role" regardless of a denomination's formal policy on female clergy. See p. 98.

275. The fact that the bishops were retired is important: they had the necessary ecclesiastical faculties to perform valid ordinations, but because of advanced age they were virtually beyond censure by the Anglican leadership.

276. National Consultation of the Episcopal and Roman Catholic Churches in the U.S.A., "The Substantial Progress of Anglican-Catholic Dialogue," *Origins* 7, no. 30 (January 12, 1978): 471.

277. Richard P. McBrien, *Catholicism*, new edition (New York: HarperCollins, 1994), 710–11.

278. Pope John Paul II, "The Vatican and Canterbury Exchange of Letters," *Origins* 16, no. 8 (July 17, 1986): 153–55.

279. Ibid.

280. Mark Chaves, *Ordaining Women: Culture and Conflict in Religious Organizations* (Cambridge, Mass.: Harvard University Press, 1999), 56.

281. Archbishop Robert Runcie, "The Vatican and Canterbury Exchange of Letters," *Origins* 16, no. 8 (July 17, 1986): 153–55.

282. Ibid.

283. For the following quotes, see Archbishop Robert Runcie's letter to Cardinal Jan Willebrands in "The Vatican and Canterbury Exchange of Letters," *Origins* 16, no. 8 (July 17, 1986): 156–58.

284. Runcie, "The Vatican and Canterbury Exchange of Letters," 156–58.

285. Willebrands, "The Vatican and Canterbury Exchange of Letters," 158–60.

286. Ibid., 156–58.

287. McBrien, *Catholicism*, 711.

288. The pontiff in 1988 reaffirmed the male-only priesthood in *Christifideles Laici* ("On the Vocation and Mission of the Lay Faithful in the Church and in the World").

289. "Vatican Responds to ARCIC I Final Report," *Origins* 21, no. 28 (December 19, 1991): 443.

290. "Archbishop of Canterbury on Vatican Response," *Origins* 21, no. 28 (December 19, 1991): 447.

291. Thérèse of Lisieux, *The Autobiography of Thérèse of Lisieux: The Story of a Soul*, trans. John Beevers (Garden City, N.Y.: Doubleday, 1957), 122–23.

Chapter 11

292. Pope John Paul II, "Holy Thursday Letter to Priests" (March 25, 1988); www.vatican.va/holy_father/john_paul_ii/letters/documents.

293. Ibid., §4.

294. Hans Urs von Balthasar, "The Uninterrupted Tradition of the Church," *L'Osservatore Romano*, English ed. (February 24, 1977), 6–7.

295. Pope John Paul II, "Holy Thursday Letter to Priests," §5.

296. Ibid. Italics added.

297. Thérèse Lisieux, *The Autobiography of Thérèse of Lisieux: The Story of a Soul*, trans. John Beevers (New York: Doubleday, 1957), 26, 58.

298. Ibid., 2.

299. Ibid., 153, 49.

Chapter 12

300. See Richard P. McBrien, "Essays in Theology: Women in the Church" (November 9, 1987); http://129.74.54.81/rm/.

301. Pope John Paul II, *Mulieris Dignitatem* ("On the Dignity and Vocation of Women") (Washington, D.C.: United States Catholic Conference, n.d.). The full text is also available in *Origins* 18, no. 17 (October 6, 1988): 261–83.

302. Ibid., 64. German theologian Ida Raming pointed out that the Latin word for "man" (*vir*) derives from *virtus*, meaning "authority" and "virtue"; the word for "woman" (*mulier*) is connected to *mollus*, meaning "soft" or "spongy," and *mollities mentis*, or "softness

of mind." See her "'Equal but Other' and Ordination of Women," *Theology Digest* 29, no. 1 (Spring 1981): 20.

303. Gail Grossman Freyne, "Women in Exile: Devout Dissent," *Studies* 86, no. 341 (Spring 1997): 9.

304. Elisabeth Schüssler Fiorenza, "Women in the Early Christian Movement," in *Womanspirit Rising: A Feminist Reader in Religion,* ed. Carol P. Christ and Judith Plaskow (New York: Harper & Row, 1979), 89.

305. The pope made no mention of Jesus' claim in Luke 21:32: "Truly I tell you, this generation will not pass away" before the coming of the kingdom of God, nor did he suggest that any "intent" of Jesus to establish the sacrament of holy orders might have been a temporary one.

306. Pope John Paul II, *Mulieris Dignitatem,* 96–97. Italics in the original. John Paul II's interchangeable use of "the Twelve" and "apostles" did nothing to clarify his claim.

307. Pope John Paul II, *Pastores Dabo Vobis* ("I Will Give You Shepherds"), *Origins* 21, no. 45 (April 16, 1992): 720, §5.

308. *Gaudium et Spes* ("The Church in the Modern World"), in Austin Flannery, ed., *Vatican II: Constitutions, Decrees, Declarations* (Northport, N.Y.: Costello Publishing Co., 1996), 185, §22.

309. "Husbands, love your wives, just as Christ loved the church and gave himself up for her, in order to make her holy by cleansing her with the washing of water and by the word, so as to present the church to himself in splendor, without a spot or wrinkle or anything of the kind — yes, so that she may be holy and without blemish. In the same way, husbands should love their wives as they do their own bodies. He who loves his wife loves himself. For no one ever hates his own body, but he nourishes and tenderly cares for it, just as Christ does for the church, because we are members of his body. 'For this reason a man will leave his father and mother and be joined to his wife, and the two will become one flesh.' This is a great mystery, and I am applying it to Christ and the church. Each of you, however, should love his wife as himself, and a wife should respect her husband."

310. Pope John Paul II, *Mulieris Dignitatem,* 86–87, 95. Italics in the original.

311. Ibid., 94–95. Here John Paul II co-opted a Pauline phrase that was actually a frequent claim of women's ordination *supporters* to show that baptism subsumes all human differences among Christ's disciples. Italics added.

312. Ibid., 100–101. Italics in the original.

313. Peter Steinfels, *A People Adrift: The Crisis of the Roman Catholic Church in America* (New York: Simon & Schuster, 2003), 299. Italics in the original.

314. Richard Viladesau, "Could Jesus Have Ordained Women? Reflections on *Mulieris Dignitatem,*" *Thought* 67, no. 264 (March 1992): 16–17. Italics in the original.

315. Pope John Paul II, *"Mulieris Dignitatem,"* *Origins* 18, no. 17 (October 6, 1988): 263–64, editorial note.

316. Pope John Paul II, *Mulieris Dignitatem* ("On the Dignity and Vocation of Women") (Washington, D.C.: United States Catholic Conference, n.d.), 21.

317. Ibid., 53.

318. Quoted from *Ein Wort* in Viladesau, "Could Jesus Have Ordained Women?" 14. Viladesau provides a brief but helpful overview of Balthasar's distinctive influence on John Paul II in *Mulieris Dignitatem.*

319. Hans Urs von Balthasar, "How Weighty Is the Argument from 'Uninterrupted Tradition' to Justify the Male Priesthood?" in *The Church and Women: A Compendium,* ed. Helmut Moll, trans. Lothar Krauth (San Francisco: Ignatius Press, 1988), 158–59. Balthasar had explored this idea at length a decade earlier in "The Uninterrupted Tradition of the Church," *L'Osservatore Romano,* English ed. (February 24, 1977), 6–7.

320. von Balthasar, "How Weighty Is the Argument from 'Uninterrupted Tradition' to Justify the Male Priesthood?" 159–60. Italics added.

321. Pope John Paul II, *Mulieris Dignitatem* ("On the Dignity and Vocation of Women") (Washington, D.C.: United States Catholic Conference, n.d.), 29, then 27. Italics in the original.

322. Ibid., 112–13. Italics in the original.

323. Ibid., 7–8. Italics in the original.

324. Ibid., 64.

325. Ibid., 85.

326. Ibid., 116.

327. Thérèse of Lisieux, *The Autobiography of St. Thérèse of Lisieux: The Story of a Soul,* trans. John Beevers (Garden City, N.Y.: Doubleday, 1957), 153.

Chapter 13

328. John Paul II, *Christifideles Laici* ("On the Vocation and Mission of the Lay Faithful in the Church and in the World"), December 30, 1988; CD Rom: *The Encyclicals and Post-Synodal Apostolic Exhortations of John Paul II,* ed. J. Michael Miller (Huntington, Ind.: Our Sunday Visitor, 1998), §49. Also at www.vatican.va/holy_father/john_paul_ii/apost_exhortations/.

329. Christine Schenk, " 'Infallibility' and Equality in Catholicism" (Cleveland: Future-Church, n.d.); www. futurechurch.org.

330. John Paul II, *Christifideles Laici,* §49. Concerning Vatican II, Hans Küng once said that bishops speak of lay participation in the *life* of the church but "they do not all like to speak, at least in official binding documents, of the participation of the laity in the *decisions* of the church." Quoted in R. Scott Appleby, "If the Church Isn't a Democracy, What Is It?" *U.S. Catholic* (May 1996): 8. Italics added. I would extend Küng's comment to include the pope's remarks in this context.

331. John Paul II, *Christifideles Laici,* §49.

332. Ibid., §50. Italics added.

333. Mary Jo Weaver, *New Catholic Women: A Contemporary Challenge to Traditional Religious Authority* (New York: Harper & Row, 1985), xiv.

334. John Paul II, *Christifideles Laici,* §50.

335. Ibid., §51.

336. Ibid., §52. The title of this section is, "The Presence and Collaboration of Men Together with Women."

337. Gerald Brown, "Dialogue Urged on Men's Gifts and Concerns," *Origins* 25, no. 9 (July 27, 1995): 143–45.

338. Regina Coll, "Introduction," in *Women and Religion: A Reader for the Clergy,* ed. Regina Coll (New York: Paulist Press, 1982), 1–2.

339. Thomas H. Groome, "From Chauvinism and Clericalism to Priesthood," in *Women and Religion: A Reader for the Clergy,* ed. Regina Coll (New York: Paulist Press, 1982), 115.

340. Elisabeth Schüssler Fiorenza, "Feminist Spirituality, Christian Identity, and Catholic Vision," in *Womanspirit Rising: A Feminist Reader in Religion,* ed. Carol P. Christ and Judith Plaskow (San Francisco: Harper & Row, 1979), 144–45. Italics added.

341. John Paul II, *Christifideles Laici,* §52.

342. Ibid., §50.

343. Richard Viladesau, "Could Jesus Have Ordained Women? Reflections on *Mulieris Dignitatem,*" *Thought* 67, no. 264 (March 1992): 15. Italics in the original. Viladesau pointed out that *Inter Insigniores* rejected this argument, holding that the priest represents the church *(in persona ecclesiae)* only because he "first of all represents Christ, the head of the Church." This claim, as Viladesau observed, begged the question. See n. 9.

344. John Paul II, *Christifideles Laici*, §51.

345. Thomas N. Taylor, *Saint Thérèse of Lisieux, the Little Flower of Jesus* (New York: P. J. Kenedy, 1927), 243.

346. Monica Furlong, *Thérèse of Lisieux* (New York: Pantheon, 1987), 130.

347. Thérèse of Lisieux, *The Autobiography of St. Thérèse of Lisieux: The Story of a Soul*, trans. John Beevers (Garden City, N.Y.: Doubleday, 1957), 153.

348. Taylor, *Saint Thérèse of Lisieux*, 241–42.

Chapter 14

349. The bishops' invitation for women to speak candidly and publicly was a groundbreaking initiative. However, no such effort was forthcoming from bishops in developing countries, where patriarchy remained a pillar of culture and religion.

350. National Conference of Catholic Bishops, "Partners in the Mystery of Redemption: A Pastoral Response to Women's Concerns for Church and Society," *Origins* 17, no. 45 (April 21, 1988): 759, §7.

351. Ibid., 757, editorial preface.

352. Ibid., 763, §39.

353. Ibid., 779, §203.

354. Canon Law Society of America, "Consensus Statement from the Symposium on Women and Church Law," in *Sexism and Church Law: Equal Rights and Affirmative Action*, ed. James A. Coriden (New York: Paulist Press, 1977), 154–55.

355. National Conference of Catholic Bishops, "Partners in the Mystery of Redemption," 781, §219.

356. P. Francis Murphy, "Statement of Bishop P. Francis Murphy," November 14, 1991 (Fairfax, Va., Women's Ordination Conference).

357. National Conference of Catholic Bishops, "'One in Christ Jesus': A Pastoral Response to the Concerns of Women for Church and Society," *Origins* 19, no. 44 (April 5, 1990): 719–40.

358. Leadership Conference of Women Religious, "Critiquing the Women's Pastoral Draft," *Origins* 20, no. 12 (August 30, 1990): 187.

359. Leadership Conference of Women Religious, "Critiquing the Women's Pastoral Draft," 185–87.

360. National Conference of Catholic Bishops, "Partners in the Mystery of Redemption: A Pastoral Response to Women's Concerns for Church and Society," *Origins* 17, no. 45 (April 21, 1988): 781, §217.

361. Leadership Conference of Women Religious, "Critiquing the Women's Pastoral Draft," 185–87.

362. Quoted in Mark Chaves, *Ordaining Women: Culture and Conflict in Religious Organizations* (Cambridge, Mass.: Harvard University Press, 1999), 88.

363. National Conference of Catholic Bishops, "'One in Christ Jesus': Toward a Pastoral Response to the Concerns of Women for Church and Society" (Washington, D.C.: United States Catholic Conference, 1992).

364. Ibid., 27. This included teaching male seminarians the reasons for denying priesthood to women. In the mid-1990s, theologian Catherine Mowry La Cugna pointed out that an irony of refusing priesthood to women is the "high number who have become educated and employed as professional theologians, who now hold tenured positions in colleges, universities and seminaries" and who educate "future priests and bishops." See Virginia Sullivan Finn, "Ministerial Attitudes and Aspirations of Catholic Laywomen in the United States," in *Religious Institutions and Women's Leadership: New Roles Inside the Mainstream*, ed. Catherine Wessinger (Columbia: University of South Carolina Press, 1996), 261.

365. Catherine Wessinger, "Women's Religious Leadership in the United States," in *Religious Institutions and Women's Leadership: New Roles Inside the Mainstream,* ed. Catherine Wessinger (Columbia: University of South Carolina Press, 1996), 25.

366. Editorial note, *Origins* 22, no. 6 (June 18, 1992): 91.

367. "Saint Thérèse of Lisieux, Virgin, Religious, Doctor of the Church, 1897" (Trinity Communications, 2002); www.petersnet.net/research/.

368. "Saint Thérèse of Lisieux," n.d.; www.catholic.org.

369. Guy Gaucher, *The Story of a Life: St. Thérèse of Lisieux,* trans. Anne Marie Brennan (San Francisco: Harper & Row, 1987), 161.

370. Thérèse of Lisieux, *The Autobiography of Thérèse of Lisieux: The Story of a Soul,* trans. John Beevers (Garden City, N.Y.: Doubleday, 1957), 136.

Chapter 15

371. United States Catholic Conference, *Catechism of the Catholic Church* (Liguori, Mo.: Liguori Publications, 1994).

372. Peter Steinfels, *A People Adrift: The Crisis of the Roman Catholic Church in America* (New York: Simon & Schuster, 2003), 289.

373. United States Catholic Conference, *Catechism of the Catholic Church,* §1.

374. Steinfels, *A People Adrift,* 290.

375. Ibid., 290–91.

376. "John Paul II to Beatify Four on Sunday," Vatican Information Service, VISen 040317 (March 17, 2004).

377. "Use Language Capable of Transmitting Positive Messages," Vatican Information Service, VISen 040405 (April 5, 2004).

378. Richard P. McBrien, "Essays in Theology: Vatican Rejection of Scripture Translations" (December 2, 1994); http://129.74.54.81/rm/.

379. John L. Allen Jr., "On the Lectionary, 11 Men Made the Deal," *National Catholic Reporter* 34, no. 41 (September 25, 1998), 3.

380. For a discussion of the ongoing conflict between the Vatican and local bishops, especially in the United States, see Steinfels, *A People Adrift,* 190–91.

381. This statement repeated *verbatim* the 1917 and 1983 codes of canon law.

382. United States Catholic Conference, *Catechism of the Catholic Church,* §1577.

383. Catholic Biblical Association of America, "Women and Priestly Ministry: The New Testament Evidence," *Catholic Biblical Quarterly* 41, no. 4 (October 1979): 608–13. At the time, the Catholic Biblical Association sold reprints of the committee's report and offered to pay the postage "on larger orders." Such intellectual commerce was to be short-lived.

384. United States Catholic Conference, *Catechism of the Catholic Church,* §1120.

385. Pope John Paul II, *Pastores Dabo Vobis* ("I Will Give You Shepherds"), *Origins* 21, no. 45 (April 16, 1992): 720, §5.

386. Henri Ghéon, *The Secret of the Little Flower: St. Thérèse of Lisieux,* trans. Donald Attwater (London: Sheed & Ward, 1934). See chapter 1, entitled "The Initial Resistance."

Chapter 16

387. Thomas J. Reese, *Inside the Vatican: The Politics and Organizations of the Catholic Church* (Cambridge, Mass.: Harvard University Press, 1996), 243.

388. Peter Hebblethwaite, *The Next Pope* (New York: HarperSanFrancisco, 1995), 164.

389. Congregation for Divine Worship and the Sacraments, "Use of Female Altar Servers Allowed," *Origins* 23, no. 45 (April 28, 1994): 777–79. Strictly speaking, this document addressed the role of the "lay faithful" on the altar, and whether certain liturgical functions could be carried out "equally by men and women." However, the document was careful to stress that bishops were free to refuse such service to females, and that even

those who did allow female altar servers should be careful to maintain the "noble tradition of having boys serve at the altar."

390. Ibid.

391. Congregation for Divine Worship and the Discipline of the Sacraments, "Concerning the Use of Female Altar Servers" (Prot. 2451/00/L)" (July 27, 2001); www.catholicliturgy.com/index.

392. Joseph D. Fessio, "Admittance of Women to Service at the Altar as Acolytes and Lectors," in *The Church and Women: A Compendium*, ed. Helmut Moll (San Francisco: Ignatius Press, 1988), 181–82. Italics added. Fessio, a student and lifelong friend of Joseph Ratzinger, added that if the "equal sacredness" of the Bible with eucharist were "thought through to its conclusion, it would raise questions about the appropriateness even of women exercising the role of lector."

393. Ibid., 184.

394. Kelley A. Raab, *When Women Become Priests: The Catholic Women's Ordination Debate* (New York: Columbia University Press, 2000), 204–6.

395. Fessio, "Admittance of Women to Service at the Altar as Acolytes and Lectors," 183. Italics added.

396. Richard P. McBrien, "Essays in Theology: Altar Girls and Dire Predictions" (May 20, 1994); http://129.74.54.81/rm/.

397. Fessio, "Admittance of Women to Service at the Altar as Acolytes and Lectors," 184.

398. Luke Timothy Johnson, "Sex, Women and the Church," *Commonweal* 130, no. 12 (June 20, 2003): 17.

399. Pope John Paul II, *"Ordinatio Sacerdotalis"* ("On Reserving Priestly Ordination to Men Alone") *Origins* 24, no. 4 (June 9, 1994): 49–52.

400. Some U.S. bishops later issued a statement saying that *Ordinatio Sacerdotalis* was "issued without any prior discussion and consultation with our conference." See their statement *in toto* in Ingrid Schaeffer's online article, "U.S. Bishops' Statement Calling the Vatican to Collegiality"; www.astro.temple.edu/~arcc.bishops.

401. John Paul II strategically avoided two words used by Paul VI: "function" and "power." Beginning in the 1970s, priestly "functions" were identified to determine the specific ways that priests could exercise "power" by virtue of their ministry, for instance, via pastoral influence or ecclesial decision-making. Over time, the counterargument evolved that priesthood was not about "power" but rather "service." In describing priesthood, *Inter Insigniores* (1976) used "function" six times and its subsequent commentary (1977) six times. *Ordinatio Sacerdotalis* (1994) used "function" only once, to declare that the apostles did not receive "only a function." The *Responsum* to *Ordinatio Sacerdotalis* (1995) did not use the word at all. *Inter Insigniores* used "power" nine times and its commentary seven times. Neither *Ordinatio Sacerdotalis* nor the *Responsum* used "power" a single time.

402. Pope John Paul II, *"Veritatis Splendor"* ("Splendor of Truth"), *Origins* 23, no. 18 (October 14, 1993): 113, 116, §§4.

403. Mary Louise Hartman, Editorial, *ARCC Light* (November–December 2001); http://arcc-catholic-rights.org/ramerman.

404. Hebblethwaite, *The Next Pope*, 160.

405. Among the documents surveyed in this book, the term "theological anthropology" appears more often in the writings of John Paul II, whereas "Christian anthropology" is used more by the U.S. bishops. For practical purposes, the terms are interchangeable.

406. *Ordinatio Sacerdotalis* referenced this remark in a footnote (no. 4): "Paul VI, Address on the Role of Women in the Plan of Salvation (January 30, 1977): *Insegnamenti*, 15 (1977), 111. Cf. Also John Paul II Apostolic Exhortation *Christifideles Laici* (December 30, 1988), n. 51: AAS 81 (1989), 393–521; *Catechism of the Catholic Church*, n. 1577."

407. John Paul II, "'Ad Limina' Address: On Parishes, Lay Ministry and Women," *Origins* 23, no. 8 (July 15, 1993): 126, §6.

408. *Dignitatis Humanae* ("Declaration on Religious Liberty"), in Austin Flannery, ed., *Vatican Council II: Constitutions, Decrees, Declarations* (Northport, N.Y.: Costello Publishing Co., 1996), 551–68. Walter Abbott translated this document as "Declaration on Religious Freedom."

409. Elizabeth A. Johnson, "Response to Rome," *Commonweal* 123, no. 2 (January 26, 1996): 11–12.

410. Hans Urs von Balthasar, "How Weighty Is the Argument from 'Uninterrupted Tradition' to Justify the Male Priesthood?" in *The Church and Women: A Compendium*, ed. Helmut Moll (San Francisco: Ignatius Press, 1988), 157.

411. See "Bishops React to '*Ordinatio Sacerdotalis*,'" *Origins* 24, no. 4 (June 9, 1994): 53–54.

412. Mark Chaves, "The Symbolic Significance of Women's Ordination," *Journal of Religion* 77, no. 1 (January 1977): 94.

413. Francis Bernard O'Connor, *Like Bread, Their Voices Rise! Global Women Challenge the Church* (Notre Dame, Ind.: Ave Maria Press, 1993), 159.

414. Patricia Zapor, "Bishop Sees Difficulties as Rome 'Ignores Reality,'" *National Catholic Reporter* 34, no. 17 (February 27, 1998), 4.

415. Christine Schenk, "Women Ministers in the Catholic Church" (Cleveland: FutureChurch, n.d.); www.futurechurch.org.

416. Thomas P. Sweetser, "Authority and Ordination," *America* 171, no. 12 (October 22, 1994): 4–7.

417. Reese, *Inside the Vatican*, 147–48.

418. Mary Fainsod Katzenstein, *Faithful and Fearless: Moving Feminist Protest Inside the Church and Military* (Princeton University Press, 1998), 152.

419. Bernard J. Lee, Barbara J. Fleischer, and Charles Topper, "A Same and Different Future: A Study of Graduate Ministry Education in Catholic Institutions of Higher Learning in the United States" (New Orleans: Loyola Institute for Ministry, Association of Graduate Programs in Ministry), 1994. Quoted in Schenk, "Women Ministers in the Catholic Church."

420. Ibid.

421. Jay P. Dolan, *In Search of American Catholicism: A History of Religion and Culture in Tension* (New York: Oxford University Press, 2002), 230.

422. R. Scott Appleby, "Crunch Time for American Catholicism," *Christian Century* 113, no. 11 (April 3, 1996): 374.

423. O'Connor, *Like Bread, Their Voices Rise!* 27. Here O'Connor quotes Maria Riley, *In God's Image* (Kansas City, Mo.: Sheed & Ward, 1985), 24. Italics added.

424. O'Connor, *Like Bread, Their Voices Rise!* 29, 94.

425. James A. Coriden, "The Canonical Doctrine of Reception" (Delran, N.J.: Association for the Rights of Catholics in the Church, n.d.), 1. This booklet provides an excellent overview, in lay language, of the doctrine of reception.

426. Richard P. McBrien, *Catholicism*, new edition (New York: HarperSanFrancisco, 1994), 65. Italics "received" in the original, and "accepted" added.

427. Ladislas Örsy, *Theology and Canon Law* (Collegeville, Minn.: Liturgical Press, 1992), 45.

428. "Declaration on Religious Freedom," in Walter M. Abbott, ed., *The Documents of Vatican II* (New York: Herder and Herder, Association Press, 1966), 680–81. Austin Flannery translated this document as "Declaration on Religious Liberty."

429. Leonard Swidler, "Democracy, Dissent, and Dialogue: A Catholic Vocation," in *The Church in Anguish: Has the Vatican Betrayed Vatican II?* ed. Hans Küng and Leonard Swidler (San Francisco: Harper & Row, 1987), 316. Italics added.

430. Pope Paul VI, *Humanae Vitae,* in Janet E. Smith, *Humanae Vitae* (Washington, D.C.: Catholic University of America Press, 1991), 269–95; also at www.vatican.va/holy_ father/paul_vi/encyclicals/documents/. Natural birth control, in its contemporary manifestation, is known as Natural Family Planning (NFP) and involves restricting the sex act to nonfertile times of the month. In 1968, this approach was known as the "rhythm" method.

431. See Richard P. McBrien, "Birth Control: An Overview," in his *Catholicism,* 989. For comprehensive treatment of activities surrounding the Papal Birth Control Commission, see Robert McClory, *Turning Point* (New York: Crossroad, 1995).

432. Dolan, *In Search of American Catholicism,* 163.

433. Joseph Fichter, "Restructuring Catholicism," *Sociological Analysis* 38, no. 2 (1977): 163.

434. James R. Roberts, *Women Priests: Reflections on Papal Teaching and Church Response* (Vancouver, B.C.: Langara College, 1994), i.

435. John Thavis, "Pope: Reject 'Extreme' Feminism," *National Catholic Reporter* 29, no. 34 (July 16, 1993), 7.

436. McBrien, "Birth Control: An Overview," 983.

437. Ibid., 984. Swidler, "Democracy, Dissent, and Dialogue," 315.

438. Peter Steinfels, *A People Adrift: The Crisis of the Roman Catholic Church in America* (New York: Simon & Schuster, 2003), 257.

439. Reese, *Inside the Vatican,* 276.

440. John H. Wright, "That All Doubt May Be Removed," *America* (July 30, 1994): 16–19.

441. Reese, *Inside the Vatican,* 276.

442. Coriden, "The Canonical Doctrine of Reception," 4. It is not too much of a stretch to say that in the case of reception, Augustine was suggesting the equivalent of "speak now or forever hold your peace."

443. Rosemary Radford Ruether, "Infallibility Is Untenable" (1996); www.womenpriests .org/.

444. By summer, nearly a thousand women were ordained to the Anglican priesthood. See Catherine Wessinger, "Women's Leadership in the United States," in *Women's Religious Leadership in the United States: New Roles Inside the Mainstream,* ed. Catherine Wessinger (Columbia: University of South Carolina Press: 1996), 25.

445. Richard R. Gaillardetz, "An Exercise of the Hierarchical Magisterium," *America* (July 30, 1994): 19–22.

446. "Pope John Paul's Pre-emptive Strike," *The Tablet* 248, no. 8026 (June 4, 1994), 691–92.

447. "Only Time Will Tell," *Ecumenical Trends* 23, no. 6 (June 1994): 1/81–2/82. Italics in the original.

448. Francis A. Sullivan, "New Claims for the Pope," *The Tablet* 248, no. 8028 (June 18, 1994), 767–69. Sullivan would not have to wait long for such a statement.

449. Commission on Woman and the Church of the Belgian Bishops' Conference, *Wie mag toeven binnen uw tent?: Vrouw en Kerk,* ed. Ann Beddeleem and Ilse van Halst (Leuven, Belgium: Davidsfonds, 1998), 55–67. Quoted here from "Who May Dwell Within your Tent?" trans. John Wijngaards, at www.womenpriests.org/teaching/Belgium. The following quotes come from this document.

450. A 1999 survey by the Women's Ordination Conference showed that 84 percent of the respondents (primarily WOC members, lay ministers, and chaplains) agreed that "decision-making in the church should be separated from ordination." See Maureen

Fiedler and Karen Schwarz, "Benevolent Subversives" (Fairfax, Va.: Women's Ordination Conference, 1999), 5.

451. See Carmel McEnroy, *Guests in Their Own House: The Women of Vatican II* (New York: Crossroad, 1996).

452. Hebblethwaite, *The Next Pope,* 171–72.

453. Jane Redmont, "The Women's Ordination Movement, Phase Two," *America* (December 9, 1995): 19.

454. "U.S. Catholicism: Trends in the '90s," *National Catholic Reporter* 29, no. 43 (October 8, 1993), 21–32. See Table 13, p. 25.

455. Leonard Swidler, "Not Resignation, but Creative Action!" in Heinrich Fries, *Suffering from the Church: Renewal or Restoration?* (Collegeville, Minn.: Liturgical Press, 1995), 13.

456. Ari L. Goldman (June 19, 1992), quoted in Roberts, *Women Priests,* 12.

457. Dean Hoge and Jacqueline E. Wenger, *Evolving Visions of the Priesthood* (Collegeville, Minn.: Pulpit and Pew, 2003), 81.

458. Michael H. Kenny, "Women's Ordination — Uneasy Questions," *America* (July 30, 1994): 16.

459. Guy Gaucher, *The Story of a Life: St. Therese of Lisieux,* trans. Anne Marie Brennan (San Francisco: Harper & Row, 1987), 80.

Chapter 17

460. United States Catholic Conference. "Strengthening the Bonds of Peace" (Washington, D.C.: United States Catholic Conference, 1995).

461. Italics added.

462. Canon Law Society of America, *The Code of Canon Law: A Text and Commentary,* ed. James A. Coriden, Donald E. Heintschel, and Thomas J. Green (Mahwah, N.J.: Paulist Press, 1985), canon 129:1.

463. Thérèse of Lisieux, *The Autobiography of Thérèse of Lisieux: The Story of a Soul,* trans. John Beevers (New York: Doubleday, 1957), 90.

464. Abbé Combes, ed., *Collected Letters of St. Thérèse of Lisieux,* trans. F. J. Sheed (New York: Sheed & Ward, 1949), 337.

Chapter 18

465. Pope John Paul II, *Letter to Women,* June 29, 1995 (Washington, D.C.: United States Catholic Conference, n.d.), 6, §3.

466. Jane Redmont, " 'Letter to Women' Bares John Paul's Isolation," *National Catholic Reporter* 31, no. 35 (July 28, 1995), 11.

467. Pope John Paul II, *Letter to Women,* June 29, 1995 (Washington, D.C.: United States Catholic Conference, n.d.); also, in "Pope John Paul II/Beijing Conference: Letter to Women," *Origins* 25, no. 9 (July 27, 1995).

468. Ibid., 16, §11. Italics in the original.

469. Ibid., 17, §11. Italics in the original.

470. See John Paul II, "Woman's Moral Nobility," April 10, 1996; www.cin.org/cin.

471. Pope John Paul II, *Letter to Women,* 4–5, §2.

472. Ibid., 8, §4. Italics in the original.

473. Ibid., 12, §7. Italics in the original.

474. Pope John Paul II, *Pope John Paul II on the Genius of Women* (Washington, D.C.: United States Catholic Conference, 1997).

475. Pope John Paul II, *Vita Consecrata* ("On the Consecrated Life"), March 25, 1996; CD Rom: ed. J. Michael Miller, *The Encyclicals and Post-Synodal Apostolic Exhortations of John Paul II* (Huntington, Ind.: Our Sunday Visitor, 1998), §34. Also

at www.vatican.va/holy_father/john_paul ii/apost_exhortations/. Theologian Lisa Sowle Cahill pointed out that the Vatican's employment practices do not provide "a great deal of confidence that the theory of the special genius of women has led to significant vocational advancement for women, or their access to positions of authority, within the church itself." See Lisa Sowle Cahill, "On Being a Catholic Feminist," *The Santa Clara Lectures* 9, no. 3 (April 27, 2003): 9.

476. Redmont, " 'Letter to Women' Bares John Paul's Isolation," 11.

477. Pope John Paul II, *Letter to Women,* 11, §§7, 10. "Being" italics in the original; "give to men" italics added.

478. Ibid., 18, §12. Italics in the original.

479. Ibid., 10, §6.

480. Pope John Paul II, "Women: Teachers of Peace," January 1, 1995, §8; www.vatican .va/holy_father_/john_paul_ii/messages/peace/index.htm.

481. Gail Grossman Freyne, "Women in Exile: Devout Dissent," *Studies* 86, no. 341 (Spring 1997): 12.

482. Society of Jesus, "Jesuits and the Situation of Women," in *Origins* 24, no. 43 (April 13, 1995): 740–42. The decree was promulgated on September 27, 1995, but it actually had been written in the early spring and sent to the pope shortly thereafter.

483. Ibid., 741.

484. Ibid.

485. Ibid.

486. Ibid., 742.

487. Ibid.

488. Thérèse of Lisieux, *The Autobiography of St. Thérèse of Lisieux: The Story of a Soul,* trans. John Beevers (Garden City, N.Y.: Doubleday, 1957), 142. Italics in the original.

Chapter 19

489. Congregation for the Doctrine of the Faith, "Doctrinal Congregation/Response to 'Dubium': Inadmissibility of Women to Ministerial Priesthood," *Origins* 25, no. 24 (November 30, 1995): 401–3. Making extreme claims against women's ordination, this document was released on the Feast Day of St. Jude Thaddeus, patron saint of desperate causes.

490. "Ratzinger's Bid for Infallible Clarity Unleashes New Round of Debate," *National Catholic Reporter* 32, no. 7 (December 8, 1995), 1. Christine Schenk quoted an objection lodged by U.S. bishops that, like other Vatican documents concerning women, the text had been published "without any prior discussion and consultation with [the U.S. bishops'] conference." Further, Ratzinger had "communicated the present statement to the head of the NCCB three hours after the close of their four-day meeting . . . with no advance warning and no opportunity for the Bishops to discuss it among themselves and provide input or reaction." See Christine Schenk, " 'Infallibility' and Equality in Catholicism" (Cleveland: FutureChurch, n.d.); www.futurechurch.org.

491. Hans Küng, *The Catholic Church: A Short History,* trans. John Bowden (New York: Modern Library, 2003), 113.

492. Pope Pius IX, *Pastor Aeternus* ("On the Magisterial Infallibility of the Roman Pontiff"), chapter 4; www.intratext.com.

493. John T. Ford, "Infallibility I & II," *Commonweal* 123, no. 2 (January 26, 1996): 8–10.

494. Francis A. Sullivan, "Recent Theological Observations on the Magisterial Documents and Public Dissent," *Theological Studies* 58, no. 3 (September 1997): 513. Italics added.

495. Walter M. Abbott, ed., *The Documents of Vatican II* (New York: Herder and Herder, Association Press, 1966), p. 125, n. 125.

496. Francis A. Sullivan, "Vatican Invokes Infallibility over Women Priests," *The Tablet* 249, no. 8103 (November 25, 1995), 1520–21.

497. "Ratzinger's Bid for Infallible Clarity Unleashes New Round of Debate," 1.

498. Richard R. Gaillardetz, "Infallibility and the Ordination of Women," *Louvain Studies* 21 (1996): 3–24. Italics added. This note was later added to the original text and reprinted at www.womenpriests.org//theology/gaill2.

499. Joseph A. Komonchak, "Response to Rome," *Commonweal* 123, no. 2 (January 26, 1996): 15–16.

500. "The Weapon of Infallibility," *The Tablet* 249, no. 8103 (November 25, 1995), 1495–96.

501. Pamela Schaeffer, "Assessing Ambiguous Infallibility Factor," *National Catholic Reporter* 32, no. 7 (December 8, 1995), 3–4.

502. Pope John Paul II, "How Authority Is Conceived," *Origins* 25, no. 34 (February 15, 1996): 572–74.

503. Leonard Swidler, "Not Resignation, but Creative Action!" in Heinrich Fries, *Suffering from the Church: Renewal or Restoration?* (Collegeville, Minn.: Liturgical Press, 1995), 13.

504. Thomas J. Reese, *Inside the Vatican* (Cambridge, Mass.: Harvard University Press, 1996), 261.

505. Ladislas Örsy, *Theology and Canon Law* (Collegeville, Minn.: Liturgical Press, 1992), 45–50, 64.

506. "An Order That Is Impossible to Obey," *National Catholic Reporter* 37, no. 34 (July 13, 2001), 28.

507. Charles Donahue Jr., "Theology, Law and Women's Ordination: '*Ordinatio Sacerdotalis*' One Year Later," *Commonweal* 122, no. 11 (June 2, 1995): 11.

508. Schenk, "'Infallibility' and Equality in Catholicism."

509. National Coalition of American Nuns, "This Teaching Cannot Be Infallible" (December 8, 1995); National Coalition of American Nuns Records, Marquette University Special Collections, Series 4, Box 2.

510. Gail Grossman Freyne, "Women in Exile: Devout Dissent," *Studies* 86, no. 341 (Spring 1997): 8.

511. Schaeffer, "Assessing Ambiguous Infallibility Factor," 3–6.

512. Komonchak, "Response to Rome," 15–16.

513. John H. Wright, "Patristic Testimony on Women's Ordination in *Inter Insigniores*," *Theological Studies* 58, no. 3 (September 1997): 516–17.

514. Nicholas Lash, "On Not Inventing Doctrine," *The Tablet* 249, no. 8104 (December 2, 1995), 1544. Italics in the original. In 1973, the National Conference of Catholic Bishops, while agreeing there was no "explicit authoritative teaching" on the matter, nonetheless wrote, "The question of ordaining women is an old one in the Church," a claim virtually unheard of in other documents. See the National Conference of Catholic Bishops, "Theological Reflections on the Ordination of Women," *Review for Religious* 32, no. 2 (March 1973): 218.

515. "The Weapon of Infallibility," 1495–96.

516. Sullivan, "Recent Theological Observations on the Magisterial Documents and Public Dissent," 511–13.

517. According to one account, several U.S. bishops, including NCCB president Archbishop William Keeler of Baltimore, "were caught off guard by the statement [*Responsum*], which was delivered by fax shortly after a four-day meeting of the National Conference of Catholic Bishops," precluding "public or even significant private discussion among them" before facing their constituencies and the press. Further, the *Responsum* was sent only to presidents of bishops' conferences, rather than to individual bishops (as is customary with

important documents). Its cover letter was dated only ten days before the document's publication in *L'Osservatore Romano*, the Vatican newspaper, making it virtually impossible to distribute it to individual bishops in time for them to study it before publication. See Joseph Ratzinger's cover letter in Schaeffer, "Assessing Ambiguous Infallibility Factor," 1, 3–6.

518. Joseph Ratzinger, "The Limits of Church Authority," *L'Osservatore Romano*, English ed., 26 (June 29, 1994), 6–8.

519. Secretariat for Doctrine and Pastoral Practices, National Conference of Catholic Bishops, "Briefing Questions on the CDF *Responsum ad Dubium* concerning the Authentic Interpretation of *Ordinatio Sacerdotalis*," n.d. Faxed from the *Denver Post* to the Women's Ordination Conference, Fairfax, Va. (November 17, 1995).

520. Joan Chittister, "Ratzinger Raised Bigger Issues Than Ordination," *National Catholic Reporter* 32, no. 7 (December 8, 1995), 7.

521. Francis X. Murphy, "Response to Rome," *Commonweal* 123, no. 2 (January 26, 1996): 18.

522. Schaeffer, "Assessing Ambiguous Infallibility Factor," 6.

523. Donahue, "Theology, Law and Women's Ordination," 12.

524. Reese, *Inside the Vatican*, 260.

525. Elizabeth Johnson, "Response to Rome," *Commonweal* 123, no. 2 (January 26, 1996): 11–12.

526. Peter Steinfels, *A People Adrift: The Crisis of the Roman Catholic Church in America* (New York: Simon & Schuster, 2003), 300.

527. Lash, "On Not Inventing Doctrine," 1544.

528. Chittister, "Ratzinger Raised Bigger Issues Than Ordination," 7.

529. National Coalition of American Nuns, "This Teaching Cannot Be Infallible."

530. Schaeffer, "Assessing Ambiguous Infallibility Factor," 5.

531. Joseph Fichter, "Restructuring Catholicism: Symposium on Thomas O'Dea," *Sociological Analysis* 38 (1977): 163.

532. Lisa Sowle Cahill, "Response to Rome," *Commonweal* 123, no. 2 (January 26, 1996): 14.

533. "Ratzinger's Bid for Infallible Clarity Unleashes New Round of Debate," 1.

534. Peter Hebblethwaite, *The Next Pope* (San Francisco: HarperSanFrancisco, 1995), 166.

535. Catholic Theological Society of America, "Study, Prayer Urged Regarding Women's Ordination 'Responsum,'" *Origins* 27, no. 5 (June 19, 1997): 75–79. The paper was dated June 6, 1997.

536. Ibid., 77.

537. Pamela Schaeffer, "Theologians Opt for Diplomacy in Dispute," *National Catholic Reporter* 33, no. 32 (June 20, 1997), 3.

538. Catholic Theological Society of America, "Study, Prayer Urged Regarding Women's Ordination 'Responsum,'" 79.

539. Ibid., 75–76.

540. "Reactions to CTSA Convention Actions Regarding 'Tradition and the Ordination of Women,'" *Origins* 27, no. 6 (June 26, 1997): 91–92.

541. Bernard Law, "The CTSA," *The Pilot* (Catholic Archdiocese of Boston: n.d.).

542. David Knight, "A Pastoral Response," *U.S. Catholic* (April 1996): 11–13.

543. V. Sackville-West, *The Eagle and the Dove, A Study in Contrasts: St. Teresa of Avila, St. Thérèse of Lisieux* (Garden City, N.Y.: Doubleday, Doran, 1944), 145.

544. Thérèse of Lisieux, *The Autobiography of St. Thérèse of Lisieux: The Story of a Soul*, trans. John Beevers (Garden City, N.Y.: Doubleday, 1957), 145.

545. Ibid., 64.

546. Ibid., 121.

Chapter 20

547. United States Catholic Conference, *From "Inter Insigniores" to "Ordinatio Sacerdotalis"* (Washington, D.C.: Congregation for the Doctrine of the Faith and United States Catholic Conference, 1998).

548. Helpful to researchers who knew where to look, the slender paperback was available only from the USCC, for $20 plus shipping and handling.

549. Cardinal Joseph Ratzinger, "Introduction," *From "Inter Insigniores" to "Ordinatio Sacerdotalis,"* 5.

550. Ladislas Örsy, *Theology and Canon Law* (Collegeville, Minn.: Liturgical Press, 1992), n. 10, 64–65. Italics added.

551. Ratzinger, "Introduction," 5. The remarks quoted here are selected from the first page of a crowded, twelve-page essay.

552. United States Bishops Committee on Women in Society and in the Church, *From Words to Deeds: Continuing Reflections on the Role of Women in the Church* (Washington D.C.: United States Catholic Conference, 1998), 14.

553. Ibid.

554. Committee on Doctrine of the National Conference of Catholic Bishops, "Ten Frequently Asked Questions about the Reservation of Priestly Ordination to Men" (Washington, D.C.: United States Catholic Conference, 1998).

555. Ibid., 2. See Richard R. Gaillardetz, "Infallibility and the Ordination of Women," *Louvain Studies* 21 (1996): 3–24.

556. Committee on Doctrine of the National Conference of Catholic Bishops, "Ten Frequently Asked Questions about the Reservation of Priestly Ordination to Men," 8.

557. United States Catholic Conference, *Catechism of the Catholic Church* (Liguori, Mo.: Liguori Publications, 1994), §1807.

558. Abbé Combes, ed., *Collected Letters of St. Thérèse of Lisieux*, trans. F. J. Sheed (New York: Sheed & Ward, 1949), 174.

559. Ibid., 175.

Chapter 21

560. John Paul II, *"Ad Tuendam Fidem"* ("To Defend the Faith"), *Origins* 28, no. 8 (July 16, 1998): 113–19. The pope's letter was accompanied by a commentary by Cardinal Joseph Ratzinger, to which we will turn next.

561. See the editorial note accompanying Ratzinger's "Commentary on the Profession of Faith's Concluding Paragraphs," *Origins* 28, no. 8 (July 16, 1998): 116–19.

562. Congregation for the Doctrine of the Faith, "Doctrinal Congregation Publishes Faith Profession and Oath," *Origins* 18, no. 40 (March 16, 1989): 661–63.

563. Quoted in Arthur Jones, "John Paul Acts to Muzzle Dissent; Bishops, Theologians Face New Rift," *National Catholic Reporter* 34, no. 34 (July 17, 1998), 14. Jones pointed out that the three levels of church teaching are often called the "hierarchy of truths."

564. Richard R. Gaillardetz, *"Ad Tuendam Fidem*: An Emerging Pattern in Current Papal Teaching," *New Theology Review* 12, no. 1 (February 1999): 44–45, 47. Italics in the original.

565. Ibid., 46. Italics in the original.

566. "Beware Murky World of 'Secondary Truths,'" *National Catholic Reporter* 33, no. 31 (June 6, 1997): 24.

567. Joseph Ratzinger, "Commentary on the Profession of Faith's Concluding Paragraphs," *Origins* 28, no. 8 (July 16, 1998): 116–19.

568. "Congregation for the Doctrine of the Faith"; see www.vatican.va/roman_curia/congregations/cfaith.

569. Ratzinger, "Commentary on the Profession of Faith's Concluding Paragraphs," 117.

570. Ibid., 116–19.

571. Richard R. Gaillardetz, "Infallibility and the Ordination of Women," *Louvain Studies* 21 (1996): 8. Gaillardetz's article concerns the CDF *Responsum* to *Ordinatio Sacerdotalis*, but much of its content is germane to the issue in general.

572. Joan Chittister, "Ratzinger Raised Bigger Issues Than Ordination," *National Catholic Reporter* 32, no. 7 (December 8, 1995), 7.

573. Ratzinger, "Commentary on the Profession of Faith's Concluding Paragraphs," 116–19.

574. Ibid.

575. Ibid.

576. Ibid.

577. Ibid., 119, n. 17. Italics added.

578. Ibid., 116–19.

579. Ibid. Italics added.

580. Richard P. McBrien, "Essays in Theology: The Vatican and Dissent" (July 20, 1998); http://129.74.54.81/rm/.

581. Quoted in Thomas J. Reese, *Inside the Vatican: The Politics and Organization of the Catholic Church* (Cambridge, Mass.: Harvard University Press, 1996), 244. For an overview of how members of the hierarchy are selected, see chapter 9.

582. Peter Hebblethwaite, *The Next Pope* (San Francisco: HarperSanFrancisco, 1995), 18–19.

583. George B. Wilson, "'Dissent' or Conversation among Adults?" *America* 180, no. 8 (March 13, 1999): 9. Italics added by Wilson.

584. Lavinia Byrne, *Woman at the Altar: The Ordination of Women in the Roman Catholic Church* (New York: Continuum, 1998).

585. "Pope Bans British Nun's Book on Women Priests," *New Women New Church* (Fall 1998): 4.

586. Byrne, *Woman at the Altar*, 9.

587. Lavinia Byrne, "Thought for the Day: Sister Lavinia Byrne Responds to the Burning of Her Book," BBC Radio 4 (August 7, 1998); www.phillipsdevaney.fsnet.co.uk/cwo/19980807. Byrne said her spirits were lifted when she read in a newspaper that the monks who own the publishing house had made an "eco-friendly" decision to put the books into the monastery incinerator so they could be "lit and fuelled by it."

588. "Saint Therese of Lisieux," n.d.; www.catholic.org.

589. V. Sackville-West, *The Eagle and the Dove, A Study in Contrasts: St. Teresa of Avila, St. Thérèse of Lisieux* (Garden City, N.Y.: Doubleday, Doran, 1944), 140.

590. Frances Parkinson Keyes, *Therese: Saint of a Little Way* (New York: Julian Messner, 1950), 77. On the back of the title page is the announcement: "This book has been read and approved at the Carmelite Convent of Lisieux."

591. Thérèse of Lisieux, *The Autobiography of Thérèse of Lisieux: The Story of a Soul*, trans. John Beevers (Garden City, N.Y.: Doubleday, 1957), 13.

Chapter 22

592. Pope John Paul II, "Address of the Holy Father to the German Bishops on the Occasion of Their 'Ad Limina' Visit," November 20, 1999; www.vatican.va/holy_father/john_paul_ii/speeches/1999/documents/.

593. The pope's allusion to the causal relationship between fidelity to Rome and eternal salvation set off a furor of its own among theologians, many of whom expressed dismay at the apparent return to the discarded belief: *extra ecclesiam nulla salus*, there is no salvation outside the church.

594. V. Sackville-West, *The Eagle and the Dove, A Study in Contrasts: St. Teresa of Avila, St. Thérèse of Lisieux* (Garden City, N.Y.: Doubleday, Doran, 1944), 152–53.

Chapter 23

595. Pope John Paul II, "Message on the Occasion of the General Assembly of the World Union of Catholic Women's Organizations" (March 7, 2001); www. vatican.va/holy_father/john_paul_ii/speeches/2001/. The Union, whose mission includes the religious education of its members, was formed in 1910 and currently has ninety international member organizations.

596. Italics in the original.

597. Patty McCarty, "Nuns Firm under Fire," *National Catholic Reporter* 37, no. 34 (July 13, 2001), 3–5.

598. "Women's Ordination Worldwide"; www.womensordination.org/pages/intern_wow.

599. Christine Vladimiroff, "Why We Said No to the Vatican Demand," *Churchwatch* (August 2001); www.cta-usa.org/watch08-01/benedictines. Italics added.

600. Ibid.

601. "Vatican Backs Down on Ban of Chittister at WOW, Dublin," *Churchwatch* (August 2001); www.cta-usa.org/watch08-01/chittister. Italics added.

602. McCarty, "Nuns Firm under Fire," 3–5.

603. Ibid.

604. Martin Browne, "Women Raise Their Voices," *The Tablet* (July 7, 2001), 1001.

605. Ibid.

606. Margot Patterson, "Saying 'No' to the Vatican: Obedience Is a Complex Matter," *National Catholic Reporter* 37, no. 35 (July 27, 2001), 5.

607. Browne, "Women Raise Their Voices."

608. "Women's Ordination Worldwide Conference: Now Is the Time." www.we-are-church.org/it/attual/Congresso.donne.prete.

609. Henri Ghéon, *The Secret of the Little Flower*, trans. Donald Attwater (New York: Sheed & Ward, 1934), 179–80.

610. Monica Furlong, *Thérèse of Lisieux* (New York: Pantheon, 1987), 96.

611. V. Sackville-West, *The Eagle and the Dove, A Study in Contrasts: St. Teresa of Avila, St. Thérèse of Lisieux* (Garden City, N.Y.: Doubleday, Doran, 1944), 126.

612. Henri Ghéon, *The Secret of the Little Flower*, trans. Donald Attwater (New York: Sheed & Ward, 1934), 119.

613. Furlong, *Thérèse of Lisieux*, 57.

Chapter 24

614. Nadya Labi, "Not Doing as the Romans Do," *Time* (November 30, 1998), 8.

615. David Markham, *The Other Side of the Street* 1, no. 16 (December 20, 1998); www.members.aol.com/tarnold23/.

616. Women's Ordination Conference, "Action Alert," November 14, 2001; online at www.womensordination.org/pages/action14.

617. Women's Ordination Conference, "Action Alert," September 16, 2002; online at www.womensordination.org/pages/action12.

618. "Priestly Ordination of South African Nun," *Catholic New Times* (November 2, 2003); 12.

619. Patricia Ann Fresen, "Why I Want to Be Ordained" (March 7, 2004); www.cnwe.org/pdf/pdf_Fresen_Ordination.pdf.

620. Letter from the National Coalition of American Nuns to Sister Patricia Fresen (January 8, 2004), courtesy of the Women's Ordination Conference, Fairfax, Va.

621. "In Their Own Words: Regarding Their Ordinations Catholic Women Share Their Reasoning for Being Ordained" (Fairfax, Va.: Women's Ordination Conference, 2002), n.p.

622. Iris Müller and Ida Raming, press release (Fairfax, Va.: Women's Ordination Conference, June 29, 2002).

623. "In Their Own Words."

624. Ibid.

625. It was later explained that the riverboat was used to avoid causing jurisdictional problems for diocesan bishops.

626. John L. Allen Jr. "Seven Women 'Ordained' Priests June 29 in Ceremony They Term 'Not Licit, but a Fact,'" *NCR Online* (July 1, 2002); http://natcath.org/NCR_Online/archives2/2002c/. Italics added.

627. "German Female Priest Ida Raming Tours U.S.," *NewWomen NewChurch* 26, no. 2 (Fairfax, Va.: Women's Ordination Conference, 2003), 4.

628. Allen, "Seven Women 'Ordained' Priests June 29 in Ceremony They Term 'Not Licit, but a Fact.'"

629. John L. Allen Jr. "Ordinations Ignite Debate over Tactics," *National Catholic Reporter* 38, no. 34 (July 19, 2002), 7. While Braschi acknowledged he had no authority to perform a Roman Catholic ordination, during the ritual he "read a prayer in Spanish that referred to *hermanos*, 'brothers.' Someone in the crowd called out 'and *hermanas*,' or 'sisters,' whereupon the excommunicated priest wheeled sharply and said: 'Today, we follow the Roman rite.'" See Allen, "Seven Women 'Ordained' Priests June 29 in a Ceremony They Term 'Not Licit, but a Fact.'"

630. Press accounts in the United States listed this pseudonym as "Angela White." A Women's Ordination Conference online history listed the more European name Angela Weiss. See "History: The WOC Story," Women's Ordination Conference, online at www.womensordination.org/pages/history.

631. According to the Women's Ordination Conference, Celeste chose to use a pseudonym because her daughter's wedding was to take place three months after the ordination, and she did not wish to cause commotion to distract from that event (personal e-mail correspondence with Women's Ordination Conference, April 15, 2003).

632. "An Open Letter to Rev. Ludmila Javorova," *National Catholic Reporter* 38, no. 31 (June 7, 2002), 17.

633. Maureen Fiedler, "Firsthand Account of Women's Ordination in Europe," June 29, 2002 (Fairfax, Va., Women's Ordination Conference).

634. Congregation for the Doctrine of the Faith, "Warning Regarding the Attempted Priestly Ordination of Some Catholic Women," July 10, 2002 (Fairfax, Va., Women's Ordination Conference).

635. "The Vatican, Women, and Excommunication: Actions Contrary to Teachings," August 2002 (Fairfax, Va., Women's Ordination Conference). For a list of the nine offenses, see the Canon Law Society of America, *The Code of Canon Law: A Text and Commentary*, ed. James A. Coriden, Thomas J. Green, Donald E. Heintschel (Mahwah, N.J.: Paulist Press, 1985), 932.

636. Congregation for the Doctrine of the Faith, "Decree of Excommunication by the Congregation for the Doctrine of the Faith Regarding the Attempted Priestly Ordination of Some Catholic Women," August 5, 2002 (Fairfax, Va., Women's Ordination Conference). Canon 1331 lists the effects of excommunication, including liturgical and ecclesiastical restrictions.

637. Canons 1732–39 provide for recourse against administrative decrees. "One cannot challenge a given law as such or its equivalent, but one can challenge its application in a particular case by an administrative decree or its equivalent." See the Canon Law Society of America, *The Code of Canon Law*, editorial note, p. 1031.

638. Congregation for the Doctrine of the Faith, "Decree on the Attempted Ordination of Some Catholic Women," in *Origins* 32, no. 34 (February 6, 2003): 566–67.

639. Sentencing in canon law takes place according to two administrative applications: *ferendae sententiae* takes effect only when it is specifically imposed by a church authority; *latae sententiae* is incurred automatically upon the commission of the offense. The CLSA pointed out that the 1917 code provided for thirty-seven different ways in which a person might ipso facto be excommunicated by virtue of one's actions, but the 1983 code lists only seven such offenses. See the Canon Law Society of America, *The Code of Canon Law,* pp. 19, 932.

640. "Statement of the Seven Ordained Women concerning the Degree of Excommunication," December 21, 2002 (Fairfax, Va., Women's Ordination Conference).

641. Fresen, "Why I Want to Be Ordained."

642. "One Year Later, Two Women Ordained as Bishops," *NewWomen NewChurch* 26, no. 2 (Fairfax, Va.: Women's Ordination Conference, 2003), 1.

643. "Priestly Ordination of South African Nun."

644. John L. Allen Jr. "Protestors in Vienna Call for Women Priests," *National Catholic Reporter* 37–34 (July 13, 2001), 5.

645. "Gender Discrimination Suit Filed Against Church and IRS," *NewWomen New-Church* 26, no. 2 (Fairfax, Va.: Women's Ordination Conference, 2003), 3.

646. Labi, "Not Doing as the Romans Do," 8.

647. Margaret Dorgan, "Thérèse of Lisieux: Mystic of the Ordinary," n.d.; online at www.showcase.netins.net/web/.

648. Pope Paul VI named Teresa of Avila and Catherine of Siena Doctors of the Church in 1970, the first women in church history to receive that title. Women make up more than 60 percent of active Catholics, yet they comprise only 9 percent of Doctors of the Church. When Vatican Radio commented in 1970 on the long delay, it explained that authorities had to proceed cautiously in order "to solve the question of whether the charism of the world, of knowledge, and of wisdom *were or were not granted to women.*" Quoted in Richard P. McBrien, "Essays in Theology: Pope John, Vatican Council Strong on Women's Rights" (December 10, 1971); http://129.74.54.81/rm/. Italics added. A decade later, Regina Coll pointed out that even when women are canonized to sainthood, they are defined by their biology. "Besides martyrs the vast majority of women saints are listed under the categories of virgin, widow, and the catch-all 'neither virgin nor martyr.'" This remains largely true today. See Regina Coll, "The Socialization of Women into a Patriarchal System," in *Women and Religion: A Reader for the Clergy,* ed. Regina Coll (New York: Paulist Press, 1982), 12.

649. Pope John Paul II, *Divini Amoris Scientia* ("The Science of Divine Love"), October 19, 1997; www.vatican.va/holy_father/john_paul_ii/apost/letters/documents/.

650. Guy Gaucher, *The Story of a Life: St. Thérèse of Lisieux,* trans. Anne Marie Brennan (San Francisco: Harper & Row, 1987), 76.

Chapter 25

651. Pope John Paul II, "How Authority Is Conceived," *Origins* 25, no. 34 (February 15, 1996): 572–74.

652. Joseph Ratzinger, "The Limits of Authority," *L'Osservatore Romano* 26, English ed. (June 29, 1994), 6–8. Italics added.

653. *Lumen Gentium* ("Dogmatic Constitution on the Church"), in Austin Flannery, ed., *Vatican Council II: Constitutions, Decrees, Declarations* (Northport, N.Y.: Costello Publishing Co., 1996), 1–95; §§12, 25.

654. Thomas N. Taylor, *Saint Thérèse of Lisieux, the Little Flower of Jesus* (New York: P. J. Kenedy, 1927), 294.

Chapter 26

655. Pamela Schaeffer, "Theologians Opt for Diplomacy in Dispute," *National Catholic Reporter* 33, no. 32 (June 20, 1997), 3.

656. V. Sackville-West, *The Eagle and the Dove, A Study in Contrasts: St. Teresa of Avila, St. Thérèse of Lisieux* (Garden City, N.Y.: Doubleday, Doran, 1944), 155.

657. Margaret Dorgan. "Thérèse of Lisieux: Mystic of the Ordinary"; n.d.; online at www.showcase.netins.net/web.

658. Sackville-West, *The Eagle and the Dove*, 155.

659. Ibid., 159.

Chapter 27

660. Pope John Paul II, *Pastores Dabo Vobis* ("I Will Send You Shepherds"), *Origins* 21, no. 45 (April 16, 1992): 722, §8.

661. Joseph Ratzinger, "The Limits of Authority," *L'Osservatore Romano*, English ed. (June 29, 1994), 6–8.

662. Joel Garver, "A Short Biography"; www.lasalle.edu/ garver/bio.

663. Elizabeth A. Johnson, "The Incomprehensibility of God and the Image of God Male and Female," *Theological Studies* 45, no. 3 (1984): 445.

664. Quoted in Leonard Swidler, "Democracy, Dissent, and Dialogue: A Catholic Vocation," in *The Church in Anguish*, ed. Hans Küng and Leonard Swidler (San Francisco: Harper & Row, 1987), 321. Italics in original.

665. Ibid., 312–13. Italics added.

666. Rose Hoover, "Consider Tradition: A Case for Women's Ordination," *Commonweal* 126, no. 2 (January 29, 1999): 17–20.

667. Gail Grossman Freyne, "Women in Exile: Devout Dissent," *Studies* 86, no. 341 (Spring 1997): 9. Italics added.

668. John Henry Newman, *An Essay on the Development of Christian Doctrine*, 6th ed. (Notre Dame, Ind.: University of Notre Dame Press, 1989), 40.

669. Ladislas Örsy, *Theology and Canon Law: New Horizons for Legislation and Interpretation* (Collegeville, Minn.: Liturgical Press, 1992), 35, 104, n. 6.

670. Anthony Padovano, "Great Saints, Two Councils Led Wayward Church Back toward Jesus the Reformer," *National Catholic Reporter* 32, no. 7 (December 8, 1995), 8.

671. Jay P. Dolan, In *Search of American Catholicism: A History of Religion and Culture in Tension* (New York: Oxford University Press, 2002), 236.

672. Dean R. Hoge, *Future of Catholic Leadership: Responses to the Priest Shortage* (Kansas City, Mo.: Sheed & Ward, 1987), 163.

673. Jane Redmont, "Communication and 'Communio,'" *America* (July 30, 1994): 22–24.

674. Libby Purves, "Break This Stained-Glass Ceiling," *The Tablet* (July 6, 1972); www.thetablet.co.uk/.

675. Francis Bernard O'Connor, *Like Bread, Their Voices Rise! Global Women Challenge the Church* (Notre Dame, Ind.: Ave Maria Press, 1993), 145.

676. In the tenth century, Bishop Atto of Vercelli wrote that in the very early church devout women had been appointed to preside over the church and to help men lead the worship because of a shortage of males. This shortage apparently had resolved itself by the mid-fourth century, when the Council of Laodicea forbade the practice. See Bernard Cooke and Gary Macy, eds., *A History of Women and Ordination*, vol. 1: *The Ordination of Women in Medieval Context* (Lanham, Md.: Scarecrow Press, 2002), 7–8.

677. Richard P. McBrien, "The Church of Tomorrow," in *Women and Religion: A Reader for the Clergy*, ed. Regina Coll (New York: Paulist Press, 1982), 132.

678. This priest shortage is paralleled by a drastic post–Vatican II drop in the number of nuns/sisters. In the "peak year" following Vatican II, 1966, there were 181,000 Catholic sisters in the United States, with some 5,000 more entering yearly. By the mid-1990s, that number stood at about 99,000. By 2002, the number was 75,000. For a comprehensive study of the reasons behind this decline, see Sister Marie Augusta Neal's landmark study, "Ministry of American Catholic Sisters: The Vowed Life in Church Renewal," in *Religious Institutions and Women's Leadership: New Roles Inside the Mainstream,* ed. Catherine Wessinger (Columbia: University of South Carolina, 1996), 238. For 2002 figures, see Peter Steinfels, *A People Adrift: The Crisis of the Roman Catholic Church in America* (New York: Simon & Schuster, 2003), 30.

679. Sociologist Mark Chaves found "that the presence of a clergy shortage is not a factor leading to the ordination of women," although it influences whether women actually perform certain tasks and fill certain roles in the congregation. See Mark Chaves, "The Symbolic Significance of Women's Ordination," *Journal of Religion* 77, no. 1 (January 1977): 112.

680. Steinfels, *A People Adrift,* 302.

681. John L. Allen Jr., "The Word from Rome" 3, no. 29 (March 12, 2004); online at www.NCROnline.org, go to "Archives."

682. Tom Heneghan, "Vatican Appoints First Female Theologians," Reuters (March 8, 2004); www.reuters.co.uk/newsPackageArticle/.

683. Mary Fainsod Katzenstein, *Faithful and Fearless: Moving Feminist Protest Inside the Church and Military* (Princeton, N.J.: Princeton University Press, 1998), 135–43.

684. Rosemary Jantzen Doherty, "Message to the Roman Catholic Clergy," *National Catholic Reporter* 33, no. 27 (May 9, 1997): 2.

685. Ibid.

686. Denise Lardner Carmody, *Women and World Religions* (Nashville: Abingdon Press, 1981), 115.

687. James Allaire. "Saint Thérèse of Lisieux inspired Dorothy Day," *Houston Catholic Worker* 16, no. 3 (May–June 1996).

688. Thérèse of Lisieux, *The Autobiography of St. Thérèse of Lisieux: The Story of a Soul,* trans. John Beevers (Garden City, N.Y.: Doubleday, 1957), 12, 17, 20.

Notes for "Strengthening the Bonds of Peace" (pp. 214–219)

Paragraph numbers have been added to this document.

1. Pope John Paul II, *Ordinatio Sacerdotalis* (*Reserving Priestly Ordination to Men Alone*) (Washington, D.C.: USCC Publishing Services, 1994).

2. Pope Paul VI, "Message of His Holiness Pope Paul VI for the Celebration of the [World] Day of Peace," January 1, 1972.

3. Pope Paul VI, *Ecclesiam Suam* (*Paths of the Church*), #81.

4. Philip Murnion, *New Parish Ministers* (New York: National Pastoral Life Center, 1992).

5. Canon 129 states: (1) in accord with the prescription of law, those who have received sacred orders are capable of the power of governance, which exists in the Church by divine institution and is also called the power of jurisdiction; (2) Lay members of the Christian faithful can cooperate in the exercise of this power in accord with the norm of law.

6. Catholic News Service, July 13, 1994.

7. See Canon 135, Code of Canon Law.

8. The Committee on Canonical Affairs, National Conference of Catholic Bishops, is currently sponsoring such a study.

9. Pope John Paul II, *Christifideles Laici* (*The Vocation and Mission of the Lay Faithful in the Church and in the World*) (Washington, D.C.: USCC Publishing Services, 1988), #12.

10. *Catechism of the Catholic Church* (Washington, D.C.: USCC Publishing Services, 1994), #1934.

11. *One in Christ Jesus,* Committee Report (Washington, D.C.: USCC Publishing Services, 1992), #12.

12. Congregation for the Doctrine of the Faith, Declaration *Inter Insigniores,* 6: *AAS* 69 (1977), 115-116. Quoted in *Ordinatio Sacerdotalis, #3.*

13. *Ecclesiam Suam,* #113.

14. *Ecclesiam Suam,* #83.

15. *Ecclesiam Suam,* #83.

Glossary

abbess (Middle English, abbesse): the superior of a community of women religious.

acolyte (Gr. *akolouthos*): a formally installed attendant at mass; in practice used to mean altar server.

ad limina visits (Lat. *ad limina apostolorum*, "to the thresholds of the apostles"): visits by bishops every five years to Rome, where they give the pope a detailed report of their dioceses.

aggiornamento (Ital., "updating"): term used by Pope John XXIII to characterize the spirit of Vatican Council II (1962–65) and the process of renewal within the Roman Catholic Church.

anthropology: the study of the origins and nature of humankind. "Christian anthropology" and "theological anthropology" are often used interchangeably to refer to various Christian understandings of divinely assigned sex roles.

apostles (Gr. *apostellein*, "to send"): witnesses to the resurrection (Acts 21:22) sent by Christ to proclaim his teaching to the world (Luke 6:13), including Paul and Mary of Magdala. More narrowly, twelve men selected by Jesus to represent the twelve tribes of Israel and to preach the gospel.

apostolic constitution: a papal or ecumenical council document used to enact a law concerning the faithful.

apostolic delegate: a Vatican representative charged with overseeing a certain area and reporting its activities to the pope.

apostolic exhortation: a papal letter encouraging the faithful to take an action.

apostolic letter: a papal or curial document used for approving religious appointments and congregations, and other routine matters.

apostolic succession: the line of lawfully ordained bishops extending from "The Twelve" apostles to present bishops. The Catholic Church teaches that Christ chose twelve men symbolizing the twelve tribes of Israel, that these men were the first bishops, and that since then bishops have inherited a divinely ordained teaching authority.

assent: see "reception and assent."

baptism (Gr. *baptizein*, "to immerse"): a sacrament of initiation that cleanses the recipient of original sin and brings the new Christian into the life of the church.

beatification: a papal declaration that a person is "blessed," allowing limited veneration of that person; final step before canonization.

bishop (Gr. *episcopos*, "overseer"): an ordained priest and successor to the apostles who is consecrated to teach, rule, and ordain priests; an archbishop is the bishop of a large or main diocese.

canon (Gr. *kanon*, measuring "rod"): in law, an official rule for church government and administration; the collection of laws is called "canon law."

canonization: declaration that a person's soul is in heaven and approval of veneration of that person, now called "saint."

Cappadocian fathers: fourth-century churchmen (Basil the Great, Gregory Nazianzen, Gregory of Nyssa) whose work to define the Trinity helped shape the Nicene Creed.

cardinal: a priest appointed by the pope to assist in the administration of the church. The college of cardinals is a group of papal advisors and administrators who head curial congregations and offices and elect new popes.

catechism (Gr. *catechesis*, "oral instruction"): summary of Catholic doctrine, often presented in question and answer form, used for teaching.

charism (Gr. *charisma*, "gift"): a gift or grace of the Holy Spirit to be used for the building up of the Christian community.

Christology (Gr. *Christos* and *logos*, "Christ" and "study"): the study of the divinity and humanity of Jesus Christ.

curia (Gr. *kyrios*, "lord," or "master," and Lat. *curia*, "court"): the body of administrative agencies and officials who assist the pope in church governance.

complementarity (Lat. *complere*, "to complete"): as used in Catholicism, a reciprocal relationship in which one sex depends upon the other.

deacon (Gr. *diakonos*, "of service"): a man who is ordained to baptize, dispense eucharist, bless marriages, read scripture at mass, officiate at funerals, and perform other liturgical actions.

definitive teaching: a doctrine concerning faith and morals which is necessary to keep and teach the deposit of faith, even if it has not been formally revealed.

deposit of faith (Lat. *depositum fidei*): the body of revelation and tradition entrusted to the church's magisterium for safeguarding and transmission to the faithful.

dicastery: a commission serving a curial congregation or office.

diaconate: the first and hierarchically lowest order in ordained ministry.

diocese (Gr. *dioikesis,* "household management"): a geographic division of the church, including its institutions, property, and people, entrusted to a bishop; the chief diocese of a province is an archdiocese.

Doctor of the Church: a title conferred on church writers, always saints, known for their great learning and holiness; a possible exception was Saint Thérèse of Lisieux (named in 1997), whose learning and writing was limited.

doctrine (Gr. *didaskelos,* "master" or "teacher"): an official teaching of the church.

– *credenda* (Lat.): a doctrine that must be believed and cannot be changed.

– *tenenda* (Lat.): a doctrine that can potentially be changed but that must be held or followed even if it is not personally believed.

dogma (Gr. *dokein,* "to think" or "to seem"): a formally stated or authoritatively proclaimed doctrine or body of doctrines concerning faith and morals.

ecclesia (Gr. *ekklesia*): gathering or assembly of the faithful, often translated as "church."

ecclesiastical: of or relating to church structure.

ecumenical council: an assembly of the world's bishops and other dignitaries meeting with the pope or his representative; its decrees are binding on all Catholics. The original use of "ecumenical" here was established prior to the Protestant Reformation (1517), hence it refers to the various Christian leaders throughout the world, East and West.

ecumenism (Gr. *oikoumenikos,* "whole world"): principles and practices of religious unity through cooperation among diverse religions.

encyclical (Gr. *enkyklios,* "circular"): a papal letter to Catholic bishops to be shared with the world's faithful; serves to condemn current errors or to inform Catholics of proper conduct.

episcopate (Gr. *episkopos,* "overseer"): the office of bishop or the body of world's bishops.

eucharist (Gr. *eucharistia,* "gratitude"): the body of Christ as both sacrament (consecrated bread and wine) and sacrifice (the mass).

ex cathedra (Lat. "from the chair"): a papal declaration of doctrine by virtue of the pope's supreme apostolic authority.

fathers of the church: early Christian writers and bishops whose works helped shape the beliefs and traditions of the church.

ferendae sententiae: an ecclesiastical penalty given after a warning.

heterodoxy (Gr. *heteros* and *doxa,* "other" and "opinion"): various opinions and beliefs, sometimes departing from established doctrine.

hierarchy (Gr. *hierarchia,* "rule by priests"): ordering of ranks of ordained clergy, beginning with the pope; this term was introduced to the church in the fifth century by Dionysius the Areopagite, a pseudo-disciple of Paul.

holy orders: the sacrament that confers on a man the grace and spiritual power to celebrate the church's sacraments.

Holy See (Lat. *Santa Sedes*): the Diocese of Rome, with the pope, curia, and the college of cardinals, and their functions and jurisdictions pertaining to the spiritual and worldly governance of the church.

Immaculate Conception: the conception of Mary in her mother's (Anne's) womb to protect her from original sin, thus making her a worthy vessel for the Son of God.

in persona Christi (Lat. "in the role of Christ"): acting as a representative of Christ.

in persona ecclesia (Lat. "in the role of the church"): acting as a representative of the church.

inerrancy: the church's freedom from error by way of God's omniscience, Adam and Eve's state of knowledge before their sin, Christ's knowledge, scripture, or the church's infallibility.

infallibility: the church's divine preservation from error when, under certain conditions, teaching on faith and morals.

laity (Gr. *laos*, "people"): the body of Catholic faithful, outside the ranks of ordained clergy.

latae sententiae: penalty incurred automatically at the time of an offense.

lector (Lat. *legere*, "to read"): a ministerial role performed by a lay person who reads the first (Old Testament) and second (New Testament) readings during the Liturgy of the Word segment of the mass.

liturgy (Gr. *leitourgia*, "public service"): public worship.

magisterium (Lat. *magister*, "master"): teaching authority of the church.
- *extraordinary:* teaching by an ecumenical council, the pope with the world's bishops, or the pope alone
- *ordinary:* teaching by the world's bishops (including the pope)
- *ordinary and universal:* agreement among the world's bishops concerning a doctrine

motu proprio ("by one's own accord"): a document written on the pope's personal initiative.

National Conference of Catholic Bishops (U.S.A.): the official conference of U.S. bishops, responsible for deciding matters of church law and issuing policy statements.

nun: a woman who has taken solemn religious vows and lives in a religious community.

Old Catholic Church: a church founded by Roman Catholics who rejected the doctrine of papal infallibility decreed by Vatican I in 1870.

ordinary (Lat. *ordo*, "an order"): most commonly, a bishop of a diocese.

ordination (Lat. *ordinatio*): to create and maintain an order.

orthodoxy (Gr. *orthos* and *doxa*, "correct" and "opinion"): right belief or teaching in accord with church direction.

papacy (Lat. *papa*, "father"): a church system in which the pope, as successor of the apostle Peter, holds supreme authority.

parish: a particular community of Catholics within a diocese.

pastor: a priest in charge of a parish or parishes; he is responsible for presiding at mass, administering the sacraments, and instructing the faithful, as well as overseeing administration of the parish.

pastoral administrator: a nonordained person who assumes the administrative duties of a pastor in a Catholic parish with no resident priest.

patriarchy (Gr. *pater* and *archein*, "father" and "rule"): organized rule by men.

pope (Lat. *papa*, "father"): the first to call himself "pope" was Bishop Siricius in the late fourth century. Until the thirteenth century, popes were called "Vicar of Peter," but Innocent III changed the tradition by calling himself "Vicar of Christ."

presbyterate (Gr. *presbyteros*, "elder"): ordained priesthood; in the early church, the governing body (presbytery).

priest: a man ordained to teach, minister, and govern; only a priest can preside over the sacrament of eucharist.

priesthood: the office of priest, or collective order of priests; priesthood can be common (all believers) or ordained (by holy orders).

revelation (Lat. *revelare*, "to draw away"): the means of knowing God's truth, including scripture and tradition.

sacrament (Lat. *sacramentum*, a military loyalty oath): a sign of sanctification and grace; the Catholic Church teaches that seven sacraments were directly or indirectly instituted by Christ: baptism, eucharist, penance, confirmation, matrimony, holy orders, and anointing of the sick.

schism (Gr. *schizein*, "to cut"): a break in church unity.

sensus fidelium (Lat. "sense of the faithful"): the collective consciousness of faith regarding an issue or question.

sister: a woman vowed to a religious order, but who may live and work outside the religious community.

subordinationism (Lat. *sub* and *ordinare*, "under" and "to order"): doctrine that women are inferior to men because of their secondary status in creation.

subsidiarity (Lat. *sub* and *sidium*, "under" and "help"): the teaching that a higher authority should not usurp power from a lower authority in matters belonging to the lower authority's jurisdiction.

Syllabus of Errors: an 1864 document by Pope Pius IX condemning eighty religious and political propositions as heresy.

synod: a gathering of church officials for the purpose of determining church law and policy.

tradition: teaching, faith, and practice from apostolic times to the present, including scripture and unwritten customs.

United States Catholic Conference: the public policy arm and executive agency of the National Conference of Catholic Bishops (U.S.A.).

Vatican (Lat. *Mons Vaticanum*, "Vatican Hill"): the hill atop which sits the papal residence; a cluster of people and places including the papal residence, Vatican City, and officials who work there.

Vatican Council I: the twentieth ecumenical (worldwide) council, called by Pope Pius IX, and convened in 1869–70; it condemned errors of modernism and defined papal infallibility.

Vatican Council II: the twenty-first ecumenical council, called by Pope John XXIII, convened 1962–65, and completed under Pope Paul VI; it implemented historic changes, including a renewal of biblical study, an alteration of popular devotions, and a participatory liturgy.

vicar: a cleric who assumes the duties in the name of another cleric; a vicar general exercises the powers of a bishop.

vocation: in religious life, a divine call (nun, brother, priest) affirmed by a superior's judgment of one's worthiness to follow that call.

Bibliography

Abbott, Walter M., ed. *The Documents of Vatican II*. New York: Herder and Herder, Association Press, 1966. A classic collection of Vatican II documents.

Byrne, Lavinia. *Woman at the Altar: The Ordination of Women in the Roman Catholic Church*. New York: Continuum, 1998. Explores Catholic feminism and contemporary Catholic women's experiences within the context of priesthood and its meanings.

Canon Law Society of America. *The Code of Canon Law: A Text and Commentary*. Ed. James A. Coriden, Donald E. Heintschel, and Thomas J. Green. Mahwah, N.J.: Paulist Press, 1985. A massive but plain-language resource for researchers of church statutes, especially as regards the history and character of church law.

Carmody, Denise Lardner. *Women and World Religions*. Nashville: Abingdon Press, 1981. Explores women's experiences in the world's religions through doctrines, symbols, and rituals.

Chaves, Mark. *Ordaining Women: Culture and Conflict in Religious Organizations*. Cambridge, Mass.: Harvard University Press, 1999. A comparative sociology of religions through the lens of women's ordination. A rare and solid resource.

Christ, Carol P., and Judith Plaskow, eds. *Womanspirit Rising: A Feminist Reader in Religion*. San Francisco: Harper & Row, 1979. Updated and re-released in 1992, this perennial collection of essays traces critical feminist thought.

Coll, Regina, ed. *Women and Religion: A Reader for the Clergy*. New York: Paulist Press, 1982. A serviceable collection of essays that have worn well over time.

Combes, Abbé, ed. *Collected Letters of St. Thérèse of Lisieux*. Trans. F. J. Sheed. New York: Sheed & Ward, 1949. An example of Thérèse's prose as rendered by nineteenth-century editors' concern for her saintly image.

Cooke, Bernard, and Gary Macy, eds. *A History of Women and Ordination*, vol. 1: *The Ordination of Women in Medieval Context*. Lanham, Md.: Scarecrow Press, 2002. This scholarly and detailed treatment offers a valuable resource for the student or researcher.

Coriden, James A., ed. *Sexism and Church Law: Equal Rights and Affirmative Action*. New York: Paulist Press, 1977. Though dated, a classic collection of informative essays written by leading scholars and edited by a leading scholar in canon law.

Dolan, Jay P. *In Search of American Catholicism: A History of Religion and Culture in Tension*. New York: Oxford University Press, 2002. A highly readable exploration of American Catholicism, including helpful statistics.

Fiedler, Maureen, and Linda Rabben, eds. *Rome Has Spoken: A Guide to Forgotten Papal Statements, and How They Have Changed through the Centuries*. New York: Crossroad, 1998. A fascinating compendium of believe-it-or-not statements from the Vatican.

Fiorenza, Elisabeth Schüssler. *Bread Not Stone: The Challenge of Feminist Biblical Interpretation.* Boston: Beacon Press, 1984. Explores biblical interpretations from a feminist hermeneutical perspective.

Flannery, Austin, ed. *Vatican Council II: Constitutions, Decrees, Declarations.* Northport, N.Y.: Costello Publishing Co., 1996. A revised translation of the council documents in inclusive language.

Fries, Heinrich. *Suffering from the Church: Renewal or Restoration?* Collegeville, Minn.: Liturgical Press, 1995. A brief treatment of the directions the church is, or is not, taking.

Furlong, Monica. *Thérèse of Lisieux.* New York: Pantheon, 1987. One of the more scholarly and serviceable treatments of a complicated young woman.

Gardiner, Anne Marie, ed. *Women and Catholic Priesthood: An Expanded Vision.* New York: Paulist Press, 1976. Traces the proceedings of the 1975 Ordination Conference in Detroit (at which the Women's Ordination Conference was formed) with more than two dozen essays by eminent writers.

Gaucher, Guy. *The Story of a Life: St. Thérèse of Lisieux.* Trans. Anne Marie Brennan. San Francisco: Harper & Row, 1987. Written by a foremost authority on Thérèse, this biography breaks through the "plaster-cast saint" mold to offer a real-life account of Thérèse. Includes numerous photos.

Ghéon, Henri. *The Secret of the Little Flower.* Trans. Donald Attwater. London: Sheed & Ward, 1934. A careful, detailed, and engaging biography by a writer who had to be convinced of Thérèse's worthiness.

Gryson, Roger. *The Ministry of Women in the Early Church.* Collegeville, Minn.: Liturgical Press, 1980. An early landmark study.

Hebblethwaite, Peter. *Paul VI: The First Modern Pope.* Mahwah, N.J.: Paulist Press, 1993. A prodigious work on the man who followed John XXIII and assumed command of an ecumenical council *in media res.*

———. *The Next Pope.* San Francisco: HarperSanFrancisco, 1995. Focuses on electing a successor to John Paul II, but offers valuable insight to the general process of electing a new pope.

Hoge, Dean R. *Future of Catholic Leadership: Responses to the Priest Shortage.* Kansas City, Mo.: Sheed & Ward, 1987. A repository of data and analyses from a premiere sociologist.

Hoge, Dean R., and Jacqueline E. Wenger. *Evolving Visions of the Priesthood.* Collegeville, Minn.: Pulpit and Pew, 2003. Traces the changes in the American priesthood from 1970 to 2000, with emphasis on priests' changing self-image from servant to cultic leader.

Hutchins, Robert Maynard, ed. *The Works of Aristotle, Volume II,* Great Books of the Western World Series 9. Chicago: William Benton, Encyclopædia Britannica, 1952. A classic reference work.

John XXIII, Pope. *The Encyclicals and Other Messages of John XXIII.* Washington, D.C.: TPS Press, 1964. A compendium of the legendary pope's writings.

Johnson, Elizabeth. *She Who Is: The Mystery of God in Feminist Theological Discourse.* New York: Crossroad, 1995. A sophisticated, substantial work of feminist theological discourse. Pursues language, symbolism, and gender toward creating an expanded image of God.

Katzenstein, Mary Fainsod. *Faithful and Fearless: Moving Feminist Protest Inside the Church and Military.* Princeton, N.J.: Princeton University Press, 1998. Explores ways in which patriotic military women and devoted Catholic women have moved the 1960s women's movement protest into the mainstream.

Keyes, Frances Parkinson. *Therese: Saint of a Little Way.* New York: Julian Messner, 1950. An emblematic work of hagiography.

Kramer, Heinrich, and James Sprenger. *The Malleus Maleficarum of Heinrich Kramer and James Sprenger.* Trans. Montague Summers. New York: Dover Publications, 1971. This official manual of the Roman Catholic Church's medieval witch-hunt offers deep insights into the religious psyche of the time.

Küng, Hans, and Leonard Swidler, eds. *The Church in Anguish: Has the Vatican Betrayed Vatican II?* San Francisco: Harper & Row, 1987. Premier theologians assess the papacy of John Paul II and the Roman curia.

Leeming, Bernard. *Principles of Sacramental Theology.* Westminster, Md.: Newman Press, 1960. An organized, scholastic approach to the sacraments that leaves no stone unturned.

McBrien, Richard P. *Catholicism.* New edition. New York: HarperCollins, 1994. One of the more readable church histories, and surely one of the most historically reliable.

McEnroy, Carmel. *Guests in Their Own House: The Women of Vatican II.* New York: Crossroad, 1996. A well-researched and unique history of women's presence at and contribution to Vatican Council II.

Meer, Haye van der. *Women Priests in the Catholic Church? A Theological-Historical Investigation.* Trans. Arlene and Leonard Swidler. Philadelphia: Temple University Press, 1973. This seminal work was the first serious favorable discussion of the ordination of Catholic women. Although dated, it remains an invaluable source of history and data concerning women's ordination.

Meyer, Charles. *Man of God: A Study of the Priesthood.* Garden City, N.Y.: Doubleday, 1974. A helpful resource, re-released by Wipf & Stock Publishers, 2002.

Moll, Helmut, ed., *The Church and Women: A Compendium.* Trans. Lothar Krauth. San Francisco: Ignatius Press, 1988. A credible and useful range of arguments against women's ordination.

Nesbitt, Paula. *Feminization of the Clergy in America.* New York: Oxford University Press, 1997. Uses biography, history, and statistics to compare and analyze career patterns in diverse denominations.

Newman, John Henry. *An Essay on the Development of Christian Doctrine.* 6th ed. Notre Dame, Ind.: University of Notre Dame Press, 1989. This classic work explores the phenomenon of doctrinal development.

O'Connell, Timothy E., ed. *Vatican II and Its Documents: An American Reappraisal.* Theology and Life Series 15. Wilmington, Del.: Michael Glazier, 1986. A scholarly but very accessible study.

O'Connor, Francis Bernard. *Like Bread, Their Voices Rise! Global Women Challenge the Church.* Notre Dame, Ind.: Ave Maria Press, 1993. A rare inclusive survey (with hard data) of beliefs about priesthood held by Catholic women around the world.

Örsy, Ladislas. *Theology and Canon Law: New Horizons for Legislation and Interpretation.* Collegeville, Minn.: Liturgical Press, 1992. A superb handbook for students and others.

Raab, Kelley A. *When Women Become Priests: The Catholic Women's Ordination Debate.* New York: Columbia University Press, 2000. A tightly packed volume intended for students familiar with the concepts and language of the debate.

Rahner, Karl. *Concern for the Church.* Theological Investigations 20. New York: Crossroad, 1986. One of Rahner's remarkably penetrating twenty-three-volume series exploring the gamut of Christian faith.

Reese, Thomas J. *Inside the Vatican: The Politics and Organization of the Catholic Church.* Cambridge, Mass.: Harvard University Press, 1996. Solid research, pithy writing, satisfying and enlightening reading.

Roberts, James R. *Women Priests: Reflections on Papal Teaching and Church Response.* Vancouver, B.C.: Langara College, 1994. Filled with information and data especially useful for the beginning student of women's ordination.

Ruether, Rosemary Radford, ed. *Religion and Sexism: Images of Woman in the Jewish and Christian Traditions.* New York: Simon and Schuster, 1974. A classic collection of essays exploring the cultural images of woman in the Jewish and Christian traditions.

——. *Women and Redemption: A Theological History.* Minneapolis: Augsburg Fortress, 1998. Explores feminist theology from the early church to the present, including often-neglected theologies in Latin America, Africa, and Asia.

Ryan, Mary P. *Womanhood in America: From Colonial Times to the Present.* 3rd ed. New York: Franklin Watts, 1983. A basic, readable introduction to the subject.

Sackville-West, V. *The Eagle and the Dove, A Study in Contrasts: St. Teresa of Avila, St. Thérèse of Lisieux.* Garden City, N.Y.: Doubleday, Doran, 1944. Offers a good background on two different women who shared a bedrock strength.

Sharma, Arvind, ed. *Women in World Religions.* Albany: State University of New York Press, 1987. A dated but perennially useful primer by an adept world religions scholar.

Smith, Janet E. *Humanae Vitae.* Washington, D.C.: Catholic University of America Press, 1991. Deftly explores every aspect of Pope Paul VI's widely rejected encyclical on birth control and the debate it spawned; written from a conservative but balanced perspective.

Steinfels, Peter. *A People Adrift: The Crisis of the Roman Catholic Church in America.* New York: Simon & Schuster, 2003. An engaging and informative survey of American Catholics in challenging times.

Stuhlmueller, Carroll, ed. *Women and Priesthood: Future Directions.* Collegeville, Minn.: Liturgical Press, 1978. An informative compilation of essays.

Swidler, Leonard, and Arlene Swidler, eds. *Women Priests: A Catholic Commentary on the Vatican Declaration.* New York: Paulist Press, 1977. This out-of-print collection of scholarly essays remains a landmark work in the study of women's ordination.

Taylor, Thomas N. *Saint Thérèse of Lisieux, the Little Flower of Jesus.* New York: P. J. Kenedy, 1927. An early hagiography.

Thérèse of Lisieux. *The Autobiography of St. Thérèse of Lisieux: The Story of a Soul.* Trans. John Beevers. Garden City, N.Y.: Doubleday, 1957. A clear, crisp translation of the saint's autobiography.

Torjesen, Karen Jo. *When Women Were Priests.* San Francisco: HarperCollins, 1994. A highly readable look at how the church's move from a private movement to a public institution gave rise to the oppression of women in the church.

United States Catholic Conference. *Catechism of the Catholic Church.* Liguori, Mo.: Liguori Publications, 1994. Official compendium of Catholic teaching.

———. *From "Inter Insigniores" to "Ordinatio Sacerdotalis."* Washington, D.C.: United States Catholic Conference, 1998. Presents full texts of both documents, but densely technical commentaries by Vatican-selected theologians limit its usefulness.

Wallace, Ruth A. *They Call Her Pastor: A New Role for Catholic Women.* Albany: State University of New York Press, 1992. A groundbreaking study of women's leadership in American parishes and responses to it.

Weaver, Mary Jo. *New Catholic Women: A Contemporary Challenge to Traditional Religious Authority.* New York: Harper & Row, 1985. A good early treatment of issues facing Catholic women in their protest of patriarchy.

Weaver, Mary Jo, and R. Scott Appleby. *Being Right: Conservative Catholics in America.* Bloomington: Indiana University Press, 1995. A solid body of up-to-date information and analysis of conservative Catholic groups by two leading Catholic studies scholars.

Wessinger, Catherine, ed. *Women's Leadership in Marginal Religions: Explorations Outside the Mainstream.* Urbana: University of Illinois Press, 1993. An exploration of the factors leading to the empowerment of women within marginal religions in the United States.

———. *Religious Institutions and Women's Leadership: New Roles Inside the Mainstream.* Columbia: University of South Carolina Press, 1996. Well-documented survey of women's entrance into leadership roles in Jewish, Protestant, and Roman Catholic faith communities in the United States; includes otherwise hard-to-obtain data.

Winter, Miriam Therese. *Out of the Depths: The Story of Ludmila Javorova, Ordained Roman Catholic Priest.* New York: Crossroad, 2001. A remarkable story of one woman's experience with faith, priesthood, and Vatican-imposed silence.

Woywod, Stanislaus. *The New Canon Law: A Commentary and Summary of the New Code of Canon Law.* New York: Joseph F. Wagner, 1918. This code of canon law, in force until 1983, offers an increasingly rare insight into the twentieth-century church.

———. *A Practical Commentary on the Code of Canon Law.* 2 vols. New York: Joseph F. Wagner, 1952. A complete and reliable commentary on the 1917 Code of Canon Law.

Index

Of Related Interest

Miriam Therese Winter
OUT OF THE DEPTHS
The Story of Ludmila Javorova, Roman Catholic Priest

The never-before-told true story of a courageous woman ordained in the Roman Catholic underground church during the religious persecutions of the communist era. This story documents Ludmila Javorova's struggle to live her priesthood with integrity within the restricted framework of the tradition and the times.

"This is a story that needs to be told. It is the story of a democratic, participatory, and prophetic church emerging in Czechoslovakian Catholicism at a moment of crisis and creativity, a church that chose to ordain women. Miriam Therese Winter is to be thanked for her gripping narration of this important story."
— ROSEMARY RADFORD RUETHER

"We need not theorize any longer about what women priests might do for the church. Miriam Therese Winter shows us Ludmila Javorova in action, ministering to the people of God in ways that few men could, as a clandestine priest in the underground Church of Czechoslovakia. This profoundly Catholic book has a bonus: a stunning portrait of a bishop with guts, Felix Davidek, Ludmila's mentor and the man who ordained her, despite opposition from the faint of heart. Davidek is a model of what a people's bishop could become in the twenty-first century."
— ROBERT BLAIR KAISER, contributing editor for *Newsweek*

0-8245-1889-6, $19.95 hardcover

Also available in Spanish
Desde lo hondo
0-8245-1975-2, $19.95 paperback

crossroad

Of Related Interest

Phyllis Zagano
HOLY SATURDAY
*An Argument for the Restoration of the Female Diaconate
in the Catholic Church*

CTA Book of the Year!

A serious effort to faithfully investigate the history and canonical viability of the female diaconate. Based on thorough research, as well as sound historical and theological analysis and reflection, this book makes a significant contribution to the discussion and development of women's roles in the modern church.

0-8245-1832-2, $16.95, paperback

Elizabeth A. Johnson
SHE WHO IS
The Mystery of God in Feminist Theological Discourse

Tenth Anniversary Edition

Winner of the Louisville Gravemeyer Award in Religion!

"As perhaps the best book of feminist theology to date, *She Who Is* is at once thoroughly orthodox, grounded in classical Christian thought, liberatingly contemporary, and rooted in women's experience."
— *Library Journal*

0-8245-1925-6 $24.95, paperback

Please support your local bookstore,
or call 1-800-707-0670 for Customer Service.

For a free catalog, write us at

THE CROSSROAD PUBLISHING COMPANY
16 Penn Plaza, 481 Eighth Avenue
New York, NY 10001

Visit our website at
www.crossroadpublishing.com
All prices subject to change.

crossroad